England, Rome and the papacy
1417–64

ENGLAND, ROME AND THE PAPACY
1417–1464

The study of a relationship

Margaret Harvey

MANCHESTER UNIVERSITY PRESS
Manchester and New York

*distributed exclusively in the USA
and Canada by St. Martin's Press*

Published by Manchester University Press
Oxford Road, Manchester M13 9PL, UK
and Room 400, 175 Fifth Avenue, New York, NY 10010, USA

Distributed exclusively in the USA and Canada
by St. Martin's Press, Inc., 175 Fifth Avenue, New York,
NY 10010, USA

British Library Cataloguing-in-Publication Data
A catalogue record for this book is available from the British Library

Library of Congress Cataloging-in-Publication Data
Harvey, Margaret (Margaret M.)
    England, Rome, and the papacy. 1417–1464 : the study of a
relationship / Margaret Harvey.
        p.   cm.
    Includes bibliographical references and index.
    ISBN 0–7190–3459–0
        1. Catholic Church—England—History.   2. Papacy—History.
    3. England—Church history—Medieval period, 1066–1485.   I. Title.
BR745.H37   1993
282'.42'09024—dc20   92–29774

    ISBN 0 7190 3459 0 *hardback*

Phototypeset in Linotron Galliard
by Northern Phototypesetting Co. Ltd, Bolton
Printed in Great Britain
by Biddles Ltd, Guildford and King's Lynn

Contents

Acknowledgements

Many people have helped in the production of this book, which has involved much travel to many libraries. In Oxford Helen Powell put up with continuous visits and Margaret Gibson frequently lent me her flat. The Heapy family exchanged houses, the younger generation even tolerating a continual, rather unsociable, presence. Professor Tilly de la Mare has been very generous in sharing information about manuscripts.

In Durham Professor Michael Prestwich encouraged my struggles with the word-processor and other things, Professor Anthony Fletcher listened sympathetically and Dr Ian Doyle has been constantly generous with information.

In Rome many specialist librarians and archivists were very helpful, but two others in particular need mention here, student librarians in the Venerabile Collegio Inglese who sacrificed leisure to supervise my labours: my thanks to Mr Sloane and Mr Massey.

Part of the work was undertaken in the midst of a family crisis; I would like to thank my brothers Donald and Peter and my sister Maura Brown for their generosity in letting me travel abroad whilst they held the fort.

Travel abroad was made possible partly with grants from the Brtitish Academy and Durham University Staff Travel Fund.

Lastly Dr Anne Orde has been a tower of support, even reading a draft. The medieval curia might have construed that heroic sanctity, material for canonisation perhaps.

Abbreviations

ACO Dijon, Archives de la Côte D'Or.

ADN Lille, Archives du Nord.

AHC *Annuarium historiae conciliorum.*

AHP *Archivum Historiae Pontificiae.*

AN Paris, Archives Nationales.

ASV Vatican, Archivio Segreto Vaticano.

BJRL *Bulletin of the John Rylands Library.*

BL London, British Library.

BN Paris, Bibliothèque Nationale.

BRUC A. B. Emden, *Biographical Register of the University of Cambridge.*

BRUO A. B. Emden, *Biographical Register of the University of Oxford.*

CB *Concilium Basiliense, Studien und Quellen,* ed J. Haller, etc.

CCR *Calendar of Close Rolls.*

CPL *Calendar of Entries in the Papal Registers relating to Great Britain and Ireland: Papal Letters.*

CPR *Calendar of Patent Rolls.*

CYS Canterbury and York Society.

DBI *Dizionario biografico degli italiani.*

DK *Annual Report of the Deputy Keeper of the Public Records,* followed by volume number.

EHR *English Historical Review.*

IE Vatican, Archivio Segreto Vaticano, Introitus et Exitus, followed by a volume number.

JEH *Journal of Ecclesiastical History.*

JWCI *Journal of the Warburg and Courtauld Institutes.*

Le Neve Le Neve, J., *Fastic ecclesiae Anglicanae,* followed by the name of the diocese.

Mandati Rome, Archivio di Stato, Fondo Camerale I, Mandati di Camera, followed by a volume number.

Mansi Mansi, J. D., *Sacrorum conciliorum nova et amplissima collectio,* with volume number.

MC *Monumenta conciliorum.*

PL   Migne, J. P., *Patrologia . . . series . . . Latina*

PPC   Nicolas, H., *Proceedings and Ordinances of the Privy Council.*

Pius II   *Privatbriefe, Amtliche Briefe, Briefe als Priester, Briefe als Bishof*: see the relevant volume in Fontes rerum Austriacarum, ed. R. Wolkan in bibliography.

PRO   London, Public Record Office.

QFIAB   Quellen und Forschungen aus Italienen Archiven und Bibliotheken.

Reg. Pen.   Vatican, Archivio Segreto Vaticano, *Registrum penitentiariae*, followed by volume number.

Repertorium Germanicum   See explanation in bibliography.

RS   Rolls Series, or more correctly *Rerum Britanicarum medii aevi scriptores.*

RTA   Reichtagsakten.

Rymer   Rymer, T., *Foedera, Conventiones*, q.v.

SC   Summary Catalogue.

TRHS   Transactions of the Royal Historical Society.

VCH   Victoria County History.

Introduction

This book is intended to fill a gap of which all scholars working on Anglo-papal relations in the fifteenth century soon become aware. A study is needed of the normal relationship before the tension of Henry VIII's divorce and continental heresy intervened, written not from the Reformation with hindsight, nor solely from an English viewpoint.

I began with the grandiose but over-ambitious idea of covering the century from 1417. Further thought convinced me that the development produced by the early Renaissance and the changed world after the French invasions of Italy should await another volume. So this book ends with the advent of Edward IV and Pius II's death, approximately at 1464.

The medieval papacy, claiming plenitude of power, had in the West embodied this in a chain of jurisdiction from subdivisions of the diocese to central organs in Rome. Christians had to apply to the pope himself for dispensations, certain pardons, redresses or rehabilitations, either in person or by proxy; some simply felt more secure in conscience or canon law with a pardon from the highest spiritual authority. The papacy needed to convey orders to the localities. Naturally most of this work was delegated. Furthermore the pope claimed the right to appoint to benefices (make provisions) throughout the church, involving lobbying for appointments and vetting of candidates, and to tax the clergy at appointment and directly. Bureaucracy was therefore ever-increasing; many churchmen needed to be in Rome. To ensure that papal appointments to high church office accorded with royal wishes, rulers also needed proctors in Rome, and popes found it expedient to have representatives in the localities. I intend to examine this system applied to England.

Relations with Rome were not confined to the 'high politics' which have most interested historians. Exclusive concentration on politics detracts from the papacy's importance as a spiritual authority. Because its claims were almost universally accepted, at least to some sort of primacy, its routine dealings with local churches were in many ways more important than the more discussed intermittent quarrels about appointments or money. To emphasise this I begin not with politics but with people: the personnel upon whom the working relationship depended, royal representatives and other English in the curia, papal representatives in England. I have tried to depict some aspects of the life of the English group in Rome, with some of the networks used.

There was also pilgrimage, where English hospices played a vital role. The book studies their function and funding, the property they rented out and their place as a centre for the English group of curial officials. There was furthermore an innumerable group of suppliants seeking the curia for grace rather than graces, for pardon from sins and misdemeanours. Only recently has the papal penitentiary opened its archives; I have been lucky enough to study the registers for this period. The first part therefore gives a picture of the routine machinery and normal workings of Anglo-papal relations.

'High politics' cannot be avoided, of course. The papal claim to appoint to benefices, especially bishoprics and archbishoprics, no less than to tax clergy whom kings also wished to milk, involved delicate international negotiations. Furthermore, in addition to being an Italian princedom, which inevitably involved international affairs, the papacy by tradition mediated between warring Christian rulers. This study begins shortly after Agincourt, with Henry V seeking allies and recogniton of his gains and his claim to the French throne. He allied with Burgundy and secured the treaty of Troyes, 1420, embodying his claim. Papal recognition of Troyes, Henry's desire, remained an aim of the council ruling England in the name of his infant son after 1422. To 1435 the English accepted papal mediation in negotiations with France. The highest spiritual authority was also the only internationally accepted power who could with any credibility declare that treaties accorded with God's will or that a publicly sworn oath was no longer binding. In the late 1420s, when the Burgundians began seriously to consider reneging on their obligations under Troyes, this became very important. In 1435 they at last repudiated Troyes, at an international congress at Arras, presided over by representatives of the pope and the general council of Basel.

The forty years before the opening of this book had been traumatic for the papacy. In 1378 the election of two popes began a schism dividing western Christendom until 1417. An attempted solution at the council of Pisa (1409), called in defiance of both popes, simply produced a third. Finally the council of Constance (1415–18), defying the popes, healed the schism except for a tiny remnant, but only by passing two decrees: *Haec sancta*, declaring that for certain matters councils were superior to popes, and *Frequens*, that councils were in future to be held at intervals to reform the church. Martin V, elected in 1417, accepted these.

During the schism secular governments obtained considerable powers over the church. The French had twice gone so far as to withdraw obedience from the pope and announced that the so-called Gallican Liberties (particularly rights of the French church over appointments) must be respected. The English never withdrew obedience but the crown dictated almost all important moves and parliament re-affirmed the statutes against provisors, fourteenth-century legislation effectively preventing the pope from appointing to benefices in England unless the king allowed. From 1407 only papal appointments to archbishoprics and bishoprics were accepted.

This book opens with the schism just ended, its effects still to be discovered. Until 1420 the pope was unable to live in Rome and, even when he returned, his political hold in Italy was weak. The spiritual and moral effect of the schism was also important, especially on the perception of obedience to the papacy.

After 1417 popes were concerned with recovery from the schism and to avoid damaging consequences from the councils, particularly Constance. Obeying *Frequens*, Martin V called a council at Pavia in 1423, but outwitted attempts to make it a reforming body undermining his power. In 1431 likewise he had to summon a council at Basel, which rapidly fell out with his successor Eugenius IV. It re-affirmed *Haec sancta*, claiming jurisdiction over the papacy and undertaking far-reaching reforms, particularly of the curia, and eventually, when Eugenius refused to accept, deposed him in favour of the duke of Savoy. No local church nor government could avoid taking some position between Basel and Eugenius; the English problem was particularly difficult because Henry VI's government wanted alliance with the Empire, where attitudes were ambiguous and divided, the most tempting being neutrality.

Eugenius finally outmanoeuvred Basel, calling a rival council for union with the eastern churches at Florence in 1439. The English were asked to participate and their interest is worth investigating. They were also involved in negotiations to end Basel (the French arranged for Nicholas V to buy off the anti-pope), because of a temporary alliance with the French, following Henry's marriage to Margaret of Anjou.

The second part of the book traces Anglo-papal diplomacy against this background, to some extent repeating what I and others have said elsewhere, but I hope here in a form more accessible to the general reader. Part of the point is to include the papal view, equally as important as the English politics usually considered. Throughout, individual appointments caused problems, but on other matters too the interests of pope and crown diverged. To 1431 the government sought papal recognition of Troyes, possibly in return for accepting mediation in the Hundred Years War, but dangling the possiblility of revocation or modification of the statutes against provisors. The pope sought abolition of the statutes and the right to raise men and money for crusade against Bohemian heretics. From 1431 to 1464 the pope's concerns were Basel, the Greeks, and a Turkish crusade (Constantinople fell in 1453), whereas English interests were France, Anglo-imperial relations and internal problems. English government became increasingly factious; Henry VI faced rebellion in 1450; loss in France accompanied his failing sanity and from the late 1440s factions dominated, Henry eventually being overthrown by Edward IV.

The theology behind the relationship is also very important. Schism and lollardy forced theologians to consider their beliefs about the papacy, but with little agreement about any aspect. I have discussed what was collected and read, as well as certain thinkers whom I consider either important or typical, without being certain that I know, even now, whether there was an 'English' point of view. Probably there was not, though I hope to show that there was a view on the role of bishops with potential as a considerable challenge to the papacy as popes perceived it.

The schism produced, and Constance crystallised, theories that councils were superior to popes: conciliarism. I offer evidence about their acceptance. Certainly more conciliar literature was read in England after Constance. But very often the conciliarism was moderate, a type on the continent often producing papalism when Basel failed.

There is need of a study of the English in the curia stretching back at least to the outbreak of the schism, to help decide how typical the years 1417–64 were. How much difference did it make that a minority council, 1422–37, was followed by a faction-ridden majority? Probably a great deal: Henry V had a more reasonable relationship with the curia than the later government, though Martin V might not have agreed, ofcourse!

Meanwhile this book is a beginning.

I have given all quotations in English, putting in footnotes the Latin or other equivalent only for works in manuscript. Where there is a printed version I have not put the Latin in a note, assuming that interested readers may check for themselves.

I
Personnel

1

The resident royal representative

To exercise authority in Europe, the papacy in the fourteenth century constructed an elaborate central administration, particularly to regulate patronage over benefices, then a major source of revenue. Consequently the European countries developed institutions at the papal court, including, by the end of our period, permanent representatives. Because the papal prince was a secular as well as a sacred ruler, the activities of these representatives were difficult to classify. The king of England regarded all the English in the Roman court as his servants, on occasion expecting them to act politically, but for most the major reason for their presence was business for clients, to secure a job or both. The task of the royal proctor was somewhat more specific. Among the English in Rome, particularly English officials in the curia, the royal representative, by far the most important, must be considered first.

Between 1417 and 1464 the English began to keep in the curia for long periods a royal proctor, to pilot royal appointments to benefices through the papal system. It was still not deemed essential for any royal representative to be retained continuously, though by 1464 the office was becoming permanent.

These resident royal *procuratores* can be distinguished from proctors sent *ad hoc* and from ambassadors. The resident proctor received a *procuratorium*, defining his function, for which that given to John Catterick in May 1413 can serve as model.[1] His task was firstly to expedite the promotion of clerks to bishoprics, as the king will inform him from time to time, and secondly to expedite 'any other business of ours at the apostolic see, however it arises'. Catterick and Thomas Polton, sent to join him in June 1414, were each specifically designated 'ambassador and proctor', whereas with the new reign Polton, when re-appointed, was only proctor and there was no resident ambassador.[2] The wording of Polton's *procuratorium*, however, is identical with his previous appointment, except that he is not called ambassador and is appointed by the royal council.

Polton was paid regularly,[3] and by 1454 Vincent Clement's letter of appointment mentioned 'with the accustomed salary and emoluments' (*cum emolumentis et salaria . . . consuetis*).[4] Francesco Coppini's *procuratorium* in November 1461 was exactly the same, including the phrase about salary, one hundred pounds a year, as for many years.[5]

Only fitfully can one observe the proctor at work. On bishoprics the letter collection of Thomas Bekynton shows Andrew Holes in action. He told the king of the promotion of John Kemp and Louis of Luxembourg to the cardinalate in 1439[6] and received secret royal instructions for the proposed reshuffle of bishoprics when archbishop Chichele wanted to resign in April 1442.[7] The bishoprics were Canterbury, Bath and Salisbury, the last for Bekynton himself. When Chichele finally died, however, Holes acted too fast on Bekynton's behalf, paying the papal tax of first fruits for Salisbury before he had firm word that William Aiscough was prepared to move.[8] Holes assumed that Bekynton would replace Aiscough, otherwise the money might be lost. Eventually Bekynton, losing Salisbury, moved to Bath and Wells.[9] Royal proctors, especially working for Henry VI's capricious government, could take nothing for granted.

'Other business concerning us arising from time to time' could be extremely varied. Holes, for instance, helped to negotiate safe-conducts from the marquess of Este for English delegates for the council of Florence,[10] and was entrusted with royal instructions about the canonisation of St Osmund.[11] He was ordered to complain to their master general about the English Carmelites,[12] and received special letters of credence with royal views on a meeting of the German electors in Frankfurt early in 1442,[13] probably required because his original mandate was not wide enough. This was a task for an ambassador rather than a proctor. We have few of his letters, but they came regularly to the king and apparently were regarded as news-sheets; extracts occur in a neat two-page 'pamphlet' in the chapter archives in Durham, presumably sent for information.[14]

The royal representative was also obliged to uphold the royal 'honour'. Delicate questions of precedence constantly arose. Polton conducted a long argument with the Castilian representative, beginning at least in the council of Constance. At Candlemas, 2 February 1422, the ambassadors of the kings of Castile and England quarrelled as to who should receive candles first. Pierre Assalbit, papal sacrist, formerly in the English nation at Constance, gave candles secretly to the English, and the pope, equally

secretly, to the Castilians. This annoyed the representatives of both the
dauphin and the king of France, who received none, there being a
problem about whom they represented.[15] At Easter 1422 an unseemly
struggle occurred in St Peter's, actually during mass, over priority of
seating between Polton and the representative of the king of Castille.[16]
Henry V protested personally to the pope in English at Polton's position
in a consistory (the equivalent of a full meeting of the royal council) less
honourable than the Castilian's, explaining that Polton was 'orator' as
well as proctor, which the pope accepted with apologies; his officers had
forgotten, since Polton had been in the curia so long.[17] In the time of
Pius II so lengthy a stay would have ensured reversion to being a simple
proctor. Martin V was trying to resist permanent ambassadors, not
amenable to curial regulations and discipline,[18] and perhaps therefore
Polton when re-appointed by the minority government was a proctor
only.

But whether called ambassador or not, the royal representative was
regarded as leader of the English in the curia. Polton's position can be
seen most clearly when Henry V's embassy arrived at midsummer 1422.
Among the English *curiales* Polton's name comes first,[19] with a place of
honour below the papal throne[20] when the embassy was heard. When
John Whethamstede of St Albans was ill in Rome in 1423, the pope
entrusted to Polton the indulgence for the sick abbot.[21] By the time of
William Gray, when there is more evidence, the proctor had a large house
and his *familiares* dominated the English hospice. He was sent detailed
instructions in 1446 on the conduct of business with the pope.[22]

In the second half of the century an education in Italy helped. Holes, a
doctor of canon law,[23] Flemming, a bachelor of theology[24] and Gray, a
doctor of theology,[25] graduated from Padua, as did Peter Courtenay.[26]
Royal proctors often already had experience of the curia; Polton, for
instance, had been working there at intervals since about 1394,[27] and
Holes had come with FitzHugh, his immediate predecessor.[28]

The post was not full-time; those who held it did other jobs. A
position in the curia itself was essential, giving access to the crucial
courts. More details will be given later about the exact significance of the
positions held, but here it suffices to point out that Polton ended his
career as apostolic protonotary,[29] as did Holes, who was also a
referendarius from 1435 and a *cubicularius*, a post in the papal household.[30] Flemming was a protonotary,[31] Peter Courtenay *referendarius*.[32]
John Lax rose from an abbreviator to being one of Calixtus III'S
secretaries.[33]

The royal proctor could also do business for others, who of course found it good tactics to employ him. Durham priory for instance always tried to employ the royal proctor; Holes, Gray and Lax worked for it.[34]

John Catterick

When the council of Constance ended there were, as we have seen, two royal representatives in the curia, John Catterick and Thomas Polton. Catterick had been appointed royal proctor and ambassador in 1413.[35] He succeeded Henry Chichele in the see of St Davids in 1414, was then translated to Coventry and Lichfield and finally, just before he died, in December 1419, to Exeter.[36] As proctor and/or ambassador he corresponded with Henry V as the curia moved back to Rome,[37] discussing Henry's diplomatic intentions in private audience with the pope,[38] as well as negotiating more routine questions concerning bishoprics in conjunction with Polton.[39] Apparently he was regarded as the senior diplomat, and remained continuously at the curia until his death on 28 December 1419.[40] He is buried in Florence.[41]

Thomas Polton

In 1414 the king added Thomas Polton as another 'ambassador and proctor'.[42] At the time he was chancellor of York, holding several valuable prebends, with the archdeaconry of Taunton,[43] but his most valuable promotions came as royal representative.[44] Letters of William Swan (to be met again) give some picture of the man: ambitious, scheming, according to Swan, not to be trusted. In 1421 Swan warned Chichele:

> For the bishop of Hereford shows in his words that he is your servant and well-wisher and zealous for your honour, but I am unable to find out how true this is, since none can ever understand him. Whatever may be the case, I do not tell him your lordship's secret business, but as far as possible it is wholly unknown to him.[45]

By then Swan had known him at the curia for nearly twenty years. Swan's letter book has evidence of Polton's attempt to conceal malpractice concerning the rectory of Pewsey, almost certainly simoniacal.[46] At the council of Pisa Polton had had this case discussed, doing his best to blacken the character of his ordinary, Robert Hallum, who was trying to prevent him holding a canonry of Salisbury.[47]

While Catterick lived, Polton appears the 'junior', who travelled to and fro to ascertain the royal will.[48] After Catterick's death he acted alone and seems to have travelled less.

Polton, ambitious, persuaded Henry V that he deserved a bishopric. In July 1420 he was given Hereford, but, despite royal support, did not obtain London, vacant in August 1421 on Clifford's death.[49] Martin V's perhaps sincere view, that London was too important to be held by an absentee,[50] probably also covered a determination to assert his prerogatives. Polton obtained Chichester in compensation.[51]

While Henry V lived, Polton's role as royal representative and chief channel of information to the king was universally acknowledged. Martin V consulted him in November 1421 when Henry complained about London,[52] acknowledging him as both proctor and royal ambassador.[53] Polton's view of the royal will evidently carried weight.[54] When Henry died Polton reverted to being royal proctor only,[55] though he retained a position as senior Englishman in the curia.[56]

With the king a minor, however, the position was ambivalent; individual members of the minority council probably employed different proctors. Polton was closely connected with Beaufort from his earliest career,[57] and fed him information.[58] This made him much less useful to other members of the government, but also vulnerable during intrigues in England. Polton wished to leave the curia in 1423 on grounds of age and the need to visit his diocese, but the government, in fact Gloucester, forbade it, saying he was needed at the council of Pavia/Siena.[59] He certainly did not attend. There is no evidence of any activity by him there and he was in Rome to greet Whethamstede,[60] but by May 1425 he seems to have left the curia, since he is not among the leading Englishmen then in Rome required to carry out the royal will.[61] Probably he thought it necessary to return to defend his own interests in the intrigues which produced for him the see of Worcester, when the government was in conflict with the papacy over the see of York.[62]

When Polton was proctor the records of the English hospice are very thin; we only know that he was a member of the confraternity of St Edmund.[63]

Polton was not replaced; from 1425 to 1429 there was no resident royal representative in Rome. This may help to explain the very strained relations which developed. On 20 June 1429, to present the reasons for using crusading money and troops in France, a proctor was again appointed.[64]

Robert FitzHugh

The candidate, Robert FitzHugh, son of Henry V's chamberlain and executor, Lord Henry FitzHugh of Ravensworth castle in Yorkshire,[65] was a theologian, who had been at the council of Pavia. In July 1424 he was appointed by the council warden of the King's Hall in Cambridge,[66] having already been chancellor of the University.[67]

At first FitzHugh led a mainly diplomatic embassy, appointed for one year, but he was being referred to as royal proctor early in 1430,[68] for business connected with peace negotiations with France. On 30 April 1431 he was promoted bishop of London.[69] Eugenius IV gave the provision, though presumably FitzHugh was being rewarded by the English government. He was consecrated at the curia in Foligno,[70] but on 3 September, 1432 was preparing to leave for England.[71] By then he had already been appointed ambassador at Basel,[72] which he reached ahead of his fellows, on 14 February 1433.

While in Rome FitzHugh most probably lived in a house belonging to the hospice of St Thomas.[73]

Andrew Holes

FitzHugh's departure again left no officially designated royal representative but certainly by 1434 master Andrew Holes, a lawyer who had come in FitzHugh's embassy in 1429, was being treated as if appointed. He said later that he acted before formal appointment.[74] On 26 October 1434, the king told him that no one was to act over the see of Rochester until Henry had made up his mind,[75] as if Holes were the leading English representative. By 1435 he was a referendary and in February 1437 was finally given official appointment,[76] from when he can be seen in action.[77] His friend Thomas Bekynton, the royal secretary, assured him of his excellent standing with the king in June 1441,[78] in the labyrinthine negotiations concerning indulgences for Eton.[79] Holes remained working hard in the curia until 29 December 1444,[80] following the pope to Florence, as well as acquiring a canon law doctorate in Padua in 1439.[81]

Holes is one of few Englishmen in the curia at this time who impressed Italian contemporaries. In the memoirs of Vespasiano da Bisticci, a famous Florentine book seller, we see him buying books, discussing theology with leading Florentine humanists and remembered for piety.[82] But he did not acquire a bishopric. Vespasiano believed, perhaps

correctly, that he had a mind above such things, but he was nominated by
Henry VI for Coutances in 1440[83] though in vain, and very probably
would not have wanted a troublesome French see. No English bishopric
was offered. Vespasiano's opinion, that he had enemies, is also very
probable. He became keeper of the privy seal after Adam Moleyns's
murder on 9 January 1450,[84] but was dismissed in April 1452, presumably to allow appointment of Thomas Lisieux, a much more obvious
royal nominee.[85] Holes then retired to his house in Salisbury cathedral
close.

In Rome he shared a large hospice house, called 'the tower', with two
other *curiales*, and was also a member of the confraternities of St Edmund
and St Thomas.[86]

William Gray

The next proctor officially designated (1446), William Gray, dean of
York,[87] was son of Sir Thomas Gray, of Heton in Northumberland and
nephew of William Gray, then bishop of Lincoln, formerly of London.[88]
When appointed he was already abroad, in 1442 in Cologne to study
theology and thence to Padua, Florence and Ferrara. From Ferrara he
came to Rome, probably during 1446, with royal orders to defend the
king and bishops against a papal tenth.[89] His patronage in Rome has
been extensively studied because he was rich, generous and an enthusiast
for Renaissance culture,[90] but his main proctorial work was not of course
collecting manuscripts but business for the king. He came and went
while in office[91] and, like Holes, helped to further the cause of St
Osmund, which the king had much at heart.[92] He became protonotary
and *referendarius*, posts discussed further in the next chapter,[93] but his
actual role in smoothing appointments is seldom apparent. He perhaps
helped obtain indulgences for Eton.[94]

Gray and many members of his household were conspicuous in the
English colony in Rome. He rented a house from St Edmund's
hospice.[95] His period of office coincided with the 1450 Jubilee, during
which he visited John Capgrave, the Augustinian author who fell sick
during his pilgrimage.[96] This was also the period of the rebuilding of the
hospice of St Thomas, and Gray was one of the guarantors of the loan for
the new building.[97] But his role was in fact much greater, as I show
later.[98] His *familiares* were crucial to the running of the hospice whilst he
was in Rome. His large house, rented from St Edmund's hospice in 1446
for 60 ducats per annum, was described as: 'A great house with a turret

and upper storey and tiled with slate and with marble stairs before it and land, garden, staircases, chambers and a stable within.[99]

William Babyngton

In March 1449 and January 1450 William Babyngton, abbot of Bury, was appointed royal proctor, on the second occasion for five years.[100] His only actions of which I am aware concerned members of religious orders coming for the Jubilee.[101] By 7 October 1453 he was dead.[102] Perhaps he was intended as an alternative to Gray.

Gray left on 13 October 1453.[103] By then the role of proctor must have become somewhat problematical, with the king's mental collapse in August;[104] Gray may have returned for advice. By early 1454 the duke of York had become protector, Thomas Bourgchier, bishop of Ely, was recommended to succeed Kemp as archbishop of Canterbury, and Gray, a loyal Yorkist, replaced him as bishop.[105] He did not return to Rome.

Vincent Clement

Gray was replaced on 4 November 1454 by Vincent Clement, whose career is discussed in the next chapter.[106] Clement was already pursuing a career in Rome and England[107] and it is unclear how long he remained royal proctor. He was appointed *de avisamento concilii*. Henry VI recovered just after Christmas 1454[108] and in March the following year Robert Flemming was formally appointed to the post.[109] Then, following Henry's defeat at St Albans on 22 May, York was again in ascendancy, until about October 1456 when the enmity between him and the queen came to a head.[110] In April 1456 English records call Clement papal collector,[111] though Flemming was not called royal proctor when appointed in August 1457 to offer the royal obedience to Calixtus III.[112] In December 1456 John Lax, a long-standing resident in Rome and secretary to Calixtus, was being called royal proctor.[113]

John Lax or Chester

John Lax's career illustrates the perils of serving the king, especially abroad, in the age of Henry VI. Lax, from the diocese of Durham, who seems to have acquired a BCL in Oxford, and DCL in Italy,[114] must first have gone to Rome in 1447 or 1448.[115] In January 1449 he was described as master of works (*magister operum*) in an arrangement for new buildings for the hospice of St Thomas,[116] and from then onwards rented a hospice house.[117]

He accumulated benefices. In 1449 he became rector of Street, Somerset, presented by Glastonbury abbey.[118] By May that year he was already an abbreviator.[119] With a dispensation to hold two incompatible benefices he added the parochial chapel of Walton in January 1450[120] and the rectory of Rickinghall Inferior, Suffolk, in June, covered by a new dispensation for three incompatibles.[121] On 20 December 1455 he became a secretary to Calixtus III, referred to as 'long known to the pope', and still held the post under Pius II.[122] He was still in minor orders, though he maintained successfully that he had papal dispensation (from 1448) to hold Street for seven years without taking major orders.[123] The dispensation had been to allow him to study, but in 1455 he claimed that business for the king and others had delayed his studies, so he had it prolonged for three more years, covering postponment for business as well as study.[124] This should have involved major orders in 1458 or 1459, of which there is no evidence.

Meanwhile he was travelling between England and Rome on business for the pope and clients.[125] In March 1457 he became, briefly, canon of Salisbury, with the prebend of Chardstock, reward for his help with the canonisation of St Osmund,[126] and on 7 September 1456 Durham Priory conferred a canonry and prebend of Hemingburgh.[127] He also, fatally, entangled himself with Cardinal Prospero Colonna. In July 1457, during litigation, he obtained Prospero's resignation of the valuable prebend of Laughton, York, estimated as worth £33 per annum, on condition that Lax paid a pension.[128] Colonna had already been disputing with Lax's predecessor, Thomas Chapman, and now accused Lax of imprisoning delegates coming to present mandates and of getting a royal order to prevent Vincent Clement from receiving papal letters.[129] An attempted compromise with Colonna failed and Lax resigned the prebend on 19 June 1459.[130] Meanwhile, however, he had added in 1458 the rectory of Dicheat, Somerset, presented by Glastonbury[131] and the provostship of St Edmund's College, Somerset.[132]

It is difficult to discover precisely what went wrong for so successful an operator. Nicholas Frome, abbot of Glastonbury, one patron, died in April 1456. Perhaps the new regime became less favourable; there had been earlier quarrels, with a Glastonbury monk,[133] and concerning the tithes owed to Street,[134], but the presentation of Dicheat in 1458 makes this unlikely. On 6 August 1458 Calixtus III died, removing presumably his strongest patron. Lax must have been in England in the earlier part of

1459 when Bekynton replaced him in both Dicheat and Street, declaring them incompatible, saying that he was not ordained.[135] On 12 September 1459 Pius II ordered him to be ordained.[136] Lax appealed against Bekynton in May 1459, alleging legislation of Pope Eugenius IV protecting resident *curiales*,[137] and in July returned to Rome to pursue the case in person.[138]

Litigation over Street and Dicheat was not his only headache. On 7 April 1452 he had agreed to take one of the largest hospice houses, and contribute 100 cameral florins for repairs, plus another 50 as a gift, provided that the *confrates* of St Thomas's contributed another 100.[139] During the litigation over Laughton, from at least 1456, he and Colonna agreed that Lax was to hold it in return for paying Colonna 20 per annum.[140] But these terms were apparently not fulfilled, probably because Lax was too poor,[141] and by June 1459 Colonna had re-acquired Laughton, though not before Lax had been condemned in Rome for gross misconduct, the penalty being sequestration of his goods and benefices for the benefit of Colonna.[142] In September 1458, his house in Rome, seized and sold to cover his debts,[143] was repurchased by the hospice for 300 gold florins, whilst Colonna claimed the use of it, presumably in lieu of cash. In the end Berard Eroli, cardinal of Spoleto, Lax's patron, undertook to pay his debts to both Colonna and the hospice.[144]

Lax must have lost a great deal, and the complicating factor was English politics. Lax was a Lancastrian. His sending to Rome in 1459 coincided with the re-establishment of the queen, and presumably he had to explain why the English were not sending delegates to the pope's congress of Mantua and why the papal legate in England, Francesco Coppini, had received rather short shrift.[145] In May 1460 Lax was on his way through Milan, bound for Rome as a royal envoy,[146] but meanwhile the situation in England had changed drastically. Coppini sided with the Yorkists who, on seizing power, tried to retain him and obtain his promotion.[147] Yet in early August 1460 the royal agent in Rome was still considered to be Lax.[148] But someone must have noticed that he was not necessarily to be trusted, because on 10 August Antonio della Torre, Warwick's agent, became the royal mouthpiece to the pope,[149] though Coppini continued to express trust in Lax.[150] By November, however, della Torre had told Pius II not to trust Lax, and the pope, though saying that Lax seemed to have Yorkist credentials and would probably side with the victors, agreed not wholly to trust Lax until he had heard from the Yorkists.[151] Perhaps Lax did decide, rather belatedly, to side with the

victors; a letter of protection for him on 22 December 1460, going to
Rome on royal business,[152] may represent Yorkist business, but would
anyway have been annulled by the battle of Wakefield (a serious defeat
for the Yorkists) on 30 December. After that there is no mention of Lax
as royal representative, and he was included in the attainder of Lancastrians in November 1461,[153] though in the curia he pleaded protection against all actions by ordinaries, as an official of the Holy See.[154]
By 9 September 1461, he had lost Dicheat.[155]

Gradually he recovered somewhat. Early in 1462 he was said to have
been pardoned in England.[156] In November 1463 he was reinstated in
Laughton, Colonna being dead.[157] In February 1465 he was again or
genuinely pardoned,[158] and on 26 August 1465 was called canon of
Utrecht.[159] By then he was litigating against the bishop of Bath and
Wells and the abbot of Glastonbury, the latter having appealed against
him.[160] In August 1465 he obtained a *monitorium* against all his
enemies.[161] But he must have lost a great deal. According to his appeal of
1465 he had not enjoyed Hemingburgh for seven years, since 1458, and
was cheated of his Salisbury prebend, Chardstock, which he did not hold
after December 1458.[162] Durham replaced him as proctor with Vincent
Clement and Thomas Hope, though his factor, Thomas Coventry, wrote
that his standing in the curia was now good and that he had begun to
recover.[163]

Professor Dobson, discussing Lax's work for Durham priory, concluded that he was dishonest.[164] Certainly his enemies in England said
so, but much more probably he was the victim of circumstances. Politics,
rather than dishonesty, caught up with him and prevented him meeting
his obligations.

Francesco Coppini

There was no attempt to keep a permanent agent in Rome until Edward
IV's government was secure. The papal legate Francesco Coppini was
actually appointed proctor, with the usual one hundred pounds salary, in
November 1461[165] but fell foul of the curia[166] and never functioned.

Peter Courtenay

In November 1463 Peter Courtenay, archdeacon of Exeter, when made
referendarius, was called proctor for Edward IV.[167] He was a lawyer
educated in Oxford, Cologne and Padua. Presumably he was still func-

tioning when Pius II died. He was one of the Devonshire Courtenays, third son of Sir Philip Courtenay, of Powderham, nephew of Lord Hungerford.

If studies of royal representatives and Anglo-papal diplomacy are combined it becomes apparent that coherent royal policy in Rome needed peace at home and a permanent representative at the curia. The times when Henry VI's government lacked such a person were either periods of strain in relations with Rome or of such internal turmoil that consistent policy would have been impossible. This lesson was learned in the subsequent reigns; royal representatives became much more permanent and important by the end of the fifteenth century.[168]

Notes

1 Rymer, IV/2, p. 31 (IX, 12). D. Queller, *The Office of Ambassador in the Middle Ages*, Princeton (NJ), 1967; B. Behrens, 'Origins of the office of English resident ambassador in Rome', *EHR*, XLIX, 1934, pp. 640–56.

2 Rymer, IV/2, p. 80 (IX, 138–9); IV/4, p. 85 (X, 266).

3 e.g. PRO, E403/636, m. 6, 7; E403/638, m. 4; E403/643 m. 6.

4 Rymer, V/2, p. 60 (XI, 359–60).

5 Rymer, V/2, p. 106 (XI, 479). Cf. Holes: PRO E404/63/97.

6 T. Bekynton, *Official Correspondence of Thomas Bekynton*, ed. G. Williams, 2 vols., *RS*, LVI, London, 1872, I, p. 50.

7 Bekynton, *Correspondence*, I, p. 149.

8 Bekynton, *Correspondence*, I, pp. 239–40.

9 Bekynton, *Correspondence*, I, pp. xliii–xliv.

10 Bekynton, *Correspondence*, I, p. 59.

11 Bekynton, *Correspondence*, I, p. 118.

12 Bekynton, *Correspondence*, I, p. 138.

13 Bekynton, *Correspondence*, I, p. 91.

14 Durham, Dean and Chapter Archives, Misc. Ch. 7246; letters to king, Bekynton, *Correspondence*, I, p. 50.

15 M. Dykmans, *Le Cérémonial papale de la fin du Moyen Age à la Renaissance*, Bibliothèque de l'Institut Historique Belge de Rome, III, fasc. XXVI, 1983, *Textes Avignonais jusqu'à la fin du Grand Schisme d'Occident*, pp. 398–9, for the text; IV, fasc. XXVII, 1985, *Le Retour à Rome ou le Cérémonial du Patriarche Pierre Ameil*, pp. 36–9.

16 J. Haller, 'England und Rom unter Martin V', *QFIAB*, VIII, 1905, pp. 249–304, esp. pp. 295–6, nos. 5 and 6; Behrens, 'Origins', p. 646.

17 Behrens, 'Origins', p. 650.

18 Behrens, 'Origins', p. 650; E. von Ottenthal, *Regulae Cancellariae Apostolicae*, Innsbruck, 1888, p. 221.

19 BL, MS Harley 861, f. 45v.

20 BL, MS Harley 861, f. 46.

21 J. Amundesham, *Annales Monasterii S. Albani a J. Amundesham*, 2 vols., ed. H. T. Riley, *RS*, XXVIII, London, 1870, 1871, I, p. 150.

22 Chapter 9, notes 301, 302.

23 G. Zonta and C. A. Brotto, *Acta Graduum Academicorum Gymnasii Patavini ab anno*

MCCVI ad annum MCCCCL, Padua, 1922, nos. 1320, 1321.

24 Zonta, no. 2198.
25 Zonta, nos. 1966, 1968, 1972–4.
26 H. Anstey, ed., *Epistolae Academicae Oxonienses, (Registrum F)*, 2 vols., Oxford Historical Society, XXXV, XXXVI, 1898, II, p. 442; R. J. Mitchell, 'English students at Padua, 1460–75', *TRHS*, 4th series, XIX, 1936, pp. 101–17, esp. pp. 106–7.
27 Below, note 42.
28 Below, note 74.
29 *BRUO*, III, pp. 1494–5.
30 *CPL*, IX, p. 82; Rymer, V/1, p. 21 (X, 620), for *referendarius*.
31 *CPL*, XI, p. 681.
32 B. Katterbach, *Referendarii utriusque signaturae a Martino V ad Clementem IX et praelati signaturae supplicationum a Martino V ad Leonem XIII*, Studi e testi, LV, Vatican 1931, p. 34, no. 16.
33 Below, note 122.
34 Below, Chapter 2, note 258.
35 Rymer, IV/2, p. 31 (IX, 12).
36 *BRUO*, I, pp. 371–2; Le Neve, *Exeter*, p. 2.
37 Rymer, IV/3, p. 88 (IX, 680).
38 Harvey, 'Martin V and Henry V', *AHP*, XXIV, 1986, pp. 49–70, esp. pp. 57, 58–9, correcting Grenfels to Ehrenfels, cf. C. Schuchard, *Die Deutschen an der päpstlichen Kurie im späten Mittelalter, 1378–1447*, Bibliothek des Deutschen Historischen Instituts in Rom, LXV, Tübingen, 1987, pp. 151–2, 226, 295.
39 Harvey, 'Martin V and Henry V', p. 59; Oxford, Bodleian Library, MS Arch. Seld. B 23, f. 68.
40 Le Neve, *Exeter*, p. 2.
41 G. B. Parks, *The English Traveller to Italy*, I, *The Middle Ages (to 1525)*, Rome, 1954, p. 301.
42 *BRUO*, III, pp. 1494–5; Rymer, IV/2, p. 80 (IX, p. 138).
43 Le Neve, *Bath and Wells*, p. 16.
44 *BRUO*, III, pp. 1494–5, for a list.
45 Quoted: H. Chichele, *The Register of Henry Chichele, Archbishop of Canterbury, 1414–43*, ed. E. F. Jacob, 4 vols., CYS, XLII, XLV, XLVI, XLVII, Oxford, 1938–47, I, p. xliv.
46 R. Hallum, *The Register of Robert Hallum, Bishop of Salisbury, 1407–1417*, ed. J. M. Horn, CYS, LXXII, 1982, no. 938; Oxford, Bodleian Library, MS Arch. Seld. B 23, ff. 52–3, and 133–5v.
47 Grimstone: cf. Le Neve, *Salisbury*, p. 57; M. Harvey, *Solutions to the Schism: a study of some English attitudes, 1378–1409*, Kirchengeschichtlichen Quellen und Studien, St Ottilien, 1983, p. 163 and note.
48 Harvey, 'Martin V and Henry V', pp. 53, 56, 57.
49 Harvey, 'Martin V and Henry V', pp. 65–6.
50 Harvey, 'Martin V and Henry V', p. 65.
51 *CPL*, VII, pp. 171, 255.
52 Haller, *England und Rom*, no. 4, p. 293.
53 Haller, *England und Rom*, no. 6, pp. 294–6 and see also below, Chapter 7, pp. 134.
54 BL, MS Cotton Cleop. C IV, f. 171, Kemp.
55 Rymer, IV/4, p. 85 (X, 266).
56 Amundesham, *Annales*, I, pp. 81, 150; H. Cnattingius, *Studies in the Order of St Bridget*, Stockholm Studies in History, VII, Uppsala, 1963, p. 134, *Episcopus Anglie* Rome, August 1423.

57 G. L. Harriss, *Cardinal Beaufort, a study of Lancastrian ascendancy and decline*, Oxford, 1988, pp. 66, 112, 156.

58 Poggio Bracciolini, *Lettere*, ed. H. Harth, 3 vols. so far, Florence, 1984–7, II, pp. 25–6, no. 9.

59 Oxford, Bodleian Library, MS Ashmole 789, f. 237, Gloucester to pope, ff. 237–7v, to cardinals.

60 W. Brandmüller, *Das Konzil von Pavia-Siena, 1423–4*, Vorreformationsgeschichtliche Forschungen, XVI, 2 vols., Münster, 1969, 1974, I, p. 30 and above note 56.

61 BL, MS Cotton Cleop. C IV, ff. 182v–3.

62 Below, Chapter 8, notes 10–17, 48.

63 'The English Hospice in Rome', sexcentenary issue of *Venerabile*, XXI, May 1962, pp. 5, 95.

64 Below, Chapter 8, notes 62, 63.

65 *BRUC*, pp. 231–2; Brandmüller, *Pavia/Siena*, pp. 32, 38. .

66 *PPC*, III, pp. 158–9; *CPR 1422–9*, p. 210.

67 *CPR 1422–9*, p. 560; *CPL*, VII, p. 255.

68 *DK*, XLVIII, pp. 262, 263; BL, MS Cotton Cleop. E III, f. 41; *PPC*, III, p. 347, IV, p. 14; Rymer, IV/4, p. 150 (X, 433), for original appointment.

69 *CPL*, VIII, p. 358; R. A. Griffiths, *Henry VI. The excercise of Royal Authority, 1422–1461*, London, 1981, p. 98.

70 Le Neve, *London*, p. 3; place: *BRUC*.

71 *CPL*, VIII, p. 280.

72 PRO, E404/48/341; A. N. E. D. Schofield, 'The first English delegation to the Council of Basel', *JEH*, XII, 1961, pp. 167–96, esp. p. 179.

73 *Venerabile*, XXI, p. 48, n. 19; English College Archives, *Liber* 232, f. 22: *Et olim stetit in dicta domo episcopus London.*

74 Holes: *BRUO*, II, pp. 949–50 and M. Harvey, 'An Englishman at the Roman Curia during the Council of Basel: Andrew Holes, his sermon of 1433 and his books', *JEH*, XLII, 1991, pp. 19–38; J. Stevenson, ed., *Letters and Papers illustrative of the Wars of the English in France during the Reign of Henry the Sixth, King of England*, 2 vols., RS, XXII, London, 1861, I, pp. 71–3.

75 *PPC*, IV, pp. 281–2.

76 *DK*, XLVIII, p. 317; PRO, E403/769, m. 3; and see note 30 above.

77 e.g. Chapter 9, notes 170–4, 206.

78 Bekynton, *Correspondence*, I, pp. 228–9.

79 Chapter 6, pp. 118–21.

80 PRO, E404/63/97; for work: Salisbury Cathedral Library, Chapter Act Book Hutchyns, mentions 1441 work in Normandy and Aquitaine too.

81 Mitchell, 'Students in Padua', p. 117.

82 Vespasiano da Bisticci, *Le vite*, ed. A. Greco, 2 vols., Florence, 1970, 1976, I, pp. 311–13.

83 Bekynton, *Correspondence*, I, pp. 14, 26.

84 Griffiths, *Henry VI*, p. 287.

85 Griffiths, *Henry VI*, p. 290.

86 BL, MS Cotton Cleop. C IV, f. 189; English College Archives, *Liber* 232, f. 29v; *Venerabile*, XXI, pp. 66, 95.

87 *BRUO*, II, pp. 809–14; Bisticci, *Vite*, I, pp. 307–10; *CPR, 1441–6*, p. 390.

88 R. M. Haines, 'The practice and problems of a fifteenth century bishop; the episcopate of William Gray', *Medieval Studies*, XXXIV, 1972, pp. 435–61.

89 Mitchell, 'Students in Padua', p. 117; R. Weiss, *Humanism in England during the Fifteenth Century*, 3rd ed., Medium Aevum Monographs, IV, Oxford, 1967, pp.

86–90; R. A. B. Mynors, *Catalogue of the Manuscripts of Balliol College, Oxford*, Oxford, 1962, pp. xxiv–xlvi; Chapter 9, notes 301–2.

90 A. C. de la Mare, 'Vespasiano da Bisticci and Gray', *JWCI*, XX, 1957, pp. 174–6; G. M. Cagni, *Vespasiano da Bisticci e il suo epistolario*, Temi e Testi, XV, Rome, 1969, pp. 120–1, esp. p. 119, referring to him, not Holes; A. C. de la Mare, 'Vespasiano da Bisticci and the Florentine manuscripts of Robert Flemming in Lincoln College', *Lincoln College Record*, 1962–3, pp. 7–16, esp. p. 11; also Humfrey, *Duke Humfrey's library and the Divinity School*, Oxford, 1988, index, p. 151; *Duke Humfrey and English Humanism in the Fifteenth Century*, Oxford, 1970, Chapter IV; *BRUO*, II, pp. 809–14; M. A. Ganz, 'A Florentine friendship: Donato Acciaiuoli and Vespasiano da Bisticci', *Renaissance Quarterly*, XLIII, 1990, pp. 372–83, esp. p. 375.

91 *DK*, XLVIII, pp. 376, 378, 382, 387, 391; PRO, E403/771, m.11.

92 A. R. Malden, *The Canonisation of St Osmund*, Wiltshire Record Society, Salisbury, 1901, pp. 95, 97, 99, 105, 110, 117, 118–19, 120, 144–5.

93 Katterbach, p. 24, no. 10; W. E. Lunt, *Financial Relations of the Papacy with England, 1327–1534, Studies in Anglo-papal Relations during the Middle Ages*, II, Cambridge (Mass.), 1962, p. 774.

94 Chapter 2, note 161.

95 English College Archives, *Liber* 272, f. 8.

96 J. Capgrave, *Liber de illustribus Henricis*, ed. F. C. Hingeston, *RS*, VII, London, 1858, p. 221; below, p. 62.

97 V. J. Flynn, 'Englishmen in Rome during the Renaissance', *Modern Philology*, XXXVI, 1938–9, pp. 121–38, esp. p. 130–3.

98 Chapter 3, note 205 seq.

99 English College Archives, *Liber* 272, f. 8.

100 *BRUO*, I, p. 86; *CPL*, X, pp. 61, 530–1; Rymer, V/2, p. 8 (XI, 226), the wording differs slightly from the norm; *CPR 1446–52*, pp. 267, 310; Anstey, *Epistolae Academicae Oxonienses*, I, no. 193, pp. 271–3.

101 *CPL*, X, p. 57.

102 *CPR 1452–61*, p. 147.

103 Malden, p. 145.

104 Griffiths, *Henry VI*, p. 715.

105 Griffiths, *Henry VI*, p. 727; Haines, 'The practice', p. 442; *PPC*, VI, p. 168.

106 *BRUO*, I, pp. 432–3; *CPR 1452–61*, p. 195; Rymer, V/2, p. 60 (XI, 359–60).

107 Chapter 2, notes 216–33.

108 Griffiths, *Henry VI*, p. 738.

109 *BRUO*, II, pp. 699–700; Rymer, V/2, p. 62 (XI, 364); *CPR, 1452–61*, pp. 227, 336.

110 Griffiths, *Henry VI*, pp. 773–5.

111 *DK*, XLVIII, p. 414; Rymer, V/2, p. 67 (XI, 378).

112 Rymer, V/2, p. 77 (XI, 403); PRO, E404/71/2/72.

113 Rymer, V/2, p. 70 (XI, 384–5).

114 *BRUO*, II, pp. 1113–14.

115 B. Dobson, *Durham Priory, 1400–1450*, Cambridge Studies in Medieval Life and Thought, 3rd series, VI, Cambridge, 1973, p. 214; Durham, Dean and Chapter Archives, *Locellus* 9 no. 30.

116 Flynn, p. 130; English College Archives, *Liber* 17, f. 11.

117 *Venerabile*, XXI, p. 67; below, note 139.

118 T. Bekynton, *The Register of Thomas Bekynton, Bishop of Bath and Wells, 1443–65*, ed. H. C. Maxwell-Lyte and M. C. B. Dawes, 2 vols., Somerset Record Society, XLIX, L, 1934–5, I, p. 109.

119 *CPL*, X, p. 49.

120 Bekynton, *Register*, I, p. 138.
121 *CPL*, X, p. 71.
122 *CPL*, XI, pp. 97, 99, 109, 597–9.
123 *CPL*, X, p. 55.
124 *CPL*, XI, pp. 98–9.
125 *CPL*, XI, pp. 115, 128.
126 Le Neve, *Salisbury*, p. 40; Malden, p. xxxi.
127 *BRUO*, above, note 114.
128 *CPL*, XI, pp. 43–4, 118; Le Neve, *Northern Province*, p. 65.
129 *CPL*, XI, p. 71; in Hope's precedent book: PRO, E36/195, pp. 128–9.
130 Le Neve, *Northern Province*, p. 65.
131 Bekynton, *Register* , I, p. 305.
132 *CPL*, XII, p. 254.
133 *CPL*, X, pp. 530–2.
134 *CPL*, XI, pp. 134–7.
135 Bekynton, *Register*, I, pp. 319–20, 327, 356–7.
136 *CPL*, XI, p. 554.
137 Ottenthal, pp. 252–3.
138 *DK*, XLVIII, p. 437.
139 English College Archives, membrane 205.
140 *CPL*, XI, pp. 43–4.
141 Le Neve, *Northern Province*, p. 65.
142 *CPL*, XI, p. 71.
143 *CPL*, XI, p. 652; English College Archives, membrane 206.
144 English College Archives, membranes 207, 208. Cardinal: C. Eubel, *Hierarchia Catholica Medii Aevi*, 8 vols., Munster, 1913, II, p. 13.
145 *CPR 1452–61*, pp. 548–9; A. N. E. D. Schofield, ' The first English delegation', *JEH*, XII, 1961, p. 73, n. 1.
146 A. B. Hinds, ed., *Calendar of State Papers and Manuscripts in the Archives and Collections of Milan*, I, London, 1912, p. 22.
147 Chapter 11, note 125.
148 Bodleian Library, MS Ashmole 789, ff. 326–7, 327, 327v.
149 Bodleian Library, MS Ashmole 789, f. 327v.
150 Hinds, *Milan*, p. 31.
151 Hinds, *Milan*, p. 35.
152 *CPR 1452–61*, p. 640.
153 *CPR 1461–7*, p. 387.
154 *CPL*, XI, pp. 597–9.
155 Bekynton, *Register*, I, p. 367.
156 Hinds, *Milan*, p. 107.
157 Le Neve, as note 141 above.
158 As note 153.
159 Cambridge, Corpus Christi College, MS 170, p. 52.
160 Cambridge, Corpus Christi College, MS 170, pp. 52, 185.
161 *CPL*, XI, pp. 597–9.
162 Le Neve, as note 126.
163 Durham, Dean and Chapter Archives, *Locellus* 25 nos. 4, 5.
164 R. B. Dobson, 'The last English monks on Scottish soil: the severance of Coldingham Priory from the monastery of Durham, 1461–78', *Scottish Historical Review*, XLVI, 1967, pp. 1–25, esp. p. 11.
165 Rymer, V/2, p. 106 (XI, 479).

166 Chapter 11, pp. 195–205.
167 *BRUO*, I, pp. 499–500; Katterbach, p. 34, no. 16; *CPL*, XI, pp. 651, 685; Mitchell, 'Students in Padua', pp. 106–7.
168 D. S. Chambers, *Cardinal Bainbridge in the Court of Rome, 1509–1514*, Oxford, 1965, chapter 1, esp. p. 1.

2

Some English *curiales*

The curia, the papal court, like that of any ruler, involved household and business offices, including the temporal business of ruling the papal states. The different functions of the offices will be described later; here I emphasise that papal bureaucracy employed many civil servants and household officials, generically called *curiales*, in an international body, theoretically employing any properly qualified men (educational and other requirements were specified). Employment was paid, except for some honorific positions, but holders often also acted for clients, piloting business through the papal system. All were excellently placed to lobby for a prime share in papal appointments to benefices. This elite international group is to be distinguished from nationals in Rome as merchants, living there as artisans or present simply to do one task for a particular employer.

The present chapter is not a complete study of every Englishman in Rome nor even all English *curiales* but a more limited attempt to identify some leading English *curiales* and sketch their careers. For a complete account a much more thorough search of the Vatican archives and Archivio di Stato would have been needed, and most probably another book. I have hoped to identify those occurring most frequently in Anglo-papal dealings, in particular those most prominent. to make a start upon which some future scholar may build.

Englishmen staying long in the curia hoped for patronage and employment. Probably always, but certainly in the fifteenth century, considerable ambiguity marked the attitudes of English clergy to a curial career. When Poggio Bracciolini, papal secretary, wrote in 1425 to Richard Petworth, Bishop Beaufort's secretary, hoping that too many benefices would not corrupt him, Petworth returned a blistering attack on Italians and the greed of the curia. Poggio replied denying that he was rich, protesting that his friend's complaints were petulant. As one courtier to another, he asked what court is pure? Simply the Roman court was more visible, and in a sense less hypocritical. But the conventional view remained that the curia was peculiarly corrupt. Bekynton warned his younger friend Richard Caunton not to learn vice there, and John Lax told the prior of Durham to stay awake, 'because in the Roman curia no one will be asleep at night.'[1]

None the less of course men went to the curia to seek posts. The heyday of employment for the English was probably under Urban VI and Boniface IX (1378–1404), though a thorough study has yet to be made.[2] When the schism ended the situation altered.

Martin V in 1418 agreed that Englishmen, if suitable, would be employed.[3] Despite distinguished members earlier, in fact, most of the more well known Englishmen had died or left before the council of Constance ended.[4]

Once the Constance delegates departed, the following 'survived': John Catterick, royal ambassador and proctor, who was also a *referendarius* (a post in the papal chancery, with a connection to the papal household, giving the right to read certain petitions and to present petitions to be read). He however died in Florence in 1419.[5] Thomas Polton was still a protonotary, a chancery official with the right to draft provisions made in the consistory,[6] and William Swan still an abbreviator of papal letters and scriptor. Swan, one of the longest-serving Englishmen, began as a proctor about 1404.[7] He had been secretary, responsible for diplomatic correspondence, to Gregory XII during the schism, remaining loyal until after the council of Pisa. He remained a secretary at Constance.[8] Polton had been in the curia at intervals since 1394, probably staying permanently after Pisa. In 1401 he had become abbreviator and finally protonotary under Pope John XXIII.[9] Another was John Haket, BCnL, first in Rome in 1406,[10] an abbreviator.[11] In the penitentiary, the tribunal dealing with all those who fell foul of ecclesiastical law and needed absolutions and dispensations, John Forster, MA, a scriptor since 1414,[12] had been in the curia since Pisa.[13] An Irishman with strong English connections was John Prene, by 1398 a judge, 'auditor of causes' in the papal camera, and in the curia thereafter.[14]

After Constance, even before returning to Rome in 1420, Martin V began reconstituting a curia. He had to accept some supporters of rival factions in the schism, though since only new appointments took an oath, it is often difficult to trace careers from the past.[15] But henceforward there is a continuous presence of Englishmen in most organs of papal government. An exception, inexplicable, is the rota, the main court. Under Urban VI and Boniface IX about eleven English auditors (judges) can be traced but none after 1417.[16]

At the centre was the consistory, equivalent to the king's council, where major appointments were made and great matters discussed by the pope and cardinals.[17] English cardinals now stayed at home, whereas Adam Easton under Richard II resided *in curia*. English opponents of cardinals Beaufort and Kemp argued that cardinals should go to the curia, and Eugenius IV certainly pressed Kemp, but, since the government would almost certainly have forced an absentee to relinquish his English see, there was every incentive to disobey.[18] Hence English influence on the consistory came through others: the royal representative, consistorial advocates, referendaries, protonotaries or, presumably, client cardinals.

I have found only one English consistorial advocate, able to argue before the consistory, Richard Broun or Cordon, in 1422 a leading member of the English group.[19] He was among those contacted by Henry VI's council in 1425 about furthering government policy to shorten the interval before the next general council,[20] and was probably 'Richard our advocate' used by Sion Abbey in late 1423.[21] But he left Rome in 1425, though never forgetting his time there;[22] thereafter English influence on the consistory had to be exercised in other ways.

The papal administration was divided into four main offices: camera or chamber, chancery, penitentiary and rota. The chamber or finance office also ran the papal states and the city of Rome. The *camerarius* and *vice-camerarius*, who from the time of Eugenius IV ruled Rome itself, presided over auditors, who heard cases before its court, treasurer and clerks of the camera, with numerous scriptors and notaries. The *cursores*, or papal messenger service, were also controlled from this office. The treasury controlled local collectors, including therefore England.[23]

Few Englishmen were attached to the camera in this period. After Constance Prene remained an auditor until at least 1425, when said to be very old.[24] When he left no further Englishmen became auditors up to 1464. Martin V at once recruited one new English chamber clerk, John Clitherow.[25] The highly coveted clerkships were the main administrative offices of the chamber, with a wide variety of duties and fingers in many pies. Clitherow, a much trusted official, thereafter fulfilled diplomatic missions, in 1422 being held to ransom in France.[26] He probably then left the curia.

Lesser officials at this early stage include Robert Aucton in 1423, a camera notary.[27]

Under Eugenius IV two English chamber clerks may be noted. Adam

Moleyns, *cubicularius*, a member of the pope's household staff, was clerk of the chamber in April 1435, perhaps as a supernumerary awaiting a vacancy. If, improbably, he actually functioned, it cannot have been for very long.[28] He had first come to Rome that year partly on royal business, for assurance that Burgundy would not be absolved from the oaths to observe the treaty of Troyes, and as agent for Thomas Bourgchier attempting to become bishop of Worcester.[29] In 1437 he travelled between England and the curia, and was rewarded by becoming protonotary in 1439,[30] but his true career was in England, chief clerk to Henry VI's royal council from 1438 to 1444 and keeper of the privy seal until killed in January 1450, during Jack Cade's rebellion. In late 1441 at the Frankfurt Reichtag, meeting to clarify imperial policy towards the pope and Basel,[31] he led the English group, ably defending a papal viewpoint. Thence he joined the curia in Florence, on royal business: commissioning cardinal Branda di Castiglione and others to look after English interests, probably in connection with the Eton indulgences;[32] the canonisation of St Osmund of Salisbury, (he was dean), because the king was interested, though the canons thought Moleyns neglectful of Osmund;[33] even the canonisation of King Alfred.[34]

During Moleyns's first stay he was attached to St Thomas's hospice, being *camerarius* in 1436,[35] and a *confrater* of St Edmund's, which considered him a protector.[36]

Eugenius also appointed as camera clerk master Richard Caunton or ap Gwillim, mentioned from 1443.[37] Fluent, he said, in English, Welsh and Latin, already DCL, after a legal education in Oxford, he had probably come to Rome in 1441 as a lawyer, following the curia (*curiam sequens*), to obtain for the king indulgences for Eton college.[38] Thomas Bekynton, the royal secretary, wrote as an older man to a younger, glad that the royal proctor Andrew Holes liked him, exhorting him not to follow the evil morals of the curia and to study oratory.[39] Evidently his friends thought him embarking on a career, yet he probably did not stay beyond early 1446. His appointment too may have been supernumerary, expecting a non-appearing vacancy.[40]

Apart from these Edmund Pollart, a scriptor in October 1447, proctor for Giovanni Opizzis, then papal collector in England, was almost certainly a German.[41] After that I have not found English names among the camera personnel up to 1464.

A *secretarius* held a position controlled from the camera, but the job included writing papal diplomatic correspondence. William Swan was certainly secretary under Gregory XII, though at resignation in 1442 designated scriptor and abbreviator.[42] The only genuine English holder during this period was John Lax, whose career, already described, culminated as secretary under Calixtus III and Pius II, appointed by Calixtus III presumably because, knowing Lax personally, he was prepared to appoint although the secretaries thereby became too numerous.[43]

Another group controlled from the camera was the papacy's own well-organised international postal service, the *cursores*, who increased from about twenty-three under Martin V to thirty-eight in the mid-century. Clerks or laymen, they held office for life.[44]

Martin V appointed one English cursor on 13 November 1417, John Wrsby, clerk, of Lincoln diocese, at the request of the English ambassadors at Constance.[45] But the cursors coming and going to England during the period of this book do not appear to be English.

In the chancery all normal papal letters were issued, including those concerning provisions to benefices. Its head was the vice-chancellor, with a subordinate *regens cancellariam*, under whom worked protonotaries, to produce 'concepts' for provisions which came before the consistory, that is those positions appointed directly by the pope, such as archbishops, bishops and abbots; then abbreviators, who produced the details for lesser benefices, and *referendarii*, described above. There were also scriptors, who wrote out the final copies, with other functionaries, including officials in the *audientia litterarum contradictarum*, where documents were read aloud and could be gainsaid.[46]

Not surprisingly the royal proctor was often a protonotary, Polton from 1414 until he left about 1425.[47] William Chichele, the archbishop's kinsman, who completed a civil law degree in Bologna in May 1423, was made protonotary in mid-1422 and came to Rome to excercise his office.[48] There in 1423 John Whetehamstede thought him one of the leading Englishmen,[49] perhaps groomed to replace Polton. In fact he died in the curia in 1424, thus sparking controversy about his archdeaconry of Canterbury, to which the pope wished to appoint a nephew, Prospero Colonna.[50] Adam Moleyns enjoyed the rank, without long exercising the office,[51] and Andrew Holes was called protonotary when leaving the curia in 1444.[52] Under Nicholas V William Gray was referred to as protonotary from 4 May 1447[53] and also as *referendarius* in 1453.[54] Robert Flemming was promoted in 1458.[55] The last three of course were royal proctors.

Abbreviators drew up the skeletons of documents for ordinary papal provisions and ensured that finished documents were legally correct and matched the intention. It was quite common to begin as an abbreviator and then move on; many did not function for long.

William Swan presumably actually functioned. His activities in Rome can be readily followed, his two letter books giving an unrivalled view of his clients (he was proctor for Archbishops Henry Chichele and John Kemp for instance).[56] Though *clericus conjugatus* (a married clerk in minor orders), his wife was not always in Rome,[57] but he rented from the English hospice of St Thomas 'a great house with a garden'.[58] At resignation in April 1442, he was called scriptor of apostolic letters.[59] Perhaps he was already absent; almost certainly he retired to England in September 1435,[60] after a brief period just before at the council of Basel. He may not have returned to the curia, though not replaced until April 1442.[61]

With Swan in the curia of Martin V worked John Blodwell, first, like many another, coming as a proctor in 1419.[62] A Welshman, dispensed as the son of a priest to be ordained and hold a cure of souls,[63] he was probably an Oxford graduate, in civil and canon law, going from there to the council of Constance and then to the curia, whence he went to Bologna, where he took a law doctorate in 1424.[64] By 1420 he was an abbreviator.[65] He died, doubtless very old, in 1462, but probably left Rome by the end of Martin V's reign.[66] I have found no evidence for his presence there after 1429. The curia thought he had laboured in the councils and convocations of England for the defence of ecclesiastical liberty and the conservation and increase of the rights of the Roman church, code for resistance to the statute against provisors, but of that I find no evidence.[67]

Under Martin V two Irish abbreviators appear briefly. Robert Holhan or de Cork, BCL from Oxford and canon of Salisbury, left no trace of a Roman career barring litigation for benefices.[68] Thomas Rossall was abbreviator by June 1428, but can be traced as a proctor for English clients from 1422, acting with Swan.[69] By 1431 he had died at the curia.[70]

Another English abbreviator, Robert Sutton, BCL, was certainly in Rome in 1425, among those notified about royal plans to shorten the time before the next general council,[71] probably there as Duke Humfrey's agent for his marital litigation.[72] By 1433 he had become abbreviator and by his death was *cubicularius*. He died in Italy before 28 September 1438.[73] Sutton played a part in the hospice of St Thomas, sharing a large house with Andrew Holes and another *curialis* from 1431 to 1435, when he probably joined the curia in Florence.[74] He was *camerarius* of the hospice in 1432.[75]

Almost contemporary was Thomas Chapman, BCL, probably first coming in 1426 as 'agent' for Bishop Flemming of Lincoln, described as Flemming's *secretarius*.[76] Thereafter he made a career, as proctor for Duke Humfrey in 1428 for instance.[77] If, as I suspect, his account is disguised under Tomasso Ciopen in the Medici bank in 1427, he was prosperous.[78] Possibly he attended Basel[79] and can be observed travelling on royal and papal business in 1442, being kidnapped en route.[80] In 1446, when Gray was arguing against the imposition of a papal tenth in England, Chapman was a *curialis* he was to take before the pope.[81] Chapman rented hospice houses between 1431 and 1445, in one of which, in rione Pontis, a Roman district, he made improvements.[82] He was also a *confrater* of St Edmund's hospice.[83] Hospice records suggest that by 1449 he was dead.[84]

Another Anglo-Irishman who moved from *curiam sequens* since at least 1435 to being an abbreviator by 1442, was John River, BCL.[85] He probably continued a career at the curia; under Pope Paul II Thomas Kemp called him *solicitator et procurator meus*.[86] Other English names occur briefly: William Wright in 1443,[87] Thomas Howys in 1449,[88] and Thomas Sollay in 1452,[89] the last probably a brief soujourner since the hospice hoped to use him in London in December 1453.[90]

Under Nicholas V John Lax, whose career is sketched elsewhere, reached this post in May 1449.[91] Thereafter, until the end of the period discussed in this book I have found no new English abbreviators.

Referendaries, already partially described, were lawyers who prepared and processed petitions, the importance of the grants controlled increasing as the century progressed. It was therefore another useful position for a royal representative. As we saw, Catterick held it in 1413,[92] but died of course before the return to Rome. In 1418, reconstructing the curia, Martin V appointed John Ixworth, DCL,[93] a long-serving *curialis*, who had left during the troubles at the end of the great schism. Ixworth regarded Odda Colonna, the future Martin V, as a patron. From London to Swan at Constance in March, probably 1416, he wrote: 'Recommend me to the most reverend father the lord of Colonna . . . Would that I were with you.' He thanks Swan 'for the diligence you have shown on my behalf with the reverend father my lord of Colonna', and for the letter in which he said 'that my lord wishes me to come to him. I would willingly come if the way were safe.'[94] Presumably the way improved; he became *referendarius*, first mentioned in 1421. In 1423, already described as seventy, he probably returned to England.[95] He was *confrater* of St

Edmund's hospice.[96] John Tybort, canon of Lincoln, called *referendarius* in 1421 is probably part of the same reconstruction.[97]

Later royal proctors were also referendaries. In 1435, before official recognition as royal proctor, Andrew Holes was already a referendary.[98] William Gray obtained the position in 1453.[99] A letter from his old tutor Guarino da Verona congratulated him.[100] In 1463 Edward IV's *procurator*, Peter Courtenay was likewise promoted.[101]

The papal penitentiary dealt with dispensations and absolutions, not only hearing supplications but issuing penitential letters, with the usual army of scribes and correctors. The basic hearing of penitents fell to minor penitentiaries, whose numbers varied, divided by linguistic areas. The English language area included Scotland, Wales and Ireland. In 1435 Eugenius IV limited the total to eleven, one for confessions of the English, but also of Scots and Irish (and presumably Welsh).[102]

An almost continuous succession of minor penitentiaries can be traced from 10 December 1426 when Thomas Mersche, Gilbertine canon of St Catherine's outside the walls of London, was appointed. Said to have studied theology at Cambridge and elsewhere for several years, he held by dispensation the parish church of Gelston in Norwich diocese;[103] he was still in office in 1427.[104] In 1428 William Certeyn, his successor, had a distinguished career: the arts in Exeter College, Oxford, law at Bologna, theology in Rome itself, a notable confessor, well-known poet and preacher before the pope, or so said Andrew Holes, preaching in the English hospice of St Thomas after Certeyn's death in 1432.[105] His activities included preaching annually perhaps for the Translation of St Thomas on 7 July. After his death Holes preached, remembering him with great respect.

Certeyn's successor was probably Thomas Morden or Saltewell, BCL,[106] with a long previous curial career, returning from the council of Constance to the curia as a proctor already in 1419.[107] He belonged to Robert FitzHugh's household when FitzHugh was royal proctor[108] and probably followed FitzHugh to Basel,[109] where he acted for Archbishop Chichele over the archdeaconry of Canterbury.[110] In 1431, if he is Thomas 'Morday', he shared a 'turret' belonging to the hospice of St Thomas with Andrew Holes and Robert Sutton.[111] He was *camerarius* in St Thomas's hospice in 1431[112] and *confrater* of St Edmund's.[113]

Morden probably held his post briefly; in January 1434 we find the appointment of John Bloxwych, BTh., a Carmelite.[114] He tried to become a bishop in Iceland, but must have failed.[115] In 1443 James Blakedon, OP and DTh., chaplain of Henry Beaufort, is mentioned[116] and then in 1444 William Symonde, licenciate in canon law, papal chaplain, and chaplain to Humfrey, duke of Gloucester, already at least a year in the curia.[117] Symonde's tenure was also short; in June 1446 Hugh Forster, a Benedictine monk with a canon law licence, was appointed,[118] and was that year *camerarius* of St Edmund's hospice.[119] He was still, or again, penitentiary in 1451.[120] From January 1448 another minor penitentiary was named, Walter Sandwych, doctor of both laws,[121] in Rome already from 1446.[122] His appointment was renewed in January 1449;[123] presumably he functioned during the Jubilee of 1450. He was active in the hospice, *camerarius* when plans for a new building for St Thomas's were approved in January 1449[124] and present as *confrater* (and minor penitentiary) when the hospice leased a house to Lax in 1452. He was also *confrater* of St Edmund's[125]

Master John Shirwood, with a canon law doctorate from Bologna, came to Rome in 1456,[126] there handing a legacy to St Edmund's hospice. In 1458 he was made minor penitentiary[127] and the following year was *camerarius* of St Thomas's.[128]

John Gunthorpe, Shirwood's successor, came to Rome from studies in Ferrara, probably in 1461, and was appointed in January 1462.[129] Probably he did not remain after Pius II's death.[130]

Apart from these, a few Englishmen held minor posts. John Forster was a scriptor in the penitentiary, appointed in 1414, though in the curia from at least the time of the council of Pisa[131] and traceable thereafter, as a messenger between pope and king in 1419, for instance.[132] John Gunyat, scriptor and notary in the penitentiary, occurs in hospice records holding a house about 1445.[133]

Various Englishmen held household posts as serjeant-at-arms, honourable members of the papal staff.[134] Most important from Martin V's accession until death in 1445 was John Ely, who was among those at Constance recognised as serving.[135] He frequently acted as confidential messenger between pope and king in the 1430s,[136] and was a leading member of the English community in Rome. He was three times *camerarius* of St Thomas's hospice and *custos* in 1442.[137] Like Swan, he was a married clerk, but his wife Riciarda – daughter of Peter or Perrinus Baker, Gascon as well as Roman citizen,[138] among the earliest members of the hospice of St Edmund's and his wife Maria[139] – certainly lived in Rome. Ely occupied a large house, with garden, upper storey, tiled, with stair, chambers and well,[140] and rented from the hospice two groves and a stable.[141] He bequeathed the house to St Edmund's;[142] as well as ensuring that it was transferred, Riciarda Ely left cloths to St Thomas's chapel.[143] Possibly Ely was succeeded in office by a son. A Guilelmus de Elense, serjeant-of-arms of the pope, figures in St Edmund's records in 1446 as an official.[144]

When John Ely died William de Astulo or Asculo, papal serjeant-at-arms, also played a part in the English community. The records of St Thomas's mention him until death, probably early in 1452; he may be identical with William de Elense.[145] He was a guarantor for a hospice loan in July 1449 for instance,[146] and responsible for paying the builder of the new building.[147] Probably with him, Guilelmus de Esculo, Salisbury records connected with the canonisation of St Osmund were left, to be collected in 1452 after his death.[148]

Apart from these serjeants an Englishman named Edward Ildriton was appointed *scutifer* of honour by Martin V in 1418[149] and on 6 December 1417 the 'noble' Thomas Gretham of Lincoln diocese was made master of the doors of the *camera paramenti*.[150] Presumably these were honorific posts. Certainly neither plays any visible part in the life of the English community thereafter.

Appointment as *cubicularius*, bestowed on several Englishmen, gave a position in the papal household, but could also be purely honorary. Some have already been noticed: Holes, Moleyns, Sutton; but others seem to have held no other rank. One was Thomas Candour or Caudour, a member of the household of Eugenius IV in 1442 and then of Nicholas V, from May 1447, when newly arrived from Padua, where in December 1446 he became doctor of canon law. He may have been there as early as 1437.[151] His shadowy persona has more substance since Professor de la Mare identified him with Thomas S. who copied many humanistic manuscripts. This explains why Poggio Bracciolini called him 'a most cultured man and bound to me by close acquaintance'. His interest in humanism involved, for example, copying Poggio's letters and Professor de la Mare traced at least fourteen volumes he either copied or annotated. He shared some interests with Andrew Holes; at least one of Holes's books bears his notes. They may have met in the curia in Florence, where he became *cubicularius* just before Holes left.[152] Candour can be seen in Rome as a proctor,[153] for, among others, Richard duke of York in 1450 and was still in the curia long after this period.[154] Nicholas V used him to convey thanks for Henry VI's part in ending the Basel schism.[155] He was *camerarius* of St Thomas's hospice when a new building was planned in 1449[156] and party to the agreement for leasing a house to John Lax in 1452.[157] In July 1452 Candour was helpful to Simon Huchyns, proctor of Salisbury, with whom he shared a house: *nobiscum est commensalis*,[158] says Huchyns.

Also made *cubicularius* in 1447 was Henry Sharpe.[159] Another law graduate from Padua, he obtained his doctorate in February 1447 and presumably came almost at once to Rome.[160] Immediately he is found as a proctor and worked with William Gray to obtain privileges for Eton.[161] In 1447 he was *camerarius* of the hospice of St Thomas.[162] A further companion of Gray's, likewise a lawyer, later certainly in his entourage, William Radclyffe, was likewise made *cubicularius* in April 1447.[163] He too was a proctor in Rome,[164] but had been there since at least 1445, sharing the hospice house 'de lilibus'.[165] With Gray he was one of the guarantors of the hospice building loan in 1449 and in 1453 testified to the quality of the work.[166]

In addition to those with official posts a penumbra followed the court, mostly lawyers acting as proctors and presumably often seeking permanent employment. Several noticed already began thus: Sutton, Morden, Chapman. Others merely came and went.

Under Martin V John Urry was a respected member of the group. He was a lawyer in 1425 in a case in Rome where William Paston was involved [167] and was a proctor in the years to 1431.[168] In 1428 he was *camerarius* for St Thomas's hospice.[169] John Estcourt, BCL, *familiaris* of Henry Chichele, was described as *curiam sequens* in 1421.[170] He had been active in Rome from at least 1403.[171] Another was Philip Newton, found in William Swan's letters and in the hospice records in 1418 called *capellanus Anglicus et Wallicus*. In 1423 he had died lately at the curia.[172]

Some were so fleetingly in Rome that they are mentioned only once in the papal registers: John Nowell, BCL, in 1423,[173] Simon Northew, canon of Chichester in 1421 for example.[174] In 1426 William Hertlant or Gertlant, rector of St Swithun's, Worcester, was proctor for several people,[175] but not found again.

Under Eugenius IV attempting a career in the curia was not easy. There was unrest in Rome and the council of Basel threatened reprisals against *curiales* who did not obey it. This may explain why in 1434–5 Ralph Hykys very briefly followed the Roman court but then returned to Oxford to study.[176]

But some people always lingered without permanent employment. Under Nicholas V Stephen Close or Cloos was proctor for several people in 1450 and 52, including for Nicholas Close, perhaps his relative.[177] In 1452 as *confrater* of St Thomas's hospice he witnessed the lease of a house to John Lax.[178] John Lasci or Lacy, *custos* of St Thomas in 1447 was still *confrater* in 1452.[179] He is found acting as a proctor.[180] Probably the

same man, canon of Southwell, was still a proctor in 1459,[181] and again
camerarius of the hospice in 1458, 1463 and 1464.[182] He may be John
Lasci who took a letter in 1460 from Henry VI to the pope concerning
Wayneflete,[183] and whom John Paston called 'another Rome-rennere' in
1473.[184]

An interesting group of non-English *curiales*, some naturalised
Englishmen, can be counted as part of the English community. They are
Johannes Ghele, Theodoric Oudencoup, Thomas Hope, Vincent
Clement and perhaps Wenceslaus Sweziko.

Sweziko, from Brandenburg diocese, was *familiaris* of Robert Hallum,
bishop of Salisbury, on his staff as a notary from 1409 until Hallum's
death at Constance.[185] He must then have joined the curia, where in
1424 he had become an abbreviator, acting as Salisbury cathedral's
proctor in the canonisation of Osmund.[186]

Johannes Ghele from Verdun came to the curia in Martin V's reign,
joining Polton's household.[187] At Polton's request in 1424 he became
procurator of the *audientia litterarum contradictarum*, where documents
were read out and disagreement invited. He held this until 1428 and may
then have gone to England. Certainly in 1430 he was admitted as vicar of
Harberton in Devon, which he held with various German and English
livings.[188] In July 1439, perhaps because of increasing English
chauvinism, he was naturalised and licensed to continue holding
Harberton,[189] but by then had returned to the curia, after a spell at Basel,
perhaps with Polton.[190] Certainly he was in Florence, where we find him
at loggerheads with Tito Livio Frulovisi, former poet and orator of Duke
Humfrey, in June 1440.[191] In 1445 back in Rome, he shared with
William Radclyffe the large hospice house 'de lilis' or 'de leonibus' and
was *confrater* of St Edmund's in 1452.[192] By November 1455, when he
had died, he had become abbreviator and papal acolyte.[193] He left
money to Harberton.

More distinguished was the career of Theodoric Oudencoup from
Utrecht. At the curia since 1429, an abbreviator,[194] he attended Basel,
where Ghele left him as proctor on returning to the curia.[195] But
Oudencoup too must have left Basel for the curia, since he was Chichele's
proctor, with Holes, in the affair of the archdeaconry of Canterbury in
1434.[196] In 1435 he is found as proctor for English clients,[197] and in
May that year Chichele gave him the church of South Malling,[198] usually
reserved for the archbishop's *familia*.[199] By 1440 Oudencoup had joined
the household of Francisco Condulmaro, the vice-chancellor, by 1443
being his secretary.[200] Before that he inhabited the hospice's great house

'de leonibus'.[201] He had died by October 1446, when, briefly, the pope tried to reserve his English benefice.[202] He remained attached to his native German community in Rome also, being *provisor* of their Anima brotherhood in 1444,[203] but his links with the English community were none the less strong.

Thomas Hope, or Hoppe, from the diocese of Worms, though his relative, Andrew Hope or Hoppe, was a native of Zurich,[204] achieved major advancement after 1464, but already by then had considerable standing. He first appears in England studying law in Oxford in 1443 and then acted as proctor for Archbishop Stafford in 1446, taking letters to the pope, becoming a notary (*tabellionatus*) in August 1447.[205] Thereafter he appears fixed in Rome. In September 1455 he acted with John Lax as proctor in the cause of St Osmund.[206] Up to 1464 a proctor,[207] at the beginning of Pius II's reign he became *cubicularius*.[208] Evidence for his English business remains in his letter book in Corpus Christi College, Cambridge and his precedent book in the Public Record Office.[209] By November 1463 he was credited with various English canonries, was *camerarius* of St Thomas's hospice and was travelling to and fro to England.[210] Apparently he sided with the Yorkists; he may have been entrusted with Edward IV's letter offering obedience to Pius II, which is among his letters.[211] Already in September 1461 the prior of Durham counselled him 'to spede ye kinges maters in all ye hast ye may'.[212] Pius II employed him with Peter Courtenay for the crusading cause.[213] He later had connections with the confraternity of St Spirito in Sassia, a fashionable Roman brotherhood,[214] and kept up his German affiliations by belonging to the confraternity De Anima.[215]

For our purposes Vincent Clement is an Englishman in Rome. From Valentia, therefore in England a Catalan, he studied in Oxford and in October 1438 was naturalised, with permission to hold benefices.[216] He was already subordinate, perhaps subcollector, to Piero da Monte, the papal collector;[217] certainly he was subcollector for the indulgence for the council of Florence.[218] Already by then he had written a work supporting the pope against Basel. By August 1440 he was in Florence presenting the pope with the king's support against Basel,[219] perhaps acting for Gloucester, as he certainly did at some point.[220] Eugenius IV thought well of him,[221] and by 1441 he was acting for the king in Florence, probably over the Eton indulgences.[222] By 28 May 1442 the pope had promoted him to subdeacon.[223] He travelled to and from the curia throughout 1443 and 1444,[224] still working on the Eton indulgences,[225] which presumably won him royal favour. In 1445-6 he played an important part in government resistance to the pope's attempt to levy one tenth,[226] and equally was prominent in the delegation from England to France and elsewhere negotiating with the anti-pope Felix V.[227]

In 1450 Clement became papal collector for England.[228] But in November 1454 and again in November 1460 he was also royal proctor, during the confused days of the change-over to Yorkist government. [229]

Clement made enemies in England. Thomas Gascoigne, a thinker we will meet again, deeply resented Henry VI's favour to him, particularly royal pressure to get him an Oxford doctorate,[230] and considered, probably incorrectly, that he had cheated the church out of money, a view temporarily shared, but later retracted, by Pius II.[231] Clement did launch a nephew, Francesco Berangarius, in the curia. Berengarius was already proctor for English clients in 1455[232] and in September 1461 Durham made him, Clement and Hope its agents in Rome.[233]

Eugenius IV maintained in 1438 that Englishmen were reluctant to join his curia because they had such problems obtaining benefices.[234] It seems true that Englishmen working in Rome were unable to make good the incomparable opportunities their presence at the centre should have afforded. The rush for provisions at a death or promotion seldom produced more than a handful of actually possessed benefices. But those working in the curia were not poverty-stricken. Andrew Holes's benefices, meticulously traced by Miss Bennett,[235] show that family interest and royal favour brought lucrative appointments, with a papal dispensation in 1440 to hold for life three cures of souls.[236] He did not obtain the archdeaconry of Northampton by provision, nor a bishopric, but one cannot call that an injury.[237]

A royal proctor might expect to do well out of office. A lesser man might do less well. An example is master Thomas Chapman. He acquired few benefices. Provision of a prebend of Hemingburgh from Martin V was ignored by prior Wessington of Durham, who wished to prevent the pope reserving the benefice.[238] A provision in 1435 of the prebend of Laughton in York, held by Prospero Colonna, produced nothing.[239] Between 1434 and 1437 he attempted to become treasurer of Limerick but failed.[240] Chapman only had one English benefice.[241] None the less he does not seem to have been poor.[242]

A further example is Richard Caunton. When first in the curia in early 1441 as a king's clerk working on the Eton indulgences,[243] he had the rectorship of the college of St Mary by St Davids, with a prebend,[244] had previously held, but now resigned, the church of Llangoedmore, in

St.David's diocese,[245] and held a cursal prebend in St David's Cathedral.[246] In November 1445 he acquired the church of Briddle in St Davids diocese,[247] but by early 1446 he had probably returned home; the last mention in Rome seems to be January 1446.[248] Thus his stay in the curia produced a cameral clerkship, a dispensation and an indulgence to help rebuild his college of St Mary.[249] The crown paid in arrears[250] and only later did he acquire lucrative benefices: archdeacon of Cardigan,[251] chancellor of St Davids,[252] archdeacon of St Davids by 1459.[253] In 1446 he had succeeded Piero Barbo in his York prebend[254] and as archdeacon of Salisbury[255] but these were by collation, not provision. Apparently he gained promotions as a royal clerk, not through work in the curia.

English *curiales* might have expected to acquire provisions in foreign churches, if not in England. My impression is that they rarely did, though Lax claimed a benefice not in English gift; in August 1465 he was referred to as canon of Utrecht.[256]

Thus a curial post did not bring the English rich rewards in provisions, nor a wider field of choice. Crown agents were not always even promptly paid and certainly were not pardoned to obtain provisions. If one chose to work in the curia, friends and influence at home remained essential, in fact perhaps even more necessary, because one was out of the English network.

Office in the curia of course was paid; proctors received retainers, with their expenses in theory reimbursed. As pointed out, the royal proctor received £100 a year.[257] Durham paid about £2.[258] These were not enormous sums and most people expected to augment their salary with benefices. Clearly for the English this was a serious problem: Eugenius was making not merely a polemical point.

Though this book is not about the Renaissance, it inevitably raises questions about contact with the curia influencing the culture of those involved.[259] Readers of Roberto Weiss's *Humanism in England* will be aware how many of his names occur here.[260] Weiss considered the Renaissance in England materially furthered by Poggio's friends Petworth and Nicholas Bildeston, by the papal collectors, especially da Monte and by those Englishmen who sought education in Italy. Humfrey duke of Gloucester's patronage was of paramount importance, but the contacts he made arose through links to the curia and Italy.

Weiss's account needs modernisation. He interpreted humanism, that portmanteau word encompassing changes of consciousness which characterised the Renaissance, purely in terms of attitudes to the pagan classics. Nowadays one would include the christian fathers and add the Christian to the pagan past in the new area of interest.[261] Secondly one would reconsider chronology. Weiss thought humanism came into England slowly in the fifteenth century from Italy, but possibly some of the influences were French, coming already from the curia at Avignon.

At the general councils well-educated people met; there was a large and thriving book market.[262] Constance gave early stimulus to humanism. At it Poggio met Beaufort and returned to Normandy and then England with him.[263] At it also Robert Hallum and Nicholas Bubwith received dedication of a copy of Serravalle's commentary on Dante's *Commedia*, which John Whethamstede, abbot of St Albans, later used from Duke Humfrey's library.[264] Basel also circulated texts later used by Whethamstede.[265] But most probably Hallum and Bubwith would not have been interested in Dante had they not already known something about him. Several *curiales* in the period before this had an education at least in part Italian.[266] Several during the schism, for instance, obtained legal degrees in Italy. Geoffrey Chaucer was not the only diplomat with a knowledge of Italy. Sir John Colvile, during the schism, spoke Italian well enough to make an elegant plea in it to the pope in 1409.[267] Cardinal Adam Easton knew of Dante from his own time in the curia, and Easton's books eventually returned to Norwich.[268]

Through inevitable contacts with the curia cultural influences would have made themselves felt in any case. But of course the Avignon curia, now acknowledged as an important centre of early humanistic culture, was very different from Rome in 1420, home of the curia at the beginning of this book. Avignon filtered into France a wealth of new learning, to influence a generation during the schism, and, mainly through the college de Navarre, to continue its influence even after the English obtained Paris (1419). Chaucer's knowledge of Boccaccio might have come from French translations.[269] By contrast, Rome under Martin V was no great centre of patronage nor culture, but none the less was beginning to attract humanists; by the reign of Eugenius IV, especially after the council of Florence, with the long stay of the pope there and the acquisition to the cardinalate of Bessarion, the curia was again of great importance in this respect.[270]

Englishmen wanting success in the curia had always been well advised to seek a legal degree in Italy; this continued. William Chichele, John Blodwell, William Certeyn, Andrew Holes, John Shirwood, Thomas Candour and Henry Sharpe are examples.[271] One slight change in this period is that a few sought more. Thus William Gray, Robert Flemming and John Tiptoft went deliberately to study with Guarino,[272] and a few fortunate souls attended not just one Italian university but copied Italian contemporaries in seeking several universities. Gray, William Babyngton and Peter Courtenay went to Cologne.[273]

Since Cologne came to be ridiculed by humanists as the epitome of everything wrong with traditional university training, one may ask why a man like Gray, obviously interested in the new learning, went there at all. The answer is partly that it lay on the route from England to Italy: hence it attracted the Scots, though the English occupation of Paris was also important.[274] But in fact very few Englishmen did obtain degrees there at this time and thus Gray's visit is rather surprising. The answer is almost certainly that Cologne was a centre of theological excellence.[275] There Thomism particularly was popular and a new method of teaching scholasticism was practised. Works of Scotus were major products of Gray's commission to his copyist Theodoric Wercken in the city. Though Gray read and collected humanistic texts in Cologne, where there was an early interest, no one would have gone there expressly for the new learning.[276] Gray was a theologian, and though interested in the new, including 'new' theology, retained respect for the old; much of his library was older works.[277] Andrew Holes is similar. From his stay in Florence he acquired many new books, some indeed the classics, but some Christian humanistic texts. He also, however, obtained works of Aquinas, perhaps indicating renewed interest in that most orthodox of saints after the council of Basel, but perhaps discovered in Padua, where in 1436 the Arts faculty made Aquinas its patron saint.[278]

A caveat against too ready a belief that Weiss said most of what was needed is the artificiality of considering any of these men 'pure' scholars, interested in humanism for its own sake. Poggio may have been such, but Gray, Candour, Holes and the others were more probably careerists with scholarly interests. Some of Holes's new books were modern canon law texts, useful, no doubt, for his work as royal proctor, referendary and protonotary.[279] Candour copied humanistic works: Poggio's letters,[280] for example and may have been the first Englishman to write a humanistic hand, but his friendship with Poggio came first from work in the curia where ability to write like Poggio was a major marketable skill. Poggio at least once used the English minor penitentiary as a scribe.[281] Bekynton advised Caunton to study eloquence in the curia, another assistance to office; in Gaspare Veronese's private school in Rome, existing from about 1445, there seem to have been English members. One Englishman actually lived with Stephano Porcari and knew

Veronese well enough to cheat him.[282] Candour had studied in Padua, but, like Holes and many others, his degree was in law, passport to a career in the papal bureaucracy.[283]

Personal contacts were a major source of cross-cultural influence, but very often were made and maintained not for shared scholarly concerns but for mutual career interests. The curial system depended above all on personal relationships. In theory the legal system depended upon correct functioning of the law; in practice the law functioned by mutual favours. Therefore those working within the system needed to cultivate contacts and keep friendships in good repair. A great deal of Bekynton's Italian correspondence is of this kind; the mutual interest is not scholarship but favours granted and acknowledged and friendships cultivated with hope of benefit.[284] Poggio's correspondence with members of Beaufort's household[285] and Aeneas Sylvius's with Adam Moleyns was the same.[286] With Beaufort, one of the most important ecclesiastics in England, Poggio had to maintain an official contact as papal secretary, responsible for a great deal of the pope's diplomatic correspondence; how much easier to commend letters to a friend in the great man's confidence.[287] Likewise Aeneas needed to ensure that letters commending a rather unpopular imperial policy reached the royal eyes. How better than to resurrect a personal contact? Presents of books were part of this; the Italians probably hoped that 'publication' on a wider scale might follow. No doubt Aeneas really believed, as he professed, that Moleyns wrote Latin excellently.[288] But flattery and present-giving were part of the normal interchange in relationships based in fact on mutual professional interests.

It does not do, therefore, to exaggerate the importance of personal contact in cultural exchange. Several of those mentioned did develope genuine humanistic interests: Gray already had before leaving England. Holes, Saxton, Bole, Candour, Flemming and Tiptoft come also to mind. But others as well placed did not: traces left by John Lax have been found so far in only one book, and that not a humanistic text.[289]

The conclusions from a study of *curiales* from England are that there were in proportion fewer than one would expect, given that England had, for the most part, a pro-papal church and state. The English in Rome at any one time, or at least the socially important English, were in fact few. G. B. Parks estimated that in 1422 the total may have been only seventy-five and in 1433 as few as twenty.[290] This must in part reflect the difficulty of obtaining benefices by provision. To some extent it also reflects increasing Italianisation of the curia, resulting from sale of office and the development of self-perpetuating groups of bureaucrats, from which foreigners were increasingly excluded.[291] By the end of Henry VI's reign there were also manifold perils in serving the government abroad; one needed to be at home to oversee one's own interests, and the problems of being a royal representative were very great indeed. Certainly long service in the court of Rome was not the best way to high favour in England, if the careers studied here are considered.

Notes

1 *Lettere*, ed. Harth, II, pp. 29–30, 34–7. Bekynton letter: below, note 39; generally: F. R. H. Du Boulay, 'The fifteenth century', *The English Church and the Papacy in the Middle Ages*, ed. C. H. Lawrence, London, 1965, pp. 197–242, esp. pp. 222–33.

2 Harvey, *Solutions*, pp. 16, 22, 29, 30, 162 for some suggestions. Very useful: C. Schuchard, *Die Deutschen*. See E. Re, 'The English colony in Rome in the fourteenth century', *TRHS*, VI, 1923, pp. 73–92. Avignon: B. Guillemain, *La Cour Pontificale d'Avignon, (1309–1376), Étude d'une Société*, Bibliotheque des Écoles Françaises d'Athènes et de Rome, CCI, Paris, 1962, pp. 612–15.

3 E. F. Jacob, 'A note on the English Concordat of 1418', *Medieval Studies Presented to Aubrey Gwynn, S.J.*, ed. J. A. Watt, J. B. Morrall and F. X. Martin, Dublin, 1961, pp. 349–58, esp p. 354.

4 Dead or left by 1418: John Fraunceys, Le Neve, Index, p. 125; Nicholas Ryssheton, *CPL*, V, pp. 267, 294; Harvey, *Solutions*; Adam Easton, *BRUO*, I, pp. 620–1; Richard Holme, *BRUC*, pp. 311–12; John Bremore, *BRUC*, pp. 90–1; W. von Hofmann, *Forschungen zur Geschichte der Kurialen Behörden vom Schisma bis zum Reformation*, 2 vols., Bibliothek des Deutschen Historischen Instituts in Rom, XII, XIII, Rome, 1914, II, p. 109.

5 Catterick: above, Chapter I; referendary: note 46.

6 Polton: above, Chapter I; protonotary: note 46.

7 E. F. Jacob, 'To and from the court of Rome in the early fifteenth century', *Essays in Later Medieval History*, Manchester, 1968, pp. 58–78, esp. p. 60; *BRUO*, III, pp. 1829–30.

8 Harvey, *Solutions*, p. 186; Hofmann, *Behörden*, II, p. 108, secretary accepted by Constance but in 1420 *scriptor* and *abbreviator*.

9 *BRUO*, II, pp. 1494–5.

10 *BRUO*, II, p. 848; English College Archives, *Liber* 232, f. 8v, renting great house, 1406; I did not find the evidence in *Venerabile*, XXI, p. 65.

11 *CPL*, VI, p. 73; *BRUO* as above, note 10.

12 *BRUO*, II, pp. 708–9; *CPL*, VI, pp. 191, 414.

13 Oxford, Bodleian Library, MS Arch. Seld. B 23, f. 52.

14 *BRUO*, III, Appendix, p. 2207; *CPL*, VII, p. 399 for him after 1418.

15 Fundamental is F.-C. Uginet, *Le Liber Officialium de Martin V*, Archivio di Stato, Fonti e sussidi, VII, Rome, 1975.

16 E. Cerchiari, *Capellani Papae et Apostolicae Sedis, Auditores Causarum Sacri Palacii Apostolici seu Sacra Romana Rota, ab origine ad diem usque 20 Septembris 1870*, 4 vols., Rome, 1919–21, II, pp. 35, 36, 37, 38, 39, 41, 138, for the earlier period.

17 Schuchard, pp. 70–91.

18 Below, Chapter 9 and notes 233–6.

19 Harvey,'Martin V and Henry V', p. 68; *BRUO*, I, pp. 486–7. Will: *Registrum Cancellarii Oxoniensis, 1434–69*, ed. H. E. Salter, 2 vols., Oxford Historical Society, XCIII, XCIV, I, 1933, pp. 299–311, esp. pp. 299, 300; H. Anstey, *Munimenta Academica, Documents illustrative of Academical Life and Studies at Oxford*, 2 vols., *RS*, L, 1868, II, pp. 639–57, esp. pp. 640, 641. Books: Anstey, *Epistolae Academicae*, I, pp. 279–80.

20 BL, MS Cotton Cleop. C IV, ff. 182v–3.

21 Cnattingius, *Studies*, p. 133.

22 *CPL*, VII, p. 16; see *Registrum Cancellarii Oxoniensis*, p. 300 and *Munimenta Academica*, p. 641.

23 Schuchard, pp. 70–2, 74.

24 *CPL*, VII, p. 399.

25 Uginet, p. 38; *BRUO*, I, p. 444.

26 *CPL*, VII, p. 10; BL, MS Cotton Cleop. C IV, ff. 171–2.

27 Lunt, II, p. 781.

28 *BRUO*, II, pp. 1289–91; Lunt, II, p. 768; *CPL*, VIII, p. 218; Cambridge, Corpus Christi College, MS 170, p. 202; P. Partner, *The Pope's Men. The Papal Civil Service in the Renaissance*, Oxford, 1990, pp. 77, 190, 241.

29 Griffiths, *Henry VI*, p. 105; J. Haller, *Piero da Monte, ein Gelehrter und päpstliche Beamter des 15 Jahrhunderts. Seine Briefsammlung*, Bibliothek des Deutsches Historischen Instituts in Rom, XIX, Rome, 1941, Beilagen, pp. 207–8, 209–10, 216–18, 218–19; Vatican Library, MS Chigi D VII 101, ff. 73–4; *CPL*, VIII, pp. 218, 282; Rymer, V/1, p. 21 (X, 620).

30 PRO, E404/51/326, E403/719, m. 18; BL, MS Cotton Cleop. E III, f. 76; Haller, *Piero da Monte*, Beilagen no. 24, pp. 210, 211; *CPL*, VIII, pp. 285–6, 317.

31 *DK*, XLVIII, p. 349; Bekynton, *Correspondence*, I, pp. 118–19; PRO, E403/743 m. 15.

32 Below, p. 119; PRO, E404/59/121.

33 Bekynton, *Correspondence*, I, pp. 117–18; Malden, p. 125.

34 Bekynton, *Correspondence*, I, pp. 118–19.

35 English College Archives, *Liber* 232, f. 34v; *Venerabile*, XXI, p. 265.

36 English College Archives, *Liber* 16, f. 10; *Venerabile*, XXI, p. 96.

37 Lunt, II, pp. 762, 794; *BRUO*, I, pp. 373–4; *CPL*, IX, p. 513, ?Taunton; also X, p. 78; Anstey, *Epistolae Academicae*, I, p. 72.

38 Bekynton, *Correspondence*, I, pp. 217–18, 227–8. Eton: p. 118, note 139.

39 Bekynton, *Correspondence*, I, pp. 229–31.

40 Privileges 1445: *CPL*, IX pp. 486–7, 501–3; proctor January 1446: Lunt, II, p. 782.

41 *CPL*, X, p. 272. Canon of Cologne, dying in Rome, May 1448, left legacy to *Anima* hospice, where buried.

42 Above, note 7.

43 Hofmann, *Behörden*, I, p. 239, n. 6; II, p. 114, 20 December 1455.

44 E. Rodocanachi, 'Les Couriers pontificaux du quatorzième au dixseptìeme siècle', *Revue d'Histoire Diplomatique*, XXVI, 1912, pp. 392–428, esp. pp. 396–403.

45 Uginet, p. 115.

46 Excellent brief account: *CPL*, XV, pp. xvi–xviii, by L. E. Boyle; Schuchard, pp. 92–121.

47 Above, Chapter 1, note 6.

48 *BRUO*, I, p. 413; *CPL*, VII, p. 2; R. J. Mitchell, 'English Law students at Bologna in the fifteenth century', *EHR*, LI, 1936, pp. 270–87, esp. pp. 270–1.

49 Amundesham, *Annales*, I, p. 81.

50 Chapter 5, notes 27–37.

51 *CPL*, VIII, p. 317, 5 November 1439, and e.g. Walser, p. 454.
52 Vespasiano (above) calls him protonotary. Referendary 1435, e.g. PRO, E30/1249.
53 Lunt, II, p. 774.
54 Katterbach, p. 24, no. 10.
55 *CPL*, XI, p. 681.
56 Bodleian Library, MS Arch. Seld. B 23 and BL, Cotton Cleop. C IV.
57 Jacob, 'To and from', pp. 71–2.
58 English College Archives, membrane 197.
59 *CPL*, IX, p. 260.
60 *CPL*, VIII, p. 286.
61 Above, note 59.
62 *BRUO*, I, pp. 202–3; W. A. Pantin, *Canterbury College, Oxford*, Oxford Historical Society, 4 vols., new series, VI, VII, 1947, VIII, 1950, XXX, 1985, III, pp. 74–80.
63 *CPL*, VI, p. 315.
64 Mitchell, 'Bologna', p. 271.
65 Chichele, *Register*, I, pp. xxxviii, 66; Lunt, II, p. 772, 1422; *CPL*, VIII, pp. 148–9.
66 Le Neve, *Welsh*, p. 72; *BRUO*, I, pp. 202–3.
67 *CPL*, VIII, pp. 148–9.
68 *BRUO*, II, p. 977, Howgan; Hallum, *Register*, pp. 66, 185, Holhan; *CPL*, VII, p. 166.
69 Lunt, II, pp. 768, 775, 784; *CPL*, VIII, pp. 57–8.
70 *CPL*, VIII, p. 376.
71 *BRUO*, III, pp. 182–3; BL, MS Cotton Cleop. C IV, ff. 182v–3.
72 Paston, *Paston Letters and Papers of the Fifteenth Century*, ed. N. Davis, 2 vols., Oxford, 1971, 1976, I, p. 6.
73 Lunt, II, p. 786; *CPL*, VIII, p. 233, 264; *BRUO*, III, pp. 1823–4.
74 English College Archives, *Liber* 232, ff. 9v, 29v.
75 *Venerabile*, XXI, p. 66.
76 *BRUO*, I, p. 389; Dobson, *Durham Priory*, p. 158.
77 *CPL*, VIII, p. 503.
78 R. De Roover, *The Rise and Decline of the Medici Bank*, Cambridge (Mass.), 1963, p. 209.
79 *DK*, XLVIII, p. 292.
80 *CPL*, VIII, p. 268; *PPC*, V, p. 203.
81 Stafford, Register, Canterbury, f. 49.
82 English College Archives, *Liber* 272, ff. 23–3v.
83 *Venerabile*, XXI, p. 95.
84 English College Archives, *Liber* 272, ff. 23–3v.
85 *CPL*, VIII, p. 236; IX, pp. 277, 278.
86 Cambridge, Corpus Christi College MS 170, p. 191.
87 *CPL*, IX, p. 334.
88 *CPL*, X, pp. 374–5.
89 *CPL*, X, p. 375.
90 English College Archives, *Liber* 17, f. 17v; Chapter 6, note 54, below.
91 *CPL*, X, p. 49.
92 Katterbach, p. xxxvi.
93 *BRUC*, pp. 329–30; Uginet, p. 63.
94 Bodleian Library, MS Arch. Seld. B 23, f. 139v.Quotations: *recommendetis me reverendissimo patri domino de Columpna ... utinam essem vobiscum..* Thanking: *de diligencia quam habetis pro me penes Rev. Pat. dominum meum de Columpna.* Acknowledging: *quod dominus meus vellet me ad ipsum venire. Libenter venirem si via*

tuta esset..
95 Katterbach, p. 8, no. 37; *Paston Letters*, I, no. 2, pp. 2–4.
96 *Venerabile*, XXI, p. 95.
97 Lunt, II, p. 784; not in Le Neve.
98 Chapter I, note 93.
99 Katterbach, p. 24, no. 10.
100 L. Capra, 'Nuove lettere di Guarino', *Italia Medioevalia et Umanistica*, X, 1967, pp. 165–218, esp. p. 185. Contact with Guarino via Robert Flemming: de la Mare, 'Vespasiano da Bisticci and the Florentine manuscripts of Robert Flemming', p. 11.
101 Katterbach, p. 34, no. 16; *CPL*, XI, p. 685.
102 The office, Chapter 6, pp. 101–2; E. Göller, *Die päpstliche Penitentiarie von ihrem Ursprung bis zu ihrer Umgestaltung unter Pius V*, Bibliothek des Königlichen Preussische Historischen Instituts in Rom, III, IV, VII, VIII, Rome, 1907, 1911, I/2, p. 123.
103 *CPL*, VII, p. 456; *BRUC*, p. 402.
104 *CPL*, VII, pp. 516–17.
105 Harvey, 'Andrew Holes'; Vienna, Oesterreichisches National Bibliothek, MS 4139, ff. 61–1v; *BRUO*, I, p. 378; Anstey, *Epistolae Academicae*, I, p. 10.
106 *Venerabile*, XXI, p. 95, from English College Archives, *Liber* 272, f. 1v.
107 *BRUO*, II, pp. 1301–2; Pantin, *Canterbury College, Oxford*, III, p. 74.
108 *CPL*, VIII, p. 480.
109 A. N. E. D. Schofield, 'England and the Council of Basel', *AHC*, V/1, 1973, pp. 1–117, esp. p. 65.
110 A. Zellfelder, *England und das Basler Konzil, mit einem Urkundenanhang*, Historische Studien, CXIII, Berlin, 1913, p. 310.
111 English College Archives, *Liber* 232, f. 29v.
112 English College Archives, *Liber* 232, f. 34v.
113 *Venerabile*, XXI, p. 95.
114 *BRUO*, III, Appendix, p. 2153; *CPL*, VIII, p. 317.
115 *CPL*, VIII, p. 499; Harth, *Lettere*, II, Book IX, no. 18, p. 379.
116 *CPR 1441–6*, p. 171; *CPL*, VIII, pp. 541–2, in 1435; *BRUO*, I, pp. 197–8.
117 *BRUO*, III, p. 1841; *CPL*, VIII, p. 319; Anstey, *Epistolae Academicae*, I, pp. 223–4; *Duke Humfrey and English Humanism*, p. 19; *Venerabile*, XXI, p. 96.
118 *CPL*, VIII, p. 320; *BRUO*, II, p. 708.
119 English College Archives, back of *Liber* 16, unnumbered.
120 *CPL*, X, p. 111.
121 *CPL*, X, p. 336; *BRUO*, III, p. 1640.
122 Lunt, II, p. 788, in 1447. For 1446: Chapter 9, note 303.
123 *CPL*, X, p. 270.
124 English College Archives, *Liber* 17, f. 11.
125 English College Archives, membrane 205.
126 Mitchell, *EHR*, LI, p. 274; English College Archives, *Liber* 272, f. 75v.
127 *CPL*, XI, p. 682.
128 English College Archives, membrane 206.
129 *CPL*, XI, p. 684; Weiss, *Humanism*, pp. 122–4; *BRUC*, pp. 275–7.
130 *CPL*, XII, p. 388.
131 *CPL*, VI, p. 414; Bodleian Library, MS Arch. Seld. B 23, f. 52. Note 12 above.
132 Lunt, II, pp. 768, 796; Harvey, 'Martin V and Henry V', p. 57 and note 59.
133 English College Archives, *Liber* 232, f. 25.
134 Schuchard, pp. 137–40.
135 Uginet, p. 104; P. M. Baumgarten, 'Miscellanea Cameralia', *Römische Quartalschrift*,

XIX, 1905, pp. 163–76, esp. p. 174.

136 IE 393, f. 82; Mandati 826, f. 138v; *CPL*, VIII, pp. 280, 282, 292; PRO, E403/719, m. 12.
137 *Venerabile*, XXI, p. 265.
138 English College Archives, *Liber* 272, f. 1; *clericus conjugatus*, Uginet, p. 104.
139 *Venerabile*, XXI, p. 84.
140 English College Archives, *Liber* 272, f. 8v.
141 English College Archives, membrane 197.
142 English College Archives, membranes 201, 203.
143 English College Archives, *Liber* 33, f. 5. Not Richard Ely, as *Venerabile*, XXI, p. 53.
144 English College Archives, membrane 204.
145 See note 144.
146 Flynn, 'Englishmen in Rome', p. 130; English College Archives, *Liber* 17, f. 5.
147 English College Archives, *Liber* 17, f. 9.
148 Malden, *Canonisation*, p. 96.
149 Uginet, p. 94.
150 Uginet, p. 101.
151 *BRUO*, III, Appendix, p. 2158; Mitchell, 'Students at Padua', p. 117; *CPL*, X, pp. 101, 274; Zonta, no. 2108; A. C. de la Mare and B. Barker-Benfield, *Manuscripts at Oxford, an exhibition in memory of Richard William Hunt, 1908–1979*, Oxford, 1980, p. 93 and nos. 2–4.
152 Harth, *Lettere*, III, p. 16; de la Mare and Benfield, *Manuscripts at Oxford*, MS 2, Oxford, Magdalen College, MS Lat. 39, with references.
153 Lunt, II, p. 772; *CPL*, X, p. 101.
154 *CPL*, X, p. 114.
155 Stafford, Register, Canterbury, f. 50v, 2 August 1449.
156 Flynn, 'Englishmen in Rome', p. 130; English College Archives, *Liber* 17, f. 11.
157 English College Archives, membrane 205.
158 Malden, *Canonisation*, p. 99.
159 *BRUO*, III, pp. 1678–80; *CPL*, X, p. 274.
160 Mitchell, 'Students in Padua', p. 117.
161 *CPR 1446–52*, p. 175; Lunt, II, pp. 764, 772, 774.
162 English College Archives, *Liber* 16, f. 1v.
163 *CPL*, X, p. 274; *BRUC*, pp. 468–9.
164 Lunt, II, pp. 762, 774.
165 English College Archives, *Liber* 232, f. 8v; Roman houses: P. Pecchiai, 'I segni sulle case di Roma nel medio evo', *Archivi*, series 2, XVIII, 1951, pp. 227–51.
166 Flynn, 'Englishmen in Rome', p. 130; English College Archives, *Liber* 17, ff. 7v, 12v.
167 *Paston Letters*, I, no. 3, pp. 4–5.
168 Lunt, II, pp. 776, 794, 814, 815.
169 English College Archives, membrane 196. John Henrici, *Venerabile*, XXI, p. 165.
170 *CPL*, VII, p. 209; *BRUO*, III, Appendix, p. 2173.
171 *Venerabile*, XXI, p. 65; English College Archives, *Liber* 232, f. 11.
172 English College Archives, membrane 190, 191; *CPL*, VII, p. 270.
173 *CPL*, VII, p. 278: 'has long followed the Roman court.'.
174 Lunt, II, p. 766; Chichele, *Register*, II, pp. 400–2.
175 Lunt, II, pp. 768, 782.
176 *CPL*, VIII, pp. 500–1, 522–3, 524; *BRUO*, II, p. 930.
177 Lunt, II, pp. 774, 776, 798.
178 English College Archives, membrane 205; *Venerabile*, XXI, p. 96.
179 English College Archives, *Liber* 16, back page, dorse, not foliated; *Liber* 17, f. 17v.

180 Lunt, II, p. 768.
181 Lunt, II, p. 768, but see also p. 774.
182 English College Archives, membrane 206; *Liber* 272, f. 77; *CPL*, XI, p. 651.
183 Cambridge, Corpus Christi College, MS 170, p. 216.
184 *Paston Letters*, I, no. 282, p. 471.
185 Hallum, *Register*, p. 10, App. E V, p. 247; *Repertorium Germanicum*, II, 1146–7.
186 Malden, *Canonisation*, pp. 8, 12; *Repertorium Germanicum*, IV, 3681.
187 *BRUO*, III, Appendix, pp. 2177–8; Schuchard, p. 144 and note 785, without English career; *Repertorium Germanicum*, IV, 1918–19.
188 E. Lacy, *Register, Exeter, Institutions*, ed. F. C. Hingeston-Randolph, London, 1909, I, p. 122; *Registrum Commune*, ed. Dunstan, V, index, p. 84, under Gele, and esp. III, pp. 114, 300.
189 *CPR 1436–41*, p. 302; PRO, E28/62.
190 *CB*, II, p. 52.
191 Haller, *Piero da Monte*, no. 145, pp. 163–4.
192 English College Archives, *Liber* 232, f. 8v. Called Greel in *Venerabile*, XXI, p. 67, and Gale p. 96.
193 *CPL*, XI, p. 24; *Repertorium Germanicum*, VI, 2919; Lacy, *Register, Exeter, Institutions*, I, p. 406..
194 Schuchard, pp. 49, 268, 332; *Repertorium Germanicum*, IV, 3516.
195 *CB*, II, pp. 55–6.
196 Zellfelder, pp. 310–11.
197 Lunt, II, p. 784.
198 Chichele, *Register*, I, p. 287.
199 Chichele, *Register*, I, p. lxxvi.
200 *CPL*, IX, pp. 136, 363.
201 English College Archives, *Liber* 232, f. 8v: *in qua nuper habitabat Theodoricus Oudencoup traject' qui obit.*
202 *CPL*, VIII, p. 310.
203 Schuchard, p. 332.
204 *BRUO*, II, pp. 959–60; *Repertorium Germanicum*, VI, 5517; VII, 2752. Andrew Hope: *Repertorium Germanicum*, VII, 109.
205 *Registrum Cancellarii*, I, pp. 102, 106, master Greek Hall, 1444, deprived 1445 for disturbance, bachelor of law; Lunt, II, p. 139; Cambridge, Corpus Christi College, MS 170, p. 208.
206 Malden, *Canonisation*, p. 150; *Repertorium Germanicum*, VI, 1052; VII, 1752.
207 Cambridge, Corpus Christi College, MS 170, p. 89; *Repertorium Germanicum*, VI, 5517, already BCL 1447; Lunt, II, p. 770, 816; Cambridge, Corpus Christi College MS 170, p. 89, *procurator causarum in Romana curia*, 6 January 1459, p. 91; Durham, Archives of Dean and Chapter, *Registrum parvum*, III, ff. 101, 106–6v.
208 *CPL*, XI, p. 654; XII, p. 391.
209 Cambridge, Corpus Christi College, MS 170, letter collection; PRO, E36/195, precedent book.
210 *CPL*, XI, p. 651. Held Combe Quinta, Wells, from 10 November 1460; Bilton, York, 1464: Le Neve, *Wells*, p. 28; *York*, p. 34.
211 Cambridge, Corpus Christi College, MS 170, pp. 218–19.
212 Durham, Dean and Chapter Archives, *Registrum parvum*, III, f. 101.
213 *CPL*, XI, p. 654; Lunt, II, pp. 145, 585.
214 Cambridge, Corpus Christi College, MS 170, pp. 236–7.
215 P. Egidi, *Necrologi e libri affini della provincia Romana*, Fonti per la storia d'Italia, Rome, 1908–14, II, p. 41: Thomas Hoppe, canon of York and Speyer, *cubicularius* of

Sixtus IV, doctor of both laws, abbreviator.
216 *BRUO*, I, pp. 432–3; *CPR 1436–41*, p. 312; PRO, E28/75 no. 10, 9 March 1445; *Epistolae Academicae*, I, p. 92.
217 Haller, *Piero da Monte*, no. 98, pp. 104–5, no. 102, pp. 110–11.
218 Haller, *Piero da Monte*, no. 121, pp. 131–2, no. 133, pp. 146–7.
219 W. Alnwick, Register, Norwich, ff. 105–5v.
220 Bekynton, *Correspondence*, I, pp. 223–4; Lunt, II, p. 820.
221 Vatican Library, MS Chigi D VII 101, f. 93v.
222 Bekynton, *Correspondence*, I, pp. 42–3, 131, 233–4.
223 Bekynton, *Correspondence*, I, p. 240.
224 Bekynton, *Correspondence*, I, pp. 231–2.
225 Bekynton, *Correspondence*, I, pp. 160–1, 174–5, 175–7, 178, 179, 185–6.
226 See Chapter 9, note 293 seq.
227 See Chapter 10, note 4 seq.
228 *CPL*, X, p. 271; Malden, p. 93, in 1456.
229 *CPR 1452–61*, pp. 195, 644; *DK*, XLVIII, p. 444.
230 Oxford, Lincoln College MS Lat. 117, p. 343; Bekynton, *Correspondence*, I, pp. 223–5; note 200 above.
231 Lunt, II, p. 435; *CPL*, XI, p. 680; XII, pp. 380–4.
232 Lunt, II, pp. 770, 796, 800, 816.
233 Durham, Dean and Chapter Archives, *Registrum parvum*, III, ff. 106–6v.
234 *CPL*, VIII, p. 263; Haller, *Piero da Monte*, Beilagen, no. 30, pp. 218–19.
235 J. A. W. Bennett, 'Andrew Holes, a neglected harbinger of the English renaissance', *Speculum*, XIX, 1944, pp. 314–35.
236 Bennett, 'Andrew Holes', pp. 319–20.
237 Bekynton, *Correspondence*, II, p. 251.
238 Dobson, *Durham*, p. 158.
239 Le Neve, *Northern Provinces*, p. 65; *CPL*, VIII, pp. 235–6.
240 *CPL*, VIII, pp. 498, 619.
241 *BRUO*, I, p. 389.
242 De Roover, *Medici*, p. 209, deposit of 1209 florins for Messer Tomaso Ciopen, July 1427.
243 Bekynton, *Correspondence*, I, pp. 217–18, 226–8, 229–31.
244 *CPR 1436–41*, p. 21; *CPL*, VIII, p. 408; IX, pp. 501–3.
245 *CPR 1429–36*, pp. 415, 603; *1436–41*, p. 21.
246 Le Neve, *Welsh*, pp. 78, 85.
247 *CPR 1441–6*, p. 377.
248 Lunt, II, p. 782.
249 *CPL*, IX, pp. 486–7.
250 *CPR 1446–52*, p. 204.
251 Le Neve, *Welsh*, p. 63.
252 Le Neve, *Welsh*, p. 58.
253 Le Neve, *Welsh*, p. 60.
254 Le Neve, *Northern Province*, p. 55, by collation.
255 Le Neve, *Salisbury*, pp. 12, 72.
256 Cambridge, Corpus Christi College, MS 170, p. 52.
257 e.g. PRO, E403/689, m. 12, FitzHugh, £100 gift.
258 Dobson, *Durham*, pp. 213–14.
259 A. Sammutt, *Unfredo Duca di Gloucester e gli umanisti italiani*, Medioevo e umanismo, XLI, Padua, 1980, bibliography.
260 Weiss, *Humanism* as Chapter 1, note 89.

261 J. F. D'Amico, *Humanism in Papal Rome. Humanists and Churchmen on the Eve of the Reformation*, Baltimore, 1983 and C. L. Stinger, *The Renaissance in Rome*, Bloomington (Ind.), 1985, most enlightening here.

262 J. Helmrath, *Das Basler Konzil, 1431–1449, Forschungsstand und Probleme*, Vienna, 1987, pp. 166–75; idem, 'Kommunikation auf den spätmittelalterlichen Konzilien', *Die Bedeutung der Kommunikation für Wirtschaft und Gesellschaft*, ed. H. Pohl, Stuttgart, 1989, pp. 116–72, esp. pp. 154–66.

263 E. Walser, *Poggius Florentinus, Leben und Werke*, Beiträge zur Kulturgeschichte des Mittelalters und Renaissance, XIV, Leipzig, 1914, pp. 47–8; M. C. Davies, 'Poggio Bracciolini as rhetorician and historian: unpublished pieces', *Rinascimento*, 2nd series, XXII, 1982, pp. 153–82, esp. pp. 173, 180–2, line 235. Beaufort with the king from 3 March 1419 at Rouen: Harriss, *Beaufort*, p. 97.

264 *DBI*, IX, Rome 1967, under Bertoldi, Giovanni de, de Serravalle; *Fratris Johannis de Serravalle . . . translatio et commentum totius libri Dantis Aldhigherii*, ed. F. B. a Colle, Prato, 1891, p. 5. Whethamstede: M. Harvey, 'John Whethamstede, the Pope and the General Council', *The Church in Pre-Reformation Society, Essays in Honour of F. R. H. Du Boulay*, ed. C. M. Barron and C. Harper-Bill, Woodbridge, 1985, pp. 108–22, esp. p. 118.

265 Harvey, 'Whethamstede', p. 121.

266 Mitchell articles, Chapter I, note 26; above, note 48

267 Harvey, *Solutions*, p. 149; J. Vincke, *Briefe zum Pisaner Konzil*, Beiträge zur Kirchen und Rechtsgeschichte, I, Bonn, 1940, p. 175.

268 Harvey, 'John Whethamstede', pp. 116, 117, 118, 120, for Easton.

269 T. Foffano, 'Umanisti italiani in Normandia nel secolo XV,' *Rinascimento*, 2nd series, IV, 1964, pp. 3–34; G. Ouy, 'Les premiers humanistes et leurs livres', *Histoire des bibliothèques françaises. Les Bibliothèques médiévales du VIᵉ siècle à 1530*, ed. A. Vernet, Paris, 1989, pp. 267–83, and articles by Ouy in bibliography here.

270 Stinger, *The Renaissance in Rome*, pp. 228–30.

271 See above, p. 10.

272 Weiss, *Humanism*, chapters VI and VII, and also above, p. 14.

273 H. Keussen, ed., *Die Matrikel der Universität Köln*, I, *1389–1475*, 2nd ed., Bonn, 1928, p. 457 no. 215/63, 64, 65, Gray and companions; p. 538 no. 247/45 Babyngton and I 75*; p. 617 no. 275/30, Courtenay.

274 R. J. Lyall, 'Scottish students and masters at the Universities of Cologne and Louvain in the fifteenth century', *The Innes Review*, XXXVI, 1985, pp. 55–73, esp. p. 55.

275 E. Meuthen, 'Die Artesfakultät der alten Kölner Universität', *Die Kölner Universität im Mittelalter*, Miscellanea Medievalia, XX, Cologne, 1989, pp. 366–93; idem, *Kölner Universitätsgeschichte*, I, *Die Alte Universität*, Cologne, 1988, Chapter V, esp. pp. 198–200.

276 Meuthen, *Die Alte Universität*, p. 205.

277 Mynors, *Catalogue*, pp. xxxi, xxxv; A. C. de la Mare, 'Vespasiano da Bisticci and Gray', pp. 174–6; H. Boese, *Wilhelm von Moerbeke als Übersetzer der Stoicheiosis theologike des Proclus*, Abhandlungen der Heidelberger Akademie der Wissenschaften, Phil.-Hist. Klasse, 1985/6, Heidelberg, 1985, pp. 23, 75, 81.

278 Harvey, 'Holes', p. 32; J. W. O'Malley, 'The feast of Thomas Aquinas in Renaissance Rome. A neglected document and its import', *Revista di Storia della Chiesa in Italia*, XXXV, 1981, pp. 1–27, esp. p. 5.

279 Harvey, 'Holes', pp. 30–1.

280 De la Mare and Barker-Benfield, *Manuscripts at Oxford*, pp. 93, 95; A. G. Watson, *Catalogue of Dated and Datable Manuscripts c. 435–1600 in Oxford Libraries*, 2 vols., Oxford, 1984, I, no. 823, p. 137; no. 834, p. 139.

281 Above, note 115; D'Amico, *Renaissance Humanism* , esp. Chapter I.

282 Gaspare Veronese: G. Zippel, ed., *Le vite di Paolo II di Gaspare da Verona e Michele Canensi*, Rerum italicarum scriptores, III, part XVI, 1904, p. xxv; E. M. Sanford, 'Juvenalis', in *Catalogus translationum et commentoriorum*, I, Washington, DC, 1960, pp. 175–240, esp. pp. 202–4.

283 D'Amico, *Renaissance Humanism*, p. 8.

284 e.g. Chapter 6, notes 166–70.

285 To Petteworth: Harth, *Lettere*, II, Book I, 11, 13; Book VIII, 2; Book IX, 2, 18; III, Book I, 1; Book II, 15. To Bildeston: II, Book V, 6.

286 Chapter 9, note 283.

287 To Beaufort: Harth, *Lettere*, III, Book I, 4; Harriss, *Beaufort*, pp. 376–7.

288 e.g. Harth, *Lettere*, II, Book IX, 18.

289 Name in Cambridge, Jesus College, MS 46. Thanks to Dr I. A. Doyle.

290 Parks, *The English Traveller*, p. 373.

291 Partner, *The Pope's Men*, pp. 208–9.

3
Hospices and pilgrims

This chapter discusses institutions already mentioned, which focused the life of the English group in Rome and to some extent acted as home from home for curial officials and pilgrims. In the later Middle Ages nearly all European countries maintained a national hospice in Rome for welcoming their own pilgrims and increasingly as centres where members of the curia from individual nations gathered for social and religious functions. England was no exception.

In 1417 there were two English hospices. The present English college began in 1362 when the English 'guild' (a confraternity) in Rome bought from John Shepherd, a chaplet seller (alias Paternoster), a house in Arenula district (rione), which Shepherd and his wife Alice then ran for the guild as a hospice. Shepherd died in 1365, leaving the hospice all his goods.[1] The second institution had existed in the fourteenth century to shelter the poor, run by the chapter of San Crisogono in the Trastevere district. In 1396 John Whyte, London merchant, persuaded the canons to allow him to lease, repair and add to it. This enterprise was also a confraternity, gradually acquiring property in the city. By 1406 it was called *hospitalis Anglicorum*, known also as the hospital of St Edmund and St Crisogono.[2]

By 1406 the confraternity of St Thomas, open to men and women, to which Shepherd had left his house, owned twenty-three houses and a palazzo, with land and vineyards.[3] By 1431 the houses had increased to thirty-one, bringing in 280 ducats rent. By 1445 thirty houses were producing 360 ducats. Rome was becoming more prosperous.[4] By then the centre was called the hospice of the Trinity and St Thomas of Canterbury, or merely 'the hospice of the English'.[5]

St Edmund's was never so wealthy, but Whyte left it his large valuable house, near the present Palazzo Farnese, and by the beginning of our period it had several other properties and a vineyard beyond St Maria del Popolo.[6] In 1449 it had nine houses and three vineyards, one unproductive.[7] By 1459 one or two more houses had been acquired,[8] producing rent of about 80 ducats a year.[9] In 1464 St Edmund's and St Thomas's were finally brought under joint management.

Probably the hospices were lay-run at first. St Thomas's had a *custos*, a chaplain and two auditors or *camerarii*, who oversaw the books. The brethren in Rome met yearly to choose these and check the accounts. Important decisions involved a meeting of all brethren, with majority vote, with a notary to record the result. *Custos*, chaplain and sacrist lived on the premises. Daily masses were said for the founders. For this period we know little of the day to day running of the houses, except that they employed some servants.[10]

Apart from rents, often from English *curiales* as noticed in the last chapter, the hospice of St Thomas had the *firma Anglie*, alms collected in England under supervision by their proctor. It is unclear how much this produced, though Mathew Crompe in 1446 sent 200 ducats for Michaelmas term that year and 400 for 1447.[11] To encourage generosity the hospice used a presentation in English, found in Archbishop Kemp's York register, first in 1426, listing the privileges of being a *confrater*. This is repeated, updated, in 1448.[12] Kemp, with other bishops, encouraged hospice questors in his diocese.[13] The aims of John Paternoster, who founded the hospice, are described as: 'in sucouring and refreshyng of pore, feble and seke men and also for pilgrymes of England that other while been robbed and spoiled by the way'. It then listed the privileges. Gregory XI allowed a chapel with a priest who could lawfully administer the sacraments to brethren and sick pilgrims. Boniface IX gave an indulgence of seven years and seven quarantines for all donating their goods, and, although this document does not say so, may also have allowed brethren choice of confessor.[14] Martin V in his fourth year, i.e. 31 March 1421, did allow the brethren to choose their confessor as often as they needed, except in cases reserved to the apostolic see and once at death for all sins.[15] Those thus privileged were obliged to fast on Friday, or, if already obliged to do so, on some other weekday or to select another penance advised by their confessor. Pope Eugenius IV agreed that brethren could, for the duration of his bull, i.e. from 25 September 1445 until 25 September 1448, choose a confessor as allowed by Martin V.[16] Nicholas V renewed this in 1447.[17]

The hospital of St Thomas in particular provided pilgrims and members with spiritual services, especially a priest speaking their own language for confession and sermons. By Eugenius IV's grant of 1445 the hospice had a burial ground, and its chaplain the right to hear confession of all but reserved sins.[18] The inventory of 1445, i.e. before its rebuilding, shows the chapel with some expensive fittings. We read also of a women's room, with a nobles' and a poor men's chamber.[19] In 1463, Pius II confirmed the hospice's rules;[20] all pilgrims in good health were to be sheltered for three days and if poor for eight. The sick had to be kept till death or recovery. The rich sick were supplied with food, doctors and medicine, the poor sick also with bedding. Gifts of bedding are included in the 1445 inventory;[21] Herman Dwerg, famous member of the German community in Rome, after considerable diplomatic dealings with England, left a bed and bedding in 1430.[22]

Membership was not said to be nationally exclusive, though in the sixteenth century members of St Thomas's had to be lieges of the king of England. But presumably for most English people membership of St Thomas's followed presence in Rome.[23]

Both hospices received properties in Rome from legacies as well as purchase, but also benefited from legacies in England.[24] Thus in July 1450 William Fygge, the *custos*, received 6 ducats left to St Thomas's by Anna, widow of Robert Tatsall, of the parish of St Swithun, London.[25] When Sir Thomas Haseley, London merchant, died, the *confratres* in Rome in late 1450 thought he had left them 100 shillings per year and tried to recover it. The present archives contain an English note of the bequest, with a Latin note that Richard Thwaytes said that Haseley's clerk had written it at Haseley's request and given it for delivery to Thwaytes.[26] Haseley had once been controller of exchange, responsible for issuing letters of exchange.[27] The various inventories of the chapel of St Thomas show gifts of valuable ornaments and cloth, though many of the most valuable come later in the century. In 1445 gifts are recorded of cloths and other things from Riciarda Ely, widow of John Ely, papal serjeant-at-arms, who himself had given a house; the prior of Canterbury; Adam Francis; Walter Hungerford (two velvet tunics); Hugh Middleton, knight and turcopelier of Rhodes (a frontal and two curtains); tablecloths from Robert FitzHugh, bishop of London; and two candelabra from Robert Botyll, prior of St John of Jerusalem, London.[28]

From the rentals one obtains some idea of types of property owned. The house given by John Whyte to St Edmund's is described thus: 'A great house with a turret, an upper storey, roofed with slate, with marble steps before it, with land and a garden and with stairs, rooms, and a stable, within the city of Rome, in the rione Arenula . . .' It had a well and was worth 60 ducats a year.[29] The house which John Ely had once inhabited was described as: 'a house with land, an upper storey and roofed, with a stair and a chamber . . . with a garden behind', worth 26 ducats a year.[30]

St Thomas's greater amount of property was also much more scattered and varied. Most magnificent was the large house 'de lilis' or 'de leonibus' in strata Armorum,[31] but there were others called *turris*, presumably typical fortified houses.[32] Many properties were also shops; in strata Armorum a shop was held successively by *barbitonsor*, *sertor*, *barbitonsor* and *recomator*.[33] A house and shop next the main door of the hospice was held in 1431 by John *Sertor*, presumably a tailor. In 1433 Gilbertus Pelliter held it, presumably Skinner or a skinner. In 1436 came Anna, the wife of the chaplet seller and Ralph *de bona ayra* and then in 1445 Johannes Sertor, followed in 1460 by Salvator Pictor.[34] In 1435 a rental names several tenants *causelare*, presumably hosier.[35] Peter, presumably a cloth merchant, son of John Ley, in 1428 resorted to arbitration when he thought the kitchen of St Edmund's was dirtying his clothes of cloth and linen (*pannos tam panni quam lini*).[36] St Edmund's was also involved in the perenial Roman practice of grinding up ancient remains for lime, using stone from its garden for use in the new building in St Thomas's.[37]

Numerous *pictores* and *paternostarii* recall the thriving pilgrim trade; sellers of holy wares rented booths near St Peter's to sell pictures, especially vernicles, and rosary beads.[38] But John Meden, brickmaker, in 1460,[39] recalls also the burgeoning building trade.

Many nationalities rented hospice houses, always of course including English, but with perhaps an increase in Italians in the second half of the century, though names do not always indicate nationality. So for instance, Jacobus de Colonia is replaced by Johannes Sartre de Brussel in 1431 and 1436 in one house,[40] and in 1431 Corradus Scerwe, *theutonicus*,[41] is in a house later rented by Johannes de Roma and then Jasper de Basilia.[42] The great house, *Scottus Turris*, where in 1431 Andrew Holes lived,[43] was in 1435 inhabited by Blasius Sancte Crucis and then in 1460 by Laurencius Francisci de Barberinis. Mathilda, *dicta Holandia*, shared a house in 1442.[44] Few English merchants are prominent in our period. Wool and cloth certainly arrived from England but Italians or Flemings usually brought it.[45] Likewise alabaster statues came, perhaps from Nottingham, but apparently brought by Italians or Germans.[46]

Some impression of increased prosperity in Rome is derived from the developing fortunes of the hospices. At the turn of the fourteenth century Rome was in a sorry state, remaining in ruins for many years.

The rent rolls of the canons of St Peter's show very large numbers of houses *in ruinis* still in mid-century.[47] In 1406 St Thomas's hospice owned a house: *in carteria sancta eundo ad sanctum Petrum* i.e. in the Borgo area, described as 'almost destroyed by wars and men at arms'. In 1431 and 1445 it was still 'vacant, almost destroyed and yields nothing'.[48] By mid-century improvements had occurred. Presumably this is the property in July 1452 rented for 2 ducats a year and repairs to master Martin Hunt, *acuarius cultellorum*, presumably a knife grinder, who seems to have worked for the curia.[49] This was no doubt part of the development round St Peter's by Nicholas V, which made property improvements there more worthwhile. But in any case the economy of the city was by then improving.[50]

Revolution in 1434 and the papal departure for Florence may explain why the hospice rents for 1435 show only 95 ducats for St Thomas's with nine houses as *vacat*, either empty or yielding no rent.[51] One, a great house with a garden 'quam inhabitat Willelmus Swan' would certainly be empty; Swan was either at the council of Basel or perhaps with the pope.[52] Roman rents always fell drastically when the papal court was absent, rising for Jubilees and imperial coronations; rental contracts reflected this. The canons of St Peter's in 1422 for instance rented a house on the understanding that if there were a Jubilee (one was due in 1423) it would pay whatever others paid.[53] Only one example can be seen in the English hospice records.[54] In November 1446 Andreas de Phano, *scutifer* of the pope, rented the great house left by John Whyte to St Edmund's at 60 ducats a year. In 1449 he asked remission of 12 ducats: 'When our holy lord the pope was absent from Rome and, so it is said, he ordered that courtiers should pay only half the rent for the rate of that half year of absence.'[55] This probably refers to the pope's departure in summer 1449 to escape plague, as for the next three years.[56]

The destructive effects of warfare on Rome can be seen; the inventory of the land of St Edmund's in 1449 recorded that when John Ely became *camerarius* of St Edmund's, probably in 1428,[57] the vineyard beyond St Peter's, 'outside the Porto Portese and beyond the chapel of Blessed Mary de la Moyle', rendered wine, 'but now is totally destroyed'.[58] Presumably the events of 1434 and later affected it.

Reconstruction can also be seen in the hospice archives. On 2 September 1425, the *magistri stratarum* declared that John Thomasson's porch was built on his own ground, not on public land.[59] These newly constituted (March 1425) officers were part of Martin V's reorganisation.[60] Presumably the recovery of the second half of the fifteenth century explains why tenancy documents often included repair agreements. Martin Hunt,[61] and John Lax have been mentioned;[62] there is also a renting to Antonius de Calais at a lower level provided he repairs.[63] Recovery also explains why, beginning in 1449, the hospice was able to rebuild, and thought it worthwhile.

The rebuilding accounts of St Thomas's would repay study by a historian of architecture. The builder, master Salvatus Andreae de Troko, perhaps a Florentine,[64] certainly using Florentine sub-ordinates,[65] had already worked for the cardinal 'of. Angers', D'Estouteville: 'I offer and exhibit the new work in the house of the reverend father in Christ commonly called the lord cardinal of Angers, which I constructed with my own hands'[66] and undertook to produce work 'like the Angers house'.[67]

He agreed that the walls would be an agreed thickness, of stone 'de tufy' (tufa?) and best lime, with space for a cellar with vault above, the front marble-faced. He promised to remove all waste to the Tiber. All wood would be good chestnut, properly seasoned. There would be a solar above the hall and lower rooms and a second solar under a roof of embossed work, on boards, painted.[68] In the end, however, the hospice complained that the finished building lacked the embossing[69] and that Salvatus had not done as he was told.[70]

Rebuilding began in January 1449. In 1450 John Capgrave described seeing the vault of the cellar, made by building over heaped earth. When the building was complete, by 1 December 1452, Salvatus had received 1,800 gold ducats.[71]

D'Estouteville's magnificent modernised palace adjoined the church of St Apollinaris. Giovanni Rucellai, during the 1450 Jubilee combining spiritual exercises with sight-seeing, admired it: 'A house of the cardinal of Angers, a Frenchman, walled in the modern style, a beautiful and noble house, and its roof extends outwards from the courtyard round four wings, and under the roof, which extends, is a floor like a balcony.'[72] Probably, therefore, it had a central cortile, an overhanging roof with the top storey a loggia, perhaps like the Palazzo Davanzati in Florence.[73] D'Estoutville's seems to have been a modernised tower house; there was a tower attached to St Apollinaris earlier in the century.[74] Modern excavation showed that the old hospice had two cortiles, one with a central cistern, as well as stabling.[75]

Money for the imposing edifice for St Thomas was first raised by borrowing from the bank of Antonio de la Casa, and then resorting to various expedients to repay him,[76] including the *firma Anglie*. The *confratres* also borrowed 100 ducats from St Edmund's, with, as pledge, one of St Thomas's houses,[77] and took lime from St Edmund's.[78]

With the hospital rebuilt they commenced rebuilding the church. In March 1456 John Lax, returning to England, was their advocate for collecting money. His letters of credence describe the existing church as 'at present . . . rather ugly and ruinous in appearance'.[79] We do not know when the new church was completed, and it seems to have been altered in 1497.[80] *Venerabile*, house journal for the English College, for the sexcentenary in 1962 produced a woodcut of 1580 giving some idea of the appearance of the final building.[81] It was brick, with brick columns with capitals and bases of travertine stone. A choir loft had organs, with a library above the left-hand aisle. In 1500 there were seven altars. In the latter part of the fifteenth century it gives the impression of being very richly appointed, but there are no inventories between 1445 and much later, and that of 1496, for instance, shows that some most valuable possessions were recent.[82]

Pilgrimage

The hospices, especially St Thomas's, were centres for welcoming and sheltering pilgrims. To go to Rome oneself, or to pay someone to go to pray for one's soul, continued to be common enough, though how popular one cannot tell. Thomas Polton wanted, when he died, a priest to spend two years making the pilgrimage and doing works of charity in the city.[83] But for the period of my study we have little first-hand evidence of the role of the hospices. Margery Kempe came just before our period, in 1414, when the papal court was absent. Travel in Italy was still very dangerous; her companions went armed,[84] and roads out of Rome were considered full of thieves.[85] There was also much poverty in the city itself.[86] Margery stayed several months, probably from autumn 1414 to just after Easter 1415. She travelled from Jerusalem, via Venice, to Assisi, because the group she was with wished to go that way.[87] In Rome she first stayed in St Thomas where she confessed and received communion every Sunday[88] and was much beloved by the master, probably John Thomasson, and all his brethren.[89] When slander from a priest in her group brought expulsion[90] she must have continued to live near St Thomas's, since she began to attend the present St Caterina in Ruota, opposite the hospice.[91] Eventually, in St John Lateran, she found a German confessor, Wenceslaus, who, she thought, had very high office in Rome, perhaps a minor penitentiary,[92] which would readily explain how he managed to act for her.

She did the stations, visiting particular churches where a special Lenten liturgy was performed,[93] made a general confession of all her sins and did penance, which included serving a poor woman and begging for her for six weeks.[94] She also attended sermons, some by Germans.[95]

Eventually the master of the hospital became convinced of her good name and received her back. She found that meanwhile the brethren had employed her former maid, as keeper of the wine.[96]

Margery was conspicuously uninterested in her physical surroundings, though evidently impressed by St Maria Maggiore and the body of St Jerome there;[97] most of her reminiscence of Rome is connected with her spiritual ideas. So, for example, she met people who had known one of her spiritual exemplars, St Bridget of Sweden, including one of the saint's maids, visiting the house where Bridget had lived,[98] very close to the hospital, in the present Piazza Farnese.[99]

In Margery's circle clergy of different nationalities spoke Latin to one another.[100] Margery could not, of course, but her close association with 'Deuche' priests and laity in Rome may be as much the result of their large numbers, especially in the area where she lived, as of her spiritual affinities with Low Country piety. For instance, her host had known St Bridget;[101] he may have been one of many German innkeepers.[102]

Jubilee years

Jubilees were special times of pilgrimage and indulgences. After its institution as a centennial event in 1300, the Jubilee had been fixed at every fifty years by Clement VI.[103] Urban VI shortened the period to every thirty-three years and one was held in 1390.[104] The next, due in 1423, is not well documented,[105] but John Whethamstede, abbot of St Albans, came to Rome for it from Siena, and was very moved when the pope sent him the indulgence when he was very ill in his Roman lodgings and, presumably, unable to perform the exercises.[106]

By 1450 the popes had again settled on a fifty-year cycle.[107] On 19 January 1449 Nicholas V announced a Jubilee for the following year. The fullest indulgence required visiting for a certain number of days four churches: St Peter, St Paul outside the walls, St John Lateran and St Maria Maggiore, and of course confessing one's sins with contrition.[108]

An increase in pilgrims and a rise in sales of holy bric-a-brac was to be expected. The English institutions expected an influx of pilgrims; hence no doubt the beginning of new buildings. The hospice collector in

England, William Knyghtcote, was sure that crowds were to be expected.[109] The English Benedictines were so troubled that large numbers of monks would take the opportunity to 'seek graces', that they obtained, through William Babyngton, abbot of Bury, the king's proctor, prohibition for monks to go without licence from their superiors, with permission for Benedictines to obtain the indulgence by contributing locally.[110]

It is impossible to say how many pilgrims came from England in 1450. There are no lists; licences to exchange money no longer appear on the patent rolls. In August 1450 Knyghtcote was finding difficulty collecting money, partly 'because of the burdens of the Jubilee' (*propter onera jubilei*); presumably those likely to pay were going on pilgrimage instead.[111] But evidently in addition the organisation in Rome proved inadequate, or money-raising for the new building was thought too greedy. Many pilgrims complained to Knyghtcote of the 'ingratitude' of the hospice members.[112] They particularly criticised the *custos* William Fygge, and said that the chaplain John Wellys was seldom there.[113] There must have been something in this, because in September 1451 the *camerarii* and a new *custos* wrote that Fygge and Wellys had been expelled. They might have absented themselves by joining the exodus from Rome at midsummer 1450 when plague broke out.[114]

Pilgrims perhaps objected to a building site instead of a comfortable hospice. But in any case Jubilee and plague proved too much for Rome.[115] Besides, 1450 was a bad year in England, punctuated by civic unrest, including, of course, Jack Cade's rebellion. Adam Moleyns, a hospice benefactor,[116] murdered in January, was only one leading political figure to lose his life, the most important being Suffolk in July.[117] Knyghtcote thought that this, combined with the Jubilee and bad organisation, made alms-collecting in England wellnigh impossible. In November he wrote: 'There never was such a year in our kingdom as this one, may God be merciful to us.'[118]

The sexcentenary issue of *Venerabile* printed lists from *Liber* 16 of the college archives, a volume including accounts for the *firma Anglie* for 1446, but mostly listing *fratres*. Each page names an English diocese and most, but not all, list individuals, the whole entitled *Liber aquittanciarum de Anglia et fratrum receptorum in Roma*. *Venerabile* did not explain that the lists are in various hands, with few dates. Here and there names have been certainly added later than 1446. For example, under Durham diocese, D. Richard Byllyngham is a later addition, the name that of Durham priory's proctor for 1464.[119] Richard Pede, called doctor of decrees, canon and dean of Hereford,[120] became doctor in 1448, but canon in 1452 and dean only in March 1463.[121] A list from Merton College, Oxford, and St John's Hall is in one hand and here we have some chance of checking dates. Several of the persons named were not members of Merton in 1446, for instance William Brygham,[122] John Wymark[123], and John Bradway.[124] One, Roger Combe, was probably not a fellow after about 1450.[125] Richard Langton was dead by July 1452[126] and John Billeston left in 1451.[127] All however were members in 1450; one may conjecture that they actually came together for the Jubilee.

From *Liber* 16 we can only be certain that on 3 July 1450, three priests from York diocese, John Dickinson, William Typton and John Wytton, delivered payment to the hospice from a *frater* of York diocese, John Lofthouse; the account notes that they lost on the exchange so Lofthouse still owed money.[128] Likewise the *custos*, William Fygge, received on 1 July from Thomas Drayton, servant of mistress Anna, widow of Robert Tatsall, London merchant, 6 ducats which her husband had left to the hospice.[129]

A few other names of Jubilee pilgrims can be gathered. Despite the prohibition of Benedictines going to Rome without licence, and warning from the prior to John Lax, Durham's proctor in Rome, that all Durham monks must show it,[130] John Byrtley obtained permission from the papal penitentiary, Cardinal Capranica,[131] and used it in spite of the prior.[132] William Partrike, monk of Durham, thorn in the flesh of Prior Wessington, organised sending his chaplain Thomas Harpur 'in this year of grace', partly to machinate against the prior in the curia, but certainly also for the pilgrimage.[133]

Harpur reached Rome,[134] but then left again to go where the pope was, Nicholas having fled the plague,[135] and Harpur there died, of plague no doubt.[136] He left as his executor in Rome a Scot, John Gray, an advocate of the Court of Arches in London. In August, when the tiny curia was sheltering in Fabiano,[137] a friar minor from Bristol also arrived there to pursue Partrike's business, lodging just outside the gates. No-one was allowed in lest they bring plague.[138]

The prior of Durham, warning about Harpur, also mentioned the following as about to set out for Rome: the bishop of St Andrews (James Kennedy); Robert Erghow, OP, formerly a monk of Durham and John Leveham, perpetual vicar of Northallerton. All had cases to pursue, but the year is no doubt also significant.

Apart from these, we know that William Taillour of London went in

August,[139] and William Strete, monk of Glastonbury, at the instigation of John Lax and Babyngton, was imprisoned, presumably for being in Rome without licence of his superior. He said he had come for the Jubilee and other business and was eventually rehabilitated.[140] John Moreton, chaplain, made his will in Oxford in April 1450, before setting off. He must have died there; it was proved in August 1451.[141]

Guide books

The only pilgrim guide to Rome written in England during this period, the *Solace of Pilgrims* by the Augustinian John Capgrave, was the product of the 1450 Jubilee.[142] It was probably written when Capgrave returned; it is undated but internal evidence shows Cardinal Beaufort recently dead (he died on 11 April 1447) and John Kemp still archbishop of York (he became archbishop of Canterbury on 21 July 1452).[143] Nicholas V was still pope.[144]

Capgrave's pilgrimage was either paid for by Sir Thomas Tuddenham, 'under whose protection my pilgrimage was specially sped', or even perhaps taken in his company.[145] Tuddenham, a Norfolk man, who figures largely and sinisterly in the Paston correspondence, was the leading henchman of the duke of Suffolk.[146]

The *Solace* gives a most interesting insight into Capgrave's attitude to pilgrimage to Rome and what he thought his readers would wish to get out of it. Of the book's three sections, the first describes ancient Rome, with subsections as in the ancient guides called *Mirabilia*, on hills, towers, bridges, palaces, arches, ending with a list of governors from the beginnings until the Empire, and of emperors from Julius Caesar to Frederick II. The second part treats the four major basilicas in the pilgrimage circuit for the Jubilee, followed by the 'station' churches, thus repeating some churches already listed. Finally, incomplete now, there was a section on lesser churches, which presumably contained the English hospital.

Capgrave explored Rome making notes, frequently saying 'as I found written there', or 'as I learned there'.[147] He 'enquired' locally,[148] noting at St Praxedis what 'the abbot said to us'.[149] This did not always produce results; at St Maria Transpontina he got no answer, 'for the dwellers are wroth anon if men ask any questions'.[150] He consulted local English informants. An English monk, probably from St Gregorio, showed him a story (on a tablet?) that at the Septizonium St Gregory kept a school.[151] At St Susannah an English friar hermit of St Augustine, who had taken part in the ceremonies, told him how Pope Nicholas had translated the body of the saint from St Peter's.[152] He distinguished carefully what he had heard from what he had read. 'Al this have I red, that whech folowith in this mater have I herd',[153] and noted where information failed: 'in this same church be many relikes whech I wrote not' at St Sabina.[154] In St Lorenzo 'many othir relikes ar shewed in this cherche of wheche I have now no fresch rememberauns for I wrote hem nowt for the prees [crowd] that was ther'.[155]

Hence the *Solace* includes a considerable amount of incidental information about the state of Rome, with frequent reference to desolation and ruined churches, St Felice[156] and St Ciriacus[157] for instance. St Susannah is 'a fair cherch . . . and a praty place annexed therto fer fro any dwellers half a mile on sum side, on sum side a hole myle'.[158] St John a Porta Latina is described: 'on the othir side of the strete is sette a fair cherch . . . but it is seldom open for there be no dwellers theron.'[159]

A map went with the *Solace*, unfortunately lost.[160] The incidentals of pilgrimage impinge from time to time. The Romans were more eager to attend the 'stations' than to make the round of all the churches because, as Capgrave understood it, mass at a station church produced as much indulgence as was available in all Rome that day.[161] He mentions crowds,[162] and 'the things they sell' when a station occurs.[163] St Maria de Palma, or *Domine quo vadis*, is 'a praty litil church and a place annexed thertoo where is commonly a taverne to the comfort of pilgrimes'.[164]

Capgrave was not uncritical. He read what he could, tackling conflicting authorities. For example in a discussion of the history of the relics of St Peter and Paul, he found his authorities giving different places of martyrdom and burial, with Martinus Polonus and a marble plaque in St Peter's differing as to what happened afterwards.[165] Capgrave's only comment is: 'Swech contradicioun is alday [common] in chronicles but for because it touchith not the articles of oure feith therfor may men chese what party thei will.'[166]

He was not influenced by humanistic archaeological concerns, but was none the less careful. He got his story about the place of St Peter's martyrdom from the *Legend* of St Pancratius, but that Peter's body had been moved from the Vatican in the time of Pope Cornelius came from Martinus Polonus,[167] whereas a marble plaque told him that this event occurred in the time of Pope Silvester.[168]

Sometimes, however, very tentatively, he ventured his own opinion. The manner of Lawrence's martyrdom was considerably disputed, with various instruments shown as relics, all seen by Capgrave, who concluded that Lawrence's torments might have been various. Lawrence's life confirmed this and Capgrave thought that if he had had at hand 'the grete book of martires whech is cleped [called] *passionarium*' he would find 'testimonies for mine opinioun'.[169] But ultimately devotion mattered more than historical accuracy, nor did he pretend otherwise.

Apart from the churches and the pilgrim round, Capgrave was most interested in indulgences and relics, preoccupations shared with his contemporary William Wey, fellow of Eton, who probably went to Rome slightly later.[170] For information Capgrave relied both on notices at churches[171] and on some book like the surviving *Staciouns of Rome*, which Wey seems also to have used.[172] Capgrave's account of the steps and the seven main altars of St Peter's, for instance, is very like the surviving *Staciouns*, though the order of the altars is not identical.[173] He distinguished indulgences of which he was sure and those based on popular opinion. At St Calixtus's catacomb: 'the comoun opinion is there of this place that who so evyr out of synne [free from] visit it that is to say clene shreve and contrite he is assoiled as clene as man may be be power of the church.'[174] He also relied on the *Mirabilia*, especially of course for understanding classical ruins.[175] To these basics he added Martinus Polonus,[176] and various *Legenda* of Saints. He had himself written saints' lives.[177]

Liturgical and social role of the hospices

The hospices, particularly St Thomas's, served increasingly as English centres and by 1464 were run by leading English *curiales*. More evidence exists for later in the century, when we have accounts of the expense of great feasts, especially the martyrdom of Becket on 29 December. The period before 1464, however, probably did not differ.

In St Edmund's the patronal feast (20 November) always figures in the accounts for special expenses.[178] In St Thomas's there are many indications that 29 December was celebrated with great expense and some evidence that Thomas's *Translatio* (7 July) may have been important also. For instance, in an inventory of 1445 (*Liber* 33) there is a mitre, worth 33 ducats 'from the goods of the courtiers for the feast of St Thomas'.[179] There exists one account for candles for the December feast, probably dated November 1433, where Thomas Cave and Andrew Holes, *procuratores* for the feast, record agreement with Sigmarictus *speciarius*, a grocer, for making torches and candles for the feast. The estimate was for six small torches and ten great candles for the main altar, with other candles for 'the light of St George' (*lumen Sancti Georgii*), for delivery before the end of November.[180] Perhaps from the same period, but most likely when the main body of the curia had left for Florence, and many for Basel, is a letter probably from William Swan, either with the curia or already in Basel, to a priest friend in Rome: 'As to the feast of St Thomas, we are here heavily taxed for it, and therefore may it please you to excuse in Rome myself and the others, because one ought not to be burdened twice.'[181]

The hospice of St Thomas also served as a poste restante and a place for safe-keeping for valuables. Andrew Holes left there with William de Esculo documents about the early stages of the canonisation of St Osmund when he finally departed.[182] The Salisbury proctor also deposited documents when he left in April 1454.[183] The hospice had a chest for valuables with three keys.[184] Security was clearly important: St Edmund's was insecure, in 1451 entrusting its money to William Gray, the royal proctor: 'because we do not have a safe place to keep money in the hospital'.[185]

A further, unexpected, function appears in the archives of the penitentiary, where on 31 October 1452, Thomas Sollay, known from elsewhere to be an abbreviator,[186] was registered confessing that he had celebrated a clandestine marriage in St Edmund's hospice chapel, 'concerning which it is doubtful whether it is consecrated or not', involving a Scotsman and a woman, neither of whose names he knew.[187]

It is difficult to envisage the life of the hospices between 1420 and 1464. Until the papacy returned and with it a flood of *curiales*, the hospice of St Thomas and its confraternity was dominated by laymen, probably artisans like the founders.[188] From about 1428 change began. That year John Ely, married clerk and serjeant-at-arms to the pope, with John Urry,[189] a proctor in Rome from 1425,[190] were *camerarii*. Henceforward officers were more likely to be *curiales*, often of some importance. The same occurred in the German hospice.[191]

Over the years too St Thomas's hospice acquired the privileges listed for potential subscribers.[192] Doubtless the privilege of choosing one's own confessor made becoming a *confrater* worthwhile. I know only two records of this. One, dated 1403, shows William Egyrton and his wife Elene, with their children, taken into the confraternity by the *custos* and brethren; Boniface IX has granted the fullest indulgences to allow them to choose their confessor to grant them fullest remission as often as they wished. The second, from 1448, is a certificate for someone who actually joined in Rome, presumably for presentation to his own parish priest to confirm his rights, countersigned at home, in Shrewsbury. According to Eugenius IV's grant of 1445, confirmed by Nicholas V, it allowed choice of confessor for three years and plenary indulgence at the hour of death.[193] William Knyghtcote in 1450, trying to resign the proctorship in England, informed the brethren in Rome that his hoped-for replacement wanted them to obtain more privileges and indulgences to encourage generosity.[194]

Property-owning inevitably involved litigation and litigation required friends. A 'great house' was bequeathed by John Whyte to St Edmund's. Some time before August 1445 the heirs of Antonio de Perusio refused to move out;[195] presumably their father had been a tenant. Litigation ensued, and we find tips to judges and notaries in the accounts.[196] Eventually the house was recovered and, from 4 August 1445 to 1 May 1446, inhabited by the archbishop of Benevento, Astorgus Agnesi, 'who pays nothing because he helped the hospice when it litigated for the said house'.[197]This was presumably a way of paying.

The tiny group of resident brethren by no means always agreed. William Swan, with a long connection to St Thomas's, preserved a petition for help to a prelate, perhaps English, dated 31 August, perhaps 1431, complaining that two *confratres*, John and Thomas, who had engaged in lawsuits and detained hospice property, were bringing the name of England into disrepute.[198]

In June 1452 Nicholas Upton, precentor of Salisbury, came to pursue the canonisation of St Osmund for his church.[199] From 1 September he leased for nine months, at 45 ducats, the largest house owned by St Edmund's, which he seems to have shared with Thomas Candour.[200] Upton stayed in the house eight months and fifteen days, doing some repairs;[201] some chapter business was done from the house.[202] On 12 May 1453 he left;[203] according to the brethren 'he withdrew secretly and did not pay his rent'. So they arrested his goods, mostly household effects, though they were apparently ready to compromise, letting him off one month's rent if he paid before he left the curia.[204] He probably ran out of money; there is no record of payment.

An influential member of the curia and his entourage could dominate the hospice. Its later history showed this, but the career of William Gray already reveals much the same. Whilst Gray was royal proctor the management of St Thomas's hospice usually contained some men already his *familiares* and others soon to become so. In 1446 and again in 1451 Richard Thwaytes, *armiger*, was *camerarius*.[205] He was marshal of Gray's household, from a family several of whose members served Gray; later he became warden of the park at Hatfield.[206] Henry Sharpe, *camerarius* in 1447,[207] like Gray, a graduate of Padua,[208] was evidently a friend, present at Gray's consecration as bishop of Ely.[209] William Stanley, later Gray's chaplain with a benefice in Ely diocese, was *custos* of the hospice in 1449 and *camerarius* in 1452.[210] John Kilvington, *nobilis*, *custos* in 1451 and 1452, received land and office later from the bishop.[211] William Radclyffe, *camerarius* in 1451 and *confrater* still in 1453, who rented a hospice house in 1445,[212] was also *familiaris* of Gray, later active in his diocese.[213]

Gray, Radclyffe, Sharpe and Thwaytes were also *confratres* of St Edmund's, with two of Gray's closest associates from his days in Cologne, Nicholas Saxton and Richard Bole.[214] When, in December 1450, the hospice was trying to recover a legacy left by Thomas Haseley, Richard Bole was one of those whom the *confratres* decided to use.[215] He accompanied Gray to Cologne and to Rome, but by February 1449 was chaplain to John Kemp, archbishop of York.[216] In late 1451 during trouble with Knyghtcote, the agent the hospice appointed to recover money was Elias Clitherow, of Gray's innermost household, his agent for sending messages to the curia.[217]

The hospices thus served very useful purposes, social and religious. They sheltered pilgrims and sick, no doubt allowing the former to orientate themselves before plunging into the world of Roman inns. They offered spiritual services in English and a safe place for valuables and receiving letters. They also provided the English at the papal court with rented housing and a social focus and were of sufficient importance by the end for it to be worth the while of William Gray to play an important part in their running. John Shepherd and John Whyte had provided better than they perhaps anticipated!

Notes

1 Best account of foundation: *Venerabile*, XXI, 1962, esp. pp. 19–42; helpful: M. E. Williams, *The Venerable English College, Rome, A History, 1579–1979*, London, 1979, esp. Appendices I, archives, and II, buildings.

2 *Venerabile*, XXI, pp. 83–5.

3 *Venerabile*, XXI, p. 54.

4 *Venerabile*, XXI, p. 54.

5 *Venerabile*, XXI, p. 49.

6 *Venerabile*, XXI, p. 85.

7 *Venerabile*, XXI, p. 88.

8 *Venerabile*, XXI, p. 88.

9 *Venerabile*, XXI, p. 88.

10 Vatican Library, MS Vat. Lat. 12159, ff. 180–6, 206 (quoting lost Book of *Acta*).

11 English College Archives, *Liber* 16, back folios.

12 Register Kemp, York, microfilm only, ff. 19, 125–5v.

13 Register Alnwick, Lincoln, microfilm only, f. 32v; Register Heyworth, Lichfield, microfilm only, f. 3.

14 I have not found evidence for Boniface IX, but see note 193 below; *Venerabile*, XXI, p. 50; Vatican Library, MS Vat. Lat. 12159, f. 206. Chapel under Gregory XI: Williams, p. 194, quoting Reg. Vat. 284, f. 56v.

15 *CPL*, VII, p. 329. See also *CPL* , VIII, p. 130, three year indult (1429) for plenary indulgence at death.

16 *CPL*, IX, p. 518, 1445, third three-year renewal. See also ibid., p. 572, right to cemetery and confessor.

17 *CPL*, X, p. 302. See notes 15 and 193: privilege lasts only three years.

18 Above for privileges; Williams, p. 194, thinks chapel newly built, not newly privileged, when Richard Hason was buried, 1446.

19 *Venerabile*, XXI, p. 58; English College Archives, *Liber* 33, f. 5.

20 *CPL*, XI, p. 651; *Venerabile*, XXI, p. 58.

21 English College Archives, *Liber* 33, f. 5.

22 M. J. Grothe, 'The Kronenburse of the Faculty of Law of the University of Cologne', *Franciscan Studies*, IX (XXXI), 1971, p. 277. Dwerg: Schuchard, *Die Deutschen*, pp. 294, 302–5.

23 Member of St Spirito in Sassia, 1447: William Pyrton, of Lincoln diocese, armiger, Egidi, p. 137. In the sixteenth century old statutes were said to have insisted that members be liegemen of the king of England, Vatican Library, MS Vat. Lat. 12159, f. 116.

24 *Venerabile*, XXI, pp. 55–6; N. P. Tanner, *The Church in Late Medieval Norwich, 1370–1532*, Pontifical Institute of Medieval Studies. Studies and Texts, LXVI , Toronto, 1984, p. 125.

25 *Venerabile*, XXI, p. 71.

26 English College Archives, *Liber* 17, ff. 1, 1v. Haseley: A. F. Pollard, 'The medieval under-clerks of Parliament', *Bulletin of the Institute of Historical Research*, XVI, 1938–9, pp. 65–87, esp. pp. 72–80; N. Ramsey, 'Scriveners and notaries as legal intermediaries in later medieval England', in J. Kermode (ed.), *Enterprise and Individuals in Fifteenth Century England*, Stroud, 1991, pp. 118–31, esp. p. 122.

27 *CPR 1429–36*, p. 282.

28 English College Archives *Liber* 33 (copy *c.* 1523), f. 5; *Venerabile*, XXI, pp. 52–3.

29 English College Archives, *Liber* 272, f. 8.

30 English College Archives, *Liber* 272, f. 8v.

31 English College Archives, *Liber* 232, f. 8v. Roman house names: P. Pecchiai, 'I segni', pp. 227–51.

32 English College Archives, *Liber* 232, ff. 19, 19v. A. Katermaa-Ottela, *Le Casetorri medievali in Roma*, Commentationes humanarum litterarum, LXVII, Helsinki, 1981.

33 English College Archives, *Liber* 232, f. 6v.

34 English College Archives, *Liber* 232, f. 8.

35 English College Archives, membrane 197.

36 English College Archives, membranes 194, 195.

37 English College Archives, *Liber* 272, f. 40v.

38 P. Pecchiai, 'Banchi et Botteghe dinanzi alla Basilica Vaticana nei secoli XIV, XV e XVI', *Archivi*, 2nd series, XVIII, 1951, p. 91. English College Archives, *Liber* 232, f. 8: Anna *uxor paternosterii*; Salvator *pictor*; f. 21: Johannes Paulus *pictor*.

39 English College Archives, *Liber* 232, f. 10; not bookmaker as *Venerabile*, XXI, p. 68.

40 English College Archives, *Liber* 232, f. 13.

41 English College Archives, *Liber* 232, f. 15v.

42 English College Archives, *Liber* 232, f. 15v, 1445, 1460.

43 English College Archives, *Liber* 232, f. 19v.

44 English College Archives, *Liber* 232, f. 6.

45 A. Esch and others, eds., *Aspetti della vita economica e culturale a Roma nel quattrocentro*, Fonti e studi per la storia economica e sociale di Roma e dello stato pontificia nel tardo medioevo, III, Rome, 1981, pp. 34, 38, 55–6, 106–7.

46 A. and D. Esch, 'Die Grabplatte Martins V und andere Importsstücke in den römischen Zollregistern der Frührenaissance', *Römische Jahrbuch für Kunstgeschichte*, XVII, 1978, pp. 211–17, esp. pp. 212–13, 214; alabaster: F. Cheetham, *English Medieval Alabasters with a catalogue of the collection in the Victoria and Albert Museum*, Oxford, 1984, pp. 45–9.

47 Vatican Library, Archivio S. Pietro, Censuali, Arm. 41/42, nos. 4 and 5.

48 English College Archives, *Liber* 232, f. 1: *est quasi destructa per guerras et gentes armarum*, and: *vacua et quasi destructa et nichil reddit.*

49 English College Archives, *Liber* 17, f. 11.

50 I. Ait, 'La Dogana di S. Eustachio nel XV secolo', in Esch, *Aspetti*, pp. 83–147, esp. pp. 97, 99, 105.

51 English College Archives, membrane 197.

52 Basel: Chapter 9, note 51.

53 M. L. Lombardo, *Spinti di vita privata e sociale in Roma da atti notarili dei secoli XIV e XV,* Archivi e cultura, XIV, Rome, 1981, p. 45; Vatican Library, Archivio S. Pietro, Censuali Arm. 41/42, no. 4, f. xvi.

54 C. W. Maas, *The German Community in Renaissance Rome, 1378–1523*, Römische Quartalschrift, XXXIX, Supplementheft, Rome, 1981, p. 79.

55 English College Archives, *Liber* 272, f. 24: *quando sanctus dominus papa erat absens a Roma, et, ut dicitur, mandavit quod curtisani solverent tantum medietatem pensionis solite pro rata illius medii anni absencie.*

56 L. von Pastor, *History of the Popes*, English ed., London, 1899, II, pp. 86–7.

57 English College Archives, membrane 194.

58 English College Archives, *Liber* 272, f. 9v: *extra portam Pertusam* (Portese) *et ultra capellam beate Marie de la Moyle* rendered wine, *modo vero est totaliter destructa.*

59 English College Archives, membrane 193.

60 Katermaa-Ottela, *Le Casetorri*, p. 80; G. Giovannoni, *Roma da Rinascimento al 1870*, part III of F. Castagnoli et al., *Topografia e urbanistica di Roma*, Bologna, 1958, p. 357; recent: M. G. Pastura Ruggiero, *La Reverenda Camera Apostolica e i suoi archivi (secoli XV–XVIII)*, Rome, 1987, pp. 100–2.

61 Above, note 49.

62 Above, Chapter 1, note 139.

63 English College Archives, *Liber* 17, f. 10v.

64 English College Archives, *Liber* 17, ff. 11–11v; M. E. Williams, Appendix II, pp. 195–6,.

65 English College Archives, *Liber* 17, ff. 9v–10.

66 English College Archives, *Liber* 17, f. 11: *do et exhibeo novum opus in domo Rev. in Christo patris et domini Cardinalis Andegevan' communiter nuncupati, quod quidem propriis manibus construxi et quod tamquam exemplar in omnibus saltem quoad ipsius formam refero .*

67 English College Archives, *Liber* 17, f. 12v: *in similitudinem domus Andegevan.*

68 English College Archives, *Liber* 17, ff. 11–11v: *cum proceribus, listis et capellaturis depictis.*

69 English college Archives, *Liber* 17, f. 11.
70 English College Archives, *Liber* 17, f. 12v.
71 English College Archives, *Liber* 17, f. 9; *Venerabile*, XXI, pp. 53, 100; Flynn, 'Englishmen in Rome', pp. 129–30, from Liber 17. J. Capgrave, *Ye Solace of Pilgrims*, ed. C. A. Mills, Oxford, 1911, p. 157.
72 G. Rucellai, *Giovanni Rucellai ed il suo Zibaldone. I, Il Zibaldone quaresimole*, ed A. Perosa, Studies of the Warburg Institute, XXIV, London, 1960, p. 76.
73 P. Murray, *The Architecture of the Italian Renaissance*, 3rd ed., London, 1986, illustration no. 34.
74 Katermaa-Ottela, no. 113, p. 38; P. Tomei, *L'architettura a Roma nel quattrocento*, Rome, 1942, p. 215. Mentioned 1510: F. Albertini, *Francesci Albertini opusculum de mirabilibus urbis Romae*, ed. A Schmarsow, Heilbronn, 1886, p. 28.
75 Williams, pp. 195–6.
76 Chapter 4, notes 51–6.
77 English College Archives, *Liber* 272, ff. 18, 23–3v.
78 English College Archives, *Liber* 272, f. 40v.
79 English College Archives, *Liber* 17, f. 4v: *in presenciarum adeo difformis et ruinosa in omni conspectu est.*
80 *Venerabile*, XXI, p. 105.
81 *Venerabile*, XXI, facing p. 106.
82 *Venerabile*, XXI, p. 106; English College Archives, *Liber* 17, f. 21.
83 Chichele, *Register*, II, p. 488, Polton; Tanner, *Medieval Norwich*, pp. 62, 86–7, 101–2, 125, others; also R. N. Swanson, *Church and Society in Late Medieval England*, Oxford, 1989, p. 295.
84 *The Book of Margery Kempe*, eds. S. B. Meech and H. E. Allen, Early English Text Society, CCXII, 1940, Chapter 30, p. 77, line 7.
85 Kempe, Chapter 42, p. 99, line 33 to p. 100, line 2.
86 Kempe, Chapter 39, p. 94, lines 23–4.
87 Kempe, Chapter 31, p. 79, lines 9–23.
88 Kempe, Chapter 31, p. 80, lines 8–12; for administration of sacraments, above, note 14.
89 *Venerabile*, XXI, pp. 66, 265.
90 Kempe, Chapter 31, p. 80, lines 13–20.
91 Kempe, Chapter 32, p. 80, lines 26–32.
92 Kempe, Chapter 33, p. 82, lines 10–30; Schuchard, p. 124 for gaps in lists.
93 Kempe, Chapter 34, p. 85, line 5; Chapter 39, p. 95, line 38.
94 Kempe, Chapter 33, p. 83, lines 7–10; Chapter 34, p. 85, lines 33–7.
95 Kempe, Chapter 41, p. 98, lines 18–19.
96 Kempe, Chapter 39, p. 95, lines 1–4.
97 Kempe, Chapter 41, p. 99, line 15; mistaken about St Lawrence, ibid. and note.
98 Kempe, Chapter 39, p. 95, lines 10–29.
99 Kempe, notes to Chapter 39 at p. 304.
100 Kempe, Chapter 40, p. 97, lines 27–8, 38.
101 Kempe, Chapter 39, p. 95, lines 18–22.
102 Maas, pp. 26–8.
103 J. Sumption, *Pilgrimage: an Image of Medieval Religion*, London, 1975, pp. 231–42.
104 Sumption, p. 245.
105 Sumption, pp. 248–9.
106 Amundesham, I, p. 143, p. 150, indulgence.
107 Sumption, pp. 253–4.
108 Lunt, II, p. 462.

109 English College Archives, *Liber* 17, f. 4.

110 *CPL*, X, pp. 57, 61; Durham, Archives of the Dean and Chapter, *Registrum parvum*, III, ff. 47v–8.

111 English College Archives, *Liber* 17, f. 3.

112 English College Archives, *Liber* 17, f. 3v, 10 November 1450.

113 English College Archives, *Liber* 17, f. 4.

114 English College Archives, *Liber* 17, f. 2.

115 Maas, pp. 92–4.

116 *Venerabile*, XXI, p. 81.

117 Griffiths, *Henry VI*, Chapter 21, pp. 610–65.

118 English College Archives, *Liber* 17, f. 3v: *numquam fuit talis annus in regno nostro qualis iam est, deus propicietur nobis.*

119 *Venerabile*, XXI, p. 70; Dobson, *Durham Priory*, pp. 211–12.

120 *Venerabile*, XXI, p. 81. *Liber* 16 adds dean.

121 *BRUO*, III, pp. 1449–50; Le Neve, *Hereford*, p. 5.

122 *BRUO*, I, p. 292, elected 1448.

123 *BRUO*, III, pp. 2119–20, elected 1448.

124 *BRUO*, I, p. 246, elected 1446.

125 *BRUO*, I, p. 474.

126 *BRUO*, II, p. 1098.

127 *BRUO*, III, pp. 332–3.

128 *Venerabile*, XXI, p. 69, reading *per*, not *in*.

129 Above, note 25.

130 Durham, Dean and Chapter Archives, *Registrum parvum*, III, ff. 33–3v.

131 October 1450, Durham, Dean and Chapter Archives, *Registrum parvum*, III, ff. 47v–8; R. B. Dobson, 'The last English monks', p. 7, note 3 for date.

132 Durham, Dean and Chapter Archives, *Registrum parvum*, III, ff. 35–5v, advice from archbishop of York, 9 March 1450; ibid., ff. 47v–8, 54–5, advice from master Richard Wetwang of York.

133 Durham, Dean and Chapter Archives, *Locellus* 9, no. 30.

134 Durham, Dean and Chapter Archives, *Locellus* 9, no. 31.

135 Pastor, *History*, II, p. 86.

136 Dobson, *Durham Priory*, p. 336; *Locellus* 9 as note 134 above.

137 Pastor, *History*, II, p. 87.

138 Durham, Dean and Chapter Archives, *Locellus* 9, no. 31.

139 *DK*, XLVIII, p. 384.

140 *CPL*, X, pp. 530–2. Poggio expected Petworth: Harth, *Lettere*, III, p. 72.

141 *Registrum Cancellarii*, I, p. 244.

142 A. de Meyer, 'John Capgrave', *Augustiniana*, V, 1955, pp. 400–40; VII, 1957, pp. 118–48, 531–75; P. J. Lucas, 'John Capgrave, OSA (1393–1464), scribe and publisher', *Transactions of the Cambridge Bibliographical Society*, V, 1969, pp. 1–35; A. Gransden, *Historical Writing in England*, II, *c. 1307 to the Early Sixteenth Century*, London, 1982, pp. 389–90. J. Capgrave, *Abbreviacion of Cronicles*, ed. P. J. Lucas, Early English Text Society, CCLXXXIII, Oxford, 1983, introduction. The only edition is *Ye Solace of Pilgrims*, ed. Mills. See Parks, *The English Traveller*, pp. 596–600.

143 *Solace*, pp. 133, 107; Lucas, 'Scribe and publisher', p. 3.

144 *Solace*, p. 123.

145 *Solace*, p. 1.

146 C. Richmond, *The Paston Family in the Fifteenth Century: The First Phase*, Cambridge, 1990, index; R. Virgoe, 'The divorce of Sir Thomas Tuddenham', *Norfolk*

Archaeology, XXXIV/4, 1969, pp. 406–18.

147 *Solace*, pp. 41, 74.
148 *Solace*, p. 123.
149 *Solace*, p. 148.
150 *Solace*, p. 161.
151 *Solace*, p. 45.
152 *Solace*, p. 123.
153 *Solace*, p. 36.
154 *Solace*, p. 87.
155 *Solace*, p. 102.
156 *Solace*, p. 11.
157 *Solace*, p. 138.
158 *Solace*, p. 123.
159 *Solace*, p. 145.
160 *Solace*, p. 2.
161 *Solace*, p. 85.
162 *Solace*, p. 102.
163 *Solace*, p. 89.
164 *Solace*, p. 162.
165 J. M. Huskinson, 'The crucifixion of St Peter: a fifteenth century topographical problem', *JWCI*, XXXII, 1969, pp. 135–61.
166 *Solace*, p. 71.
167 *Solace*, p. 70.
168 *Solace*, p. 71.
169 *Solace*, p. 102.
170 W. Wey, *The Itineraries of William Wey, fellow of Eton College, to Jerusalem AD 1458 and AD 1462: and to St James of Compostella*, Roxburghe Club, 1857, pp. 142–52.
171 *Solace*, p. 166.
172 *The Stacyons of Rome*, ed. F. J. Furnivall, in: *Political, Religious and Love Poems*, Early English Text Society, XV, 1866, pp. 143–73; or *The Stacions of Rome*, ed. Furnivall, Early English Text Society, XX, 1867, esp. pp. 30–4, none identical with Capgrave.
173 *Solace*, p. 63.
174 *Solace*, p. 69.
175 R. Weiss, *The Renaissance Discovery of Classical Antiquity*, 2nd ed., Oxford, 1988, pp. 6–8; Sumption, pp. 225–6.
176 Martin of Troppau, *Chronicon pontificum et imperatorum*, ed. L. Weiland, Monumenta Germanica historica, Scriptores, Hannover, 1872.
177 List with bibliography: *Abbreviacion*, pp. xcix–ciii. Most recently: K. A. Winstead, 'Piety, politics and social commitment in Capgrave's *Life of St Catherine*', *Medievalia et Humanistica*, new series, XVII, 1991, pp. 59–80.
178 English College Archives, *Liber* 272, passim.
179 English College Archives, *Liber* 33, f. 5: *de bonis curtisanorum pro festo Sancti Thome*.
180 BL, MS Cotton Cleop. C IV, f. 189.
181 BL, MS Cotton Cleop. C IV, f. 184v: *Quantum ad festum sancti Thome, nos sumus hic graviter pro eo taxati ideoque placeat vobis me et aliis dominis meis excusare in Roma quia quis non debet bis gravari.*
182 Malden, p. 96.
183 Malden, pp. 147–8.
184 English College Archives, *Liber* 33, f. 5.
185 English College Archives, *Liber* 272, f. 52: *pro eo quod non habuimus locum tutum ad custodiendum ipsas pecunias in prefato hospitali.*

186 *CPL*, X, p. 375.
187 *Reg. Pen.* 3, f. 388v: *de qua dubitatur utrum dedicata existit aut non.*
188 *Venerabile*, XXI, pp. 264–6, gives list.
189 *Venerabile*, XXI. p. 265, has Henrici.
190 *Paston Letters*, ed. Davis, I, pp. 3–5.
191 Maas, pp. 94, 175.
192 Above, note 12.
193 1403 document: is PRO SC1/43/147, brethren grant what Boniface IX allowed: *cum plenissimis indulgenciis vobis concedit potestatem elegendi ydoneum et discretum presbiterum in confessorem qui totiens quotiens vobis fuerit oportunum omnium peccatorum vestrorum plenam remissionem vobis concedere valeat quarum summam indulgenciarum nemo nescit nisi deus.* 1448 document: H. E. G. Roper, 'A Salopian pilgrim to the Hospice in 1448', *Venerabile*, X, 1942, pp. 265–8, to Thomas Peyton, chaplain, St Chad's, Shrewsbury.
194 English College Archives, *Liber* 17, f. 3.
195 English College Archives, *Liber* 272, f. 12v.
196 English College Archives, *Liber* 272, f. 12v.
197 English College Archives, *Liber* 272, f. 10: *qui nichil solvit quia adiuvavit hospitale quando litigavit pro dicta domo*; f. 14v: *stetit in domo magna propter hospitale S. Thome* from 4 August 1445 to 1 May 1446; Archbishop: Eubel, II, p. 116.
198 BL, MS Cotton Cleop. C IV, ff. 148–9v.
199 Malden, pp. xxii, 94.
200 English College Archives, *Liber* 272, f. 58v; Malden, p. 99.
201 English College Archives, *Liber* 272, f. 61.
202 Malden, p. 134; should read *in regione Arenula*.
203 Malden, p. 140.
204 English College Archives, *Liber* 272, f. 62v: *qui secrete recessit et non solvit pensionem.*
205 *Venerabile*, XXI, p. 265.
206 R. Haines, 'The associates and *familia* of William Gray and his use of patronage while Bishop of Ely (1454–78)', *JEH*, XXV, 1974, p. 241.
207 *Venerabile*, XXI, p. 265.
208 Mitchell, *TRHS*, 1936, p. 117; Zonta, nos. 1993, 2108, bachelor of laws in 1446, 2126, 2127, doctor of civil law in 1447; *BRUO*, III, pp. 1678–80.
209 Haines, 'The associates', p. 226.
210 Haines, 'The associates', p. 235 ; *Venerabile*, XXI, pp. 67, 96, 265; Flynn, p. 129, 132.
211 Haines, 'The associates', p. 241; English College Archives, *Liber* 17, ff. 2, 5v.
212 *Venerabile*, XXI, p. 265; English College Archives, *Liber* 232, f. 8v.
213 Haines, 'The associates', pp. 226, 229.
214 *Venerabile*, XXI, pp. 95–6; Mynors, *Catalogue*, pp. xlvi–xlix; *Duke Humfrey and English Humanism*, p. 24; G. M. Cagni, *Vespasiano da Bisticci e il suo epistolario*, Temi e testi, XV, Rome, 1969, p. 120, Saxton acting for Gray.
215 Flynn, p. 126; English College Archives, *Liber* 17, f. 1.
216 *Duke Humfrey and English Humanism* p. 24; Nigota, p. 391.
217 Flynn, p. 134; Haines, 'The associates', pp. 239–40; *Paston Letters*, ed. Davis, I, pp. 54–5, no. 37.

4
The English network

The curial system depended on a supporting network in England, with papal collectors and subcollectors, for gathering payments. The financial organisation in England has been more than adequately discussed by Dr Lunt in volume two of *Financial Relations of the Papacy with England*[1] but personnel are only incidentally considered. There was also need to export large sums to Rome, the largest being service taxes for greater prelates; because of English exchange regulations this involved Italian merchants and banks with London branches. Moreover, English proctors in Rome required trustworthy agents in England to contact clients and act as postmen for letters and money. The *curiales* needed a safe courier system for conveying confidential information too. For purposes of clarity I divide the couriers from the exchange system, though they often involved the same people.

Papal collectors

In this period there was almost always a papal collector resident in England, frequently, though not invariably, Italian. Later one, Pietro Griffi, wrote a treatise on his job which still survives, though Walter Medford, the first appointed by Martin V, wrote one for his successors, based upon the work of *his* predecessor, Paolo de Capo Grassi.[2] Though it is lost, we can gather from the actions and comments of the incumbents and their masters at this time how they saw the task.

Each newly appointed collector was given a careful outline of his powers, with an array of privileges, allowing him to grant certain favours. Typical powers were given to Piero da Monte in 1435:[3] to collect all money due to the pope, from every rank, including goods confiscated, for instance from heretics, but not the common and petty services, payable on major benefices directly; to act as judge in all cases concerning the moneys due, even involving bishops; to arrest goods, use ecclesiastical censures, order obstructors to appear before the pope and invoke the secular arm if necessary. Delay for payment was limited to one year; there was a limit to the number of subcollectors he could employ and he rendered account to the papal camera.

Da Monte had in 1435 the privilege of creating a number of notaries, to dispense a fixed number of people from defect of age, from defect of birth, to be married within the fourth degree of relationship, grant a fixed number of confessional letters and portable altars, give a fixed number of dispensations for marriage within the third degree of relationship and for absence from benefices to study. The numbers allowed were always limited (averaging fifteen of each) and with each renewal the limits were specified.[4] These favours were valuable because the recipients could obtain them without having to apply to Rome. Prior Wessington of Durham had a coveted portable altar.[5]

During preparations for the council of Pavia/Siena cardinals responsible for suggesting reforms noted the necessity of sending to England as collector a notable, prudent, upright, excellent prelate with adequate income to sustain an honourable estate, whose task would be[6] 'the bringing back of that kingdom to former practice [*morem*] and obedience, the renunciation of the statute [against provisors] and the recovery of Peter's pence and other rights of the Roman church'. They thought it was:

> a great detriment that that unique sign, which represents the Apostolic See in that kingdom, has been removed. The pope was wont to be faithfully informed by the collector of everything happening in that kingdom but now he cannot have information of those parts unless the king's proctor wishes, to the great loss of the church and the clergy of that kingdom.

The last collector, sent back to the pope by Henry V, had not yet returned. This represents the curia's continuing view of the collector's task: as well as gathering money, not now a very large amount, he was the curial eyes and ears.

Because of the statutes against provisors the money handled by the collector had dwindled. Lunt calculated that Hugo Pelegrini between 1349 and 1358 collected in total £6711, including £4958 from annates, for provisions, whereas da Monte's total for a five-year collectorship was £3689, including at least £2459 from indulgences; the bulk of ordinary revenue was from Peter's pence, and a few other small dues. In a normal year the amount owed would be about £250 from England.[7]

Qualifications for the job do not seem to have been specified. The

Italians were lawyers but had held different curial posts: Simon of Teramo, consistorial advocate; Giovanni Opizzis, auditor of the sacred palace; da Monte, protonotary.[8]

A complete list of the holders can be made, and it is possible to see a little of the work they did.

The first after the schism, a local man, Walter Medford, bachelor of law, had been appointed in 1417, as part of Martin V's reconstruction of the papal finances, having held no curial post.[9] He held office until 1420.[10]

On 6 September 1420 Medford was replaced by Simon of Teramo.[11] The government of Henry V returned him to Rome on 19 July 1421,[12] to be spokesman for the English attitude about the anti-provision statutes. The government paid him a handsome allowance,[13] but meanwhile the pope had no agent in England, hence the comments on the task of the collector mentioned above.

So back came Teramo in May 1423,[14] accompanied by a nuncio with a more limited task. Teramo's stormy career[15] ended with an attack on his attitude to Duke Humfrey's marriage problems and Richard Flemming's promotion to York. He was recalled.

On 25 January 1425 Giovanni Opizzis was appointed[16] After the troubles leading to Chichele's suspension as *legatus natus*,[17] his position improved. After 1429 he was allowed to, and did, hold benefices.[18] Eugenius IV re-appointed him in November 1431[19] and presumably he held office until replaced.

In April 1435 he was succeeded by Piero da Monte.[20] Monte regarded his task as rather to uphold papal authority than collect money, though he advised on appointments and collected for indulgences,[21] as well as doing all in his power to counteract the council of Basel. We may have an exaggerated view of his importance because he left a letter book presenting an incomparable view of his working life, available for no other collector.[22] Monte held office until late 1441.[23]

His successor, appointed 2 March 1442,[24] was Giovanni di Castiglione, nephew of Cardinal Branda, regarded as a friend of England,[25] but perhaps because he could not at once come, in September Adam Moleyns, da Monte's subcollector, was appointed until 1443[26] and seems to have functioned.

Castiglione, however, was collector in England and Ireland from 1443 to 1445. In 1444 he was trying to ensure the payment of the crusading tenth, for instance,[27] but in July 1445, after becoming bishop of Coutances,[28] was replaced.

His successor from August 1445 was Opizzis again,[29] seen at work during 1446.[30] Then there is a gap. Perhaps failure by the pope to collect a tenth caused temporary suspension of the system, or simply the records are lacking.[31] In any event the next certain date is not until 1450.

Vincent Clement, appointed by Nicholas V on 6 January 1450, and confirmed by Calixtus III in June 1455, had probably been da Monte's subcollector.[32] He was called collector when the king appointed him proctor in the curia in 1454.[33] He seems to have been active, in England only, between 1453 and 1456, but was confirmed in office by Pius II on 16 November 1458, and was still officially collector when the period ended.[34] For some of his time in office he used his sister's son Bonifacius Berengarius, a Catalan merchant, as deputy.

Despite spectacular quarrels with Teramo and Opizzis, relations with the collectors were usually good. Clearly Italians were expected to play politics, but the crown equally regarded them as useful channels of communication with the pope, as the cases of Teramo and Opizzis show.[35]

Ecclesiastical rewards in the country of work could be expected for a collector, though the statutes complicated appointments in England. It became usual for the royal council to allow the collector to hold benefices up to a certain sum, often £100. Teramo and Opizzis held English benefices, and took some interest. John Colet showed Griffi the window in Stepney parish church placed by Opizzis in 1431.[36] Clement of course was naturalised anyway,[37] and Castiglione was rewarded in France, as much for his uncle's sake as for his own. Da Monte did not get quite what he wanted, but held benefices.[38]

Subcollectors can seldom be seen at work and only some are known. They were sometimes foreigners but English names also occur. Opizzis used John Carleton in York diocese;[39] da Monte, Vincent Clement and Adam Moleyns.[40] Collecting indulgence money in 1439 in Durham diocese, Monte had two Italian sub collectors: Bartholemew and Urban, of the order of the Holy Spirit in Rome. He also had Antonio Beccaria, described as clerk of Humfrey, duke of Gloucester and subcollector, who quarrelled with the others over their powers.[41]

The exchange system

Dr Lunt thoroughly explored the system for transporting money to the Roman court. From 1390 export of bullion was forbidden; money for Rome had to be paid to merchants in England who arranged payment abroad by letters of exchange.[42] Italian merchants selling letters were obliged to buy, within three months, English merchandise to the value of the letters issued.[43] The crown tended to sell to one merchant a temporary monopoly for issuing letters and there was a crown tax of 2*d* for every noble exchanged.[44] Buyers were also charged by the merchant a fee for each letter and needed royal licence to use them. But attempts to carry coin would have been unwise. William Wey explained carefully the money needed for going from England to Italy in 1458, with the rate of exchange, adding: 'tak none Englysch gold with yow from Bruges for ye schal lese in the chaunge and also for the most part of the wey they will not chaunge hyt.'[45]

All this, of course, added to the client's costs. For example the Medici in 1455 received money from their branch in London for indulgences for the knights of St John. The Introitus and Exitus accounts in the Vatican archives, the documents the Medici presented to the papacy as its bankers, have the following:[46]

> Note that the society de Medicis conceded to the king of England for bringing the money out of England 400 pounds sterling, making 2000 cameral florins. And furthermore the society promised to bring out of the said kingdom within the year merchandise to the value of the said sum. And if they make less on the said merchandise the camera promises to make it good both for the merchandise and the florins paid to the king.

The largest payments were service charges for great prelates, several of which Dr Lunt examined. They were in two parts, firstly common services, one-third of the estimated gross income of a bishopric or abbey whose holder was appointed in consistory; secondly petty services, payments to cardinals present when the appointment was made. There were also a host of other small gifts to various curial officials, often making a large sum. For example: London was assessed at 3000 florins, whereas York was 10,000, and St Asaph 470, for the common services, to which other payments, including for the pallium in the case of York and Canterbury, would be added. Prelates could be excused if, for instance, the see had been vacant too recently; they might borrow or get permission from the pope to raise revenue locally from the clergy. Compared with Italian sees the English were wealthy, but these levies from the clergy were a major source of complaint.[47]

Other transactions also involved payments, both in the Roman court, in charges, fees to proctors and lawyers and tips of all kinds, and also in England to obtain possession of the bull when finally delivered. Usually, of course the bull or grace was handled by an agent in Rome, either sent *ad hoc* or a permanently resident lawyer. Payment for bulls was often made in Rome by the Italian merchants, who delivered them in England when the client had paid the bank's English agent. Thus English permanent residents in Rome did business with Roman banks having branches or agents in London. So Friar Nicholas Walsh in 1449 obtained in Rome a bull required (by the crown) and pledged himself and Henry Sharpe in Rome to redeem it in London in four months.[48]

Merchants who paid in Rome and recouped in England would be helped by the curia with ecclesiastical penalties to recover the money. From 1431 the curia usually exacted cash on delivery for provisions to all great prelates, abolishing the former system of payment by instalments.[49] Merchants paid in Rome all the charges for these prelates and collected cash on delivery or returned the bull to the camera, recouping losses if payment was late.[50]

The hazards for the clients resulting from the exchange system are beautifully illustrated in letters for 1450–2 in the English college in Rome, to the hospice representative in England, William Knyghtcote.[51] In 1449, when the *confratres* in Rome decided to build, they borrowed 600 ducats from Antonio de la Casa, former manager of the Medici bank in Rome, at that time running his own firm.[52] They promised to repay 600 gold ducats *de camera* in London, in seven months. For every 2 ducats they agreed to pay one noble (one-third of a pound sterling) and for every noble 12 pence. 'Which nobles, reckoned with the aforesaid exchange' came to £115 sterling (345 nobles). In the reckoning, it appears, Anthony was to keep 'the exchange', a charge of 12 pence per noble. This money they promised to have paid in London by Knyghtcote, proctor for the *firma Anglie*, their alms.

Knyghtcote, however, instead of actually paying in London, sent letters of exchange drawn by Felice Fagiano in London, expressed in ducats or florins and apparently including a charge (which the hospice called the exchange) by Fagiano of 10 pence per noble. When the first letter reached Rome de la Casa refused to accept because he wanted payment in England to Jacopo de Salviatis, Borromeo representative in London,[53] not to Fagiano. He also said that if he was paid in Rome he required repayment at 2 ducats for every noble of the £115 (thus receiving the charge himself), and he did not want the charge in London for the transaction included in the sum. The hospice explained what happened when the first letters of exchange were taken to de la Casa:

The said Anthony wished to have had for every noble of the £115 which the
hospital owed him in England 2 ducats here in Rome, and because he did not
wish to have any reckoning of the exchange paid to his colleagues in England
and thus by this reckoning if the hospice paid two ducats per noble and lost
the exchange the hospice would lose 64 ducats in the payment of the debt,
which it would not lose if the exchange of 10 pence per noble was counted in
the sum, which exchange our proctor William Knyghtcote pays in England,
i.e. always 2 ducats for every noble and 10 pence. And because then Anthony
de la Casa said 'I cannot make a reckoning or account with the hospital
concerning the exchange because the hospital has paid to Felice de Fagiano
and not to Jacob de Salviatis as was agreed, and thus Felix de Fagiano enjoys
that exchange and not I Anthony,' and because the letters of exchange made
mention of ducats and not of nobles, marks or pounds . . .[54]

there was a problem.

Apparently the hospital, finding that Fagiano would charge less, was
trying to get Anthony to accept the lesser charge, but he was only willing
provided he received all the money. Much, however, is obscure; one is
left feeling uneasily, like the hospice, that someone was cheating!

The first two letters of exchange from Knyghtcote were dated late
1450; when de la Casa refused to accept, the hospital returned them,
telling Knyghtcote to deal with Salviatis and to redo the transaction,
strictly adhering to the instructions about payment in London, in
sterling. Nothing happened because Alessandro de Palestrellis in
London, Jacopo Borromeo's partner, hung on to the instructions, trying
to deal directly with de la Casa, so that Fagiano would benefit. Meanwhile the hospice could only obtain a testimonial from de la Casa
accepting delay. He agreed that if Knyghtcote paid Borromeo in nobles,
marks or pounds and a letter to that effect was sent to Anthony, saying
that payment was from the hospital, he would settle. Knyghtcote then
sent the balance in early 1451, but expressed in florins, drawn on Fagiano
and postdated 24 June. Again de la Casa refused to accept. The exas-
perated hospice wrote to Knyghtcote:[55] 'Go to Felice Fagiano and say
that he drew that letter badly', ordering him to get a refund, 'with losses,
expenses, and interest . . . and place it in the Borromeo bank, because
Antonio de la Casa wishes to be answerable for them'. Knyghtcote must
not accept a letter of exchange from the bank but say that he wished to
pay the hospice debt to de la Casa in London.

In the end the *confratres* reckoned that, instead of 600 ducats, de la
Casa had had quittances worth 720.[56]

Banks and merchants

Knyghtcote's sufferings underline the importance of banks and merchants. To 1436 the Alberti merchants dominated the transactions between England and Rome; then their bank collapsed and the Medici inherited their role, but other banks and individual merchants in London can be found, involved in Anglo-Roman business.[57]

Individual Englishmen in Rome favoured particular banks and did their business mainly through one, not necessarily that used by their English clients. Though Salisbury, his client, used the Medici, Lax did not.[58] William Swan mainly used the Alberti; the only other firm he employed was the Vettori.[59] In 1435 Alessandro Ferrantino, Alberti factor in London, was Swan's English attorney, with Swan's nephew John.[60]

John Lax at first used the Baroncegli bank of Florence. Its London agent in 1456 was Rainaldo Baroncegli[61] and in Rome in 1455 Raimondo Baroncegli.[62] In 1463 Lax relied in London on Lionardo di Boninsegna, a Florentine merchant,[63] acting for the bank of Baptista de Alleata in Bruges, 'a notable and trustworthy man'.[64]

In the 1440s the Borromeo bank figures prominently in the records. Vincent Clement used it dealing with the Eton indulgences.[65] The Rome branch was in operation from 1431 and although their London branch is thought by Biscaro to have functioned only from September 1435 to about 1441[66] their (?former) agent Alessandro de Palestrellis in London was transferring money to Clement in Rome in October 1443[67] and in 1447 and 1448 transferred for the government money for a pension to the vice-chancellor of the curia.[68]

The Medici bank naturally figures very prominently especially from late 1436. In December 1448 the Bruges branch claimed sole responsibility for completing the monetary transaction concerning the see of London for Thomas Kemp,[69] threatening to return the bull to the camera if his uncle John Kemp did not pay promptly. Salisbury used the Medici bank to pay for the canonisation of St Osmund in 1452.[70] In 1456 they were relying on Simon Nori: 'respondent in the kingdom of England for the society de Medicis',[71] to organise sending letters, despite the unstable political climate. When Durham, in 1461, replaced Lax with master Thomas Hope, Hope was also in touch with Nori, by then perhaps in Bruges.[72]

Agents in England

Lawyers permanently in the curia did not rely solely on Italian merchants. They needed permanent, reliable English agents in London to receive letters, forward cash, and deal with bankers and government. The agent and attorney in 1449 for William Gray, king's proctor in Rome, is an example: 'the seyd Clederro sendith maters and letters owth of Ingeland to his seyd master every monith etc. He is well knowe in London and among the Lombardis'. This is Elias Clitherow, Gray's receiver general, still in 1457 forwarding Gray's letters to John Free in Italy.[73] William Swan used members of his family: his brother Richard, a skinner of Southflete and later John Swan, perhaps a nephew, as well as John Launce, rector of his parish church.[74] These not only collected and arranged the dispatch of Swan's money but also sometimes served as distributors, even on occasion of official letters.[75] The Swan house in Southflete was in fact the English centre of William's business.

John Lax's confidential agent and attorney was his cousin William Lax, by 1455 priest of St Olave's church in London.[76]

Proctors in Rome also needed reliable messengers to carry confidential letters and messages by word of mouth. Of course any known, reliable agent would serve, but some people seem to have come and gone frequently. These may be what John Paston II called 'Rome-runners' in 1473.[77] In the 1450s John Lax used Hugh Spalding as messenger to the dean and chapter of Salisbury and to Durham.[78] Spalding, described by Salisbury, writing to Lax, as 'your chaplain' (*capellanus vester*), later had a minor career in the English community in Rome, ceasing to be Lax's friend.[79] In the 1460s Lax relied on Thomas Coventry, 'my familiar' (*familiarem meum*),[80] who defended his master to the prior of Durham when Lax was being attacked in the early 1460s.[81]

Lawyers

A group of lawyers who specialised in curial practice might have developed in England. This did not happen, presumably because, though canon law and chancery regulations could indeed be studied anywhere, the intricate network of personal relations which constituted the curia and was as essential to success as a good legal case, needed lawyers on the spot. Good lawyers in England could indeed produce cases to be argued in Rome. For instance, Archbishop Kemp outlined for William Swan legal arguments for use against his chapter.[82] William

Paston, in 1426, sought advice at the Parliament of Leicester about the legality of instruments in his case with the priory of Bromholm 'from the wysest I coude fynde', including master Thomas Brouns, Chichele's chancellor and Nicholas Bildeston, Beaufort's chancellor, who had some experience of the Roman court.[83]

But there was no substitute for the lawyers with a present or recent curial practice. At the Leicester parliament Paston also consulted master Robert Sutton, 'a courtezane of the court of Rome' and master John Blodwell, 'a weel lerned man holden and a suffisant courtezan of the seyd court'. Both were temporarily in England: Sutton embarking on a distinguished career in Rome; Blodewell there since at least 1419.[84]

Advice about assembling the correct evidence was much more likely to come from Rome than England. The priory of Durham in 1442, as ever litigating about its daughter house of Coldingham, sent its proctor merely excerpts from its papal bulls.[85] Lax, when dealing with the case, sent long and detailed instructions about documents required, stressing that all the bulls about Coldingham must be fully copied in a book.[86] In the final stages of the canonisation of St Osmund Salisbury employed as proctor Lax, then papal secretary; better still, Andrew Holes, former royal proctor, who had become their chancellor with a house in the close, was able to give them advice. He had been concerned with the case in the curia in 1442, though without an official proxy.[87] In 1452 the chapter envoys reported Pope Nicholas V enquiring cordially of Holes's well-being 'and attaches great trust to what he says'.[88] Holes, who no doubt had known Tomasso Parentucelli in the court of Eugenius IV, duly wrote, asking Nicholas to canonise Osmund. He also explained to the chapter how to obtain a properly authenticated copy of the commission to cardinals to enquire into the case in Florence in 1442 – 'such commissions always used to remain in the custody of one of the notaries' – so there was no need for the chapter representatives in Rome to scurry about to locate copies of documents left by Holes.[89]

A great corporation like Durham priory, doing regular business with Rome, also needed confidential agents in London, who understood the exchange system and knew the merchants. In the 1440s and 1450s the prior of Durham used master Robert Roke, vicar of St Lawrence in London, sending money and letters to and fro by his steward, Robert Rodes, a Newcastle merchant.[90]

The postal system

In this period there was no regular royal messenger service to the curia, despite the system within the kingdom.[91] The curia, however, had a properly constituted college of *cursores* who went all over Christendom, sometimes carrying private letters both from *curiales* and back to the curia.[92] Solemn letters from the king to the pope, of course, were usually taken by full diplomatic missions, but routine correspondence and private letters to the royal proctor were apparently entrusted to merchants, usually, or to household servants. When roads were really dangerous friars seem to have been more likely to arrive.[93] Other correspondents with the curia relied heavily on the merchants or entrusted letters to any traveller

The royal method is easy to observe. Carriers include a valet of the royal household, Hans van Pruce.[94] In July 1443, however, letters to Clement concerning Eton were entrusted to Frederick, almost certainly a returning papal *cursor*.[95] Other correspondence about Eton, however, reached Clement via the Borromeo bank;[96] the Borromeo London agent, Alessandro de Palestrellis, delivered letters to Bekynton.[97] The Alberti were similarly used. Their London agent, Alessandro Ferrantino, was charged in early 1430 with delivering instructions to Robert FitzHugh, royal proctor in Rome,[98] and Alessandro's use for conveying letters is evident in the royal accounts.[99] A royal esquire organised sending routine correspondence. In 1441 Richard Alrede had the task.[100]

Salisbury sent letters using the Medici bank,[101] explaining in May 1456 that Simon Nori, the Medici agent, would arrange a special messenger to Bruges and thence to Rome. Nori estimated the journey from Bruges to Rome,[102] and in July 1456 John Lax that from Rome to Calais, as about twenty days for routine letters.[103] In 1452 Simon Huchyns said he had collected from the Medici bank in Rome on 30 June the letter sent by Salisbury on 6 June.[104] In 1419–20 letters were taking much longer, from seven to eight weeks, but then the routes were very unsafe.[105]

The papal *cursor* system can be seen routinely working throughout the period. When Baptista of Padua, bishop-elect of Concordia, came to England in July 1444,[106] a series of *cursores* followed: Giovanni Castrato;[107] Giovanni di Francia;[108] a *caballarius* delivering his letters from England paid in February 1445; and Michele de Francia going to the bishop.[109] In May Nicolo Castrato was paid for coming from England[110] and Andrea de Brabantia paid in July for going there, carrying bulls.[111] Sometimes messengers were too lowly, and presumably the business too routine, for them to be named: 'for two *caballarii* sent to England'.[112] The service could be very fast indeed. On 5 September 1439, *cursores* with news of union with the Greeks and the bull of indulgence set out,[113] and the news was being sent round England two weeks later.[114]

Routes and dangers

Medieval correspondents were well aware of 'the dangers of the way'. William Swan and his correspondents are typical in repeating information in several letters, beginning with a recital of correspondence received, date written and list of letters dispatched.[115] As well as the obvious hazards of thieves, robbers and dishonest companions,[116] war and political enmity added dangers between 1417 and 1464.

The English traveller to Italy usually went to Middleburg, along the Rhine via Cologne, to Constance and thence over the Alps. This was Margery Kemp's way in 1414–45, from Yarmouth to Zierekzee and back via Middleburg to Yarmouth.[117] In 1419 William Swan and Walter Medford were returning to the curia in Florence, via Constance, when Medford was robbed.[118] John Whethamstede, travelling to the council of Pavia/Siena in 1423, gives a very full account, with a list of journey times and towns passed: Calais, through Flanders and Brabant to Cologne, Mainz, where he encountered the legate, Cardinal Branda, via Trent to Verona and Cremona to Siena.[119]

While the English remained in France, particularly Henry V in person, there was frequent communication between Rome and England via France, messengers from Rome sometimes calling on the king or Bedford before crossing to England.[120]

Both routes were highly dangerous, but of course more at some times. Whilst Henry V was actually fighting the French, nothing protected a messenger. In late 1419 master John Forster, probably already a *scriptor* in the papal penitentiary, who acted as go-between for both curia and king, was kidnapped on his way from Normandy to the curia, though protected by French and Burgundian safe-conducts. He had a verbal message from the king about filling the see of Lisieux.[121] In May 1422 master John Clitherow, cameral clerk, travelling from Rome to England via the king in France, was kidnapped and held to ransom despite a papal safe-conduct.[122]

The Rhine route became temporarily safer once the English became firm allies of the Burgundians. Bedford seems normally to have relied upon French messengers to the curia. Kidnapping does not seem to have been a problem between 1422 and the council of Basel, but once Basel quarrelled with the pope, papal messengers were seriously at risk. In April 1432 Eugenius IV sent Giovanni Ceparelli de Prato to England[123] with bulls dissolving Basel,[124] but in May he was captured, delivered to the council and his bulls taken.[125]

Once the Burgundians broke off their English alliance in 1435 the Rhine route became and remained for several years extremely hazardous for any English messengers. There were regular kidnappings of messengers to and from Cologne and the Emperor. Burgundy was also at enmity with the latter, which made the situation worse.[126] Hence the English feared that a large delegation to the council of Ferrara/Florence would encounter great hostility, fears confirmed when Giovanni Opizzis, coming from the curia in late 1438 with the necessary safe-conducts for English envoys to the council, was captured by the duke of Burgundy. Indignantly writing to the duke, Eugenius IV admitted that Opizzis would have been better with a safe-conduct, but the pope had thought this unecessary since he was a noble Luccan, member of the curia and travelling for the papal council. In other words Opizzis was not an English agent.[127] But kidnapping and seizure of letters continued[128] and Henry VI was quite right to plead that John Kemp could not come safely to Rome for his cardinal's insignia; routes were too dangerous and safe-conducts no protection.[129] Sea routes were no better: we hear of several seizures by pirates of letters to the pope.[130]

The comparative easing of tension by a truce did not necessarily lessen the dangers. In May 1442 master Thomas Chapman was sent from England to Andrew Holes in the curia, almost certainly about the indulgences for Eton.[131] The Anglo-French truce should have meant safe travel, but he was seized in Brabant, handed over to the local seigneur, the lord of Auxi, and was still captive in August.[132]

Travel then eased until relations between France and England broke down again in the later 1450s; by then in any case the situation in England was also deterring many people from leaving the country.

An interesting footnote is that even at the most dangerous times friars got through, thanks perhaps to their international connections; this may explain their frequent use as royal messengers.[133]

In the dangerous conditions Englishmen doing business in Rome took precautions to ensure against fraud, theft and loss. It was essential to keep check on documents sent. Thus, sending Richard Byllingham to the curia in February 1464, Durham priory listed all the documents he took.[134] It was also vital to be seen attempting to comply with legal requirements, even unsuccessfully. When in 1428 the proctor of the prior of Lytham left for the curia, his departure from Durham was recorded by notaries. He went, they wrote: 'On the highway commonly called Elvetpath . . . in his right hand holding a walking stick with a cap on his head, with some acts and letters . . . in a certain bag'. And they noted that: 'Over the bridge of Shynkely [Shincliffe] . . . he receded from our sight'.[135]

Sensitive correspondence often appears in Swan's letter book with cryptic subscription, known only to the receiver presumably. Thomas Polton, in his quarrel with Robert Hallum, signs 'by him whom you know well enough' (*per quem satis noscis*).[136] Chichele used a secret seal for very private letters to the pope.[137] Some letters are so cryptic as to be now almost wholly unintelligible, for instance some of Bekynton's correspondence.[138] Very often, the really important part was left for delivery by word of mouth: 'The bearer can tell you news of us and something of what is going on in Basel', writes the royal chancellor to Swan in 1431, just when we want him to say more.[139] But he knew how unsafe that would be and so we are left uninformed.

Hidden costs

There were of course standard charges for almost all the graces and favours in Rome and for royal services, like letters of exchange. But in both Rome and England the wheels were oiled by tips and presents, adding greatly to costs. In Rome gifts in kind were essential courtesies. In May 1441 Bekynton organised sending to Florence, via the Florentine galleys, undyed white cloth, for Richard Caunton to have dyed and given to the pope.[140] The papal secretary Biondo of Forli acknowledged similar cloth from Bekynton.[141] Juan de Mela, an auditor, quite openly specified to William Swan his wishes.[142] In 1423 Thomas Fishbourne, in Rome on business for Sion Abbey and the Bridgettines, made gifts to the pope, Ardiceno de Novara, the advocate mentioned elsewhere, Herman Dwerg, the most influential German in the curia, an apostolic protonotary, and several cardinals.[143]

In England too there were tips. The prior of Durham tipped Thomas Coventry, Lax's *familiaris*, one mark, 'for a simpill reward'.[144] Hugh Spalding was tipped by Salisbury for carrying letters from Lax.[145] Small gratuities were the norm, greatly increasing expenses.

Here described is the mechanics of a system for dealing with a distant court, with very complex rules and regulations, but also very complicated personal relations. Clearly the novice and the amateur could be out-manoeuvred in dealing with it. It was essentially a world of experts, adept at using the mechanisms provided. Dealing with the exchange system, for instance, one can see why some contemporaries became easily convinced that they were being cheated: it is not easy to understand now what some of the transactions involved; we may assume that contemporaries under-stood their business better than we do, but some of them seem to have found the system baffling enough, if poor Knyghtcote is typical. The complication of getting business done in Rome probably goes some way to explain why the curia was viewed with such mixed feelings.

Notes

1 Lunt, II, passim, esp. pp. 429–32, 695–7, 700–1.
2 Pietro Griffi, *De Officio Collectoris in regno Angliae di Pietro Griffi da Pisa (1496–1516)*, ed. M. Monaco, Uomine e dottrine, XIX, Rome, 1973. List of collectors, pp. 212–14, 311–15, for this period; pp. 257, 390, Medford's book.
3 Haller, *Piero da Monte*, pp. 187–90.
4 *CPL*, VIII, for 1435: pp. 282–4; for 1438: pp. 292–3; for 1439: pp. 254–5.
5 Durham, Dean and Chapter Archives, *Locellus* 21, no. 40.
6 *CB*, I, p. 176.
7 Lunt, II, pp. 379, 436.
8 Teramo: W. Brandmüller, 'Simon de Lellis de Teramo. Ein Konsistorialadvokat auf den Konzilien von Konstanz und Basel', *AHC*, XII, 1980, pp. 229–68, and in idem, *Papst und Konzil im Grossen Schisma. Studien und Quellen*, Paderborn, 1990, (which I use), pp. 356–96, esp. p. 362; Opizzis: *CPL*, VII, p. 35; da Monte: Haller, *Piero da Monte*, p. *46.
9 Uginet, p. 30.
10 *BRUO*, II, pp. 1252–3. Replacement, next note.
11 Griffi, pp. 212, 312.
12 Harvey, 'Martin V and Henry V', p. 64.
13 PRO, E404/39/339; and below, p. 143.
14 PRO as note 13 above; Lunt, II, p. 420; R. Foreville, *Le Jubilé de St Thomas Becket du XIIIe au XVe siècle (1220–1470)*, Paris, 1958, pp. 64–5, 181–2.
15 Chapter 8, notes 8, 23.
16 *CPL*, VII, p. 35; Vatican Library, MS Chigi D VII 101, f. 25v; ASV, Arm. XXXIX 5, ff. 320v–21; Griffi, p. 213.
17 Chapter 8, notes 53–8.
18 Harvey, 'The benefice as property', *Studies in Church History*, XXIV, 1987, pp. 161–73, esp. pp. 169–70.
19 *CPL*, VIII, pp. 278–9, 316.
20 *CPL*, VIII, pp. 221, 282–4; Haller, *Piero da Monte*, Beilagen, no. 2, pp. 187–90. Latest: D. Quaglioni, *Pietro da Monte a Roma. La tradizione del Repertorium utriusque juris (c. 1435). Genesi e diffusione della letteratura giuridico-politica in età umanistica*, Studi e fonti per la storia dell' Università di Roma, III, Rome, 1984.

21 e.g. Chapter 9, notes 209, 246.

22 ed. Haller, as Chapter 2, note 29.

23 Lunt, II, p. 130; see Haller, *Monte*, no. 161, pp. 181–4; Bekynton, *Correspondence*, I, pp. 34–6.

24 *CPL*, VIII, p. 318.

25 *DBI*, XXII, pp. 156–8 by F. Petrucci; Foffano, 'Umanisti', pp. 13, 17, 18, 32.

26 *CPL*, VIII, p. 318. Not in Griffi.

27 Lunt, II, pp. 132, 135, 436; *CPL*, VIII, p. 299.

28 Eubel, II, p. 150; Griffi, p. 213; Bodleian Library, MS Ashmole 789, f. 262v, Henry VI to pope reccommending him and Zeno after Branda's death.

29 *CPL*, VIII, p. 319–20; Lunt, II, p. 135.

30 Lunt, II, pp. 136–7; Griffi, p. 314.

31 Griffi, p. 315.

32 Griffi, p. 315 Vatican references: p. 214 details; *CPL*, X, pp. 205–7, 222, 227–8, 271, 273, for 1450; XI, p. 192 for 1455.

33 *CPR 1452–61* p. 195; see May 1458, *DK*, XLVIII, p. 427.

34 Lunt, II, pp. 141, 435–6; Harvey, 'The benefice', p. 168; Griffi, p. 315; *CPL*, XI, p. 682.

35 Above, notes 12, 30.

36 Harvey, 'The benefice', pp. 169–70; Griffi, pp. 312–13.

37 Above, Chapter 2, note 216.

38 *PPC*, V, p. 44.

39 Durham, Dean and Chapter Archives, Misc. Ch. 4367.

40 Clement: Chapter 2, notes 217, 218; Moleyns: *CPL*, VIII, p. 318.

41 Durham, Dean and Chapter Archives, *Registrum parvum*, II, f. 124; *Locellus* 19, no. 75.

42 Lunt, II, pp. 204–6; M. J. Barber, 'The Englishman abroad in the fifteenth century', *Medievalia et Humanistica*, XI, 1957, p. 71.

43 Lunt as previous note. Examples: *CCR Henry V*, II, *1419–22*, pp. 216, 230; *Henry VI*, I, *1422–29*, pp. 49, 145.

44 *CPR 1416–22*, p. 135; *1429–36*, p. 282; *1436–41*, p. 139.

45 Lunt, II, p. 207; Wey, *Itineraries*, pp. 1–2, quotation p. 2.

46 IE 432, f. 45v: *Et est notandum quod dicta societas de Medicis pro habendo summam suprascriptam extra regnum Anglie concesserunt regi Anglie quadringentas libras sterlingorum facientes duo milia florenas de camera. Et ultra hoc promisit dicta societas extrahere tot mercantias de dicto regno infra annum quot ascenderi ad dictam summam, et casu quo ipsi habebunt dampnum de dictis mercatis camera promittit eos conservare indempnes tam de dictis mercantii quam de dictis 2000 floren' concessis regi.*

47 Lunt, II, chapters 5 and 6.

48 PRO, E404/65/88.

49 Lunt, II, p. 193.

50 Lunt, II, pp. 194–5, 210–11.

51 Flynn, 'Englishmen in Rome', pp. 130–3, from *Liber* 17, English College Archives.

52 De Roover, pp. 211, 216; English College Archives, *Liber* 17, f. 7v: *que nobilia una cum prefato cambio simul computata.*

53 P. Hurtubise, *Une Famille-Témoin: les Salviati*, Studi e testi, CCCIX, Rome, 1985, pp. 51–2.

54 Fagiano: PRO, E28/74, no. 17; E404/65/94. Quotation, English College Archives, *Liber* 17, f. 5v: *et quia tunc Antonius voluit habuisse pro quolibet nobili de £115 quos hospitale debuisset solvisse dicto Antonio in Anglia duos ducatos hic in Roma, et quia dictus Antonius noluit habere aliquam racionem de cambio soluto sociis suis in Anglia et sic per*

istam racionem si hospitale solveret duos ducatos pro nobili et perderet cambium, hospitale perderet in solucione dicti debiti 64 ducatos, quos non perderet si cambium x denariorum pro nobili computataretur in dicta summa.

55 English College Archives, *Liber* 17, f. 2: *Vadas ad Felicem de Fagiano et dicas quod ipse male fecit illam literam,* with refund: *cum damnis, expensis et interesse . . . et ponas in banco de Boromeis, quia pro ipsis vult Antonius de la Casa respondere.*
56 English College Archives, *Liber* 17, f. 6.
57 G. A. Holmes, 'Florentine merchants in England, 1346–1436', *Economic History Review,* 2nd series, XIII, 1960, pp. 193–208; Lunt, II, pp. 198–9; De Roover, pp. 47–8, chapter 9, passim.
58 Below, note 61.
59 Holmes, 'Florentine merchants', p. 204, note 8.
60 BL, MS Cotton Cleop. C IV, f. 189v.
61 Durham, Dean and Chapter Archives, *Registrum parvum,* III, f. 77–7v.
62 Malden, p. 153.
63 A. Grunzweig, *Correspondance de la Filiale de Bruges des Medici,* Commission royale d'Histoire, Brussels, 1931, p. 116; *CPR 1461–7,* p. 270.
64 Durham, Dean and Chapter Archives, *Locellus* 21, no. 16: *qui est vir valde notabilis et fidelis.*
65 G. Biscaro, 'Il Banco Filippo Borromei e compagni di Londra (1436–39)', *Archivio Storico Lombardo,* 4th series, XL, 1913, pp. 37–126, esp. p. 39. Holes paid via others, 1443: PRO, E404/59/251. See *DBI,* XIII, under Borromeo, Filippo and Vitaliano, by G. Chittolini, pp. 45–6, 72–4.
66 Biscaro, p. 49. Safe-conducts etc.: PRO, E28/66, nos. 26, 27; E28/64, 24 October 1440 and February 1441.
67 Bekynton, *Correspondence,* I, pp. 185–6; PRO, E28/73, no. 75, 1444.
68 PRO, E403/771, m. 10; E404/64/98.
69 Grunzweig, pp. 13–5, no. 8.
70 Malden, p. 150.
71 Malden, p. 162; and index, under Nori.
72 Durham, Dean and Chapter Archives, *Registrum parvum,* III, f. 101. Grunsweig, pp. viii, xxviii–xxix.
73 *Paston Letters,* ed. Davis, I, no. 37, pp. 54–5; above Chapter 3, note 217. Parks, *English Traveller,* pp. 557, 558, for Free. Edition of letters: J. E. Spingarn, 'Unpublished letters of an English humanist', *Journal of Comparative Literature,* I, 1903, pp. 47–65, esp. pp. 55, 56 for Cliderow; letter from him pp. 57–9.
74 E. F. Jacob, 'To and from', pp. 69, 70–1.
75 M. Harvey, 'England and the Council of Pisa: some new information', *AHC,* II, 1970, pp. 263–83, esp. p. 266.
76 Bekynton, *Register,* I, pp. 138, 109; Durham, Dean and Chapter Archives, *Registrum parvum,* III, ff. 48v–9, 91–1v; Malden, p. 214.
77 *Paston Letters,* ed. Davis, I, no. 282, p. 471.
78 Malden, pp. 153, 161; Durham, Dean and Chapter Archives, *Registrum Parvum,* III, ff. 130v–1.
79 *Venerabile,* XXI, index, p. 305.
80 Durham, Dean and Chapter Archives, *Locellus* 21, no 16.
81 Durham, Dean and Chapter Archives, *Locellus* 25, nos. 4, 5.
82 BL, MS Cotton Cleop. C IV, f. 166v.
83 *Paston Letters,* ed. Davis, I, no. 4, pp. 6–7.
84 As note 83 above.
85 Durham, Dean and Chapter Archives, *Registrum parvum,* II, ff. 151–1v; Misc. Ch.

1024.

86 Durham, Dean and Chapter Archives, *Locellus* 21, no. 16.
87 Malden, pp. xvii–viii, 99.
88 Malden, p. 99.
89 Malden, p. 111.
90 Dobson, *Durham Priory*, pp. 44–5, 129–31; Durham, Dean and Chapter Archives, *Registrum parvum*, III, ff. 88v, 89.
91 M. C. Hill, *The King's Messengers, 1199–1377*, London, 1961.
92 Schuchard, pp. 88–91; Rodocanachi, 'Les couriers', pp. 396–403 for this period.
93 O'Heyn, 1437: Chapter 9, note 184; Thomas Bird to emperor, July 1438: PRO, E403/731, m. 15, E403/733, m. 10, 12; Bird sought Waterford, July 1439, 1440, 1441, Bekynton, *Correspondence*, I, pp. 236, 237, 238–9; Bird to Mainz, 1441: Chapter 9, notes 259–65; John Kegill sent to Rome 1440, *Correspondence*, I, pp. 121–2.
94 PRO, E403/671, m. 3; E404/48/311.
95 Mandati 829, f. 26; IE 406, f. 78; 1443: Bekynton, *Correspondence*, I, pp. 185–6.
96 Bekynton, *Correspondence*, I, pp. 175–7.
97 Bekynton, *Correspondence*, I, p. 178; Biscaro, pp. 49, 55.
98 BL, MS Cotton Cleop. E III, f. 43.
99 PRO, E403/706, m. 19.
100 PRO, E404/57/293; E 403/743, m. 3.
101 Malden, p. 150.
102 Malden, p. 162.
103 Malden, p. 167.
104 Malden, p. 96.
105 Jacob, 'To and from', p. 66.
106 Lunt, II, p. 132; below, Chapter 9, notes 285–7.
107 IE 410, f. 167v; Mandati 830, f. 88v.
108 IE 410, f. 177v; Mandati 830, f. 100v.
109 IE 410, f. 177v; Mandati 830, f. 100v; IE 412, f. 116v; Mandati 830, f. 120.
110 Mandati 830, f. 111v.
111 Mandati 830, f. 126v.
112 IE 406, f. 124; Rodocanachi, p. 402.
113 G. Hofmann, *Acta Camerae Apostolicae et Civitatum Venetiarum, Ferrariae, Florentiae, Januae de Concilio Florentino. Concilium Florentinum documenta et scriptores*, series A, III/i, p. 77; Mandati 828, f. 230.
114 Lacy, *Registrum Commune*, II, pp. 160–3; Rodocanachi, p. 397.
115 e.g. BL, MS Cotton Cleop. C IV, f. 168v.
116 e.g. Jacob, 'To and from', pp. 74–7.
117 Kempe, *The Book*, pp. 60, 101.
118 Jacob, 'To and from', p. 74–7.
119 Amundesham, *Annales*, I, p. 129. Wey, *Itineraries*, pp. xxi–xxii, and 79–89, 1458. In 1462, he avoided Cologne. Wey translated: Parks, *English Traveller*, pp. 550–3.
120 Polton: Harvey, 'Martin V and Henry V', pp. 53, 57.
121 Pantin, *Canterbury College*, III, pp. 75, 76, 78, 80; Jacob, 'To and from', p. 65.
122 *CPL*, VII, p. 10; BL, MS Cotton Cleop. C IV, f. 172.
123 IE 393, f. 60v; Mandati 826, f. 87.
124 Schofield, *AHC*, p. 16.
125 *PPC*, IV, p. 160; below, Chapter 9, note 47.
126 Master Stephen Wilton and Sir Robert Clifton, captured by Burgundy, September 1435, released 10 April, 1438: *PPC*, IV, p. 308, V, p. 79; Rymer, X, 626–7; *DK*,

XLVIII, pp. 308, 321; PRO, E403/721, m. 11; E364/78, m. 9 dorse; E404/62/108; Haller, *Monte*, pp. 12–13, no. 20. Thielemans, p. 74, n. 51, capture of letters from king to pope, emperor etc., April 1436. Bekynton, *Correspondence*, I, pp. 220–1; *PPC*, V, p. 86, for Danker Petersen, messenger from Cologne, captured by pirates, September 1437.

127 Haller, *Monte*, no. 89, p. 93; Beilagen, no. 38, pp. 226–7.

128 PRO, E403/734, m. 15, in July 1439 letters of Hartank van Klux from Cologne seized at Sluys; E403/736, m. 16; E28/63, nos. 77, 78: emperor's messenger sent letters from Antwerp via merchants; secret messenger to congratulate emperor on election: Bekynton, *Correspondence*, I, pp. 105–6, 107–8; E403/739, m. 7; pilgrims to Jerusalem captured mid-1440, released at request of Cologne: Bekynton, *Correspondence*, I, pp. 93–4.

129 Bekynton, *Correspondence*, I, pp. 48–50.

130 Bekynton, *Correspondence*, I, pp. 238–9, Henry's letter to pope seized by pirates mid-1441. Also note 126 above.

131 PRO, E404/58/154.

132 E. Scott and L. Gilliodts van Severen, eds., *Le Cotton Ms. Galba B I*, Collection des chroniques belges inédites, Brussels, 1896, p. 449, no. 184; *PPC*, V, p. 203; *CPL*, VIII, p. 268.

133 Note 93 above.

134 Durham, Dean and Chapter Archives, Misc. Ch. 1066.

135 Durham, Dean and Chapter Archives, *Locellus* 9, no. 40: *in alta via vocata vulgariter Elvetpath . . . in manu sua dextera baculum tenens itineralem ac capellam in capite, una cum nonnullis actis, literis . . . in quodam sacculo.* And the notaries recorded that: *per pontem de Shynkley a visu nostro recessit.*

136 Bodleian Library, MS Arch. Seld. B 23, ff. 75v, 76.

137 BL, MS Cotton Cleop. C IV, ff. 144–5v: it had Emmanuel.

138 Below, Chapter 6, notes 140, 141.

139 BL, MS Cotton Cleop. C IV, f. 180v: *Nova parcium nostrarum et aliquid de disposicione eorum que agunt in Basilea, novit lator referre.*

140 Bekynton, *Correspondence*, I, pp. 227–8, 231.

141 Bekynton, *Correspondence*, I, pp. 241–2; for the man *DBI*, X, pp. 536–59, by R. Fubini.

142 BL, MS Cotton Cleop. C IV, f. 191.

143 Cnattingius, p. 133; Dwerg: above, Chapter 3, note 22; Ardiceno: Chapter 7, note 60.

144 Durham, Dean and Chapter Archives, *Registrum Parvum*, III, ff. 112v–3.

145 Malden, p. 214, if Stallyng.

5

Rewards

Apart from receiving fees and rewards in kind, those in the curia, whether Englishmen or foreigners, hoped to be rewarded with English benefices. In this period appointments to bishoprics, which always concerned 'high politics', never went to foreigners. In fact Francesco Coppini's promise of some selected English bishopric as reward for services to the Yorkists was unprecedented for the fifteenth century, though a portent of easing attitudes.[1] Later in the century it became usual for at least one bishopric to be, in effect, reserved by the crown for Italians who had done good service, but between 1417 and 1460 this was unheard-of.[2]

From the papacy, the obvious payment was by papal provision, equivalent, when money was very short, to reward in kind.[3] In England of course the statutes against provisors stood in the way. The law was clear, particularly for lesser benefices.[4] Anyone seeking a provision, attempting to introduce a bull or to litigate in Rome, would suffer the penalties. The law could be modified by royal licence to go to Rome for graces and/or by pardon for having gone, but after 1407 pardons were only to be granted for provisors to archbishoprics and bishoprics. Generally the law was observed.[5]

Licence to go to Rome to sue for benefices was therefore very rare in this period and even more rarely produced the desired benefice. An example was John Spencer, BCL, Sc Th., given permission in September 1439 to sue in Rome for benefices, when already pardoned for obtaining permission to become a beneficed religious (he had been a monk of Muchelney).[6] But I can find no record of his success. Another example is the struggle over the deanery of Wells in 1446–7. When John Forest, the dean, died on 25 March 1446, licence to elect, sought on 28 March, was granted on 1 April.[7] There were two contenders: the queen's secretary, Nicholas Carent (whom we will encounter in the penitentiary archives), whom the chapter elected on 22 August and Bishop Bekynton confirmed, with, as rival, the royal almoner, John de la Bere, the king's candidate, who had permission to sue in Rome for the deanery, with a provision, and royal pardon for accepting it, as well as a letter from the king asking Bekynton's favour.[8] The chapter tried to protect itself by obtaining from the royal council permission not to execute any provision and Bekynton protested against the curia that de la Bere had not shown his provision when claiming the position.[9] Evidently this was a struggle among the government factions. De la Bere did not obtain the deanery, receiving instead the bishopric of St Davids in September 1447.[10]

Petitioners still thought it worth obtaining provisions, presumably because these gave a papal guarantee and thus more security of tenure. An insight is offered by the provision of John Ixworth, a *curialis* of long-standing, on 10 October 1422 given a bull stating that, whereas he lately had an expectative for the prebend of Biggleswade, Lincoln, on the expected resignation of Philip Morgan, elect of Worcester (1419), he had meanwhile been collated (actually on 2 January 1420), by Philip Repingdon, and 'seeing that the said John, for certain reasons, desired to make use of the bishop's collation rather than the pope's mandate . . .' he wanted to accept collation, with papal confirmation.[11] In fact Ixworth was displaced in 1423 by master John Forster, a royal candidate, after judgement in the royal court. Forster of course was another *curialis*.[12]

To the papacy compliance with a papal command was a matter of obedience. To a bishop it was never so straightforward, as shown by the example of Walter Medford's benefices. Medford, collector until 6 September 1420, had died by 14 July 1423, at the council of Pavia/Siena.[13] John Kemp promptly (23 July) conferred the prebend of Cadington Minor, in London, on his chaplain John Bernyngham.[14] Martin V was very displeased. On 11 January, 1424, he conferred the benefice on William Pencrych, canon of Exeter, in the curia, declaring the benefice reserved.[15] Alerted by William Swan, Kemp denied that the benefice was reserved; the reforms of Constance reserved only benefices of *curiales* in office at death.[16] Though this was not in the English agreement with the papacy in 1418, since English law considered reservations invalid in any case, from the pope's angle the Constance rule was universally valid; he may have considered death at a general council equivalent to death in service. In any event he reacted very severely, pointing out to Kemp that his promotion to London involved supporting Martin's provisions.[17] Kemp did not yield and Pencrych did not get his benefice. But Thomas Gascoigne (whom we will meet again) accused Kemp, as archbishop of York, of appointing evil aliens and *curiales*.[18] This had its grain of truth. In November 1426 Martin V allowed Kemp to fill the York benefices vacant by the promotions of Bishops Alnwick, Gray and Rickinghall.[19] Kemp had already filled some of these before the permission but into one he put the pope's nephew, Prospero Colonna.[20] In general Kemp cleverly walked the tightrope between placating the pope and keeping the law of the land. Even when an appointment was made by papal prompting it apears in the register as a straightforward episcopal grant, as Ixworth's would have done, had it succeeded.[21]

A papal provision would not be needed if a bishop could be persuaded, or pressurised, into collation. Chichele found this in February 1428, when he was most anxious to please the pope. He had been informed that letters from the curia had just come, saying that master Richard Jordan (?Cordon) had died and that the pope had conferred his Chichester prebend (probably Eartham) on master John Urry.[22] Chichele, 'believing that in this he would please his holiness, lest some adversary should be had in the said prebend, contrary to apostolic intention', had written to the bishop, John Rickinghall, 'that, in consideration of our said lord [the pope] and in respect of our prayers' he would confer the prebend on Urry. But eight or nine days later a letter from William Swan came, saying that the provision had in fact gone to Swan's nephew and asking him to alter his letter for Urry. Chichele said that he could not but that Swan himself could negotiate with Urry, 'now present in the curia'.

The most likely suppliants for provisions were not Italian cardinals nor other aliens but English *curiales*; from time to time, when a glaringly obvious vacancy occurred, there would be a crop of claims. The struggle for promotion to the see of Worcester between Bourgchier and Brouns in 1433 is one example.[23] Eugenius IV had made plain his displeasure at the promotion of Bourgchier, pointing out to king and council that it behoved them in reply to withdraw any obstacles to the liberty of the apostolic see; Henry received a long lecture on reserved benefices.[24] The *quid pro quo* was a series of papal provisions which Eugenius expected to succeed. This bid was only partly successful, but the little group of provisions was mainly the result of petitions by Englishmen at the curia.[25]

Different problems arose when a foreigner tried to obtain an English benefice. A bishop might find himself torn between a desire to please pope, foreigner, king or all three, and a self-preservation instinct to prevent the benefice from becoming permanently reserved, which was not legally acceptable in England but would be claimed by the pope.

The attendant problems can be seen clearly in the case of the archdeaconry of Canterbury. When Chichele, at the hieght of his troubles with the papacy, wrote: 'notwithstanding solemn embassies and apostolic demands even under diverse censures, there is none in the kingdom, save myself, who grants promotion to aliens', the statement was not wholly true;[26] if anything Chichele was more niggardly than most of his fellows in collating foreigners, but he probably had the archdeaconry in mind.[27] The benefice had been held by cardinals in the past and probably to avoid reservation Prospero Colonna's immediate predecessor had been Chichele's own kinsman, William Chichele. But he died in the curia, in office; thus according to the chancery rules of Constance the benefice was reserved.[28] Martin V made provision for Prospero on 24 June 1424.[29] His proctor for the benefice would be the papal collector, Giovanni Opizzis.[30] The complicated politics of the appointment have been discussed elsewhere. Not until April 1426 was Prospero given permission to hold benefices by provision worth up to £500, though holding the archdeaconry was hedged with many caveats to prevent reservation.[31] Even so parliament complained about foreigners in English benefices.[32] This was a benefice which Colonna lost when his family was excommunicated for revolting against Eugenius IV in 1431. Chichele reclaimed it, inserting another relative, Thomas Chichele.[33] The archbishop fought at Basel and at the curia to prevent Prospero recovering the benefice when reinstated, and Propero lost, but had to be compensated.[34] By 1437 he was holding the rectory of Charing and the vicarage of Lydde, for which Thomas Chichele acted as his proctor.[35] The papacy also granted him a pension from the archdeaconry, until he obtained comparable benefices. Such pensions to foreigners were unusual in England, though common elsewhere, probably because the English resisted them along with provisions.[36] Perhaps the struggle was worth it to Chichele, though the consequences can still be seen after this period, with Paul II still trying to persuade Edward IV to allow a cardinal to enjoy the pension.[37]

One disadvantage of allowing the archdeaconry to be held by a foreigner was that it brought patronage of seven vicarages and one chantry, thus allowing Colonna (or his proctor) to make appointments in England, which Opizzis certainly did.[38]

But fear of perpetual reservation was probably the most potent objection to any appointment of a cardinal or foreign *curialis*. Salisbury made Marino Orsini archdeacon of Wiltshire in 1451, no doubt with a view to his promised services for the canonisation of St Osmund.[39] The appointment of Vincent Clement and Peter Courtenay as his successors may have been a prudent way of keeping friends in the curia without allowing the benefice to become permanently alienated.[40] The archdeaconry of Northampton showed what could happen. On 1 May 1431, as a result of the promotion to London of Robert FitzHugh, and his consecration at the apostolic see, the pope declared his benefices reserved and appointed Ardiceno della Porta to this one.[41] Ardiceno was a valued friend of England who acted in English interests on many occasions, but papal reservations were unacceptable.[42] So the royal council reacted by granting him the archdeaconry, but treating it as equivalent to his former annual pension, certainly not allowing his provision.[43] Even so he had difficulty obtaining possession.[44] When he died, by then a cardinal, in April 1434, Eugenius IV at once claimed the benefice as reserved, and to emphasise the point, provided Andrew Holes.[45] The bishop, William Gray, had been in charge of the delegation to the curia in 1428 to discuss modification of the statutes.[46] He did not appoint Holes, but rather, as the pope put it, 'notwithstanding the reservation, nor considering the authority of us and the apostolic see, and wholly unmindful of the promise which you lately made in the name of the king to Pope Martin our predecessor concerning English benefices vacant in curia', appointed his nephew William.[47] Holes failed; Eugenius was in no position to insist on his rights in 1434.

Thus provisions alone seldom suceeded and even with permission were difficult to implement. Ardiceno's nephew, Stefano of Novara, advocate of the English at Basel in 1435–6, was rewarded with the right to hold benefices like his more distinguished uncle, but I have found no evidence that he held any, certainly no prebends.[48] Foreigners depended much more upon the goodwill of individual bishops and appointments by them depended on a mixture of self-interest and (probably) fear of the consequences of annoying the pope too much.

It became usual for the collector to be allowed to hold benefices by collation. In 1421 Simon of Teramo obtained from Richard Flemming the prebend of Coringham in Lincoln and sucessfully collected Bedwyn in Salisbury on Medford's death.[49] In the latter he had a curial rival, with a provision: the bishop must have been delighted to avoid the statute whilst, presumably, pleasing the pope.[50] Opizzis (with others) had special permission in 1429 to hold benefices by collation or provision, presumably as a sweetener to Martin V at that very critical juncture.[51] Thereafter he held by collation the prebend of Bilton in York, in 1432,[52] the prebend of Combe Prima in Bath and Wells in 1434, until 1449,[53] with at least one parish church from 1430.[54] Da Monte had permission to hold up to £100 in benefices,[55] and obtained the rectory of Ivychurch, in Canterbury diocese but never the prebend he wanted.[56] Giovanni di Castiglione was made bishop of Coutances on 2 September 1444, and was a pillar of support for English rule in Normandy until Charles VII forced him to swear allegiance in September 1449.[57]

Other cases where Italians held benefices, such as Marino Orsini, or Ardiceno della Porta, were examples of rewards for very specific services. Piero Barbo's prebend of Grindale in 1437 was more probably an attempt to please the pope through his nephew, as was Piero's briefly held archdeaconry of Salisbury.[58] Barbo failed to add to his benefices, despite powerful pressure from his uncle.[59] When in 1446 he resigned Grindale the bishop quickly collated Richard Caunton, who had also succeeded him in the archdeaconry, presumably because Caunton was considered able to withstand any attempt to reserve the benefice.[60]

The king attempted to thank those who helped with the Eton indulgences. The vice-chancellor, Francesco Condulmaro, had tried already in 1435 to obtain a Lincoln prebend, but had been defeated by William Gray, the bishop's nephew.[61] He was allowed in January 1448 to hold benefices up to £100, but obtained no prebend.[62] In the end a pension was his reward, as for others who had helped.

Thus the rewards in England either for service in the curia by Englishmen or for foreigners who helped there, were few and far between, as Poggio discovered.[63] Open defiance of the pope was less common than evasion and sheltering behind the statutes, but as far as one can tell cases where apparent appointment by a bishop hid compliance with the papal will were not very common; they did occur, but must have been a matter of luck. The statutes were most effective and protected England from some of the most abusive and hated results of the papal benefice system.

Notes

1 Chapter 11, esp. note 143.
2 A. H. Thompson, *The English Clergy and their Organisation in the Later Middle Ages*, Oxford, 1947, pp. 26–7; Du Boulay, 'The Fifteenth Century', 1965, p. 222.
3 Harvey, 'The benefice', passim.
4 R. L. Storey, 'Clergy and common law in the reign of Henry IV', *Medieval Legal Records, Edited in Memory of C. A. F. Meekings*, eds. R. F. Hunniset and J. B. Post, London, 1978, pp. 341–408, esp. pp. 353–408.
5 Lunt, II, pp. 381–408.
6 *CPR 1436–41*, p. 337; *CCR 1435–41*, p. 145.
7 Le Neve, *Bath and Wells*, p. 5.
8 *CPL*, VIII, p. 308; Lunt, II, p. 432; *CPR 1441–6*, pp. 442, 447; *Letters of Queen*

Margaret of Anjou, ed. C. Monro, Camden Society, 1st Series, LXXXVI, 1863, no. 33, pp. 57–8, no. 63, pp. 93–4.

9 Lunt, II, p. 432; Historical Manuscripts Commission, *Calendar of Manuscripts of the Dean and Chapter of Wells*, Cd. 7106, London, 1914, II, pp. 675–7; Bekynton, *Register*, II, p. 434.

10 Le Neve, *Bath and Wells*, p. 5; idem, *The Welsh Dioceses*, p. 55; *CPL*, X, p. 295.

11 Ixworth: Chapter 2, notes 93–6; Biggleswade: Le Neve, *Lincoln*, p. 37; quotation: *CPL* VII, p. 213.

12 Above, note 11.

13 Above, Chapter 4, notes 9, 10; death: ASV, Arm. XXXIX 6, f. 160; 4, ff. 313–13v; AN, LL 4ᵃ, f. 135.

14 J. A. Nigota, 'John Kemp, a political prelate of the fifteenth century', Ph.D for Emory University, 1973, p. 157; Le Neve, *St Paul's, London*, p. 26.

15 *BRUO*, III, pp. 2205–6; Vatican, Ms Chigi D VII 101, f. 52v.

16 Nigota, p. 157; Constance: C. J. Hefele, *Histoire des Conciles*, Paris, 1916, VII/1, p. 542.

17 Haller, *England und Rom*, p. 253, n. 1; MS refs., note 13 above.

18 Nigota, pp. 380–1; T. Gascoigne, *Loci e Libro Veritatum*, ed. J. E. T. Rogers, Oxford, 1881, p. 38; Oxford, Lincoln College, MS Lat. 117, p. 388.

19 Nigota, p. 380.

20 Le Neve, *Northern Province*, p. 61.

21 Nigota, p. 383.

22 BL, MS Cotton Cleop. C IV, ff. 174–4v: *domino sanctissimo per hoc conplacere credens, ne videlicet aliquis in dicta prebenda contra intencionem apostolicam haberetur adversarius.* To Rickinghale he wrote: *qui contemplacione dicti domini nostri et precium nostrarum intuitu* he would act. E.g. also, Wittrisham, 1425: *CPL*, VII, p. 403; Chichele, *Register*, I, p. 227.

23 Chapter 9, notes 110 seq.

24 Haller, *Piero da Monte*, Beilagen, no. 21, pp. 207–8.

25 Chapter 9, notes 126–32.

26 BL, MS Cotton Cleop. C IV, f. 145: *non obstantibus ambassiatis solemnibus ymmo et requisicionibus apostolicis eciam sub censuris diversis, non est in regno qui quemquam in promocionibus extraneorum exaudiverit nisi solus ego..*

27 Harvey, 'The benefice', p. 167.

28 Above, note 16.

29 Chichele, *Register*, I, pp. xlv, 239–42.

30 Chichele, *Register*, I, pp. lxii–lxiii.

31 R. G. Davies, 'Martin V and the English episcopate', *EHR*, XCII, 1977, pp. 309–44, esp. p. 331; Rymer, IV/4, pp. 119–20 (X, 354).

32 *Rotuli Parliamentorum*, IV, pp. 304–5; Lunt, II, p. 424.

33 Chichele, *Register*, I, p. 282.

34 Zellfelder, pp. 120–9, documents, pp. 306–11.

35 Chichele, *Register*, I, pp. lxii–lxiii, 295, 312.

36 *CPL*, IX, pp. 166–7. Pensions: B. M. Hallman, *Italian Cardinals, Reform and the Church as Property, 1492–1563*, Berkeley 1985, (Cal.), esp. pp. 46–64.

37 Cambridge, Corpus Christi College, MS 170, p. 210.

38 Chichele, *Register*, I, pp. 254, 264, 269, 277 for Doddington; 248 for Hackington; 271 Linsted; 253 Lympne; lxiv, 274 Sandwich; 252, 253, 259, Teynham; 252, 265, 269, 274, 276, chantry; 218, 264, 275, 278, West Hythe.

39 Malden, p. 95; Le Neve, *Salisbury*, p. 14.

40 Le Neve as note 39. Above, Chapter 2, for Clement and Courtenay, pp. 15, 18.

41 *CPL*, VIII, p. 359.

42 Chapter 7, note 60; advocate of Sion, 1423, Cnattingius, *Studies*, p. 133.

43 Pension: *PPC*, III, p. 339; grant: Rymer, IV/4, p. 173 (X, 494); *CPR 1429–36*, p. 107. PRO, E404/48/127 paid for notable services for the last two years *precedens la date de son avancement par nous a luy nadgaires fait de lerchedaconry de Northampton*.

44 *PPC*, IV, p. 118; Rymer, IV/4, p. 179 (X, 509).

45 Eubel, I, p. 34; Le Neve, *Lincoln*, p. 11.

46 Chapter 8, notes 58, 59.

47 Bekynton, *Correspondence*, II, pp. 251–2.

48 PRO, E28/55 no. 38, 14 June 1435.

49 Le Neve, *Lincoln*, p. 54; *Salisbury*, p. 9.

50 Harvey, 'The benefice', pp. 168–9; he was Richard Cordon.

51 Rymer, IV/4, p. 143 (X, 415); *PPC*, III, p. 339.

52 Le Neve, *Norther Province*, p. 34.

53 Le Neve, *Bath and Wells*, p. 23.

54 Harvey, 'The benefice', p. 170.

55 *PPC*, V, p. 44.

56 Chichele, *Register*, I, pp. 309–10.

57 *DBI*, XXII, p. 156; Bekynton, *Correspondence*, I, pp. 162–4, 164–5.

58 Le Neve, *Northern Province*, p. 55; *Salisbury*, p. 12.

59 Chapter 9, note 263.

60 Above, note 58.

61 Le Neve, *Lincoln*, p. 117.

62 Rymer, V/1, p. 185 (XI, 195); *CPL*, X, p. 480.

63 Walser, pp. 76–7.

6

Using the system

The penitentiary

Many people approached the papacy for forgiveness; of sins either technical – breaches of canon law, technically barring a man from holding office, for instance – or all too real and immoral. Dr Thomson, in a pioneering article, described many aspects of the system at work as depicted in the grants found in the *Calendar of Papal Letters*[1] but stressed that it would be more enlightening to study the supplications behind the grants. What follows is based on a study of some of the registers of the papal penitentiary, though these seldom contain the full documentation, that is the very first communication, the polished supplication and then the final grant.[2] Only by comparing these could the full story of each petition be given, and even then, as we shall see, the truth is sometimes very different.

The penitentiary archives are very extensive and even nowadays the full range is closed to scholars, but the registers of supplications for this period can be consulted. Some cases there might be expected to have been dealt with elsewhere, but the penitentiary was extending its jurisdiction in this period, which may explain why some grants were made by it.[3] Whether penitents came to the office in person or by proctor a formal statement had to set out their case, with their request. These documents are not the *ipsissima verba* of the supplicant, but are carefully couched in correct legal language, to obtain what was required. They were then examined either by the cardinal penitentiary himself, his deputy or even by a minor penitentiary, the last seeing individuals in person, and the resulting decision entered on the document. This petition, with its various endorsements, was the basis of whatever document finally went to the penitent. Frequently a small charge was made for the certificate requested and a record of cost sometimes entered in the register.[4] But there are also petitions like that of John Kayscolor of Ely diocese, present and petitioning for ordination and to hold a benefice, despite illegitimacy, who asked for letters 'free for the sake of God' (*grates pro Deo*) because he was too poor, as he was prepared to swear. His petition is signed: 'Let it be done if he swears' (*fiat si jurat*).[5]

The registers contain miscellaneous summaries of petitions, with a few letters sent and other documents.[6] Sometimes the summary is very summary indeed. There are long lists of requests to choose one's own confessor or for dispensations for illegitimate people, to allow them to be ordained and hold benefices, or to allow young men to be ordained under age, usually at twenty-four. Many, probably most, of these do not appear elsewhere, but are exactly the type whose end product provided the basis of Thomson's study.[7]

More interesting here are less routine cases where much, probably most, of the original petition is transcribed, usually beginning 'It is explained on behalf of X . . .' (*Exponitur pro parte X . . .*), though sometimes the whole petition has been copied, with its *exordium*, often presenting the curia as the seat of mercy. If the petitioner is present in the curia in person the fact is noted. At the end of the petition the decision is written, in various legal forms, as we shall see.[8] The supplication volumes do not include all the cases before the penitentiary; some were so confidential that they resulted only in penance and absolution,[9] with perhaps a private document, letters close, given personally to the penitent. Furthermore a great deal seems to have been lost; there are, for instance, no registers now for Martin V's reign. But what remains contains a great deal of English material, very enlightening about attitudes.

Let us take cases concerning secular clergy first. The registers contain innumerable examples of men wishing to be ordained priest under age, usually at twenty-three or twenty-four. Petitioners commonly professed an ardent desire, and sometimes a religious house explained that it was short of priests, a routine legal reason for allowing the dispensation.[10] Almost as frequently men asked permission to be ordained by any bishop. Here, when a reason is alleged, it is usually the acquisition of a benefice which must be served by a priest, need to become one within the year and no ready access to one's own bishop.[11] Often this must have been because the petitioner was already in the curia.[12] A note may be made of the bishop to whom the matter is to be committed.[13] This last type, of course, was open to abuse; there are examples of men who ask absolution for using a fictive title to a benefice in order to be ordained. Thomas Cawsai of Brinkburn Augustinian Priory, Durham diocese, not only left his order without permission but then 'by reason of a certain commission which he obtained, had himself promoted to all orders in the Roman curia by the bishop of Folien', using a fictitious title.[14]

The curia provided a ready market place for fraud, this being one reason why it was so disliked. Roger Brese of Lincoln diocese, priest, registered his petition on 19 March 1439, that while in minor orders in the curia, having no title to a benefice, a friend, John Runeling, a poor clerk, of the diocese of Trier,[15] said that as proctor of the priory of Santeo in Trier he had presentation of the church of Arovilla in the diocese, which Nicolas de Brugge had resigned. With promise of this church Brese obtained from Martin V provision to it,[16] and with this title was ordained by the archbishop of Corinth[17] 'in the chamber of the arch-bishop himself, secretly' (*in camera ipsius archiepiscopi secrete*). Recog-nising his fraudulent title, he confessed to the major penitentiary, Giordani Orsini, cardinal bishop of St Sabina,[18] obtaining absolution with letters testimonial sealed by him, but, worried lest this be inadequate, he had his rehabilitation confirmed in Eugenius IV's reign.[19] Here the signature reads: 'Let it be done according to the special powers given to the penitentiary, and he is to be forbidden to serve the altar for a time' (*fiat de speciali, interdicto sibi ministerio altaris ad tempus*).

Those seeking permission for ordination in spite of illegitimacy included the offspring of many unions: priests and unmarried women, priests and married women, two unmarried people,[20] even Patrick Cantwell of Dublin diocese, son of a bishop, probably Richard Cantwell, bishop of Waterford, who died in 1447.[21] The signature there reads: 'Let it be done according to the special powers, and let it be entrusted to the archbishop of Cologne because the suppliant is in that diocese at present.'

One sad example shows the penitentiary soothing scruples of con-science. On 24 March 1439, the registers record that Richard Coppefield, priest from the diocese of London, thinking there was no impediment, had had himself ordained and then:[22] 'The mother of this said suppliant, in her death agony called her son to her and said to him "My son, you are not the child of my husband but of such and such a priest," and with these words she died.' According to Coppefield no one else heard her, but evidently his conscience troubled him; a bastard should not have been ordained. The signature is revealing: 'Let it be done according to the special powers, in the forum of conscience' (*Fiat de speciali in foro consciencie*); thus no public document, but rehabilitation for his own peace of mind.

There are also numerous petitions for priests to be non-resident for study,[23] or to be allowed to study civil law[24] and men wishing to postpone ordination to the priesthood (presumably for study) whilst holding their benefice. Here we find a signature 'Let it be done according to the special powers, but limited to seven years' (*Fiat de speciali in limitatione ad septennium*),[25] for a man who apparently specified no such limit.

Uncommon, and revealing, is a plea from the old parish priest of Meltham, Yorkshire, John Vallis, to be allowed to employ as house-keeper Agnes Myly, who was at least sixty.[26]

Petitions from the non-beneficed occur in a form exemplified by the case of Edmund Freman de Hersey (=Hesset?), a priest of Suffolk, who explains: 'in the kingdom of England there are certain provincial and synodal constitutions which cause fear that priests without benefices with cure can be compelled to serve the benefices with cure of other priests even if they are unwilling.'[27] Freman was unbeneficed and felt he could not conscientiously serve, asking dispensation. This was granted *de speciali*. Similar dispensations occur, which, if effective, must seriously have annoyed the local ordinaries. William Lyndwood, a contemporary commentator, whom we will meet again, assumed that some affected by the local legislation could be serving private chaplaincies, but also that they would not normally be chaplains to nobles and kings.[28]

Petitions about physical defects were also quite common. Thomas Clyff, priest of York, suffered occasionally from falling sickness and wished to celebrate mass, whereas some said that he should not.[29] The penitentiary allowed this 'if it is so' (*si est ita*), implying careful enquiry locally, where doubtless there was gossip, and he was told not to cele-brate, if possible, eight days before and after an attack. William Drant, priest of Lincoln diocese, feared that because of injury to his foot when aged two he should never have been ordained, whereas he had been, and so sought rehabilitation.[30]

There remain numerous petitions from religious. A most common reason driving members of religious orders to the penitentiary was that without permission they had left the order to wander about the world, often settling into the parish system and ministering without absolution. Frequently petitions for rehabilitation included a request to be allowed to enter a different house of the same order,[31] presumably because their behaviour had been too disruptive. Monks came to Rome without permission, for example Thomas Cawsai quoted above, who also sought ordination,[32] or John Gisborne or Nightingale, of Whitby, who, as he explains in a letter registered on 7 February 1442, with the consent of some fellow monks but not his abbot, went to the curia and cited his abbot before Cardinal Branda da Castiglione. The abbot died before the citation took effect and his successor refused to receive Gisborne back, so he simply left the order. Gisborne's innocence becomes slightly suspect when one finds that he was also petitioning to become a beneficed religious, notoriously a device for avoiding the discipline of the cloister.[33] Thomas Elkyngton, OSB, monk and priest of Bardney, Lincoln diocese, in a petition registered in 1449, said that his abbot had simply conceived a prejudice against him, refusing to do him justice, so he came to the curia to ask for rehabiltation and permission to enter another Benedictine house. Here again the reality may have been a little different. Bardney was torn by strife between 1438 and 1440, as epicopal visitations reveal; Elkyngton, described as 'of unfree blood', may have been involved.[34] John Baret, canon of the Gilbertine house of Shouldam, Norwich diocese, not obtaining his requested permission to come to the curia, simply came, not, he points out as he was obliged to do, putting aside his habit. Having come, he wished 'to remain a little while afterwards in the curia in the city of Rome' (*aliquandiu postmodum in curia in urbe Romana permanere*), to function as a priest and only afterwards return to his order or a stricter house. This may have been perfectly innocent, but could be the prelude to seeking a benefice.[35]

Sometimes one can discover more behind these stories. William Elkilington, OSA, of Wellow (Grimsby), in 1457 petitioned that he had permission from his superior to come to Rome but when he was unable to do so, for what he says were good and sufficient reasons, his superior refused to allow him back until he had done so. That may have been because he was required to seek a pardon in the penitentiary. So he absconded, gave up his habit and said mass as a secular priest. In 1457 he sought absolution from both the apostasy and excommunication, with permission to enter a different house.[36] But when Wellow was visited by Bishop Alnwick in 1440, the abbot, Henry Sutton, said that Elkilington had had leave to go to Rome and returned, being re-admitted. He left again without leave and was again re-admitted. Leaving yet again, he had not then returned. In 1440 the bishop ordered the convent to bring him back, but in January 1442 he obtained permission to hold a benefice.[37] Nothing of this appears in Elkilington's 1457 petition.

Professor Dobson notes similar examples where a man would be sent specifically by his superiors to the penitentiary.[38] The prior of Durham registered that a particular monk has been much better disposed since returning from Rome, though we know it did not last.[39] The priory archives contain certificates allowing men to go to Rome for good and sufficient reasons, to return within a year and promising to do nothing to injure the house, paid for by their friends.[40] All too often, however, the result was licence to hold a benefice or transfer. One may note the Canterbury monk William Pouns in 1441, who had bulls allowing him to hold a benefice proclaimed at St Nicholas Shambles in Newgate Street, but then faced a writ of *praemunire* sued by the abbey. He was eventually pardoned and allowed to join the Cistercians of Boxley.[41]

Religious sought unusual dispensations. Under 28 July 1440 is registered the request of William Walsche, priest and monk of St Peter, Westminster, OSB, presumably the man who became a monk in 1416 and was prior in 1441,[42] asking permission to use linen, since 'because of uncleanness and great fastidiousness about vermin he suffers grave anxiety and disquiet of mind'.[43] Brother Thomas Waltham of St Botolph's priory, Lincoln, OFM, at sixty, professed physical weakness and was given permission to eat meat, eggs and milk,[44] *de speciali* 'and let it be left to his conscience.'

Religious seeking reinstatment after absconding often pleaded their youth at the time of first vows. Robert Burg of Lincoln diocese, in the Franciscan convent in Nottingham at ten, by persuasion of some of the brethren entered the order. Lest his parents found out, the *custos* and brethren sent him to Reading, where he spent a year, making his profession, though not yet twelve. Then he left without permission, but since had come and gone into houses of the order. At nineteen the order had him ordained but finally he left completely and worked as a parish priest. He now, in March 1448, wished to return completely to the order, to some house where he would find well-wishers.[45] John Hymeslay, priest of York diocese, says in his petition of June 1460 that having entered the Franciscans at seven 'by the will of his parents' amd worn the habit for three years, though without vows, he wanted to be freed. The registers say 'let it be committed to his ordinary who says he knows about this'.[46] Presumably therefore the ordinary had sent him in the first place.

The laity also applied in large numbers. Probably the most numerous routine petitions concerned the right to choose one's own confessor, so frequent from clergy and laity that the registers merely suumarise.[47] Next most frequent were varieties of applications for dispensations to marry, or absolutions for having married, within various prohibited relationships, most commonly the spiritual relation of godparenthood.[48]

Some dispensations, however, are far from routine. William Park, layman of York diocese, explained how he exchanged words of present consent with a woman to whom he was related within the prohibited degrees and then, led by simplicity, because he had not consummated that union, made another 'marriage' with Elizabeth Boterwile, to whom he was not related within the prohibitions. He applied for rehabilitation and dispensation to return to the first union.[49] The signature, 'Let it be done if it is so' (*fiat si est ita*), implied the need for local investigation. John Dunford, another layman of York, contracted marriage and then as he, or his proctor, puts it, 'from levity of mind and instability' (*ex quadam animi levitate et instabilitate*) had himself ordained and even acted as a priest. The woman sued him and he was obliged to remain married. He now asked dispensation from his promise to say the hours.[50] William Andrew, of Belrford, Worcester diocese, married Margaret Lediis of the parish of Coryngton (= Corringham), Lincoln diocese, and lived with her for ten years.[51] Whilst she was still alive he committed adultery with Isabel Draper of Lincoln diocese and then actually 'married' her, by obtaining a separation from Margaret by use of false witnesses. When Margaret died Isobel and William confessed and were told that they must cease to cohabit, which they obeyed for eight years. William, interestingly, seeking absolution from the penitentiary, wanted a declaration that his second marriage to Isobel was invalid. Presumably he now wished to marry another?

Another couple, Walter Grant and Agnes Felse, of Lincoln diocese, had married by words of present consent in a church ceremony and had children. They were related by consanguinity but neither seems fully to have understood the impediment. Presumably something revealed it, because their petition, in 1458, says: 'at present expelled by their parents and present in the curia, they are as it were banished and poor'. Their wish to regularise their union was granted 'by special and express powers' (*de speciali et expresso*, powers granted *viva voce* by the pope understood). The resulting bull in Bishop Chedworth's register, presumably because he had to investigate *si est ita*, does not say that the couple had had to come to Rome in person to obtain it.[52]

Priests were bribed to overlook impediments,[53] or celebrated marriages without proper banns, in an unconsecrated building, as Thomas Sollay did, in the chapel of St Edmund's hospice.[54]

A most pathetic story under the date of 4 June 1442 concerned Joan Radcliffe of the diocese of London.[55] When about twelve, and therefore old enough technically to consent, she was persuaded to marry, by words of present consent, with proper banns, John Lichtfoot or de Dyssington, a man of about fifty. About five months later, for no good cause, (a phrase very revealing about the law),[56] he began to use harsh, cruel language and physical violence, and after three years she ran away. She stayed away about three weeks and was then persuaded by their friends to try again, John promising to behave better. But instead he: 'kept the said Joan for a fortnight bound by one leg with an iron chain in a certain chamber'. At length about three weeks later, helped by some compassionate neighbours, she again escaped and joined a convent in Somerset, remaining six years, wearing the veil and obedient to the abbess. Aged about twenty-one she left, went to London and thence to Winchester, there meeting and 'marrying' John Ryall, who knew nothing about her past. They cohabited about four years, having four children, when, fearing that the truth might get out, she told Ryall the whole. He continued to live with her, fathering two more children, when word came that Lichtfoot was dead. So the couple confessed to a religious priest who said that Joan must not continue to live with Ryall until the matter was resolved in Rome. She requested validation of her marriage and legitimation of her three living children. No one knew the story except herself, Ryall and the priest. The request was granted in the presence of the cardinal penitentiary himself, and presumably no further public ceremony was needed to validate the marriage.

Vows came under the jurisdiction of the penitentiary. By the end of the period people were applying to it for permission to go to the Holy Land. John Tiptoft, earl of Worcester, was licensed to go to the holy sepulchre with nineteen people, registered on 18 November 1457.[57] Commutation might be sought also. Thomas Mayland came to Rome to have his vow to go to the Holy Sepulchre commuted to other good works to be decided by the penitentiary.[58] Aline Skipwiche, widow of John Skipwiche of Lincoln diocese,[59] in a petition registered on 19 January 1440, explained that she and John, vowing to make pilgrimage to Jerusalem, reached only Rhodes and they could go no further. Without consulting anyone they sent a member of a religious order in their place. In 1440 John was dead and Aline's 'conscience was troubled because of the vow'. At eighty she clearly could not fulfill it, but wished to expend the money not spent in Jerusalem on some other good cause. The signature reads: 'Sign with "let it be done by the special power" and whatever more she would have spent if she had gone personally let her spend in the usual way': an arrangement by which she worked out what more they would have spent in person, to give to some approved cause, often the crusade.

Many petitions by lay people concerned violent crimes against clergy; equally violence and shedding of blood by clergy or aspiring ordinands would produce a petition to the penitentiary or even a visit in person. Under 27 September, probably 1439, Henry Dabilis,[60] was given absolution and public penance to be performed in two or three places in Rome, requested by his ordinary, the archbishop of Canterbury presumably, who had probably also sent a letter of explanation. Under 5 July 1438 are registered two petitions, concerning a clerk and two laymen, involving the same incident.[61] The laymen, William de Printe and William Roger, alias Pastoral, and the clerk, John de la Nonee, all of York diocese, on a Sunday after divine service burned and totally destroyed a church wherein some of their mortal enemies were killed. Absolution was: 'granted in form in the presence of the cardinal penitentiary. And let it be committed to the bishop of Dol because, for fear of a person, they have not true access to the ordinary'. Probably the incident, involving both murder and sacrilege, had created terrible local tensions.

Killing in self-defence might produce a petition where a scrupulous clerk or would-be clerk felt he had been responsible for shedding blood. A few examples out of many will show the type of problem.

Under 18 May 1441 was registered the petition of Robert Peacock, subdeacon of London diocese.[62] who, studying at Cambridge, had had a *familiaris* who after about two years asked a salary.[63] Peacock replied that he had never promised payment but had given 'board and friendship' (*victum et amiciciam*) and 'kept him with him in the schools for the sake of learning' (*secum in scolis causa discendi tenuisse*). The *familiaris*, very angry, told his brother and both brought an armed group to Peacock's lodging 'in a certain hospice in the city of London' (*in quodam hospitio in civitate Londinien*). In an ensuing affray the brother 'broke a certain staff on the head of the exponent in several pieces' (*quendam baculum super caput ipsius exponentis in pluries pecias fregit*). Peacock, unable to flee, seized a dagger and defended himself. He and another fell to the ground. The brother rose: 'and who, or how or in what way he was wounded' (*et quis[sic], vel quomodo, a quali vulneratus fuit*), Peacock did not know but he died of his wounds in three weeks. Peacock did not know if he was responsible but, wishing to be ordained priest, he wanted also to silence any who might say he was debarred and requested a dispensation for shedding blood.

Another example, signed 'Let it be done according to the special powers in the presence of the lord cardinal' (*fiat de speciali in presencia domini cardinalis*), registered on 20 June 1441, concerned Richard Mitchill 'alias multum', priest and monk of Crowland, who by December 1440 had obtained a dispensation to hold a benefice. He may have petitioned to ensure that he was not debarred.[64] He explained that, sent by his monastery, he traded with John Faynhaed of the diocese of Therouanne, who claimed, whilst Mitchill denied, that he had sold Mitchill goods. Blows followed, during which Faynhaed put his hand on his knife. Mitchill's words, 'Friend, think better of this and go away, thus to burst out like this against me for what you have done', merely inflamed Faynhaed, so Mitchill, seizing a small stick in self-defence, hit the layman on the head, without drawing blood. At this point by-standers separated the contenders and for the rest of the day Faynhaed went about his business apparently well, eating and drinking as if nothing had happened. In the evening however, to reach his hospice, he had to cross a river in a ship, in which 'there came on the layman a chilliness' (*supervenit eidem laico aliqualem infrigilitatem*), so that the sailors and others took him to a hospital and put him to bed. And: 'so it is said, at night there came upon the layman a vomiting, so that he cast up things by his mouth', causing those with him to say he must have had internal injuries[65] and that night he died. Mitchill was granted absolution and permission to continue in holy orders.

In a final example Thomas Cok, priest of the diocese of Lichfield, and probably chaplain to the nobleman he mentions, registered a petition on 7 April 1438.[66] The nobleman had lawsuits (*lites*) with a knight. Coming to the parish church to divine service, with some neighbours 'for his protection' (*pro sui tuicione*), some entered to see if the knight was inside. Finding him, prompted 'by a devilish spirit' (*spiritu diabolico*), they insulted him, and joined by the noble and his bodyguard, an affray occurred. Two laymen with the knight were killed and Cok, with the nobleman, wounded in the head another of the knight's party, a layman, though he soon recovered. Subsequently Cok went to Calais, which was surrounded by capital enemies, probably therefore in 1436, when the Burgundians besieged it. With other priests and laymen Cok helped to defend Calais, participating in taking booty, in rapine, burning etc. 'he resisted as far as he could for the defence of the town, his country and the right of his king.' Many were killed, though he knew of none personally killed or wounded by him. He never sought absolution, continuing to say mass. He now sought to rectify this.

The military struggles of the fifteenth century were a fruitful source of violent deeds and scruples of conscience like Cok's, as well as of technical breaches of canon law. Thomson mentions qualms of Robert Gilbert, later bishop of London, about his role as chaplain on Henry V's campaigns.[67] The penitentiary has several such cases. Registered under 25 May, probably 1439, is the case of Robert Westerin, priest of the diocese of Durham, who at about twenty 'went to Hainault with a certain noble man whose familiar he was and carried the arms of his lord',[68] probably in Humfrey, duke of Gloucester's, Hainault expedition of late 1424. Westerin did not participate in any killing, but later, without declaring his past, though otherwise rightly, was ordained to all orders, which he now feared was irregular, presumably because of the remote involvement in bloodshed. Peter William, priest, of Bordeaux diocese, responding when summoned by his archbishop, with his fellow clergy and laymen when the French invaded, had been involved in an accident, killing a boy with a crossbow.[69]

Individuals on all sides, of course, felt equal qualms. A Breton[70] and a Castilian[71] reveal their scruples about their behaviour in fighting England, and on the Welsh borders clergy could become involved in fighting. William Heroll de Valia, clerk, of the diocese of St Davids, had two matters on his conscience, one a knife fight with a layman over some hose, leaving one party unable to work with his hands for a long time. The other concerned invasion of the kingdom of England by capital enemies, when the king ordered certain captains to raise men, including William's brother who ordered William to accompany him. No one was killed but he none the less sought absolution.[72]

Bishops in Wales tried to use the penitentiary as the ultimate sanction against unruly subjects. John Aperlly Ecciis, a layman of St Davids diocese, must have been dismayed to find himself applying to Rome. His petition, registered on 15 January, some time in the reign of Pius II, explained that his bishop had excommunicated thieves of his horses, cows and other animals, putting his subjects on oath to respect this. None the less John had stolen two horses and thus was guilty of perjury and excommunicate. The petition was granted and the case committed to a minor penitentiary since 'he cannot approach the ordinary for fear of a person'.[73] Other examples from St Davids occur in the same register.[74]

Simony, understandably a most obscure crime, is illuminated in the registers, especially when one can add evidence from elsewhere to discover the true situation.[75]

Suppliants might quote the latest canons they feared or knew they had broken, showing that the law did have some effect, though perhaps legal advisers were aware of it rather than their clients. Richard Lambert, rector of St Michael's church Aston (Tiroll), in Salisbury diocese, Thomas Caylart of the parish church of Seroblyghby, Lichfield diocese, and Thomas Coper of St Mary de Wiggenhale, Norwich diocese,[76] referred to the constitution *Multe contra symoniacam* of 12 March, 1418, issued by Martin V in the last stages of the council of Constance, which nullified simoniacal elections, postulations, confirmations or provisions and *ipso facto* excommunicated the perpetrators; and also Eugenius IV's bull of 1434, *Cum detestabile scelus*, by which the simoniacally ordained had to make restitution of the fruits of their benefice. Simony became a sin reserved for papal absolution; to conceal it incurred excommunication.[77]

The variety makes interesting reading. John Steppe or Stappe, priest, rector of the parish church of Landulph, Cornwall, in Exeter diocese, explained in 1439 that his father had become 'the lord at farm' (*dominum ad firmam*) of the church of Landulph. Lyndwood understands this as letting a church for a time without giving up *dominium*. It was forbidden to laymen. Presumably the father paid, since the normal patrons were the earls of Devon, 'with the intention, as is believed, and as the suppliant afterwards understood',[78] of presenting his son to the living. When the church became vacant, the boy being still under age, his father presented one Peter, on condition that Peter resigned when John came of age, and only received £11 sterling a year from the church. Peter did resign and John, duly presented to the bishop of Exeter, had now held the church for several years, but had begun to think the transaction simoniacal. Here we can reconstruct at least some of the story. In 1433 Peter Thomas was presented to Landulph by John Stappe, presumably the elder, and others, patrons *hac vice*. In 1435 John Stappe, the younger, had dispensation to hold a benefice at twenty-two. In March 1436, young Stappe was presented to the bishop of Exeter, as incumbent of Landulph. But here Stappe's petition may differ slightly from the truth, because the bishop then ordered an enquiry into how the church was vacant. Discovery may have prompted the qualms of conscience which Stappe felt in 1439.[79]

Thomas Caylart, who also thought that he had breached recent legislation, had paid the noble patron for presentation.[80] The signature reads *concessum de speciali in presencia d. cardinalis*, and 'sign by let it be done according to the special powers, he having first given up the benefice' (*per fiat de speciali, dimisso dicto beneficio per prius*). Shortly afterwards, in the same register, dated 4 June 1440, Caylart, having resigned, asks that if the benefice be conferred on him again, lawfully, he may keep it.[81] This too was granted in the presence of the cardinal. Thomas Coper,[82] vicar of St Mary de Wiggenhall, appropriated to Castle Acre Priory, explained that his predecessor, probably Robert Hammond, found holding this living, had agreed to resign the benefice into the hands of a third party, with the agreement of the bishop, and a certain sum of money was paid to a layman, referred to as 'the mediator and third party in this agreement' (*in eadem convencione mediator et interposita persona*); the suppliant gave the layman a house worth 26 marks sterling. Thus Coper got the benefice, though the mechanics of the exchange were not discussed. The penitentiary absolved him *fiat de speciali*, but on 13 August a further petition was registered.[83] The first could not yet have taken effect, but he wanted a dispensation either to hold another benefice or be properly reappointed to St Mary's. This was granted, provided that he restored the fruits received and freely resigned the benefice first. In the Norwich registers, however, we find first the 'simoniacal' appointment when Coper, or Cowper, is instituted to Wiggenhall, by the free resignation of his predecessor Hammond on 5 October 1432. Then, on 17 July 1441, a new vicar is instituted, with no reference to the past. So Coper did not succeed in recovering Wiggenhall.

Another variant is the case of Richard Lambert, already mentioned, registered in 1454.[84] Here the villain, Nicholas Carent, dean of Wells, told Lambert: 'Act according to my counsel and I will make you rector of Aston church.' Lambert agreed and swore on the gospels. Three days later William North, presumably Thomas Bekynton's chaplain and later registrar,[85] brought presentation of the church sealed, explaining that he must swear to resign to the ordinary 'for the utility of' (*ad utilitatem*) Thomas Smyth, whenever North or Carent asked. And so the transaction was done and Lambert thought he had committed simony. He was absolved 'by the special and express powers' (*de speciali et expresso*). In Richard Beauchamp's register, Aston, in the gift of Witham Charterhouse, was given to Thomas Smyth, MA, on 3 January 1455. He was resident in Oxford, and already had had presentation of the same church on 14 February 1450.[86] This looks like a case where a church was held for someone as yet unable to reside.

A final example, registerd on 7 May 1455, concerned Thomas Barnabe of York diocese, priest and perpetual vicar of the parish church of Darfield,[87] petitioning that after the previous vicar, John Atlain, died, Robert Barnabe, Thomas's brother, paid 120 florins from Thomas to a certain knight (*armigerus*), and thus Thomas held the living for two years, until, troubled in conscience, he resigned to the vicar general of the archbishop of York. He now asked pardon for his simony and permission to hold the benefice. This was granted 'by the special and express powers' (*de speciali et expresso*). From other sources it transpires that the advowson of the church of Darfield belonged to the hospital of St John of Jerusalem.[88] When Thomas Barnaby's predecessor, John Atlain, died on 20 February 1451,[89] Robert Botyll, prior of St John, presumably the bribed *armigerus*, then presented Thomas. Thomas was re-presented on 20 September 1453, presumably after confessing to the vicar-general.[90] In the records no reason is given for this second presentation, inexplicable without the penitentiary registers.

In the penitentiary the curia had its most characteristic office, which, in many ways, performed its most important spiritual services. The registers reveal the office supplying great needs; many consciences must have been soothed, in situations where the local spiritual powers were too familiar or too threataning to serve. But the snags are also evident. It was too difficult to check the stories. Often penitents only arrived because already discovered, and some of the examples suggest also that, as the local religious authorities complained, Rome could shelter those anxious to escape the local discipline of their religious superiors. It is quite clear why Prior Wessington of Durham did not wish his monks to be free to go to Rome, though he wished to be able to apply there himself when necessary!

Canonisation

Canonisation of a saint also required attendance at the curia. This seemingly esoteric pursuit was not infrequent in this period. By the fifteenth century the curia had long successfully asserted its exclusive right to canonise. The long, complex and expensive process meant that few saints were finally officially acknowledged, but that did not stop people trying. In the first half of the fifteenth century only one new English saint was recognised officially by Rome: Osmund, bishop of Salisbury, who had died in 1099. His recognition was remarkable: the cause had begun in the thirteenth century and could then be said to have failed. It revived during the schism probably because of the zeal of the chapter under Bishop Hallum, prompted perhaps by the usefulness of Osmund to Hallum as a symbol of episcopal reforming zeal. The longueurs of the ensuing process probably reflect the unwillingness of the post-schism papacy to canonise this English bishop whose chief claim to sanctity, apart from miracles, was work for his own diocese, the endowment of his cathedral and the Sarum rite, as Richard Ullerston claimed in a sermon for his cause in Salisbury in 1416.[91] Nor was Osmund a mendicant. In the course of the process a cardinal mentioned a bias towards them, as well as Nicholas V's reluctance to do for Henry VI what he was unwilling to do for Aragon or France over Vincent Ferrer.[92]

Many causes failed. Henry VI petitioned for King Alfred,[93] unavailingly, and various petitions for English kings in the fourteenth and fifteenth centuries (Edward II, Henry VI himself), failed too.[94] Canterbury's campaign for Anselm[95] succeeded only in 1494. The same happened to causes pressed by other nations.

Meanwhile many unofficial saints were honoured locally in England, where canonisation mattered less. The curia linked canonisation and acknowledgement of its authority. The consistorial advocate employed by Salisbury in 1452 urged the Salisbury representative in Rome to stress that the inhabitants were eager to canonise Osmund on their own authority: 'If this were inserted in the letter of the lords, it would cause the pope more quickly to incline towards his canonisation, because such a fact might cause our area to withdraw from obedience to him and the pope fears this greatly.'[96]

The process was both lengthy and expensive: over £700 in the last stages spent in Rome, but it was worth the money because, according to canon law, only a duly canonised person could enjoy an official cult: this was recognised, for instance, by those promoting the cause of Richard Rolle.[97] Thus to promote an official pilgrimage, grant indulgences, or insert a holy man into the church calendar required canonisation. Ultimately therefore canonisation was not just a matter of prestige, though that too was clearly involved.

The process can be seen clearly in the Osmund dossier.[98] 'Fame of holiness' (*fama sanctitatis*) was essential, preferably letters from local bishops and rulers, which Salisbury collected from Henry VI,[99] Margaret of Anjou, Archbishop Kemp, and tried to acquire from the universities of Oxford and Cambridge.[100] The chapter also entertained in Salisbury curial personnel in England: Poggio saw the library; James, bishop of Trieste, had as one task collecting evidence; Roberto Cavalcantibus promised help but did nothing; they hoped to use both him and Piero da Monte in the curia, though Holes thought both too preoccupied; Marino Orsini, declaring himself impressed, said he would use his influence.[101]

Much depended on the quality and expertise of the representatives in the curia, and therefore on the envoys sent to manage the business. Salisbury used Adam Moleyns, to co-operate with Andrew Holes, their chancellor as well as royal proctor.[102] By the time Moleyns arrived, in 1442, Holes had persuaded the pope to commission a committee of three cardinals: Domenico Ram, called Tiraconensis, Guillaume d'Estouteville, called of Angers, and Domenico Capranica, of Fermo, to examine the case. Moleyns however, for whatever reason, did not raise the case with the pope, and because Holes lacked full proctorial authority the commission proceeded no further under Eugenius IV.[103] In 1444 Holes left, finally retiring to Salisbury cathedral close, from where he continued to help, writing letters and providing advice about tactics.[104]

By 1452 the chapter must have felt it had the necessary friends. It sent as representatives Nicholas Upton and Simon Huchyns.[105] Marino Orsini, bishop of Taranto, in England the year before, had promised help. William Gray, now royal proctor, *confrater* of Salisbury, also offered aid and, best of all, Nicholas V admired and trusted Holes.[106] Holes duly wrote to Nicholas in August 1452 to commend the cause.[107]

Yet still nothing happened. Protracted Roman procedures were bad enough, partly deliberately to deter applicants,[108] but worse, the pope purposely procrastinated for political reasons. The French and Aragonese, both quarrelling with Nicholas, were pressing canonisation of Vincent Ferrer, so, to avoid making concessions to any king, the pope referred the English case *ad partes*, for enquiry into local, recent, miracles.[109]

The complications of procedure make fascinating reading. On arrival in June 1452 the Salisbury proctors called on Orsini who offered help but needed various proxies to show breadth of support, which the representatives were awaiting, via the Medici bank.[110] They called on William Gray, who offered help but they were delayed until they could recover documents of the case to date, left by Holes with William de Asculo of the English hospice and with Cardinal Capranica.[111] On 8 July they finally obtained audience with the pope, through Orsini and Gray. Pope Nicholas explained that these matters tended to take a long time. They told him the history of the case, begun in 1228.

All contacts and influences were useful. The Salisbury proctors shared lodgings with Thomas Candour, who was in touch with someone 'who is very secret with the Holy Father' who gossiped that Orsini was actually doing little for them.

One month later the documents were all assembled, except for a commission for two cardinals in Florence, which they could not find.

They commissioned Andreas de Sancta Cruce, a consistorial advocate, who had been involved in Ferrer's cause and the recent canonisation of Bernardino of Siena. By 6 August, on his advice, Huchyns had prepared a supplication.[112] On 11 October the pope set up a commission of cardinals Capranica (Fermo) and Alfonso Borgia (Valentino). On 3 November they began to hear the case.[113]

On 31 January the chapter recalled Upton,[114] telling him to leave all muniments either with Huchyns or in the English hospice 'in some sure place suche as clothes of silk and the best juelx of that howse be kept in'. In February 1453 the chapter constituted Huchyns and Gray its proctors, though Upton did not in fact leave until 12 May 1453.[115] But meanwhile the hearings were held up again. Gray would not act 'for envie that ye have your trust on Tarentyn [= Orsini]', but Orsini had fallen out of papal favour, having left the curia on 3 February, 'not with most worship', for suspicion of involvement in the Porcari conspiracy.[116] Capranica (Fermo) also explained the delay by the pope's reluctance to canonise Ferrer.[117] Once Orsini left, however, Gray was again willing to act.[118]

By 28 August Huchyns had enlisted John Lax, whom the chapter had decided to employ in January and whose excellence Huchyns praised.[119] When Gray left on 13 October, Lax and Huchyns were acting together.[120] Further delay followed. Fermo had promised Gray speed but after Constantinople fell (29 May 1453) he became totally occupied in raising forces against the Turks and left work entirely to Borgia (Valentino), finally departing altogether on a crusading legation. Lax tried promising d'Estouteville, 'which is the grettyst doer in the court', 300 ducats, but in November 1453 Fermo's departure had effectively halted the whole proceedure, despite an attempt to enlist Cardinal Barbo.[121] In April 1454 Huchyns deposited all his documents in the hospice for safekeeping and left Rome.[122]

The cause was resumed under Calixtus III, who, of course, had been involved as Cardinal Borgia, in September 1455,[123] largely, it would seem, because John Lax was papal secretary and friend of the new pope.[124] The dean and chapter were now using as their proctors Lax and Thomas Hope.[125] By 6 January 1456 the canonisation was proceeding well,[126] with Cardinal Capranica again in charge, though the chapter worried because, if the elderly pope died before the case ended, the whole business would have to start again.[127] Henry VI's letters of support were delayed, on which the pope did not fail to comment both to Lax in July and to the bishop on 30 August 1456, pointing out that as yet no envoys from England had offered him obedience, suggesting that England lacked devotion to him.[128] Doubtless the delay was caused by the king's mental collapse and the first battle of St Albans. One letter comments:[129] 'May it please your wonted prudence to note the instability of the state of the world, especially with us.' Lax himself may even have suffered a temporary fall from favour whilst York was in power,[130] but by 23 July 1456 was again acting for the chapter.[131] The cardinals had to agree,[132] but finally on 13 December 1456 Calixtus III told the chapter that Osmund would be canonised on the following 1 January.[133] Lax was given much credit for this success.

The time, expense[134] and complexity explain why so few English saints were canonised in this period. The happy coincidence of the election of Calixtus III and his familiarity both with the case and with John Lax made the difference to the cause of Osmund.

Privileges for Eton and King's

Rome was also a source of privileges: graces allowing institutions and persons exemptions and extras not normally allowed by canon law could be obtained only from the curia – for a price. A most telling example of the system at work in this period was Henry VI's collection of indulgences for his new foundations of Eton and King's College, Cambridge

Henry VI's determination to endow his new foundations with extensive papal privileges and indulgences was astonishing, and dismaying, partly because very expensive.[135] The energies of several royal nuncios were engaged in the 1440s and their activities are very illuminating for anyone wishing to understand the Roman system.

Requests from Henry, which produced a papal licence to found Eton College and confirmed its endowments, were granted by the pope in bulls dated 28 January 1441 and must have been managed initially by Andrew Holes.[136] Henry then requested an indulgence for Eton. The first agent specifically for this was Richard Chester,[137] royal chaplain and a theologian, with commendations to Cardinal Marco Barbo, the pope's nephew, and Zeno di Castiglione, bishop of Bayeux, a notable anglophile.[138] The king also sent Richard Caunton; both worked with Holes.[139] Letters betweeen them and Bekynton reveal that Holes mistrusted Chester;[140] there was misunderstanding, or worse, among the three.[141]

There were exchanges of presents with pope and cardinals and then,

on 28 May 1441, a bull,[142] giving in perpetuity to any who came to Eton
church on the feast of the Assumption of the Virgin (15 August), and
contributed to its repair, an indulgence modelled on (*ad instar*) that of St
Peter ad Vincula in Rome, on 1 August, i.e. plenary.[143] Henry worried
that the plenary nature of this unusual grant would not be recognised
and, late in 1441, Vincent Clement was also sent to work on it.[144] He
was very diligent. On 9 May 1442 another bull likewise gave plenary
indulgence to anyone who contributed on the Assumption, but provided
that three-quarters of the money was for use against the Turks.[145] This
lasted only for Henry's life.[146]

Henry was not satisfied. Adam Moleyns was working on the
indulgences in Rome in 1442 and in mid-1443 Clement was back there,
trying to have the grant altered. Apparently the king wanted the
indulgence perpetual with almsgiving not compulsory. Clement was
enquiring the cost of alterations. The mechanics can be seen fitfully: he
worked on the papal chamberlain, Cardinal Jean le Jeune and on
Bartolemeo Rovarella, whom he calls the 'secret' *cubicularius*, very close
to the pope.[147] In August Bekynton, commiserating, said the king
preferred a perpetual indulgence to a greater one limited in time.[148]
Henry himself had given the instructions. In October we learn that 1,000
ducats had been banked for Clement.[149] He had a list of four possible
indulgences, with orders to work from the most desired to the least. In
December Clement complained to Bekynton, overwhelmed by a flood of
letters and instructions from the king, Suffolk and Chichele, that new
clauses had been suggested in the royal letter delivered on 14 December,
specifying powers for confessors and to dispense ecclesiastical persons
from irregularities and commute vows.[150] Each suggestion presented
new difficulties. He suspected slander in England, complaining that
Eton was preparing to entrust its demands to its own envoy. In January
he again complained about terrible difficulties, though now working
with Cardinal Condulmaro (the vice-chancellor) as well as with le Jeune
and Roverella.[151]

Bekynton replied on 6 March, assuring Clement of his good will and
that the reports had cheered king and archbishop.[152] As a reward for all
his labour the king had requested the duke of York to help Clement
achieve provision to the chapel of St Peter Montfort in Rouen diocese,
vacant because Louis of Luxembourg, now dead, had held it *in commendam*.[153]

Finally on 11 May 1444 a new bull was issued, repeating the clauses
about the division of the money, with some for the crusade, which

remained a compulsory part of the indulgence, but adding a perpetual clause allowing confessors to absolve from all but reserved sins.[154] Not all that the king had wanted, but an improvement.[155]

Early in 1446 Eugenius IV, prompted no doubt by William Gray,[156] extended the indulgence to other feast-days when visitors could have seven years and seven quarantines. Priests hearing confessions then could absolve from all but reserved sins and on the Assumption could commute vows of pilgrimage, except to Jerusalem, Rome and Compostella.[157] This may be what Clement had wanted earlier.

This expensive process had taken many months' work by several agents. Richard Chester, who worked for Eton and King's College in other ways too, collecting books for instance,[158] was granted 12 pence a day for ten years in November 1442,[159] and then two tuns of wine yearly in 1449.[160] Caunton was paid £600 from customs in September 1448.[161] The actual cost of the bulls was much greater. As we have seen, Clement had 1000 ducats at his disposal.[162] The issue rolls show that on 22 June 1442 £158 6s 8d was paid in the curia for, presumably, the second indulgence.[163] The money spent in Rome by Moleyns in 1442–3 was carefully listed. He was seeking various bulls: allowing Henry VI to marry within the prohibited degrees, with various privileges for the royal chapel and protecting Eton's property in various ways, but the payments were typical.[164] Advised by Andrew Holes he paid various door-keepers, at 24 ducats. To speed two bulls for Eton and two for the king he paid Theodoric Oudencoup 200 ducats for the pope. Abbreviators and scriptors had 200 ducats. The *solicitator* of the vice-chancellor had 20 ducats as a tip. Flavio Biondo, the papal secretary concerned, had 100 ducats, Bartolemeo Rovarella, the 'secret' *cubicularius*, 50 and the vice-chancellor 200. For this Moleyns changed nobles into ducats. Writing cost 6 ducats and messengers to Flanders and Bruges 32. Every ducat exchanged cost 2d. The total, including the cost of the exchange, was £145 12s[165]

While Clement worked on the second bull various people received presents. When Angelo Gattola, *scutifer honoris* of the pope, brought John Kemp his cardinal's insignia late in 1440[166] he must have alerted Bekynton to the value of cultivating the friendship of Flavio Biondo of Forli, one of the closest aides of Eugenius IV.[167] By June 1441 the two were corresponding,[168] Bekynton sending greetings via Biondo to Piero da Monte, Gattola and Clement. This was Bekynton's way of bringing himself to the pope's notice.[169] Clement 'introduced' Bekynton to Rovarella[170] and Biondo, Gattola and Rovarella together worked on

Bekynton's promotion to a bishopric.[171] It is thus not surprising to find the trio working on the Eton privileges.

Consequently also pensions were paid to various cardinals. Moleyns was authorised by Henry VI late in 1441 to appoint persons in Rome to oversee English affairs. He chose Cardinal Branda,[172] with a pension of 100 marks per annum, and the vice-chancellor, Francesco Condulmaro, with the same.[173] In 1447 Condulmaro was allowed to hold benefices. Holes thought him the main agent for Moleyns's business.[174] In July 1443 the cardinal of St Eustache, Alberto de Albertis, involved in early negotiations,[175] received 50 marks per annum.[176] There were also presents of fine cloth, in lieu of money.[177] The payment of pensions continued until at least 1449.[178]

The papal privileges for King's College were equally costly. The provost was allowed £40 by the king in 1445 for his labour in seeking bulls in Rome[179] and Matthew Crompe was said in July 1448 to have spent thirty-two months on the matter and was paid £101.[180] The result was an array of nine bulls giving extensive immunities.[181]

Was the result worth the money? Eton attracted crowds at first, but extra confessors had to be entertained and the college did not make more than £30 a year, less than the cost of privileges. In this case, then, perhaps not, in monetary terms, but not all contemporaries, including the king, computed it thus.[182] King's, however, became, and remains, an ecclesiastical peculiar, with accademic immunity, in its own terms well worth having.[183]

In the foregoing section I have tried to describe the main institutions and the chief people responsible for the day to day relations between England and the papacy and to illustrate some business. But in fact the smooth running of the machinery depended very much on good relations between crown and pope at the level of 'high' politics. Political tension might hold up seemingly lowly or purely spiritual transactions. Thus 'diplomatic' relations between crown and pope could be of great importance to the local church. To these we must therefore turn.

Notes

1 J. A. F. Thomson, 'The Well of Grace'. Englishmen and Rome in the fifteenth century', *The Church, Politics and Patronage in the Fifteenth Century*, ed. R. B. Dobson, Gloucester, 1984, pp. 99–114; Du Boulay, 'The fifteenth century', pp. 227–33.

2 I would like to thank Mgr de Magistris of the Apostolic Penitentiary for granting me permission to examine the Registers.

3 Standard: E. Göller, *Die Päpstliche Penitentiarie von ihrem Ursprung bis zu ihrer Umgestaltung unter Pius V*, Bibliothek des Königlichen Preussische Historichen Instituts in Rom, III, IV, VII, VIII, Rome, 1907, 1911. Essential until promised book: F. Tamburini: 'Il primo registro di suppliche dell'Archivio della Sacra Penitenzieria Apostolica (1410–1411)', *Rivista di Storia della Chiesa in Italia,*, XXIII, 1969, pp. 384–427, p. 388 for Göller; 'Nota Diplomatiche intorno a suppliche e lettere di Penitenzieria (sec. XIV–XV)', *AHP*, XI, 1973, pp. 149–208; and bibliography below, under Tamburini.

4 e.g. Reg. Pen. 2, f. 17v, margin '*g° ii pro penitenciariis*'. Complete supplication: Anstey, *Epistolae Academicae*, I, p. 8.

5 *Reg. Pen.* 6, f. 112v, 15 September 1457.

6 I examined *Registri* 2–11, including 2bis. Summary index: Vatican archives, consultation on request. Registri 12 and 13 may contain material for reign of Pius II.

7 Thomson, 'Well of Grace', p. 101.

8 Tamburini, 'Nota', p. 153.

9 Tamburini,' Il primo', p. 389.

10 After *Reg.* 1 and 2 I recorded only unusual instances. English examples: *Reg. Pen.* 2, f. 2v, 8, 28v, 46v, 47v, 57v. Religious houses claiming priest shortage: *Reg. Pen.* 6, f. 326v, Osney abbey, 4 May 1449, for three canons' ordination at twenty-three.

11 e.g. *Reg. Pen.* 2, f. 12v, Richard Rowe, acolyte of Norwich, granted: *concessum in presencia cardinalis* [= penitentiary] de speciali (= by special powers given him by the pope), Ferrara, 10 January 1438; *Reg. Pen.* 6, f. 346, three *qui racione dictarum ecclesiarum arctati promoveri infra annum*, ask ordination at curia by any Catholic bishop, *c.* 1458.

12 See previous note. Other examples: *Reg. Pen.* 5, f. 300, William Waid, acolyte, Canterbury diocese, John Grynn, acolyte, Norwich diocese, John Urwhen, acolyte, Lincoln diocese, 12 September 1456.

13 In petition in note 12 *signatura* reads: *fiat de speciali et expresso* [= the pope had given express permission] *et committatur epsicopo Alexandrino* (= Marco Cattaneo, Eubel, II, p. 96).

14 *Reg. Pen.* 6, f. 356v. R. Swanson, 'Titles to orders in episcopal registers', *Studies in History Presented to R. H. C. Davis*, ed. H. Mayr-Harting and R. I. Moore, London, 1985, pp. 233–45, esp.p. 238, suggesting penitentiary dispensations disappear after 1345, noting only *CPL*, VIII, p. 90, 1429.

15 See note 19; not in Schuchard, but see *Repertorium Germanicum*, IV, no. 2321.

16 No record found.

17 Possibly Petrus Rainaldi, OP, Eubel, I, p. 210.

18 Göller, *Penitentiarie*, I/1 (Bibliothek, III), p. 96.

19 *Reg. Pen.* 2bis, ff. 129v–30.

20 After *Reg.* 2 I recorded only unusual examples. Cases reserved to pope: W. Lyndwood, *Provinciale*, Oxford, 1676, repr. Farnborough, 1969, I, tit. IV, *De Temporibus ordinandorum*, c. *in primis* p. 29.

21 *Reg. Pen.* 6, f. 126v, 3 May, Calixtus III, probably 1457. Bishop: *Handbook of British Chronology*, 3rd ed., London, 1986, pp. 337 and 377.

22 *Reg. Pen.* 2bis, ff. 130–30v.

23 e.g. *Reg. Pen.* 5, f. 291v, 30 May 1457, Nicholas Michil, perpetual vicar of Bosall, York diocese.

24 *Reg. Pen.* 2, ff. 88v–9, William Wortham, rector of Basingham, Lincoln diocese, in gift of Corpus Christi College, Oxford, already bachelor of both laws, to continue studying law for five years more, for doctorate in civil law, 1 July 1438. Not in *BRUO* or *BRUC*.

25 *Reg. Pen.* 9, f. 147, 3 April, *c.* 1461, John Caister, perpetual vicar of St Botolph's, Lincoln diocese.

26 *Reg. Pen.* 2bis, f. 134, John Vallis, rector of 'Melchamb', York diocese, 10 April, probably 1439.

27 *Reg. Pen.* 3, f. 58v, 31 January 1453; *quod in regno Anglie quedam constitutiones provinciales et synodales existunt quibus caveri dicitur quod presbitri non habentes beneficia curata ad serviendum aliis beneficiis eciam curatis aliorum presbitorum eis eciam invitis conpelli possunt.* Lyndwood, *Provinciale*, III, tit. XXIII, *De celebratione missarum,* c. *affrenata*, pp. 238–40.

28 e.g. *Reg. Pen.* 3, f. 384v. Lyndwood, *Provinciale*, p. 239.

29 *Reg. Pen.* 2, ff. 137v–8. Lyndwood, *Provinciale*, p. 29.

30 *Reg. Pen.* 5, f. 61, 17 June 1455.

31 e.g. *Reg. Pen.* 11, f. 168, Thomas Cowper, Bonhommes of the Blood of Christ (= Ashridge, Bucks.), OSA.

32 Above, note 14.

33 *Reg. Pen.* 2, f. 238v, 9 January, seeking rehabilitation; f. 239, 7 February, full story. Both signed *fiat in forma*, i.e. according to normal power of the penitentiary. *VCH, History of the County of Yorkshire*, III, pp. 101–5, for Whitby, p. 104 for person; *CPL*, IX, p. 214, dispensation to hold benefice, 24 January 1442.

34 *Reg. Pen.* 3 f. 7v, 27 February, 1449. *Visitations of Religious Houses in the Diocese of Lincoln, 1420–49*, II *Records of Visitations held by William Alnwick . . . (1436–49)*, ed. A. Hamilton Thompson, 2 vols., CYS, XXIV, XXXIII, 1919, 1927, I, pp. 10, 16, 20, cellarer 1437–8; probably absent 1440, p. 28. Former serf: *CPL*, IX, p. 423. Bardeney: *Documents illustrating the activities of the General and Provincial Chapters of the English Black Monks 1215–1540*, ed. W. A. Pantin, 3 vols., Camden Society, 3rd series, XLV, XLVII, LIV, 1931–37, III, no. 267, pp. 109–10.

35 *Reg. Pen.* 3, f. 28bis, 15 April 1448.

36 *Reg. Pen.* 5, f. 296v, 30 August 1456.

37 *Visitations*, II, pp. 391, 393–4. Dispensation: *CPL*, IX, p. 218, 31 January 1442.

38 *Durham Priory*, p. 74.

39 Durham, Dean and Chapter archives, *Registrum Parvum*, III, f. 25, John Dorward, *ex quo a Curia Romana repatriavit et ad nos rediit in corde contrito et humiliato inter suos confratres . . . bene, religiose et laudabiliter conversatus est.* Ibid., ff. 3, 3v, wandering again, ff. 63v–4.

40 Durham, Dean and Chapter Archives, *Registrum Parvum*, II, ff. 86–6v, for John Heworth, but see Dobson, *Durham Priory*, p. 76.

41 *Literae Cantuarienses. The letter books of the monastery of Christ Church, Canterbury*, ed. J. B. Sheppard, 3 vols., *RS* LXXXV, 1887, 1888, III, pp. 172–6; bull: *CPL*, IX, p. 206, under Powas, 2 August 1441.

42 E. H. Pearce, *The Monks of Westminster*, Cambridge, 1916, p. 135.

43 *Reg. Pen.* 2bis, f. 163v.

44 *Reg. Pen.* 9, f. 125v, 1 February 1461.

45 *Reg. Pen.* 3, f. 22, 20 March 1448.

46 *Reg. Pen.* 8, f. 214v, 5 June 1460.

47 *Reg. Pen.* 2, f. 28v, 23 January 1438, for John Hopton, his wife Margaret, John Sharpe, priest, Robert Barellis and wife Margaret, of Halbeswort (= Halesworth, Suffolk?), Norwich diocese.

48 R. H. Helmholz, *Marriage Litigation in Medieval England*, Cambridge Studies in English Legal History, Cambridge, 1974, pp. 77–87.

49 *Reg. Pen.* 2, ff. 120–20v, undated, probably 1438.

50 *Reg. Pen.* 2, f. 134.

51 *Reg. Pen.* 2, ff. 143–3v.
52 *Reg. Pen.* 6, f. 208, 28 April 1456: *in presenti de parentibus expulsi et presentes in curia tamquam relegati et pauperes existunt.* Register of Chedworth, Lincoln (microfilm only), f. 35 gives bull.
53 *Reg. Pen.* 11, ff. 234–4v, after 1463, 28 August.
54 *Reg. Pen.* 3, f. 388v, 31 October 1452.
55 *Reg. Pen.* 2bis, f. 237. Quotation: *dictam Johannam per quindenam ligatam tenuit cum catena ferrea per unam tibeam in quadam camera sua.*
56 Helmholz, *Marriage Litigation*, pp. 101–7, esp. p. 105 for degree of *saevitia*, cruelty, for separation.
57 *Reg. Pen.* 5, f. 414; *BRUO*, III, pp. 1877–9; R. J. Mitchell, *John Tiptoft, 1427–70*, London, 1938, p. 27.
58 *Reg. Pen.* 5, f. 335.
59 *Reg. Pen.* 2bis, f. 114. Quotation: *eius conscientiam propter dictum votum gravari*, and *Signanda per fiat de speciali et illud plus quod expendisset si personaliter accessisset solvat ut in forma consueta.*
60 *Reg. Pen.* 2 bis, f. 80v, 27 September, probably 1439.
61 *Reg. Pen.* 2, f. 231. Two entries because crime different for clerk, Lyndwood, p. 29. Quotation: *concessum in forma in presencia Cardinalis Penitentiarie. Et committatur Episcopo Dol quia propter metum persone non patet ipsis verus ad ordinarium loci accessus.* Bishop was Alanus Spervier, Eubel, II, p. 161. .
62 *Reg. Pen.* 2bis, ff. 229–9v. Note 61 for law.
63 Peacock not in *BRUC*. Servants sharing master's education: *History of the University of Oxford*, I, *The Early Oxford Schools*, ed. J. I. Catto, Oxford, 1984, pp. 169, 183.
64 *Reg. Pen.* 2bis, ff. 239–9v. Dispensation to be beneficed: *CPL*, IX, p. 221, 30 December 1440. Quotation: *Amice cogita melius et vade pro factis tuis contra me ad talia sic prorumpere*, and *ut asseritur, de nocte eidem laico supervenit certus vomitus, ex quo per os suum plura emisit.*
65 *Aliquid a postrema debuisse fuisse sibi ab intra ruptum et apertum.*
66 *Reg. Pen.* 2, ff. 71–1v. Cok in Calais: *pro ville et patrie predictarum ac juris sui regis defensione in quantum poterat resistebat.*
67 Thomson, 'Well of Grace', p. 104.
68 *Reg. Pen.* 2bis, f. 62: *ad Hanonan', cum quodam nobili viro cuius familiaris erat se transtulit et arma sui domini portasset.*
69 *Reg. Pen.* 2bis, f. 399v, 11 December 1442.
70 *Reg. Pen.* 2bis, ff. 256–6v, 16 August 1441; f. 284v.
71 *Reg. Pen.* 5, f. 353, 4 June 1457.
72 *Reg. Pen.* 2bis, f. 85v, 1438 probably.
73 *Reg. Pen.* 11, f. 141: *ad ordinarium adire non valet propter metum persone.*
74 *Reg. Pen.* 11, f. 182.
75 Swanson, *Church and Society*, pp. 55–6, 65–6; Lyndwood, *Provinciale*, I, tit. IV, *De temporibus ordinandorum*, c. *in primis*, p. 30. Renouncing benefice showed necessary repentance.
76 *Reg. Pen.* 2bis, f. 148, 30 May 1440 for Caylart; Coper, ibid., f. 157, 15 July 1440. For Lambert, *Reg. Pen.* 3, f. 367v, 16 March 1454.
77 *Decrees of the Ecumenical Councils*, 2 vols., ed. N. P. Tanner, London and Washington, DC, 1990, I, p. 448, for Constance. *Bullarium Diplomatum et Privilegiorum Sanctorum Romanorum Pontificum*, Turin, 1860, V, pp. 16–17, for *Cum detestabile scelus*, 18 May 1434.
78 *Reg. Pen.* 2bis, ff. 49–50, 17 September 1439: *ea intencione, ut creditur, et ut ipse exponens postmodum intellexit.* Lyndwood, *Provinciale*, III, tit. IX, c. *ut vere*, pp. 152–3.

79 Lacy, *Registrum Commune*, V, index; esp. I, p. 332, presented 26 March 1436, bishop orders enquiry; II, pp. 47, 193, licence to be absent for study. Benefice at 22: *CPL*, VIII, p. 530, 27 June, 1435. Peter Thomas: *Registrum Commune*, V, p. 200, index; Lacy, *Institutions*, ed Hingeston–Randolph, I, p. 153, Landulph vacant, 1433, Thomas instituted, with patron *hac vice* including John Stappe; p. 209, Thomas resigned.

80 Above, note 76.

81 *Reg. Pen.* 2bis, ff. 148v–9.

82 Above, note 76. Lyndwood, *Provinciale*, p. 30 for mediators.

83 *Reg. Pen.* 2bis, f. 161v; F. Blomfield, *An Essay Towards a Topographical History of the County of Norfolk*, 11 vols., ed. C. Parkin, London, 1805–10, IX, p. 172. Alnwick, Register, Norwich (microfilm), f. 58, 5 October 1432, Cowper instituted after free resignation of Robert Hammond. Lyhert, Register, Norwich (microfilm), f. 60v, 17 July 1441, new vicar, Roger Ely, instituted, no cause given.

84 *Reg. Pen.* 3, f. 367v, 16 March, 1454. Quotations: *Vis tu facere secundum consilium meum et ego faciam te rectorem dicte ecclesie de Aston.* Advowson: *VCH Berkshire*, III, pp. 455–6; Beauchamp, Register, Salisbury (microfilm), I, f. 36v. Smith: *BRUO*, III, pp. 1719–20.

85 Bekynton, *Register*, I, p. xviii.

86 See Beauchamp, Register, as note 84.

87 *Reg. Pen.* 5, f. 31v; Aiscough, Register (microfilm), f. 122v.

88 A. H. Thompson and C. T. Clay, *Fasti Parochiales*, I, Yorkshire Archaeological Society, Record Series, LXXXV, 1933, p. 73, for moiety B.

89 *Fasti Parochiales*, p. 80.

90 *Fasti Parochiales*, p. 80.

91 A. Vauchez, *La Sainteté en Occident aux Derniers Siècles du Moyen Age, d'après les procès de canonisation et les documents hagiographiques*. Bibliothèque des Écoles Françaises d'Athènes et de Rome, CCXLI, Rome, 1981, esp. p. 55 for Osmund. Dossier: Malden, *The Canonisation*; sermon: ibid., pp. 236–42.

92 Malden, pp. 134, 144. In general: J. R. Bray, 'Concepts of sainthood in fourteenth-century England', *BJRL*, LXVI/2, 1984, pp. 40–77; A. M. Kleinberg, 'Proving sanctity: selection and authentication of saints in the later Middle Ages', *Viator*, XX, 1989, pp. 183–205. Ferrer: H. Fages, *Histoire de Saint Vincent Ferrier*, 3 vols., Paris, 1901–4, II, pp. 316–44.

93 Bekynton, *Correspondence*, I, pp. 118–19.

94 Swanson, *Church and Society*, pp. 100–1 with references.

95 Malden, pp. 106–7.

96 Malden, p. 109.

97 Vauchez, p. 111; R. M. Woolley, *The Officium and Miracula of Richard Rolle of Hampole*, London, 1919, p. 12.

98 Miracles: Malden, pp. 35–46, 56–84, 142–3.

99 Bekynton, *Correspondence*, I, pp. 117–18.

100 Malden, pp. 99, 109–10, 120, 131, 144.

101 Poggio, *Lettere*, ed. Harth, I, no. 7, pp. 19–20. Cavalcantibus and Orsini: Malden, pp. 94–5; Trieste: Malden, pp. vii, 5, 14, 15–18, 21, 22, 26, 230.

102 Above, Chapter 1, pp. 13–14.

103 Malden, pp. 97–101, 101–2.

104 Above, note 102; Malden, pp. 187, 213.

105 Malden, pp. xviii–xxii.

106 Malden, p. 99.

107 Malden, p. 105–6.

108 Vauchez, pp. 73–80.
109 Malden, pp. 134–6, 142–3.
110 Malden, pp. 94–7.
111 Malden, pp. 96, 103.
112 Malden, pp. 106–8, 108–10. St Croce and Ferrer: Fages, II, p. 318. King Alfonso gave evidence, III, pp. 447–8.
113 Malden, pp. 122–4.
114 Malden, pp. 114–18.
115 Malden, pp. 140–1.
116 Malden, p. 131. Tarentino: Eubel, II, p. 270.
117 Malden, pp. 134–6. Ferrer was canonised 1455.
118 Malden, p. 138.
119 Malden, pp. 141–2.
120 Malden, pp. 143–5.
121 Malden, pp. 143–5, 145–6.
122 Malden, pp. 147–8. Lax *camerarius* p. 147. Upton: *BRUO*, III, pp. 1933–4. Witnesses: Richard Coper, Wills, *presidens hospitalis, capellanus*, John Kybow, *capellanus hospitalis*, p. 148, to add to *Venerabile*, XXI, p. 266.
123 Malden, pp. 148–50, 153.
124 Malden, pp. 151–2.
125 Malden, p. 150.
126 Malden, pp. 152–4; 163–4.
127 Malden, pp. 161–2.
128 Malden, pp. 93–4; 165.
129 Malden, p. 162.
130 Malden, pp. 163–4, 28 January 1456, to bishop of Salisbury, Beauchamp, defending Lax.
131 Malden, pp. 165–7.
132 Malden, p. 167.
133 Malden, pp. 167–9.
134 Expenses: Malden, pp. 187–215.
135 Griffiths, *Henry VI*, p. 247.
136 Bekynton, *Correspondence*, II, pp. 270–93.
137 *BRUO*, I, pp. 407–8.
138 Bekynton, *Correspondence*, I, pp. 136, 218–20; Foffano, 'Umanisti', pp. 3–34.
139 Bekynton, *Correspondence*, I, pp. 228–9.
140 Bekynton, *Correspondence*, I, pp. 225–6.
141 Bekynton, *Correspondence*, I, pp. 226–31.
142 Bekynton, *Correspondence*, II, pp. 297–9.
143 Lunt, II, pp. 511–12.
144 Bekynton, *Correspondence*, I, pp. 131, 240, 242–3.
145 Bekynton, *Correspondence*, II, pp. 299–302, 302–3; Lunt, II, p. 512.
146 Bekynton, *Correspondence*, II, p. 302.
147 Bekynton, *Correspondence*, I, pp. 179, 231–2; Eubel, II, p. 8.
148 Bekynton, *Correspondence*, I, pp. 160–1.
149 Bekynton, *Correspondence*, I, pp. 185–6.
150 Bekynton, *Correspondence*, I, pp. 175–7.
151 Bekynton, *Correspondence*, I, p. 179.
152 Bekynton, *Correspondence*, I, p. 178.
153 *CPL*, IX, p. 392.
154 Bekynton, *Correspondence*, II, pp. 306–9.

155 Lunt, II, p. 513.
156 Above, Chapter 1, note 92.
157 Bekynton, *Correspondence*, II, pp. 309–11.
158 H. C. Maxwell-Lyte, *A History of Eton College*, 4th ed., London, 1911, p. 27; A. N. L. Munby, 'Notes on King's College Library in the fifteenth century', *Essays and Papers*, London, 1977, pp. 27–36, esp. 28–30.
159 *CPR 1441–46*, p. 132.
160 *CPR 1446–52*, p. 209.
161 *CPR 1446–52*, p. 204.
162 Above, note 149.
163 PRO E404/58/168; Maxwell-Lyte, p. 24, note 6: payment to Nicholas Wyllughby for labours in Rome.
164 *Historical Manuscripts Commission*, 9th Report, Eton College Manuscripts, London, 1883, p. 351.
165 PRO E404/59/121.
166 Bekynton, *Correspondence*, I, pp. 37–8.
167 A. Kraus, 'Die Sekretäre Pius II', *Römische Quartalschrift*, LIII, 1958, pp. 25–80, esp. p. 30; *DBI*, X, pp. 536–559, by R. Fubini, esp. p. 541.
168 Bekynton, *Correspondence*, I, pp. 169–70.
169 Bekynton, *Correspondence*, I, p. 170.
170 Bekynton, *Correspondence*, I, pp. 173–4.
171 Bekynton, *Correspondence*, I, pp. 161–2, 172–4.
172 PRO, E30/1436.
173 PRO, E30/425.
174 *CPR 1446–52*, p. 125. Holes: Salisbury Cathedral Library, Chapter Act Book, Hutchyns, p. 127.
175 Bekynton, *Correspondence*, I, p. 227.
176 *PPC*, V, p. 300; Rymer, XI, p. 43; *CPR, 1441–6*, p. 237.
177 e.g. Bekynton, *Correspondence*, I, p. 227.
178 e.g. PRO, E403/759, m. 5 (Albertis); 767, m. 14 (Condulmaro); 771, m. 10 (Condulmaro) ; 773, m. 14; 775, m. 2 (Albertis).
179 PRO, E403/759, m. 8.
180 PRO, E403/771, m. 10.
181 *CPL*, VIII, pp. 258–9; IX, pp. 478–9, 482–3, 511–12 with one other: *VCH, Cambridgeshire*, III, *The City and University of Cambridge*, London, 1959, pp. 376–94, esp. p. 377 for bulls, p. 385 for effect; D. R. Leader, *A History of the University of Cambridge*, I, *The University to 1546*, Cambridge, 1988, pp. 227–8.
182 Maxwell-Lyte, p. 25.
183 *VCH, Cambridgeshire*, III, pp. 377, 385.

II
Diplomacy

7
Martin V and Henry V

Odda Colonna, Pope Martin V, elected at the council of Constance, was crowned on 21 November 1417.[1] The council continued for discussion of reform, but the new pope immediately began re-establishing an administration, particularly for finances, seriously damaged by the schism. In 1417–18 the dangerous Italian situation prevented the curia returning to Rome. The first consideration therefore was to regain control of the papal states; the next to re-establish sound finances and administration.

On 5 December 1417 Martin signalled his intentions to England by re-appointing a papal collector in the person of Walter Medford.[2] Martin was also reconstituting a papal court, re-employing, among others, the English ambassadors, John Catterick and Thomas Polton, who were also *curiales*.[3]

Before the close of the council various general reforms were accepted and agreements for local reforms signed with the various nations. Some of the English provided themselves and the king with free copies of the English agreement before leaving for home, with dates varying from 29 May to 21 July 1418. It consisted largely of undertakings by the pope to refrain from abusive interference with the local church. Nothing was said about appointments to benefices.[4]

Already by then it must have been clear in England that Martin V intended to assert his right, lapsed since the deposition of Pope John XXIII in May 1415, to appoint at least to bishoprics there, though Henry V insisted that petitioning to Rome was not to begin until he and the new pope had corresponded,[5] but the system whereby the pope normally appointed those for whom the king petitioned was not long in reappearing,[6] once Martin's accession was known in England, in mid-November 1417.[7]

On 18 December 1417, however, Martin made a much more controversial move: the appointment of Henry Beaufort as a cardinal and legate *a latere* for life, with Winchester *in commendam*, that is to be held at the same time.[8] It is not certain how soon Henry V knew of this, though Thomas Polton visited him in early April 1418,[9] but thanks to K. B. McFarlane we know that the news produced immediate strong resistance and threats to Beaufort of the full penalties of the statutes against provisors until he relinquished the honour and, in effect, bought a pardon.

In late February 1418 also Martin sent formal notification of his accession to Henry V at Caen and to England, conveyed by Richard, count of Modigliano.[10] The count was also to request the promotion of Richard Flemming, notable at Constance, particularly for urging the council to a speedy election.[11] He had had the task of presenting to the council the English volte face in 1417, which had helped to resolve deadlock, moving the English nation from refusing papal election before reform, to urging speedy election with only minimum reform beforehand.[12] Flemming had been intended as a papal envoy to England in January 1418, with Abbot Thomas Spofforth of York, but neither came, probably because Henry was deeply displeased over the Beaufort affair. Both were Beaufort supporters.[13] In the end Flemming[14] achieved at that point only an appointment as *cubicularius*.[15]

Thus in early 1418 the scene was set for tension between king and pope over appointments, though no worse than that between the curia and the king of France over the same matters.[16] In fact the English situation was in many ways easier for the papacy. In France civil war left the Burgundians (and later the English) as champions of papal rights, with the Armagnacs (and later the dauphin), as champions of 'the Gallican Liberties' i.e. restrictions on the right of the pope to make provisions. Thus, paradoxically, in France the English always favoured sharing appointments to benefices with the papacy, based, in 1418, on the arrangement made with the French nation at Constance.[17] This, unlike that with the English, reserved for five years certain benefices to the pope, and for the rest prescribed an 'alternative' system, whereby alternating appointments fell to pope and ordinary collator.[18] French (Armagnac) resistance was unacceptable to Martin V, who devoted great efforts to persuading the French to change their minds, but civil war in France considerably complicated all attempts to achieve a settlement.

Martin V also took seriously his role of peacemaker, a role the English certainly acknowledged.[19] In April 1418 he sent two legates to France to discuss possible peace terms.[20] Guillaume Fillastre, cardinal of St Mark, later stood out as a supporter of the dauphin against Henry V, but

Giordano Orsini had been a friend of the English at least since the council of Pisa (1408–9), championing the Burgundians when at Constance the duke was accused of murder in the affair of John Petit.

In April and May 1418 Fillastre talked diligently to the French, while Orsini finally came to meet Henry V before Louviers on 21 June.[21] Later in the year, while Henry besieged Rouen, Orsini travelled to and fro between English and Burgundians, whilst the English continued also talking to the dauphin, and apparently made needless difficulties until Rouen fell on 19 January 1419. We know little of communications with Martin V, though evidently Henry V was in touch with both Polton and Catterick at the curia.[22] Polton came to see the king in April 1419.

Orsini returned to the curia in new year 1419[23] and on 11 July, at Pouilly, Burgundy and the dauphin actually came to an agreement, though clearly a very insecure one.[24]

In June 1419 the pope prepared to try again to introduce genuine peace negotiations in France. Now for the first time, however, he introduced the question of 'ecclesiastical liberty', papal parlance for the repeal of the statutes against provisors. On 13 June Catterick and Polton announced the sending of Henry Ehrenfels, apostolic protonotary, a man, they told Henry, influential with the imperial electors.[25] His instructions must have involved peace negotiations and a request for the abolition of the statutes, as well as orders to seek information on Henry's attitude to ecclesiastical appointments in the territories he was rapidly acquiring.

Henry in fact was willing to allow appointment of papal candidates in Normandy, where usually the alternative system prevailed.[26] What he resisted was appointment of hostile Frenchmen.[27]

Thus Ehrenfels was sent back to the curia accompanied by Richard Flemming. In the instruction given on 16 October 1419, Ehrenfels was to express to the pope the king's eagerness for peace, but to say that the king could not abrogate the statutes without the assent of the three estates. He had been too occupied for two years to seek this.[28] Flemming was to seek the see of Lisieux for John Langdon, the royal candidate whom the pope was resisting,[29] but, much more importantly, his letters of credence were a detailed account of the warfare and negotiations in France since Martin's accession and even before,[30] to justify Henry's present stance. Catterick, Polton and Flemming were to present Henry's case before the pope.

By the time the English were given audience by Martin V, even before Ehrenfels and Flemming left France, the whole diplomatic scene had been altered by the murder of the duke of Burgundy by the dauphin's followers at the bridge of Montereau. The murder on 10 September not only dissolved the treaty of Pouilly but loosed a flood of propaganda, Burgundy trying to blacken Charles the dauphin and the latter trying to defend himself. By 25 December Anglo-Burgundian talks had produced an agreement.[31] All sides lobbied the pope, Burgundy wishing Martin to declare Charles a murderer and a perjurer,[32] Charles declaring his innocence but offering concessions on the liberty of the church.[33]

On 28 December Catterick died,[34] so it must have been Flemming, now bishop of Lincoln, and Polton, who were given audience by the pope, with the dauphinists, on 27 December. On that occasion or perhaps earlier Polton, or if earlier perhaps Catterick, made a long speech before the curia closely based on Flemming's instructions.[35] The object was to stress Henry V's zeal for peace and his innocence. The text was *Expectabimus pacem et ecce turbacio* (Jeremiah 13 v. 19) and inevitably the French were accused of insincerity, deliberate delaying tactics and prevarication. On 27 December both sides defended their governments. One account, by Guillaume Fillastre, thought the English short of money and in need of papal mediation,[36] but a merchant of Lucca recorded a heavily ironical reply from Martin V to both parties, showing considerable scepticism about all these protestations for peace.[37]

Martin V did not condemn the dauphin, nor did he acknowledge Henry's right to the French throne. Anglo-Burgundian negotiations continued and there followed in June 1420 the treaty of Troyes, with the marriage of Catherine and Henry (2 June) and a declaration that the dauphin was disinherited for his crimes.[38]

Burgundy and Henry now became very anxious to have this treaty accepted by the pope. This may explain why Cardinal Branda di Castiglione and not John Langdon eventually obtained the see of Lisieux, thus cementing a relationship going back to Constance between the English and Branda, of great importance in future.[39] Martin V later said that Henry himself requested this provision.[40]

Realisation that he had something which the English very much wanted toughened Martin's attitude. On 6 September 1420 he replaced Walter Medford as collector with an Italian, Simon de Lellis of Teramo, who began work (April 1421) by addressing Canterbury convocation on provisions and had a conversation with the king on the same subject.[41] The address must have been delivered in an atmosphere of some uneasiness. Teramo can be seen trying, and failing, to obtain benefices for Poggio Bracciolini, Beaufort's employee.[42] Bishop Nicolo Albergati was trying to obtain the archdeaconry of Lincoln[43] and the pope urged Richard Clifford, bishop of London, to uphold ecclesiatical liberty.[44]

Convocation over, Henry sent ambassadors to Rome, where the pope had now returned, with instructions probably concerning peace.[45] Then on 19 July Teramo was dispatched there as government representative, with instructions about the statute. He was paid by the English government throughout his ensuing stay in the curia.[46]

In Teramo's instructions Henry again emphasised that the statutes were the work of his predecessors with the consent of parliament. Revocation needed parliamentary consent. In newly-conquered territories the king had made no innovations. The statutes could not be discussed in the current parliament, which was overfilled with pressing business, but to show his good intentions, he offered, 'not offered otherwise' (*alias non oblata*), that when he next returned he would have the matter discussed by the estates to see if the statutes ought to be kept.[47]

On 2 October 1421 the pope reacted by sending Urban de Florencia, a Carthusian *familiaris* of Albergati, used in secret negotiations with France,[48] writing that he was delighted to hear from Teramo that Henry was anxious to conserve the liberties of the church, especially in the new territories, and was intending to try to have the stautute revoked.[49] It may be significant that the dauphin was provoked at the same point, late autumn 1421, into sending an embassy to Rome to complain that Martin was insufficiently supportive of his right to the French throne, but also offering to abolish the French anti-papal legislation.[50]

On 17 November 1421, Martin further asserted his prerogatives by appointing John Kemp by provision to the see of London, to replace Richard Clifford. Thomas Spofforth was to go from Hereford to Chichester, Kemp's former see, and John Langdon to Rochester.[51] Henry at first refused to accept; he wanted Thomas Polton, whom the London chapter duly elected, but Martin insisted that it was unsuitable for London to be ruled by an absentee (Polton of course remained in the curia). A lively correspondence with lobbying and slander ensued, continuing throughout 1422. After the king's death Kemp, with Bedford in France, told William Swan, his proctor in Rome, that he at last obtained royal consent. This is possible, if unlikely, but Kemp retained London in the aftermath of Henry's disappearance.[52]

Martin was behaving with equal severity to the dauphin. Despite Charles's promises, French anti-papal legislation was not abolished but renewed. Martin therefore refused to accept Charles's candidate for the see of Toulouse, Denys des Moulins, whom he considered the main instigator of the royal policy.[53]

Simultaneously Martin began again to conduct peace negotiations, apparently assured by Urban de Florencia that Henry was favourable.[54] On 8 February 1422 Nicolo Albergati, bishop of Bologna, a saintly Carthusian, was appointed nuncio.[55] He began work in France on 25 April and soon, on 13 June, wrote optimistically of progress with help from the duke of Savoy, uncle of the duke of Burgundy.[56] The various French parties were to meet; the dauphin was full of good intentions about the liberties of the church.

On 24 June 1422 Henry and Burgundy sent an embassy to the curia.[57] It consisted of Gilles de Duremort, abbot of Beaubec, Philibert de Montjeu, Henry V's candidate for the see of Paris, a Burgundian greatly devoted to England, and Jean Fouquerel, with the seigneurs of Vezelay and Romulles and Gautier of Bauffrement or Ruppes, seigneur of Soyes and Trichastel, chamberlain and councillor of John the Fearless, as well as master Jean of Almans, Pierre Morice and Nicole Davy. Thus all were French or Burgundian and the aim peace.

The ambassadors were away from 24 June to 24 November 1422. An account of part of their business exists in the collection about the English title to the throne of France made by Thomas Bekynton, later royal secretary to Henry VI. This piece was probably a letter to England by Richard Cordon, advocate in the consistory, who explains that he was an eyewitness.[58]

Duremort made a speech before the pope outlining the benefits brought by the treaty of Troyes. The same evening the pope, seven cardinals, the ambassadors, many Armagnacs and Scots, heard a counter-attack by a dauphinist, defending Charles's title, attacking the legitimacy of Troyes, and outlining the evils it had caused. Gautier de Bauffrement urged one Anglo-French ambassador to denounce this, but their instructions forbade such arguments. The pope left amid uproar.

The English group at the curia, Cordon, Polton and master John Blodwell, an abbreviator,[59] decided on a public reply, and employed Ardicino della Porta of Novara, a curial advocate well known at Constance for his defence of Burgundy in the Petit case.[60] They organised another hearing, at which Cordon noted meticulously the positions of all the protagonists, including Denys des Moulins who seems to have led the French party. Arguments for and against Troyes were again exchanged in an atmosphere of increasing acrimony, with offers of violence in varying languages. The vivid little scene ended with the pope walking out. But he had not accepted Henry's claims.

What would have been the outcome of Albergati's mission and Henry's lobbying if the king had lived we cannot know. Even the extent of the bargaining remains shadowy; most of what is said was recollected later when memory may have rewritten events to favour politics. In May 1422 ambassadors of the duke of Savoy had come to see Henry V[61] and looking back a year later the duke thought that Henry was being too demanding.[62] But in 1435 the Burgundians remembered that Henry genuinely wanted discussions and maintained that at his request the duke of Savoy had been called in, because war had become too expensive in lives and money.[63]

Notes

1 Chapter based on my 'Martin V and Henry V', without all its documentation but adding some new.
2 *CPL*, VII, p. 1; ASV, Arm. XXIX 7, f. 249; Lunt, II, p. 429.
3 Chapter 2, p. 26; Uginet for discussion, with list.
4 Edition: A. Mercati, *Raccolta di Concordati*, I, *1098–1914*, Vatican City, 1954, pp. 165–8; also Jacob, 'English Concordat', passim.
5 Harvey, 'Martin V and Henry V', p. 52; BL, Add. MS 17402, f. 12, royal letter.
6 Harvey, 'Martin V and Henry V', pp. 52–3.
7 Chichele, *Register*, III, p. 33, report to convocation, 26 November.
8 K. B. McFarlane, 'Henry V, Bishop Beaufort, and the Red Hat, 1417–21', *England in the Fifteenth Century*, ed. G. L. Harris, London, 1981, pp. 78–113, esp. p. 80. Also Harvey, 'Martin V and Henry V', p. 53; Harriss, *Beaufort*, pp. 94–9.
9 *Calendar of Signet Letters of Henry IV and Henry V (1399–1422)*, ed. J. L. Kirby, London, 1978, no. 826.
10 *CPL*, VII, p. 5; further, Harvey, 'Martin V and Henry V', p. 53, note 26.
11 C. M. D. Crowder, 'Henry V, Sigismund and the Council of Constance', *Historical Studies*, IV, 1963, pp. 93–110, esp. p. 107, note 62; BL, MS Cotton Tib. B VI, f. 57v.
12 Crowder, 'Henry V', p. 105.
13 *CPL*, VII, p. 5.
14 Chapter 2, p. 34.
15 H. E. Salter, ed., *Snappe's Formulary and other Records*, Oxford Historical Society, LXXX, 1924, pp. 139–40.
16 Harvey, 'Martin V and Henry V' p. 54 for bibliography.
17 French agreement: Mercati, pp. 150–7. For misleading term concordat: Brandmüller, *Papst und Konzil*, p. 275, note 52.
18 System: N. Valois, *Histoire de la Pragmatique Sanction de Bourges sous Charles VII*, Archives de l'histoire religieuse de la France, Paris, 1906, pp. ii–v, x–xi; also C. T. Allmand, 'The relations between the English government, the higher clergy and the papacy in Normandy, 1417–1450', Oxford university DPhil., 1963.
19 *Petitiones* of Richard Ullerston: H. von der Hardt, *Magnum Oecumenicum Constancientie Concilium*, 4 vols., Frankfurt and Leipzig, 1700, I, cols. 1126–71; and below, Chapter 12.
20 Harvey, 'Martin V and Henry V', pp. 54–5.

21 Harvey, 'Martin V and Henry V', p. 56.
22 Harvey, 'Martin V and Henry V', p. 57.
23 B.-A. Poquet du Haut-Jussé, *La France gouverné par Jean Sans Peur*, Paris, 1959, p. 261, no. 991.
24 G. du Fresne de Beaucourt, *Histoire de Charles VII*, 6 vols., Paris, 1881–91, I, p. 300.
25 Not Grenfels, as Harvey, 'Martin V and Henry V', p. 58, see Schuchard, *Die Deutschen*, pp. 151, n. 842; 226, n. 237; 295, n. 9.
26 Allmand, 'The relations', esp. pp. 219–20. I am very grateful to Dr Allmand for allowing me to use his thesis and for much other help.
27 Harvey, 'Martin V and Henry V', p. 59 for Lisieux.
28 Rymer, IV/3, pp. 136–7 (IX, pp. 806–7).
29 See note 27.
30 P. Chaplais, *English Medieval Diplomatic Practice*, Part I, *Documents and Interpretation*, 2 vols., London, 1982, II, no. 240, not used in 'Martin V and Henry V', p. 60.
31 V. Martin, *Les Origines du Gallicanisme*, 2 vols., Paris, 1939, II, p. 230. Best account of what followed: P. Bonenfant, *Du Meutre de Montereau au Traité de Troyes*, Brussels, 1958. Treaty: Chaplais, *Medieval Diplomatic Practice*, II, no. 266.
32 Bonenfant, p. 103, note 4; p. 104, note 7.
33 Valois, *Pragmatique*, p. xii and pièces no. 1; Martin, *Les Origines*, II, p. 234.
34 Le Neve, *Exeter*, p. 2.
35 Oxford, All Souls College, MS 47, fols. 274–8v, incipit: *Ecclesie Militantis*, not used in 'Martin V and Henry V', p. 61. Unlikely to have been delivered by Flemming, since *Dominus Lincoln*' is referred to on f. 277. Flemming became bishop of Lincoln by provision on 20 November. For MS see below, Chapter 12, p. 217. January 1420 'articles' sent to pope and others, Chaplais, *Diplomatic Practice*, Part I/ II, nos. 345, 240[c].
36 Beaucourt, I, pp. 328–9.
37 Harvey, 'Martin V and Henry V', p. 61, note 95.
38 Troyes: Chaplais, *Diplomatic Practice*, Part I/II, no. 292[a].
39 Harvey, 'Martin V and Henry V', p. 62.
40 Vatican Library, MS Chigi D VII 101, f. 53; K. A. Fink, 'Martin V nach den Brevenregistern', *QFIAB*, XXVI, 1935–6, no. 196; Pantin, *Canterbury College*, III, pp. 78–90.
41 Chichele, *Register*, III, p. 66; Lunt, II, p. 419.
42 Harvey, 'The benefice' p. 169.
43 Oxford, Bodleian Library, MS Arch. Seld. B 23, f. 81v, quoted Chichele, *Register*, I, pp. xliii–xliv.
44 BL, MS Royal and Kings, 10 B IX, f. 57v.
45 A. Morosini, *La Chronique d'Antoine Morisini: extraits rélatifs a l'histoire de France*, 4 vols., ed. L. Dorez and G. Lefevre–Pontalis, Société de l'Histoire de France, Paris, 1898–1902, II, pp. 223–4, n. 7; J. H. Wylie and W. T. Waugh, *The Reign of Henry V*, 3 vols., Cambridge, III, 1929, p. 375; Harvey, 'Martin V and Henry V', p. 64.
46 Dates: Harvey, 'Martin V and Henry V', p. 64; instructions: BL, MS Cotton Cleop. E II, ff. 368v–9.
47 Quotations: Harvey, 'Martin V and Henry V', p. 64.
48 *CPL*, VII, p. 9; P. de Töth, *Il Beato Cardinale Nicolo Albergati ed i suoi tempi, 1375–1444*, 2 vols., Viterbo, 1934, II, p. 174.
49 O. Raynaldus, *Annales*, Lucca, 1752, VIII, pp. 538–9; Fink, 'Breven', no. 174.
50 Valois, *Pragmatique*, Pièces no. 5 and p. xiv.
51 Harvey, 'Martin V and Henry V', pp. 65–6. Here I disagree with Davies, 'Martin V', p. 314.

52 Details: Harvey, 'Martin V and Henry V', p. 66.
53 Details: Harvey, 'Martin V and Henry V', p. 66. Du Moulins: H. Müller, *Die Französen, Frankreich und das Basler Konzil, 1431–1449*, Konziliengeschichte, Reihe B, Untersuchungen, 2 vols., Paderborn, 1990, pp. 422–31.
54 Töth, II, pp. 174–5.
55 Töth, II, p. 170, n. 1; Harvey, 'Martin V and Henry V', p. 67, note 133. Albergati: *DBI*, I, Rome, 1960, pp. 619–621, by E. Pasztor.
56 Fink, 'Breven', no. 260.
57 Full documentation Harvey, 'Martin V and Henry V', pp. 67–8 and notes. Membership of embassy with dates: Paris, BN, MS fr. 20590, f. 21. Further: Müller, index under Philibertus.
58 I used BL. MS Harley 861, ff. 43–48. See Harvey, 'Martin V and Henry V', p. 68, note 143 for other MSS. For Cordon, above, Chapter 2, notes 19–22.
59 Blodwell: above, Chapter 2, notes 62–7.
60 Harvey, 'Martin V and Henry V', p. 68, note 146 and below, Chapter 8, note 42.
61 Beaucourt, I, p. 339.
62 Beaucourt, II, pp. 318–29. esp. 318, 322; Paris, BN, Collection de Bourgogne 70, f. 4, Savoy unwilling to deal with Bedford, *considere le response que fist a ses ambaxadeurs feu le roy dengleterre.*.
63 Printed: J. G. Dickinson, *The Congress of Arras, 1435. A Study in Medieval Diplomacy*, Oxford, 1955, pp. 209–10.

8

Martin V and the minority government

The sudden death of Henry V on 31 August 1422, followed on 22 October by that of his father-in-law Charles VI, caused important changes in the context of Anglo–papal relations, posing serious problems for both pope and English government.[1] The pope now faced a situation where decision-making in England was collective; no individual on the royal council had decisive power. Furthermore the collective task was to transfer intact power and possessions when the new king came of age, so that alterations to statutes or definitive peace treaties became wellnigh impossible.

Martin probably did not fully understand this. He wrote at once to the council asking the members to bring up the child in the fear of God, make peace, and revoke the statutes.[2] He continued to urge the last two, without perhaps, at first at least, wholly understanding the problems. His determination was a measure of his continued need for money to re-establish his authority and status.

The minority government, in so far as it had a collective view, shared the aims of Henry V: to be able to appoint its candidates to bishoprics and to obtain papal recognition of the treaty of Troyes. The means deployed, however, were much less effective than his. With no single ruler to oversee appointments the post of royal proctor in Rome lapsed,[3] opening the way for more than usually bitter intrigues.

Henry's death brought changes very quickly. The English/Burgundian delegation at the curia had returned by 24 November;[4] the papal legate Nicolo Albergati rapidly found John, duke of Bedford, determined not to negotiate for peace. In early April 1423 Bedford and Burgundy had made a new alliance in the treaty of Amiens.[5] So by late 1423 Albergati had returned to Rome.[6]

In February 1423 the English government reappointed Thomas Polton royal proctor;[7] at much the same time the pope sent back his collector, Simon of Teramo, with instructions to work in England for the revocation of the statutes. Simon was accompanied by James, bishop of Trieste, as nuncio.[8] Martin was always conscious of the need to uphold 'ecclesiastical liberty'; at the same time he was involved in a very similar struggle with the dauphin.[9]

The first major problem confronting pope and government concerned Martin's desire to appoint Richard Flemming, bishop of Lincoln, to York, vacant in October 1423, when the royal council wanted Philip Morgan, bishop of Worcester.[10] Flemming supported the pope's viewpoint at the council of Pavia/Siena (1423–4) but had no political base in England.[11] In the background, usually with Bedford in Normandy, lurked John Kemp, who eventually got away with the prize.[12] The intrigues became extraordinarily complex, intertwined with the desire of Humfrey, duke of Gloucester, that the pope should annul the first marriage of Jacqueline of Hainault, whom he considered his wife; the equal desire of Philip, duke of Burgundy, that the pope should not;[13] the pope's desire to have the statutes revoked; and Bedford's to achieve the widest degree of control over the church in France, coupled with his need not to offend Burgundy (his chief ally), whilst not humiliating his brother Humfrey. Not all these desires were compatible but the lack of a central guiding policy in England allowed the quarrels to get quite out of hand. It is certain, however, that none of this can be seen only in terms of intrigues in England: the French and Roman dimensions were evidently important also, even if much less visible to us.

Omitting details unnecessary here, one needs to stress that while the archbishopric of York was causing a struggle in England, the regime governing benefices in the English areas of France, set up by the agreement at the end of Constance, was due for renegotiation at the time of the council of Pavia/Siena; the chief agent of the triumph of the pope there had been Jean de Rochetaillée, also Bedford's agent.[14] At the end of the council, in February 1424, Rochetaillée left for the curia with a list of requests to reward Bedford's loyalty: a group of French cardinals, a special arrangement for appointments to benefices in the French territories while the war continued, recognition by the pope of Troyes, that the pope desist from interference in the Humfrey/Jacqueline marriage since Bedford and Burgundy had now been recognised as arbitrators.[15] Meanwhile Flemming returned to England, to find himself threatened by the statute against provisors: refusal of York and even deprivation of the see of Lincoln, until he agreed to back Philip Morgan and Humfrey's marriage claims.[16] In Rome Thomas Polton was almost certainly no longer at the centre of affairs. The last mention that I know is early 1424. He was certainly in England in October 1425 and perhaps even in August.[17] Meanwhile Bedford's chancellor, Kemp, also in England machinating on his own behalf, was attempting to satisfy the pope's desire for 'liberty' by making direct appointments of papal candidates in his diocese, not provisions.[18] And everyone, including the Burgundians, who spent enormous sums in the curia, bombarded the pope with good advice about Hainault.[19]

In April 1424 the pope in effect refused Bedford's requests.[20] In the second half of 1424 and in 1425 therefore Bedford and the English council set out to pressurise the pope. This involved moves to activate a new general council and complaints in France about money flowing to Rome.

In July 1424 diplomats were sent by England to the Spanish peninsula (including to Alfonso, king of Aragon, who had his own quarrel with the pope), to the Empire (Sigismund was also quarrelling with Martin), and to Lithuania, Poland, Denmark and the Teutonic Knights, to enquire whether these countries would support an early general council.[21] In October Bedford connived at a vociferous attack in the French parlement about money draining to Rome.[22] In October also Humfrey bitterly complained to the pope about the papal collector, saying that he had been linking a verdict against Humfrey in the marriage case with the repeal of the statute (i.e. saying that if Humfrey lost his case in Rome his enemies would repeal the statute).[23] Whatever the truth, Martin V had been linking ecclesiastical liberty with Humfrey's success, using every means to insist that Flemming should have York as well as pressing other cases concerning 'liberty'.[24]

Early in 1425, the embassies sent to canvass the allies about a council returned with favourable replies.[25] The emperor urged on Martin V his duty to call an early council, claiming English support.[26] Alfonso of Aragon told Sigismund that he had been in touch with the English and would send ambassadors to the curia.[27] The English government ordered its nationals in Rome to obtain the support of representatives of other nations there.[28] Sigismund sent a mission to press his point,[29] and the English an embassy containing one French representative, two Englishmen and a councillor of the duke of Burgundy, to meet the emperor's representatives to put the case jointly to the pope.[30]

What did all this mean? Some have seen it as a conversion of the English government and Bedford to conciliar theory, that is belief in the superiority of councils over popes.

In the case of Bedford it surely was not so, whatever the convictions of his subordinates. Most probably the secret is his continued attempts to obtain the most favourable terms in government dealings with the church in Lancastrian France. In spring 1425 the pope sent Juliano Cesarini to Bedford to refuse modified proposals but apparently to suggest alternatives.[31]

Accompanying this was a breakdown of the alliance system constructed by Henry V and Bedford after Troyes. After the battle of Verneuil, 17 August 1424, Bedford was in one sense much stronger, but precisely because of this his allies were wavering or falling away. By March 1425 Artur of Brittany had defected to the French, becoming constable of Charles VII. Jean, duke of Brittany, Artur's brother, had also temporarily joined Charles. The comte de Foix had also gone. By early 1424 Charles VII had made him lieutenant general in Languedoc and by late 1425 he had been definitively bought.[32] By early 1425 too relations between Humfrey and Burgundy had so deteriorated that Humfrey challenged Philip to single combat.[33]

Meanwhile Franco-papal relations, having been very bad, were improving. On 10 February 1425, at Chinon, Charles VII granted the pope full rights over benefices in France, denying for the moment the Gallican Liberties, which hitherto he had sworn to uphold. This promise went to Rome with a solemn embassy about Easter 1425.[34] The delegates also took a series of requests for favours, including that those vassals who had taken oaths as allies of the enemy might be absolved by the royal confessor. Meanwhile Burgundy and Charles were negotiating, using the good offices of Savoy.

This, very threataning to Bedford, must all have been well known to Martin V, who cannot but have thought that a Burgundy disenchanted with an English alliance would be likely to reconcile with Charles VII. In April 1425 therefore Martin V not only forbade the duel between Humfrey and Philip but also sent a messenger to exhort Bedford, Burgundy and Charles to talk peace.[35] In May he wrote again to Philip that he had heard that the French were anxious to offer terms, begging Philip to exhort the English to listen, but also reminding him that promises were not to be kept if they did not please God.[36] Probably at about the same time, May 1425, cardinal Branda di Castiglione in Rome consulted Cesarini and others about the obligations of allies after Troyes.[37] Although Bedford may not have realised this, Cesarini's conclusions favoured the French.

Bedford's support for an early council is therefore fairly easily explained. The support in England is probably similar: Martin V was still refusing to budge on York. In fact, however, by mid-1425 he was preparing to give way.

On 20 July the curia yielded on York, with a new plan for disposing of the vacant English bishoprics.[38] Martin had evidently decided that Bedford was the key figure to be placated; in September he sent an important embassy to the duke, keeping the Anglo-imperial embassy in Rome waiting unheard whilst he awaited a reply from France.[39]

The papal delegation consisted of Jean de Rochetaillée, Bedford's protégé at the council of Pavia/Siena, who had first taken his requests to Rome and Jean Vivian, the duke of Burgundy's proctor at the curia, who had worked, in Burgundy's interest, on the Gloucester marriage case.[40] They brought a new papal plan for benefices in English France, which was accepted on 26 November.[41] One can see it taking effect at once: despite opposition from the parlement a papal provision hitherto blocked was forced into effect on Bedford's insistence.[42] Rochetaillée and Vivian also brought John Kemp's appointment to York,[43] and announced the papal prohibition of the duel between Humfrey and Burgundy.[44] We know all this from letters from John Kemp to William Swan, his proctor in the curia. Kemp showed a great desire to please Cardinal Branda, who must have been one of the important figures in all these manoeuvres.[45]

Kemp had still to achieve acceptance in England. There relations between Humfrey and Beaufort had become so bad that Beaufort was refusing to attend council meetings.[46] Humfrey had returned from Hainault defeated and angry and Beaufort wrote to Bedford to ask him to intervene.[47]

Bedford duly crossed to England, late in 1425, and immediately the impasse over bishoprics was sorted out: on 26 February 1426 the curia ratified a slightly modified version of its own plan.[48]

This left the embassies in the curia high and dry. Martin V finally granted them audience and the eloquent pleas for an early council remain, but on 17 December 1425 the pope said he would do his duty when the time came: in other words he refused.[49]

The delegates returned home and the matter dropped.[50] There seems no reason to suppose that the governments concerned were converts to conciliarism.

Gloucester's marriage also faded out of the picture. By September 1425 Humfrey had tired of Jacqueline and Philip was defeating her in the field.[51] The day the consistory ratified the English arrangements about bishoprics Cardinal Orsini also pronounced an interim judgement that

Jacqueline had been wrong to leave her first husband.[52] By then it mattered less in English politics.

In this more favourable climate Prospero Colonna was allowed to hold English benefices, Beaufort and Rochetaillée became cardinals, Beaufort with his bishopric *in commendam*, and Martin V decided to try again to have the statutes revoked.[53] In April 1426 he sent Juliano Cesarini to England. We do not know what he achieved but Martin believed that Humfrey then promised to have repeal discussed in the next Parliament.[54] When nothing happened Martin became fierce; early in 1427 Chichele was suspended as *legatus natus*. Gloucester had the papal collector arrested for trying to deliver the bull, but in desperation Chichele appealed to a general council.[55]

Martin won that round: the matter was discussed in parliament in late January 1428.[56] Historians have concluded, mistakenly, that Martin was utterly defeated. Kemp and Chichele, however, certainly thought that Martin would be pleased with the results of the parliament.[57] In August 1428 an embassy was sent to the pope, led by the bishop of London, William Gray.[58] Later Eugenius reminded him (by then bishop of Lincoln) that he had conveyed a promise that benefices vacant in curia would be open to provisors.[59] This was probably agreed by the royal council as a result of the parliament of 1428.

Little seemed to change, nevertheless, probably because Martin ceased further bargaining, since he now began to need English support for his crusade against the Hussites.[60] Chichele was restored to his legateship even before the offers of the English can have been known in the curia[61] and the months from May onwards were dominated on the papal side by the raising of men and money for the crusade, to be led by Beaufort. And then, in June 1429, the English used the troops and money against the French, after the severe defeat at Patay.[62]

Papal anger was acute. In June 1429, for the first time since about mid-1425, the English set about establishing a permanent representative in Rome in the person of Robert FitzHugh.[63] On 15 July he was given the task of explaining to the pope this diversion of men and money, but Martin at once showed his hostility by blocking the council's canididate for the see of Chichester.[64]

By 1429 too peace negotiations in France were again looming. In August the French offered Burgundy generous terms; although he refused, he, Bedford and Beaufort agreed that they would again accept papal mediators from the next year.[65]

Thus early in 1430 FitzHugh was ordered to ask the pope to send cardinals as mediators and to suggest Beaufort as one. He was also to request the pope not to heed demands by the other side for release from oaths to keep the treaty of Troyes.[66]

The pope was deeply hostile to any such plan. Letters from him point out that Beaufort ought not to be involved in the papal effort at mediation. Martin said that Beaufort's presence could only exacerbate tension caused by the misuse of the papal army. This was despite Beaufort's sending of Nicholas Bildeston to repeat the request.[67]

By the time Martin V died, early in 1431, he had indeed commissioned Nicolo Albergati to go to France 'as an angel of peace', largely, it seems, because preparations for the forthcoming general council of Basel, which he was obliged to call according to the decree *Frequens* passed at Constance, made European peace highly desirable.[68] But Anglo-papal relations were tense; Martin was less and less inclined to favour England's French pretensions. In that climate the long preparations for the peace congress of Arras were begun.

On the two questions – liberty of the church and the treaty of Troyes – neither pope nor government had gained much up to Martin's death. Martin had a promise of concessions on provisions and a possible lever in the renewed need of his mediation in the peace process. The royal council had not given much on the statute: the true meaning of its offer had yet to be tested but papal aid was needed in negotiations with the French. It remained to be seen what a successor could make of the situation Martin had left.

Notes

1 Chapter based on my 'Martin V and the English, 1422–1431', *Religious Belief and Ecclesiastical Careers in late Medieval England*, ed. C. Harper-Bill, Bury St Edmunds, 1991, pp. 59–86.

2 Fink, 'Breven', no. 187.

3 See above, Chapter 1, notes 59–62.

4 BN, MS Fr. 20590, f. 21; see also BN, MS Fr. 4491, f. 26 (new notation), f. 37; BN, MS Fr. 4485, f. 360.

5 Beaucourt, II, p. 333; R. Vaughan, *Philip the Good. The Apogée of Burgundy*, London, 1970, p. 9.

6 Töth, II, pp. 192–5; P. Partner, *The Papal State under Martin V*, London, 1958, pp. 77–8.

7 Rymer, 4/4, p. 85 (X, 266); detained in Cologne ?1423, Chaplais, *English Diplomatic Practice*, I/I, no. 191.

8 PRO E404/39/339; *CB*, I, p. 176; Lunt, II, p. 420; Foreville, *Le Jubilé*, pp. 64–5, 181–2.

9 Harvey, 'Martin V and the English', p. 62.

10 Harvey, 'Martin V and the English', pp. 63–4. See esp. Davies, 'Martin V', pp. 309–44 and Harriss, *Beaufort*, pp. 153–5.

11 Brandmüller, *Pavia–Siena*, I, pp. 30–36, 130–1.

12 Kemp: Nigota, 'John Kempe'.

13 R. Vaughan, *Philip the Good*, most helpful here.

14 Constance agreement: above, Chapter 7, note 17. Pavia/Siena: Brandmüller, *Pavia–Siena*, I, pp. 30, 116, 224; C. T. Allmand, 'Un conciliariste Nivernais du XVe siècle, Jean Beaupère', *Annales de Bourgogne*, XXXV, 1963, pp. 145–54, esp. pp. 146–7.

15 Brandmüller, *Pavia–Siena*, I, p. 224; Valois, *Pragmatique*, pp. xxii–xxiv; printed: E. du Boulay, *Historia Universitatis Parisiensis*, V, Paris, 1668, p. 366. I used Paris, AN, P. 2298, pp. 815–25.

16 Brandmüller, *Pavia–Siena*, I, p. 233 for departure; Davies, 'Martin V', pp. 323–4 for return.

17 Above, note 3.

18 Nigota, p. 14.

19 Vaughan, pp. 32–49. See ADN, B 1929, ff. 57v–8, 148v; B 1931, ff. 96, 96v, 97v. B 1935 (1430), ff. 151v–2, estimates 3925 livres of Flanders, with list of expenses.

20 Paris, AN, P. 2298, pp. 815–25.

21 Alfonso: K. A. Fink, *Martin V und Aragon*, Historische Studien, CCCXL, Berlin, 1938, pp. 108, 111, 116–18. Sigismund: note 29 below. Jean Gentil to Portugal, Castille, Leon and Aragon: PRO, E364/58, m. 2 dorse; E 101/322, no. 8. John Stokes to Sigismund: J. Ferguson, *English Diplomacy, 1422–1461*, Oxford, 1972, p. 112; PRO, E364/58, m. 2 dorse, E403/666, m. 14; *RTA*, VIII, pp. 385–7; Sigismund's letter to Henry VI: University of Uppsala, MS C I, ff. 365v–6r (photocopy only; reference thanks to Dr I Doyle). John Norton to Lithuania, Poland, Denmark and Prussia: PRO, E 364/58, m. 2 dorse, E404/58/77; J. Caro, 'Liber Cancellariae Stanislai Ciolek', *Archiv fur Oesterreiches Geschichte*, XLV, 1871, pp. 319–545, esp. p. 404, no. xlvii.

22 S. Luce, *Jeanne D'Arc à Domremy*, Paris, 1885, no. lxxix, pp. 127–8; Fauquembergue, *Journal de Clément Fauquembergue, Greffier du Parlement de Paris 1417–35*, ed. A. Tuetey, Société de l'Histoire de France, CVIII, 3 vols., Paris, 1909, II, pp. 143–6, 148.

23 Bekynton, *Correspondence*, I, pp. 279–80.

24 E.g. Harvey, 'Martin V and the English', pp. 70, 71.

25 Dates of return: PRO, E364/58, m. 2 dorse.

26 Sigismund: note 21 above and Ferguson, *English Diplomacy*, pp. 89–90.

27 Fink, *Martin V und Aragon*, p. 125 and note 21.

28 BL, MS Cotton Cleop. C IV, ff. 182v–4; quotations: Harvey, 'Martin V and the English', p. 73, note 86.

29 C. J. H. Walravens, *Alain Chartier*, Amsterdam, 1971, pp. 28–33; P.-M. Perret, 'L'ambassade de l'Abbé de Saint Antoine de Vienne et d'Alain Chartier à Venise', *Revue Historique*, XLV, 1891, pp. 298–307.

30 Jean Picart, abbot of Ourscamp, William Sulbury, abbot of Beaulieu and Sir Walter de la Pole; joined by Pierre de Romulle councillor of duke of Burgundy, in August. Sulbury and Pole: PRO, E364/59, m. 5; E404/41/331, 332, 346; E403/671, m. 1, 8, 13; E403/673, m. 7. Ourscamp and Romulle, (not Roville as Ferguson, p. 16): BN, MS Fr. 26048, no. 447, 449, 450. Royal letter: H. Koeppen, ed. *Die Berichte der Generalprokuratoren des Deutschen Ordens an der Kurie*, Veröffentlichungen der Niedersächischen Archivverwaltung, XXIX, 3/2, *Jehan Tiergart*, Göttingen, 1971, no. 298.

31 Valois, *Pragmatique*, pp. xxv–xxvi and n. 1; Fink, 'Breven', no. 197; Paris, AN J 653, no. 15. Cesarini: H. Fechner, *Giuliano Cesarini (1398–44) bis zu seiner Ankunft in Basel*

am 9. September 1431, Berlin, 1907 and *DBI*, XXIV, Rome, 1980, pp. 188–95, by A. A. Strnad and K. Walsh. Payments ASV, IE, 382, f. 176v; 383, f. 55v.

32 Brittany: G. A. Knowlson, *Jean V, duc de Bretagne et l'Angleterre*, Cambridge/Rennes, 1964, pp. 126–32; Beaucourt, II, pp. 73–84; E. Cosneau, *Le Connetable de Richemont (Artur de Bretagne) 1393–1458)*, 2 vols., Paris, 1886, I, pp. 82–90. Foix: M. G. A. Vale, *English Gascony 1399–1453*, Oxford, 1970, pp. 95–6.

33 L. Devillers, ed., *Cartulaire des Comtes de Hainault*, 6 vols., Collection de chroniques Belges inédites, Brussels, 1889, IV, pp. 443–5, 448–51, 452–3, 454–5.

34 Martin, *Les Origines*, II, pp. 255–68.

35 Emperor: Stevenson, *Letters and Papers*, II, pp. 412–14; Bedford: Fink, 'Breven', no. 24; delivery to Bedford: Stevenson, II, p. 414. Urban de Florencia to ask for peace: ASV, Arm. XXXIX 6, f. 124v; Fink, no. 198, *mutatis mutandis* to Charles VII, Brittany, and Bedford, 27 March 1425. In April Richard Cordon returned from curia: *CPL* VII, p. 16. 11 May Hans van Pruce, valet of king's household, to Rome: PRO, E403/671, m. 3; E404/48/311.

36 ACO, B 11897/2, 11 Kal. June, year 8 = 21 June 1425. Wrongly dated Fink, no. 170 and Harvey, 'Martin V and Henry V', p. 69, note 147. Also Fink, no. 168.

37 T. M. Izbicki, 'The canonists and the treaty of Troyes', *Proceedings of the fifth international Congress of Medieval Canon Law*, eds. S. Kuttner and K. Pennington, Monumenta iuris canonici, series C, Subsidia VI, Vatican City, 1980, pp. 425–34, esp. pp. 425–30.

38 ASV, Acta Misc. I, f. 157v.

39 Albizzi, *Commissioni di Rinaldo degli Albizzi per il Commune de Firenze dal 1399–1433*, ed. C. Guasti, 3 vols., II, Florence, 1869, pp. 442, 444, 467, 480–1.

40 BL, MS Cotton Cleop. C. IV, f. 191v; Harvey, 'Martin V and the English', p. 75.

41 Valois, *Pragmatique*, p. xxvii; BL, MS Cotton Cleop. C IV, ff. 170v, 155v–6, letters of Kemp.

42 Appointment of Ardicino della Porta of Novara to prebend of Saint Germain l'Auxerrois: Fauquembergue, II, pp. 113, 196–7; Valois, *Pragmatique*, pp. 19, 21. Legislation: Fauquembergue, II, pp. 199, 200–2, 203, 204, 209–10, 215–16, 230–1, 272–3.

43 BM, MS Cotton Cleop. C IV, ff. 164v–5.

44 Stevenson, II, p. 414.

45 Letters in Cotton Cleop. C IV: Harvey, 'Martin V and the English', pp. 77–8; MS, ff. 158–8v for this.

47 Harriss, *Beaufort*, Chapter 7; Griffiths, *Henry VI*, pp. 73–81; MS Cotton Cleop. C IV, f. 159.

48 *PPC*, III, pp. 180–1 council plan for bishoprics, with Cotton Cleop. C IV, ff. 167–7v, Kemp to Swan. Consistory decision: ASV, Acta Misc. I, f. 162v.

49 Albizzi, II, pp. 490, 493–4, 515. Speeches: E. Brown, ed., *Fasciculi rerum expetendarum*, 2 vols., London, 1690, I, pp. x–xxi, from Oxford, Bodleian Library, Ashmole MS 789, ff. 243–52v, probably de la Pole's own copy; Koeppen, *Die Berichte*, no. 251 and note 12; no. 298.

50 Sulbury: above, note 30. Ourscamp: add also C. T. Allmand, 'The relations', p. 196; N. Valois, *La Crise religieuse du XVe Siècle: Le Pape et le Concile, 1418–50*, 2 vols., Paris, 1909, I, p, 85 note 1; BN, MS Nouvelles Acqu. Fr. 7626, ff. 473–4. Circulation of speeches: Harvey, 'Martin V and the English', p. 78, note 124. To MSS there add Württembergische Landesbibliothek, Stuttgart, Cod. Poet. et Phil. 4° 31, ff. 260–71, Ourcamp to pope and cardinals. See also below, pp. 222–3.

51 Vaughan, above, note 13, for progress of struggle.

52 Devillers, *Cartulaire*, IV, pp. 539–41.

53 Harvey, 'The benefice', p. 167; Fink, 'Breven', no. 213; Harriss, *Beaufort*, pp. 155–6.

54 *CPL*, VII, pp. 16, 34; Raynaldus, *Annales*, IX, p. 44; Fink, 'Breven', no. 221; ASV, IE, 383, f. 78; 385, f. 129v. Cesarini: Poggio Bracciolini, *Opera Omnia*, ed. R. Fubini, Turin, 1964 reprint, II, pp. 728–9. Martin's reaction: *CPL*, VII, p. 36; D. Wilkins, *Concilia Magnae Britanniae et Hiberniae*, 4 vols., London, 1737, III, p. 479; MS Ashmole 789, f. 207.

55 Davies, 'Martin V', pp. 339–40, 342. Letters in Ashmole 789 and Library of the Inner Temple, MS Petyt 538 no. 55, also used by E. F. Jacob, Chichele, *Register*, I, pp. xlv–xlvii. I must thank the librarian of the Inner Temple for allowing me to use this MS.

56 Wilkins, *Concilia*, III, pp. 483–4 from Ashmole MS 789, ff. 209–9v and Petyt, ff. 97–7v, notarised account of Chichele's address.

57 Kemp and Chichele about outcome: Cotton Cleop. C IV, ff. 169–9v, 174–4v; also Stafford: ff. 173v–4. See also G. Holmes, 'Cardinal Beaufort and the crusade against the Hussites', *EHR*, LXXXVIII, 1973, pp. 721–50, esp. p. 732, note 1.

58 Embassy: PRO, E404/44/328, 340; E404/48/312; E364/65, m. 9; Cotton Cleop. C IV, ff. 162–3, 163–3v, 198–9; Rymer, IV/4, p. 140 (X, 405); *PPC*, III, pp. 301, 311.

59 Bekynton, *Correspondence*, II, p. 251.

60 Holmes, 'Cardinal Beaufort', p. 732; Harriss, *Beaufort*, pp. 173, 175–8, 182, interprets differently.

61 Chichele, *Register*, I, pp. xlvi–xlvii; *CPL*, VIII, pp. 64–5; Oxford, Bodleian Library, MS Tanner 165, f. 69.

62 Holmes, p. 742; Harriss, *Beaufort*, pp. 184–5.

63 PRO, E404/45/148; *PPC*, III, pp. 330, 339, 437.

64 Rymer, IV/4, p. 150 (X, 433); Griffiths, *Henry VI*, pp. 81–3; *CPL*, VIII, p. 114; Anstey, *Epistolae Academicae*, I, pp. 50–1, no. 46; ASV, Arm. XXXIX 5, ff. 302v–3v.

65 Vaughan, p. 21; C. A. J. Armstrong, 'La double monarchie et la Maison de Bourgogne 1420–1435: le declin d'un alliance', *Annales de Bourgogne*, XXXVII, 1965, pp. 81–112, especially pp. 104–12; also in idem, *England, France and Burgundy in the Fifteenth Century*, London, 1983, pp. 343–74; Harriss, *Beaufort*, p. 188; Beaucourt, II, pp. 412–13; Stevenson, II/ii, pp. 126–7.

66 *PPC*, IV, pp. 12–15; PRO, E404/46/170.

67 Cotton Cleop. C IV, ff. 222–3, 221v–2 to Beaufort, ff. 225v, 226–7. PRO, E404/46/172, to Billesdon; cf. Harriss, p. 188 disagrees.

68 Beaucourt, II, p. 438; Töth, II, p. 200.

9

Anglo-papal relations 1431–47

It is particularly difficult to write a history of Anglo-papal relations during the reign of Eugenius IV because, whereas the council of Basel is very well documented, the history of the papacy, and particularly of the curia, is not.[1] Yet there was more to the relationship than English participation or non-participation in the council, important though that was. England never withdrew obedience from Rome and so the relationship continued, though sometimes with great strain; curia and England continued to seek each other's help.

There were three main themes in papal policy concerning England: the council, the papal peace initiative and an area including these but with other aspects: papal assertions of jurisdiction, largely concerning benefices, of course, but also including taxation. These cannot be disentangled; they influenced one another. The English desired to avert a clash between pope and council. There seem to have been few 'root and branch' conciliarists, though several supporters of the superiority of general councils over popes.[2] There existed also determination to keep the statutes against provisors and desire to use papal mediation in the war with France, without, however, making permanent peace.

Eugenius was elected on 3 and crowned on 11 March 1431. Robert FitzHugh, resident royal proctor, in April was made bishop of London by provision, to be consecrated in Italy in August.[3] He must have witnessed, as did William Swan, the very tense change-over to the new regime.[4] 'Un grand conte d'Inghilterra', probably a knight of St John, was one of the guardians of the conclave.[5] Perhaps because of the unusual tension, a copy of the election capitulation, claiming a great deal of power for the cardinals, was sent to England.[6] William Swan's collection includes letters about the unrest in Rome after Martin's death,[7] and about the Colonna revolt, when Martin's nephews seriously disrupted civic order in their desire to keep their former power, with the immediate effect in England that Chichele had an excuse to deprive Prospero

Colonna of the archdeaconry of Canterbury.[8]

Swan, probably acting for Chichele, was entrusted with a letter of congratulation for the new pope.[9]

Eugenius's early actions made signals about policy. He confirmed Juliano Cesarini as president of the newly summoned council at Basel, thus indicating that he was intending to observe *Frequens*,[10] and, at the end of April, 1431, confirmed Albergati's position as nuncio with power of legate to treat for peace between England, France and Burgundy.[11]

The peace must have been most important to the English. Reappointment of Albergati came when Burgundy, suffering serious reverses, was calling for more English help.[12] In May 1431, before Bedford and some others of the council joined Henry VI in France for his coronation, there was discussion as to how Albergati was to be received.[13] Ominously, the group rejected a lasting peace before Henry's majority, considering a truce the best that could be hoped for. Troyes had forbidden any treaty without consent of the estates of France and England.[14] What if a truce was unacceptable to the French estates? The conclusion in the council was that any papal legate was to be welcomed and heard and a reasonable truce accepted, unless some way of successfully prosecuting the war could be found. A Burgundian embassy, with Philip's plea that without England's aid the war would be lost, must have been in England when these conclusions were reached; the members were absent from 20 April until 14 May.[15] Concurrently Philip sent ambassadors to the king at Rouen with similar complaints, discussed when Beaufort joined the king in mid-May.[16]

Albergati set out in early July 1431,[17] travelling via Savoy, to whose Duke he had letters of introduction,[18] and reached Charles VII at the end of September. He became party to lengthy discussions already under way since April; by 8 September Philip and Charles VII concluded a three-year truce for Burgundy and Champagne, followed by, on 21 September, a limited truce for the Bourbonnais area.[19] Charles and Philip had already agreed to discuss peace and on 1 October Charles, referring to Albergati's mission, named ambassadors to discuss either a general truce or a general peace with Burgundy, to include England if she agreed.[20]

Albergati then went on to meet Henry VI. A discussion in the English council, involving Bedford and Beaufort, resulted in a statement that the English were ready to accept 'all amicable, reasonable and honest' means to peace, having also taken counsel of Burgundy as Troyes required. Representatives then discussed a truce with Albergati, which the English said they were ready to accept, provided Burgundy agreed. 'De nos queles responses il se est monstre estre tres content et joyeux.' Albergati intended to proceed to Burgundy, calling on Charles VII either before or after.[21] Some of his entourage may have gone to England.[22]

At the same time the English were defending themselves in Rome. In late 1431 and early 1432 Charles VII had an impressive embassy there, headed by the archbishop of Tours.[23] One of the group, Jean Juvenal des Ursins, later recalled that when the archbishop defended Charles against Troyes, citing Digest 2.24.1.42 – 'a son, therefore an heir' (*Filius ergo heres*) – the bishop of London, proctor of the king of England (i.e. FitzHugh) replied with 'I deny that' (*Ego nego*) and supported himself by citing Troyes. But the pope replied 'Be silent. Would that there were a good peace between our son Charles, the Christian king of France, and your king.' Des Ursins understood that Eugenius thought the treaty 'wicked and unreasonable' (*inique et deraissonable*).[24]

The anecdote rings true. In 1443, Piero da Monte, trying to persuade Charles VII not to support a potentially anti-papal third general council, recalled the many benefits conferred on the king by the pope: that Eugenius had never consented to his adversary but always tried to persuade the English to remain content with England. Despite the pope's notorious poverty, said da Monte, he kept Albergati almost three years in France, at very great expense.[25] The last was certainly true: Albergati was paid regularly for a very costly mission.[26]

While French and English argued in Rome, Albergati went to Flanders for an impressive reception in Lille in November.[27] The result was a six-year general truce signed on 13 December between France and Burgundy, in which Burgundy formally saved the obligation to supply Bedford with troops, but of course had not notified Henry VI beforehand nor even attended his coronation.[28]

Albergati, ill on his return journey to Henry VI, communicated by letter, carried by his auditor the prior of St Innocent in late November or early December 1431.[29] To this Henry VI replied on 3 December,[30] to fix time and date for final peace talks. Henry knew that Burgundy had agreed, and declared: 'We always were, are and will be prepared for all friendly, reasonable and honest means of peace', accepting between 1 and 8 March next, in the region of Cambrai. Meanwhile however he would not desist from fighting. On 25 December he repeated this for Burgundy, adding that the prior had been told of other venues if Cambrai would not do and also informing the duke that Cesarini and Basel had now urged him to send a notable embassy to the council 'which we have decided to do' (*ce qua avons conclu de faire*), and suggesting that Burgundians and Anglo-French should co-operate at the council. The invitation must have come in the bull *In ecclesia Dei* of 24 September, seeking English participation in Basel.[31]

Meanwhile Philip, having warned Henry on 12 December that a truce was imminent for lack of aid,[32] finally on 29 December informed him of the six-year truce.[33]

On 14 December Albergati travelled to spend Christmas in Dijon and thence to meet Charles VII.[34] Philip was in secret communication with him in January[35] and from Chinon on 23 January the cardinal wrote to the pope.[36]

By then Eugenius IV was quarrelling seriously with Basel and trying to disband it. This tension probably prompted the pope to try to persuade both Beaufort and John Kemp to come to the curia at this point.[37] The quarrel of Basel with the pope diverted both parties' attention from peace-making, leaving Albergati to struggle on.

An English report to the parlement of Paris, on 31 March 1432, explains what happened to the peace conference.[38] Charles VII refused to accept Cambrai as a meeting-place but offered alternatives. On 25 February, perhaps in a personal interview with Albergati, whose arrival he seems to have been awaiting on 20 February,[39] Bedford offered to send delegates to Corbeil on 1 May, if the French would assemble at Melun, with Albergati at Brie Comte Robert. Failing that, he offered an alternative. But neither proved acceptable and Bedford came in person to Corbeil, where on 31 March Albergati also seems to have been, to offer alternatives, with details of the security needed. Bedford specifically asked Albergati not to treat separately with the adversary.

By mid-March 1432 Burgundy had decided to send delegates to Basel and encouraged Henry VI to hear the delegation coming from the council and to send an embassy.[40] Albergati was at Melun on about 2 April, presumably anticipating the changed venue of the peace congress.[41] On 7 April Philip told Basel that he was keeping their representatives whilst he awaited the French 'from day to day' (*de die ad diem*).[42] They must have arrived soon afterwards, perhaps next day, and Albergati also arrived.[43] The outcome was the suggestion that all parties would meet in Auxerre on 8 July.[44]

Philip's proxy for this meeting, dated 8 May, was accompanied by very enlightening instructions.[45] His ambassadors were to hear what the French and English had to say about a general peace, but, very significantly, the delegates were to support the right of the English allies to the crown of France only as founded on 'the final treaty of peace' (*traité de la paix finale*) i.e. Troyes, but not 'the old English quarrel' (*l'ancienne querele dangleterre*). They were to hear the French statement about the murder of Philip's father and accept a general peace only if satisfactory both on the murder and on the crown. If the English did not come to Auxerre Philip still wanted his representatives to listen to Albergati and work towards a general peace. He was willing, if this meeting failed, to try for another at Basel or elsewhere.

In short: very limited support for England's claims and very evident desire for a general peace.

This was the background to the reception in England both of delegates from the council of Basel[46] and of the pope's representative, Petrus de Mera, who was in England by 2 July 1432, a precursor having been arrested on the way.[47] Divisions among the cardinals concerning the correct attitude to Basel and the desperate situation in Rome are referred to in letters in William Swan's collection, which shows close following of the movements of the emperor, who was, of course, trying to mediate.[48] Andrew Holes seems to have journeyed to England early in 1432, returning in early May. English sources contain the pope's letter to the emperor on the former's dissolution of Basel, and Sigismund's reply, with his *Avisamenta*, whilst Cesarini's opinions, unfavourable to the pope, were certainly known.[49] On 10 May, from Rome, Swan explained how Basel was pressing *curiales* to join it,[50] and, albeit very briefly, he listened, though Holes of course did not.[51]

Eugenius's representative in England, de Mera, a Fleming, was the leading 'German' in the curia, a rota auditor and *curialis* of long standing.[52] No doubt he brought Eugenius's defence, certainly received by the archbishops and Bedford.[53] De Mera was carefully chosen to ensure a sympathetic hearing, yet his reception was evidently somewhat cool. To the pope on 2 July Henry VI said he was keeping Petrus until he heard the ambassadors of Basel, but he lamented the dissolution of the council and asked the pope to think again, though saying that he would support the pope's projected new council if this plan did not succeed. As a result of the pleas of the ambassadors of Basel, proctors were organised for the council; there was no boycott as the pope requested.[54]

Dr Schofield considered that pursuit of heresy and, less importantly, desire to march with the emperor, induced the English to attend Basel.[55] Swan's letter book certainly shows close observation of the emperor's views, but in any case the role of Basel as a venue for peace-making meant that the English could not ignore it once Burgundy had sent delegates.

Furthermore, even officially the government did not wholly approve of Eugenius's behaviour.

On 3 September 1432, FitzHugh, the royal proctor, was returning home prior to being sent to Basel,[56] so the situation in Rome must have become known in England. The ultimatum from the council, issued on 18 December, giving the pope sixty days to rescind his dissolution or face suspension, was certainly soon known there.[57]

An English delegation left for Basel whilst the peace negotiations limped. We know about the latter largely from a letter from Albergati to Philip of Burgundy on 15 December 1432.[58] Albergati had gone to Semur on his way to Auxerre and there fell ill. On 15 June Philip told his chancellor that he and Albergati had notified Henry VI of the meeting and knew that the English intended to come.[59] They informed Philip that they wanted a limited general truce. Long delays occurred, over the English safe-conducts and the inevitably slow arrival of delegates.[60] Finally on 27 November the French arrived and at once began to make difficulties. Before that, however, in August, a preliminary discussion had been held in Semur between the French and the Burgundians, after which Philip's representatives sought advice.[61] Albergati had listened to what the French and Burgundians had to say in Semur and advised that if the English did not arrive by 30 September a separate peace should be made without them. The Burgundians had no power for this. They believed, however, that Albergati favoured it, for which he had 'express and special commission' (*expresse et especialle commission*) from the pope. But they believed also that Charles VII was not serious, but intent merely on dividing Burgundy and England.

Philip told his representatives to stay for the Auxerre meeting and try for a general peace, since a separate peace was not expedient.[62] If safe-conducts could not be obtained he wanted a further meeting, if necessary at Basel. Above all, he wanted Albergati convinced that he was doing all in his power for peace.

When the French finally reached Auxerre, about 27 November,[63] they immediately asked that 'the kingdom of France would freely and in peace be given over to their lord as due by hereditary right'. Not surprisingly the English said that this touched the royal majesty 'as devolved by hereditary right' (*tamquam jure hereditario devolutum*), but secretly the French told Albergati that they wanted the duke of Orleans and other hostages held in England present at the negotiations. The English, with no orders about the hostages, but considering that the request might be reasonable, said they needed to report back and meanwhile suggested a general truce. The French refused. So Albergati fixed a further meeting for 21 March, with hostages present, somewhere between Corbeil and Melun.

Meanwhile the English government had had a plan to send delegates to the curia, headed by Archbishop Kemp. This had been first mooted at Canterbury convocation in September 1432, which had thought that some delegates to Basel should go first to the curia[64] and the plan persisted in the first quarter of 1433.[65] Some did in fact go to the curia, for instance the subprior of Canterbury, John Salisbury, who also went to Basel, acting as go-between for Thomas Polton at Basel and William Swan, now back in Rome,[66] but the majority did not.

Various developments altered the plans. On 27 February 1433, Eugenius sent his serjeant-at-arms, John Ely, 'with bulls of the celebration of the council' (*cum bullis celebracionis concilii*),[67] probably the sheaf of letters to Kemp and others dated 16 February, explaining that he no longer intended to move Basel.[68] Though Eugenius had yet again forbidden *curiales* to leave, they continued to go.[69] The total disarray in Rome must have been reported by Ely and the refusal of the council to accept the pope's terms became known too.[70] English reaction was far from favourable to Eugenius.

On 7 July 1433, if not before, in the presence of probably all the cardinals still in Rome, Andrew Holes, the nearest to an English royal representative left in Rome, preached a sermon notably backing the viewpoint of the cardinals who wanted the pope whole-heartedly to accept Basel.[71] We do not know how well informed Holes was about the attitude of the government, but on 2 June Kemp had written to Eugenius and the cardinals lamenting that it now appeared that Eugenius, far from accepting Basel, was failing to get on with it and begging him, in tones of devotion, to behave humbly.[72]

Kemp had not come to the curia because he had become involved in the peace plans. The projected meeting in spring 1433 had taken place at Seine Porte; discussions lasted many days.[73] By 10 April Albergati's auditor told Chancellor Rolin of Burgundy that the English were prepared only to bring the hostages to Dover, whereas the French wanted them at Rouen. Finally it was agreed that they would be brought to Calais and the meeting would occur nearby. Albergati 'taking it badly' (*egre ferens*) decided to interview Charles VII yet again, but was gloomy.[74]

In August Henry VI reminded Burgundy that Bedford had met Albergati in Corbeil. The English regarded the French replies as 'frivolous and useless' (*frivoles et inutiles*)[75] and presumably it was then that Louis of Luxembourg, chancellor of English France, refused to sign draft peace terms presented by Albergati.[76]

As a result of these discussions the English council met its Anglo-French counterpart in Calais in May 1433.[77] Copies of past truces between England and France were prepared[78] and on 19 May Albergati was expected in a few days. The hostages were at Dover. A conference had been arranged at St Omer to settle any differences between Burgundy and Bedford, with Beaufort the mediator; Gloucester entrusted to Beaufort and Bedford settlement of outstanding differences between himself and Burgundy. On 19 May Kemp and Hungerford were awaiting instructions to take or send to Basel, but the royal council thought that the English parliament must first be consulted. The instructions therefore must have concerned peace.[79]

In the end Albergati merely brought Charles VII's offer of a four-month truce without an offer to speak with the hostages, which seemed to Henry VI merely a way of preparing more hostilities.[80] The true result of the Calais meeting was to re-charge the English campaign in France with money from Beaufort, who was readmitted to the English council.[81] Not unnaturally Kemp did not leave for the curia nor Beaufort for Basel; that neither would go was clear by 20 July.[82]

Meanwhile Burgundy was pressing Henry VI for either a general peace, a general truce or more adequate men and money.[83] On 7 July, pleading his own great expenses, Henry offered to consult parliament, as well as arranging for it to discuss Albergati's latest suggestions. If the dauphin refused a general peace or a truce of at least a year he would defend his crown and lordship of France. Meanwhile he would not believe malicious rumours of the noble and honourable duke.

Burgundy's envoys, however, prepared a tripartite report, concerning Henry's reply, their own interview with Orleans and general comments.[84] They noticed that there were already people in England favouring a general peace to be accompanied by marriage between Henry VI and a daughter of Charles VII. Much evidently depended on parliament's willingness to finance further hostilities. Warwick told them that Philip's failure to visit when Henry was in France had been unfriendly;[85] the ambassadors countered by complaining of ill-will in England.

On the way home the ambassadors met in Calais a gentleman who had been with Charles VII. He told them that the way to a general peace was the release of Orleans 'in such a way that the English do not have the crown for he [the dauphin] must not hear a word of that . . .' They assured Burgundy that Bedford was his advocate.

During these negotiations Albergati's whereabouts are unknown, though in July he was at Chappes,[86] perhaps near Troyes, and that month wrote to Basel in despair; there was no hope of peace because both sides were assembled for war.[87]

By 14 August 1433 the English had arranged for Orleans to summon a convention for 15 October in Normandy or elsewhere, and Henry asked Burgundy to attend.[88] But Albergati had given up. On 9 September he re-entered Basel and on 16 reported complete lack of progress.[89]

The meeting in Normandy did not occur, though Philip summoned a delegate from Basel for it and treated it seriously. Either the French were waiting to see how the Burgundians fared in the field or trying still to lure them into separate negotiations.[90]

Consequently the centre of interest in the peace process moved to Basel and the curia. In Basel the English had fallen foul of the council over incorporation and the failure to establish voting by nations, which would have allowed them considerable power. On 14 August Henry ordered his ambassadors to withdraw to Cologne to await the resolution of the incorporation problem.[91] Before that order arrived, Henry's letter (written on 17 July) rebuking the council for its violent language against the pope and protesting about the oath of incorporation had been read out (17 August).[92] This, calling Henry king of France, provoked French protests[93] and Burgundian replies. When Philip in October sent a new, much larger, delegation he objected strongly to the cries of 'Burgundian traitors' which had greeted his delegates' objections.

Philip's new delegates brought new instructions.[94] He desired peace by 'reasonable ways and means' but the meetings with Albergati had not produced this, though Burgundy's six-year truce had been intended as preliminary to a general peace. His ambassadors were to ask the council to send Albergati and one other cardinal to work with the duke of Savoy for a general peace. They were also to work with the Savoyards to remove the processes against the pope.

In June the English co-operated with the rest to delay the council's actions against Eugenius; on 10 August he wrote to Henry praising English resistance to his suspension.[95] But the English no longer counted for much in Basel. Philip's delegates reported acting with the Savoyards and Albergati on the matter, though noting that Henry's letter placed him on their side.[96] The full representation from Savoy, expected to help in peace talks, arrived only on 29 September and only on 2

October did Albergati and Rochetaillée obtain them a hearing to plead for peace.[97] The archbishop of Tours, for France, publicly welcomed this initiative and Cardinal Castiglione, president of the session, was also delighted. It remained for those at Basel to make concrete progress.

The Emperor Sigismund reached the council on 11 October. By then many English had withdrawn as ordered by the government,[98] but the prior of Norwich remained to welcome him on 12 October in their name and beg him to help reconcile pope and council and organise the council by nations.[99] English were among those (including Burgundians, Savoyards and Venetians) who worked with Sigismund to present a formula on 13 October to gain more time for the pope.[100]

While the council concentrated more on its quarrel with the pope than on peace-making, a further local attempt at self-help occurred in France. In February 1434 the French were yet again sounding the Burgundians about a separate peace,[101] and Philip, at a family wedding, had been approached by the duke of Savoy with offers to mediate,[102] after which he sent yet more ambassadors to England.[103] A Breton group, also in England, offered mediation.[104]

Henry's reply to the Burgundians on 11 June 1434 shows that there were still hopes for a meeting in Calais, but he added that prompted by emperor and council he had now sent a further embassy to Basel 'instructed, among other things, on the said matter of peace' (*instruits entre autre choses en la dicte matiere de paix*), and asking for co-operation between the two delegations, especially in defending Henry's right to the French crown, which Philip had warned him the French intended to attack at Basel.[105] Tentative moves for conveying Orleans to Calais continued.[106] The council had sent an embassy to Henry in October 1433 and he had promised a further delegation.[107] Convocation discussed this in November and December,[108] and agreed to send delegates, though the clergy were less enthusiastic than the government, for which, of course, peace talks were more important.[109]

Relations with Eugenius IV, however, were not at all good in late 1433 and early 1434. On 31 August 1433 Thomas Polton died at Basel. On 24 September, surely the earliest that Eugenius could have heard, he told Henry that he had provided Thomas Brouns, who had failed to obtain Chichester in Martin V's time because Martin had been determined on Simon Sydenham.[110] Brouns was at Basel[111] but the appointment was unwelcome to the royal council, particularly to Beaufort, and on 22 November a letter to the curia commended Thomas Bourgchier, twenty-three-year-old half-brother of Humfrey, earl of Stafford,

Beaufort's brother-in-law.[112] In the curia Andrew Holes must have had the thankless task of presenting the royal wishes. Eugenius refused to rescind but promised Bourgchier the next vacancy,[113] between 15 and 30 April 1434 writing numerous letters pointing out that Bourgchier was under age, castigating the Worcester chapter for electing him, and alleging the prohibitions of Constance against under-age elections.[114]

His determination is shown by his reaction to the vacancy of the archdeaconry of Northampton, on the death of Cardinal Ardicino della Porta.[115] On 16 May the bishop of Lincoln, William Gray, appointed his nephew William, though Eugenius had already conferred it, as vacant in curia, on Holes.[116] The bishop had led the embassy which in 1429 promised Martin V that the government would exempt such benefices from the statutes. Eugenius asserted that he would allow no one to fill benefices vacant by the death of a cardinal,[117] but of course was in no position to insist. Rome was wracked by civic unrest; on 4 June 1434 he had to flee. He was followed shortly afterwards by Andrew Holes and eventually reconstituted a much depleted curia in Florence. On 7 August he sent John Ely again to England, probably to explain the changed situation, though also to convey further protests about the still-vacant see of Worcester.[118]

Meanwhile however the second English delegation had reached Basel, where Brouns remained, and rapidly became embroiled not in peace talks but in quarrels over the English title to be a nation.[119]

The gordian knot of Worcester was finally untied by the death, on 30 September in Basel, of John Langdon, bishop of Rochester.[120] As soon as the news was known in England, on 26 October, the king told Holes in the curia that no one was to be provided to Rochester until he had made a decision,[121] protested to the pope again about Worcester[122] and forbidden Brouns, if tempted, to accept provision to Worcester.[123] Then, on 14 November, the royal council asked Eugenius to give Rochester to Brouns.[124] The message went with Adam Moleyns, a Beaufort man, who by 23 March the following year had persuaded Eugenius to accept. The pope exhorted Bourgchier, who got Worcester, to justify the honour done to one so young.[125]

But Eugenius was not prepared to yield meekly, so he promptly declared Bourgchier's benefices vacant in curia and conferred them on various *curiales*. In March 1435, returning Moleyns, upon whom he had conferred Bourgchier's prebend of Colwich in Lichfield, Eugenius exhorted Beaufort to work for the liberty of the church.[126] Henry received a long letter about reserved benefices and liberty of the church, menaced by the statutes, with a copy to the royal council.[127] Most of the provisions were fruitless. John River, BCL a lawyer *curiam sequens*, received on 12 March Bourgchier's prebend of Wells, but on 8 May the ordinary, John Stafford, conferred it on Richard Petworth, Humfrey's secretary.[128] Petworth received Bourgchier's prebend in York but almost certainly did not obtain it,[129] any more than Moleyns obtained Colwich.[130] At the same time Eugenius asked Kemp to help obtain the prebend of Laughton in York for an English *curialis*, Thomas Chapman, litigating with Prospero Colonna, but he failed too.[131] From all the benefices vacated by these promotions only one successful provision resulted. Robert Sutton, a *curialis* of long standing, obtained, though technically by collation, the prebend of Langford Manor in Lincoln, vacant by Broun's promotion.[132] Even Holes did not obtain his archdeaconry.

Tension between England and the pope in late 1434 and early 1435 was unwise because peace negotiations were about to recommence. The second English embassy to Basel was empowered to deal with peace.[133] The embassy was ordered to emphasise the king's co-operation with Albergati, to blame the failure hitherto on the French, but to say that, out of reverence for the council, the ambassadors were empowered to listen to what the council might offer and themselves offer acceptance of neutral arbitrators in a neutral spot, not too far off, where princes of the blood from both sides might attend. They were also to ask the emperor, or some other neutral party, to negotiate a truce of some years. Langdon, who died shortly after arrival, had special instructions about a truce. On all these matters the envoys were to co-operate with the embassies from Lancastrian France, Burgundy and Brittany.[134]

Some of these suggestions were hardly serious. It was, for instance, unlikely that the emperor could have any standing in the matter. Sigismund had meanwhile allied with France against Burgundy in a local quarrel about Austria[135] and this no doubt explains why an English envoy, John Stokes, was with him between 12 July and 17 November 1434.[136]

But England's inability to produce peace terms acceptable to the Burgundians ensured that by autumn 1434 various separate truces began to be made in the Franco-Burgundian theatres of war[137] and in December a French embassy approached Philip, who assembled a formidable group to meet the French at Nevers in January 1435, to lay the basis for the congress of Arras.[138] At Nevers it was decided that Charles VII would offer 'honest' peace to Henry VI and would deal separately with Burgundy if Henry refused the terms. A congress was to meet at Arras on 1 July presided over jointly by conciliar and papal representatives.[139]

In December 1434 Philip empowered his embassy at Basel to deal with peace,[140] so some of the negotiations before Arras were conducted by the English and Burgundians at Basel. Philip's messenger to England after Nevers fell ill, so his announcement of the meeting did not reach England until 8 May.[141] But Philip had also written to the English at Basel, about 22 February, and there seems to have been a French suggestion that some English at Basel might attend Arras.[142] Though the English delegates at Basel said their powers were insufficient to discuss peace terms, they too wrote to England.[143] On 23 April Eugenius IV empowered Albergati to go to Arras as his representative;[144] John Ely came to England on 30 April with papal notification and on 20 June the king wrote to Eugenius accepting, saying he had also informed Basel and the emperor.[145] Thus began the meeting which led to the outmanoeuvring of the English by the French and the beginning of the end of English dreams of French conquest.[146]

Thus the history of Anglo-papal relations in the period 1431-5 was dominated by peace negotiations. After Arras the English bitterly blamed Albergati, but they trusted him till then. There is little evidence before this date that they championed the papacy against the council; apart from anything else the council was too useful as a venue for peace talks to be abandoned. Nor is there much evidence that attitudes to the papacy were any less pragmatic than under Martin V. When Eugenius was at his weakest the government still refused to grant requests for provisions. And Kemp's role as a negotiator overrode his duty to the pope.

After Arras

The aftermath of the congress of Arras was a very new world. Already early in 1435 Eugenius IV must have been conscious that Anglo-papal relations were strained. When a new collector, Piero da Monte, was appointed on 21 April, with the usual wide powers,[147] his own view of his task was that he must uphold and defend the authority of the apostolic see; despite the pope's chronic shortage of money, collecting was not the main task.[148]

In the second half of 1435 much toing and froing to the Curia by Adam Moleyns and John Ely was almost certainly connected with

Arras.[149] From Florence on 16 July the pope told Henry that Moleyns with Andrew Holes and the bishop of Amiens had presented royal letters; Henry was assured that no French princes had been released from their oaths (i.e. the oath taken by Burgundy to observe Troyes), but was urged to talk peace,[150] a letter Henry later used against the Burgundians. On 7 September, the day after Beaufort left Arras,[151] the final French offer went to England,[152] accompanied by requests from the cardinal of Cyprus, representing Basel,[153] and from Philip,[154] that Henry would accept. On 26 October Henry told Basel that he would consider these requests,[155] but he circulated copies of Eugenius's letter of 16 July, in a document denouncing Burgundy.[156]

Yet Eugenius was not blamed, though his representative was. This may indicate how at this time Basel was the centre of affairs, with the pope very much on the sidelines.

Arras left the English very vulnerable to criticism and attack. They needed to justify their refusal to accept the terms and to acquire allies against Burgundy, who had to justify her change of heart by a show of hostility against former friends.

In later December Moleyns left for Basel and the curia[157] with Henry's letter denouncing Burgundy.[158] At the same time to the emperor, the archbishop of Cologne, the bishop of Liége, the duke of Guelders and the count of Mörs went master Stephen Wilton and Sir Robert Clifton,[159] to gain support against the now-hostile Burgundy, especially from the Rhine princes. The memories of Aeneas Sylvius show that Albergati was thoroughly hated in England for his supposed bias at the peace conference.[160] If, as seems probable, Aeneas's Scottish journey just after Arras, when he experienced this hostility, had as one aim inciting the Scots to a diversionary attack on England, the English were right.[161]

The aftermath of Arras was indeed highly dangerous for England. The messengers to the emperor, captured by Burgundy, were imprisoned for two years.[162] In April 1436 English letters for the emperor, pope and others, captured by Burgundian sailors, were delivered to Philip.[163] Messengers continued to go to and fro from the emperor and presumably the pope, but routes were precarious in 1436 and 1437.[164]

By 4 March 1437 ambassadors of the archbishop of Cologne were in London negotiating an alliance and oath of vassalage, in return for a pension. Cologne was to be the centre of a system of alliances against France and Burgundy on the Rhine.

Attempts to please the pope were also made. When Moleyns went to the council and curia in December 1435,[165] taking the letter of Henry VI mentioned above, he carried privy seal letters allowing Piero Barbo, the pope's nephew, to hold English benefices worth 1200 ducats.[166] For Basel Moleyns must have taken Henry VI's letters read out there on 7 January 1436,[167] denouncing the council. By then of course the English no longer had official representatives at Basel, though the government maintained contact with Jean Beaupère, Simon of Teramo, the former collector, and Stefano of Novara, relative of Ardicino della Porta, who was even allowed benefices.[168]

Church unity must have been part of the exchanges with the Germans and the council, as well as with the pope, though we have little evidence of Anglo-papal contacts in 1436.[169] The king's coming-of-age made a difference. Now Henry himself controlled policy, intervening much more personally from 1437. One result was probably the formal recognition of Andrew Holes as royal proctor on 27 February 1437.[170]

One purpose of Holes's appointment must have been to have a properly accredited agent, the better to oversee appointments to bishoprics, which continued to cause problems.

On 25 October 1435 Philip Morgan, bishop of Ely, died and Robert FitzHugh, though elected, then died before he could take office. Royal support then went to Thomas Rudbourne, probably Beaufort's candidate,[171] but the chapter wanted Bourgchier, whom they elected in August 1436 and for whom a provision was obtained on 27 August.[172] The pope was willing to translate Rudbourne from St Davids to Worcester, but Henry's government, almost certainly prompted by Beaufort, changed its mind. The chancellor of France, Louis of Luxembourg, archbishop of Rouen, had been left almost penniless after Arras and in April 1437 Henry's government petitioned the pope for Louis to hold Ely *in commendam*, Bourgchier's provision to be annulled. Eugenius resisted.[173] On 22 June Henry repeated his request, with further letters to various cardinals and by September Eugenius had yielded, though Louis had great difficulty in persuading Chichele,[174] who retained old-fashioned prejudices about *commendams*.

Eugenius was still in no position to resist the English government. On 31 July 1437 Basel sent him a *monitorium* giving him sixty days to accept or be deposed. He retaliated on 18 September by transferring the council to Ferrara.[175] This news, with information about the bishoprics, came with John Ely[176] and Roberto de Cavalcantibus, an auditor, legate to England and Scotland, who acted with da Monte.[177] The royal council discussed the *monitorium* on 21 October[178] with da Monte present for some of the discussions.[179] The conclusion, according to him, was to send a royal letter to Basel to denounce the *monitorium* and to the emperor and other allies to solicit support for the pope.[180] The collector suggested to Eugenius that the English be sent a special invitation for his new council of Ferrara, to meet the Greeks coming to discuss church unity. News of the granting of Ely to Louis of Luxembourg came in time for da Monte to tell Henry whilst all this was being discussed.[181]

The English committed themselves to co-operation with the Empire to solve the problem of the council of Basel. The government wished neither to break with the pope, nor with the Empire, particularly not with Cologne. But bitter divisions in the Empire made the policy very difficult, if not impossible. Some reformers also hankered after Basel for reform, if this could be had without schism.[182] In practice foreign policy overrode the claims of the pope; the relationship with Cologne was maintained even when the archbishop had quarrelled with Eugenius. Meanwhile the inconsistencies of German policies about the council made the English look even more uncertain than perhaps they were.

Between 3 and 7 November 1437 the electors, at Frankfurt, tried to arrange a compromise between pope and council.[183] The pope was to accept the major reforming decrees of Basel, with the principle of the supremacy of general councils, whilst Basel returned to organisation by nations and accepted the pope's council to meet the Greeks. There was no hope of either party accepting, but the terms shaped negotiations for the next months.

On 29 November Henry dispatched to the emperor, Basel and the pope, a friar, John O'Heyne, with a sheaf of letters.[184] To Basel Henry expressed abhorrence of the *monitorium* and asked the council to accept Ferrara as a site to meet the Greeks, pointing out that otherwise union with the Greek church would be jeopordised.[185] He included a very strong plea for the right of secular princes to play a role. To the emperor he deprecated the *monitorium*, questioning its legality since the few cardinals still at Basel had not accepted it.[186] Eugenius had then moved the council to Ferrara and the council had retaliated by selecting Avignon, which Eugenius would surely reject. In the circumstances princes had a duty to act; Henry recalled Sigismund's importance at Constance. Henry had begged Eugenius to choose another city and to do nothing further until the secular rulers had been consulted. Much the same went to the elector of Cologne.[187] The letter to Eugenius asked him to try patiently to avoid schism and to select another city,[188] but, whilst it abhored the *monitorium*, it did not express wholehearted support for the pope's sufferings. We are left uncertain whom to blame for the quarrel or what the government intended if the schism became final: probably they had not yet decided.

Sigismund died on 9 December, before O'Heyne left, but although the royal council discussed representation at his funeral and other possiblilities,[189] no further messengers went to Germany[190] until in February the nuncio of the archbishop of Cologne, arriving belatedly after being kidnapped,[191] was sent back with requests for the elector to alert the newly elected emperor to the English desire for alliance. O'Heyne was probably the English *nuncius* present at the electoral diet at Frankfurt in March,[192] where the electors agreed before choosing Albrecht, duke of Austria, as emperor that they would remain neutral at present in the quarrel of Basel with the pope.[193] On 20 March the electors notified Henry VI of this and of their choice of emperor. The messenger probably also brought the elector's reply that the newly elected emperor had been informed of Henry's desire for an alliance, as with Sigismund.[194]

Henry now prepared to send ambassadors to the electors.[195] Information on their stance was coming not only from official sources but also from the papal representative at the diet, Antonio di Altan, bishop of Urbino, writing to da Monte.[196] In late May Roberto di Cavalcantibus returned to the curia, taking messages from da Monte and the English government.[197]

It is usually supposed that the English government was firmly pro-papal by this time, yet in May 1438, when representatives of Basel were again in England to persuade the government to accept their viewpoint in the quarrel with the pope, opinion in the royal council was divided. Da Monte considered the royal council on the pope's side, whereas the representatives of Basel thought there was a strong possibility that support would be for them.[198]

Enigmatic notes from royal council discussions suggest an intention to send messengers both to the emperor and to Basel to enquire their intentions, though to refuse for the moment to take sides in quarrels with the pope. Yet meanwhile the royal council was also preparing to send envoys to the papal council of Ferrara. The intention was solely to support moves for unity with the Greeks.[199] Until the English could ascertain the outcome of the German squabbles they were trying to remain neutral in the struggle between pope and council. Cavalcantibus must have reported this to the curia in late May.

On 30 June Henry urged the newly elected emperor to labour for union with the Greeks in spite of the divisions in the western church.[200]

The letter was delivered by master Thomas Bird, OFM., whose main task was to organise safe-conducts and escorts for a large delegation to the Empire.[201] Discussions with ambassadors of the elector of Cologne still continued.[202]

Relations with the pope were still strained, with provisions causing difficulty. Piero Barbo had permission to hold English benefices but obtained none. He had a provision and da Monte thought a prebend in Lincoln would result, but the ordinary, Bishop Alnwick, refused him possession, fearing the statute and refusing to appoint him directly. Similarly, da Monte's attempts to obtain for Barbo one of William Aiscough's prebends, when Aiscough was promoted to Salisbury in February 1438, failed.[203] And still in July that year Louis of Luxembourg had not obtained possession of Ely.[204]

In July 1438 the English government sent Giovanni Opizzis to talk to the pope, both about prebends for Barbo and about safe-conducts for the English delegation to Ferrara.[205] Eugenius sent Opizzis back with a sheaf of letters intended to solve the problem of the prebends. The Lincoln prebend of Sutton, which Barbo wanted, had still not been conferred because the king wanted it for Bekynton, the royal secretary. A papal *cubicularius*, master Robert Sutton, had recently died at the curia, so the pope now conferred his prebend of Langton in Lincoln on Bekynton,[206] thus asserting the right to reservations as well as satisfying Barbo; there is no evidence that Bekynton obtained it. Eugenius complained bitterly about the statutes and the poor rewards for English *curiales*. Andrew Holes, according to the pope, now alone upheld the honour of England in the curia;[207] the scarcity of Englishmen was not surprising, rewards were so poor. Eugenius offered to share with Henry reserved benefices as a reward for royal servants, if the king would only yield a little.

This was the first time that Eugenius suggested a bargain with the king of England over benefices, of a kind much more common as the council of Basel ended. But the English could do better with their local legislation, and Eugenius needed them more than they needed him. Eugenius's willingness to make the offer is yet another indication that he did not think the loyalty of England certain. There is no evidence of follow-up and Barbo failed.[208] The prebend had already been conferred on another; on 1 October da Monte told Barbo that England was a hopeless place for benefices.[209]

Opizzis's papal letters were delayed because he fell victim to the hostility of Burgundy, being captured on his return journey, to the pope's indignation.[210] But by 12 February 1439 the first payment occurs to an English Carmelite at the papal council in Florence.[211] Finally there was a modest English presence, financed by the pope, but Holes must have been the only official national representative, probably because sending large groups from England had become too dangerous. Interest in the outcome was limited to a few, and once union had been made there was little further concern.[212]

Meanwhile the debate in the Empire had moved on. In March/April 1439, in the presence of representatives of the council of Basel, the princes at the imperial diet at Mainz decided to accept the main reform decrees of the council.[213] While the newly elected Albrecht asked Henry to accept the solution of a new general council,[214] in July representatives of Basel from Mainz met Beaufort at Calais. Probably they brought a request from Basel that Henry and his French subjects should, like the Germans, accept the reforming decrees of the council.[215] Kemp's address to the Baslers was relatively mild, exhorting them to relinquish schism but refusing discussion of the relative positions of pope and council, for which there was a time and place, but admitting that opinions differed.[216] Not a categorical insistence on the papal position; perhaps some sections of clerical opinion still hankered after Basel as a source of reform.

On 16 May 1439 Basel declared councils superior to popes, denying the pope's power to dissolve it,[217] following this on 25 June by deposing Eugenius IV.[218] This, if not conveyed to the Calais meeting, was certainly being publicised by da Monte by 24 July.[219] Though gloomy about possible reactions, da Monte supposed that this extremism might return to the pope even supporters of the superiority of general councils. He pointed out to Nicholas Bildeston, at Calais with Beaufort, whom he knew to be one, that the council had now gone too far.[220] On 30 August Henry rebuked Basel for its attitude to Eugenius, begging it not to elect another pope,[221] and asked the emperor for help, pointing out that the deposition might ruin the newly achieved union with the Greeks.[222] Da Monte in fact wrote this last letter.[223]

Da Monte also of course spread the joyful news of union with the Greeks;[224] multiple copies of the decree were sent to England.[225] On 3 October Henry VI was enthusiastic,[226] but his and others' enthusiasm did not necessarily mean equal support for all Eugenius IV's policies.

By the time da Monte's letter from Henry to the emperor had been delivered Albrecht II was dead.[227] Contact with the electors was maintained through Cologne, whose elector had representatives in London in

October and November.[228] They were certainly discussing the elector's vassalage but must also have considered the church. At a Reichtag in mid-November, when the Empire declared itself neutral between pope and Basel (the council had by now elected an anti-pope), English representatives were present.[229] The ambassador of Cologne finally took the concluded treaty, made on 12 December, with a request for the archbishop to work for the peace of the church.[230]

The election of an anti-pope ended all official English contacts with Basel. The *monitorium* against Felix V from the council of Florence appears in English sources; in spring 1440 representatives of Basel seeking English endorsement of the new pope were rebuffed; on 23 April 1440 England formally refused to accept Felix. Vincent Clement took to the curia Felix's letter to the king and the king's to Eugenius, deeply deploring the appointment.[231] Clement delivered this with a much-admired speech, expressing the devotion of king to pope, returning with a very flattering request for Henry to gather support.[232] Officially, therefore, from the advent of the anti-pope English support for the papacy was unwavering.

There was a difference between enthusiasm for the council of Ferrara, hostility to Felix V and unwavering support for Eugenius IV, however, as can be seen in the government's attitude to Kemp's cardinalate. On 18 December 1439, Kemp was made cardinal, with York *in commendam*, but letters patent allowing him to keep York were not issued until 4 February.[233] There was probably hostility in England and very soon Eugenius also began to make problems for Kemp, whose presence in the curia he very much desired. Eugenius, asserting there were too few Englishmen in his court, requested not, it appears, an *ad limina* (courtesy) visit, but Kemp as a resident curial cardinal.[234] The pope at first refused the cardinal's insignia and the attempt to drive Kemp from England had support from some of the new cardinal's enemies,[235] but by 13 August the pope had relented.[236] The change may have resulted from Kemp's appointment as a government representative at the forthcoming diet of Mainz, scheduled for February 1441,[237] though on 25 December 1440 Henry changed his mind.[238] More probably, however, Eugenius realised that he must support Kemp as a cardinal, against attacks both on him and on Beaufort in England and that, however much he desired curial cardinals, summoning Kemp played into the hands of anti-clericals in England.[239]

Whilst the pope and Kemp argued about his status, events in the Empire had moved on. On 4 February 1440 Frederick III had been elected emperor[240] and Henry sent William Swan and Hartung van Klux to renew his alliance and discuss church unity.[241] Swan turned back at Cologne but Hartung presumably arrived.[242]

In July or August the archbishop of Cologne and Frederick had envoys in England.[243] The known discussions, in a stay lasting ten weeks, concerned the treaty with Cologne, but when the ambassadors left on 2 September, Cologne was told that Henry would do all in his power to further the archbishop's laudable zeal for church unity and would send envoys to wherever a diet was held to discuss this.[244] The ambassadors presumably outlined Cologne's ideas on unity, but these were unclear; the elector supported Basel. Kemp was to attend this diet.

During 1440, whatever the concerns of the government, the papacy impinged on the common people of England chiefly through the preaching of an indulgence to defray the costs of the Greeks in Florence and for defence against the Turks.[245] This was Piero da Monte's chief concern from November 1439. The bulk of the money had come in by mid-June 1440, a little trickling in up to 31 December.[246] The cause was fairly popular; a reasonably large sum was collected, though some critics in convocation questioned the legality of the indulgence, and da Monte noted some anti-papal feeling associated with hostility to papal dispensations for plurality of benefices and connected with the burning of the lollard Richard Wyche.[247] There was little interest in the papal council once unity had been achieved and the indulgence money collected. In October 1440 da Monte left England,[248] and thereafter Henry VI's government concentrated its ecclesiastical concerns on attempting to co-ordinate policy with the Empire and seeking from the pope indulgences and privileges for Eton and King's Colleges, spending a great deal of effort and money, as we have seen.

The emperor was committed to a diet to discuss unity of the church in November 1440. Before the envoys sent in the summer reached Germany, the emperor had again written to Henry[249] and probably in connection with this, a message about church unity, the esquire Edward Hull went secretly to the emperor and Cologne on 2 December, ordered to follow the lead of Cologne.[250] For the diet, now postponed till January, representatives were preparing to go to the emperor in early December, but seem to have stayed in England.[251] In late December envoys from the archbishop came again for the final stages of the Cologne treaty[252] and early in the new year William Swan set off to return to the curia, with letters to deliver on the way to Cologne and the emperor.[253] The letter of credence for the pope suggests that Swan's task was discussion of the religious question with the Germans.[254]

By the time the treaty with Cologne was signed news must have reached Henry VI that the diet to discuss the Acceptation of Mainz and neutrality in the schism had been rearranged for 6 January 1441.[255] English representatives with Hartung van Klux at Nuremburg in January could be Hull and Swan,[256] but on 30 December Frederick rearranged the meeting for February.[257] By 3 February at the latest the true date was known to Henry VI.[258]

Henry decided to send John Beke and Thomas Bird, a Franciscan. Beke was his envoy also to the emperor, with orders first to accompany Bird to Mainz.[259] Henry's attitude to the substance of the conference – the Acceptation of Mainz and neutrality in the church conflict – is unclear, but England did not stand out as a champion of Eugenius IV. In the Empire England's attitude was still questioned.[260]

The English reached the conference in early April,[261] when the terms for Eugenius's recognition in the Empire, *Avisamenta moguntina*, had already been agreed by all, except the elector of Cologne, still supporting Basel. The electors offered recognition if Eugenius agreed that general councils were superior to popes and gave them substantial privileges. The emperor preferred neutrality, or, if the worst happened, a further general council. When the emperor's representatives and the French suggested meeting to discuss this projected council, the English countered with a document proving the difficulty, or impossibility, of choosing an acceptable site, though not rejecting a new council totally; presumably they might have accepted if Eugenius had agreed and it were not held on French soil.[262] But on 7 April all at Mainz (the English not among the signatories) agreed to a preliminary meeting.[263]

From Mainz Beke went to the emperor in Vienna, arriving in late May.[264] Bird joined him in early June.[265] In early July the emperor, returning Beke, told Henry that he had noted Beke's message about church unity.[266] Beke must have been present in Vienna when Frederick rejected the plan presented by the princes, refusing the *Avisamenta*.[267] He brought safe-conducts for an English delegation to the next diet to discuss church unity.[268]

Preparations to send people, being made in October/November 1441, were probably never completed because it became known that the emperor did not intend to go.[269] Finally the definitive diet was arranged for Frankfurt in June 1442[270] and Henry deputed John Botyll, turcopolier of Rhodes,[271] with John Lowe, bishop of St Asaph, Reginald Boulers, abbot of Gloucester, and Adam Moleyns, the leader,[272] to visit the pope afterwards.

In the diet, from June to August 1442,[273] the English were active from about 8 July.[274] Moleyns's speech, as leader of the group, merited a special reply from Thomas Ebendorfer, a leading Viennese theologian, chief spokesman for the legitimacy of Basel.[275] On 10 July the English explained their refusal to accept a new general council, declaring firm adherence to Eugenius IV.[276] They then left. By 27 July Moleyns was in Rome, organising cardinal 'protectors' for English interests.[277] By 14 August Lowe and Boulers were in England,[278] reporting to the royal council on 21 August.[279] After they left the emperor and the electors agreed to hold a new general council, which the English had resolutely opposed, at least until a neutral meeting-place could be found.[280] To secure support, no doubt, messengers of the emperor were in London in August.[281]

No support was forthcoming. The pope rejected the imperial plan,[282] and continued letters from Aeneas Sylvius, the emperor's secretary, to Moleyns, failed to interest the English government.[283] In the mid-1440s the English government had other interests, but in any case the diet must have convinced it that to be pro-papal was no longer compatible with co-operation with the divided German allies on the church question. Probably the attempt had never had any chance of success. But in the seeming incompatibility of their aims the English were no different from the Germans, whose policies towards the pope and Basel also appear contradictory.

Despite the appearance of complete loyalty to the pope, however, relations with Eugenius could still become very strained. This was all too apparent when in January 1443 he announced an income tax of one-tenth from the clergy for his projected crusade to aid the Greeks, promised at Florence.[284] In England the collection began only when the papal collector, Giovanni di Castiglione, and a papal nuncio, Baptista of Padua, bishop-elect of Concordia, were given the task.[285]

Early in 1445 Baptista had an interview with the king, in which Henry demurred at a papal levy, but, consulting the archbishop of Canterbury and other bishops, agreed that the clergy could make an offering 'from sheer goodwill' (*mera liberalitate*), thinking this might raise 6000 ducats.[286] On 12 March 1445 the bishop of Bath, Thomas Bekynton, the abbot of Gloucester, Boulers, and Vincent Clement, who acted as interpreter, told Baptista the plan. Apparently the intention was to raise the money at once. The nuncio was told that, to raise 6000 ducats, the bishops would publicise indulgences and the king would try to obtain papal help to produce Anglo-French peace. Baptista assured them that the pope had no wish to coerce them and that pope and curia understood their difficulties.[287] The problem was, of course, that money was short for the war with France. In June 1445, after Baptista left, Eugenius replied to the king and the archbishop of Canterbury, Stafford (Clement also wrote) that he had now heard from his envoy, assuming that 6000 ducats had already been collected,[288] though Stafford's register records that Stafford and Clement had written that peace with France was an essential preliminary.[289] Professor Lunt has traced Stafford's attempts to raise the money,[290] which by no means amounted to one-tenth.

Eugenius was dissatisfied. On 24 and 26 June 1446 he wrote to Stafford, giving his understanding that 6000 ducats had been promised by the king, in part payment of one-tenth, with delay granted in its collection. The account of what had happened, however, differs slightly in the two letters.[291] He sent these with Louis of Cordona, to co-operate in the collection with the new collector, Giovanni Opizzis, since the bishops said they were too burdened.[292] Eugenius was quite clear that Henry VI had consented, at least to a levy of 6000 ducats. Somehow the pope had misunderstood.

Louis of Cordona came to the archbishop at Croydon on 25 September 1446; the letters from Eugenius were read in the presence of Vincent Clement and the registrar of Canterbury. The archbishop said that he wished to obey the pope, but the laws of the kingdom stood in the way and royal permission was needed for any such levy, as well as discussion with his fellow bishops. Cordona was asked to wait in London for a reply. The king was informed on 1 October and asked the archbishop to cause the nuncio to wait till the king could see him.[293] Despite Clement's attempts at explanation, Cordona thought he was being fobbed off.

Early on 21 October, at Lambeth, the archbishop consulted Adam Moleyns, now bishop of Chichester, Opizzis, Cordona and Clement, about certain clauses in the papal bulls which seemed inconsistent or misinformed.[294] Meanwhile all the bishops met in London. Next day Cordona, in advance of a meeting already arranged in Moleyns's house, called on Clement to stress that Cordona understood the collection had been agreed; it would be a mortal sin to refuse to pay the tenth, tithes being an obligation under divine law.[295] Not unnaturally Clement was very troubled and, before the group met in Moleyns's house, told Stafford. The latter 'somewhat troubled' (*aliquantulum turbatus*), insisted that only the actual wording of the bulls was for discussion. After much coming and going, with much discussion of the events of 1445 described by the pope, the meeting in Moleyns's house was cancelled.

On 11 November Cordona finally came before the king, privately, at Westminster, to present the Golden Rose, a great compliment, with a papal letter thanking him for the tenth.[296] After flowery speeches, Cordona renewed the request for one-tenth. On behalf of the king Stafford promised a reply.

On 30 November Stafford, as Chancellor, finally delivered the answer, in the presence of the court. While the king promised to send orators, nothing was to happen as to the tenth. Louis asked whether there was any hope of a tenth at all and Archbishop Kemp simply replied that royal letters would explain. Stafford added that Cordona, secretary to Baptista, knew what had happened, which Cordona denied. On 6 December, meeting Stafford, Clement and William Biconyl, Cordona made a last attempt to insist that the tenth be collected, but Clement cut him short, telling him that the pope had appointed him, confident of his wisdom and prudence, not to incite discord. In Rome he need only retail the truth.[297]

The royal letter to Eugenius on 5 December,[298] thanked him for the Rose, complained of troubled times and promised envoys. To ensure that his version reached the pope, Stafford himself, on 8 December, wrote to Eugenius, and two copies of the royal letters were made, one entrusted to Stafford's own messenger, Thomas Hope,[299] to be presented by William Gray, the royal proctor, two or three days before Hope himself had audience.

Stafford's letter explained that Cordona's request had been contrary to English law; such a tenth needed royal licence. Henry would send envoys, but meanwhile had forbidden collection.[300]

To Gray, one letter from the king, dated 6 December, in English, simply told him to help Hope,[301] another, from the archbishop, gave instructions about what Gray and Hope were to do and say.[302] If necessary Gray was to take before the pope the leading Englishmen in Rome, named as Sandwich, Schapman (Chapman) and Gueyll (Ghele or Neel?);[303] to keep reminding Eugenius that envoys were coming; and to inform Stafford of all that happened. Stafford also sent 'certain remunerations' (remuneraciones aliquas, no doubt sweeteners). And nothing more was paid.[304]

Thus it would be impossible to describe Henry VI's government as enthusiastically pro-papal. Eugenius's offer to share reservations was not apparently followed up; the government, in the tense situation in the

1440s, was not prepared to help the pope financially; and there was considerable hostility to Kemp's position as cardinal. Though Henry was enthusiastic for privileges for Eton, there is little evidence of official sympathy for Eugenius's problems. Schism would not be supported but neither would crusade.

Notes

1 Best account: J. Gill, *Eugenius IV, Pope of Christian Union*, London, 1961.
2 Chapter 12, passim.
3 *CPL*, VIII, pp. 338, 358; *CPR 1429–36*, p. 145; Le Neve, *St Paul's, London*, p. 3.
4 W. Brandmüller, 'Der Übergang vom Pontifikat Martins V zu Eugen IV', *QFIAB*, XLVII, 1967, pp. 598–629; reprint in idem, *Papst und Konzil*, pp. 85–110, which I use.
5 Brandmüller, 'Übergang', p. 99.
6 BL, Add. MS. 14848, f. 115.
7 Cotton Cleop. C IV, f. 202v.
8 Cotton Cleop. C IV, f. 204–4v. Revolt: Brandmüller, 'Übergang', pp. 91 to end, and *DBI*, XXVII, Rome, 1982, pp. 267–9, under Colonna, Antonio, article by F. Petrucci. Archdeaconry: Chapter 5, pp. 95–6.
9 Cotton Cleop. C IV, ff. 179–80.
10 *MC*, I, pp. 106–7; Christianson, pp. 20–1.
11 *CPL*, VIII, pp. 277–8; U. Plancher, *Histoire générale et particulière de Bourgogne*, . . . 4 vols., Dijon, 1739–81, IV, *Preuves*, no. LXXVII, p. lxxxvii; ACO, B11898/13; O. Raynaldus, *Annales*, IX, *ad annum* 1431, p. 100. In general: J. Toussaint, *Les Relations diplomatiques de Philippe le Bon avec le Concile de Bâle, 1431–1447*, Louvain, 1942, pp. 73–9.
12 Vaughan, *Philip the Good*, pp. 62–4. Anglo-Burgundian alliance: ibid., pp. 62–74; C. A. J. Armstrong, 'La double monarchie France–Angleterre et la Maison de Bourgogne 1420–1435: le declin d'une alliance', *England, France and Burgundy in the Fifteenth Century*, London, 1983, pp. 343–74, esp. pp. 366–74; reprinted from *Annales de Bourgogne*, XXXVII, 1965, pp. 81–112. Plancher, *Preuves*, IV, no. LXXV, pp. lxxxv–lxxxvi and Beaucourt, II, p. 437, Burgundian pleas; Harriss, *Beaufort*, Chapters 10, 11, 12.
13 *PPC*, IV, pp. 95–6, with date: Griffiths, *Henry VI*, p. 192.
14 Troyes: Chapter 7, note 37.
15 ADN, B 1942, ff. 131v, 132–2v.
16 Stevenson, II/1, pp. 188–93; ADN, B 1942, ff. 117, 122. 24 May letters from Rouen to Lille: *touchans la venue de Mons. le Cardinal d'Angleterre audit Rouen*; Harriss, *Beaufort*, p. 209.
17 Töth, II, p. 201; Morisini, *Chronique*, III, pp. 347–8.
18 ASV, Arm. XXXIX 7a, ff. 194–4v.
19 Vaughan, *Philip the Good*, pp. 63, 65; Beaucourt, II, pp. 439–40.
20 ACO, B11898/102.
21 Plancher, *Preuves*, IV, no. LXXXI, pp. xciv–xcv, from Henry VI to Burgundy, 6 October. Harriss, *Beaufort*, pp. 210–11, for situation.
22 Veronese and Porcari: Zippel, *Paolo II*, pp. xxiv, xxv; A. Andrews, 'The lost fifth book of the Life of Pope Paul II by Gaspar of Verona', *Studies in the Renaissance*, XVII,

1970, pp. 7–45; E. M. Sanford, 'Gaspar Veronese, humanist and teacher', *Transactions and Proceedings of the American Philological Association*, LXXXIV, 1953, pp. 190–209, esp. 193–4. Cf. ADN, B 1948, f. 284, gift to Porcari's nephew.

23 Valois, *Pragmatique*, p. lvii.

24 J. J. des Ursins, *Écrits politiques de Jean Juvenal des Ursins*, ed. P. S. Lewis, Société de l'Histoire de France,, 2 vols., Paris, 1978, 1985, II, p. 56; date, p. 1.

25 Vatican Library, MS Vat. Lat. 3878, ff. 65–5v: *inter quos hoc perhenne esse debet memoriale: quod adversario regis non paucas post promissiones consentire numquam voluit, quin super eum ut regni Anglie possessione contentus sit inducere conatur* . . . Therefore the pope kept . . . *notoria sua non obstante egestate, reverendissimum cardinalem Sancte Crucis, propriis sanctitatis gravibus in expensis, in regno isto spacio fere trium annorum.* Haller, *Piero da Monte*, p. *94, note 248 for MS and speech.

26 IE 392A, f. 45; 395, f. 33; 397, f. 73; 398, f. 82; Mandati 826, ff. 55, 116v, 117v, 152, 163v; 828, ff. 33, 84v.

27 17 October, Hugh de Lannoy summoned to Brussels, ADN, B 1942, f. 114; elaborate preparations, ff. 118–18v; assembly, ff. 128, 128v, copies of previous discussion with Charles, f. 128v; at Lille 12 November.

28 ACO, B 11898/90, 91, 92, 93, 94b, 95.

29 ACO, B 11898/17.

30 ACO, B11898/15; Plancher, *Preuves*, no. XXIX, pp. xxxiv–xxxv, wrongly dated 1424, see Töth, II, p. 204.

31 Schofield, *AHC*, pp. 6–7; copies: BL, Add. MS 14848, ff. 93–3v; Cotton Cleop. E III, f. 56. Basel's messenger representative of prior of St Martin des Champs, Paris: *MC*, I, p. 125; in Burgundy ADN, B 1942, f. 144.

32 Stevenson, II/1, pp. 196–202.

33 ADN, B 11898/14.

34 Töth, II, pp. 204–5.

35 ADN, B 1945, f. 50.

36 ADN, B 1945, f. 74, at Chinon. Töth, II, p. 205, note 3 for letter, quoting ASV, Arm. XXXIX 7a, f. 117.

37 Haller, *Piero da Monte*, Beilagen nos. 15, 16; summons to Beaufort: Durham, Dean and Chapter Archives, *Registrum Parvum*, II, f. 56v; copy: BL, MS Royal 10 B IX, ff. 58–8v.

38 Paris, AN X¹ᵃ 8605, ff. 21v–2.

39 Paris, BN, MS Lat. 1575, ff. 55–5v and 54–5. See PRO, E404/48/155, payment 28 February for letters to *le Cardinal de St. Croy* and our council in France, *pur la traite du pees perentre nous et le Dauphin a Cambray*; also PRO, E403/700, m. 17.

40 Toussaint, *Les Relations*, p. 6; idem, *Bulletin de la Commission Royal d'Histoire*, CVII/part I, Brussels, 1942, nos. 27, 28, pp. 109–15.

41 ADN, B 1945, f. 74v.

42 E. Martène and U Durand, *Veterum scriptorum et monumentorum . . . amplissima collectio*, 9 vols., Paris, 1724–33, VIII, cols. 105–6 and *MC*, II, pp. 184–5. Hugh de Lannoy's views: B. de Lannoy, *Hughes de Lannoy, Le Bon Seigneur de Santes*, Brussels, 1957, pp. 226–30.

43 ADN, B 1945, f. 55v; Plancher, *Preuves*, IV, p. cxxiii, letter 25 June; Martène and Durand, VIII, col. 114; Beaucourt, II, p. 445.

44 Plancher, *Preuves*, IV, no. XCIX, p. cxvi–cxvii; ACO, B 11899/98.

45 Plancher, *Preuves*, IV, p. cxxiii–cxxiv.

46 Schofield, *JEH* XXI, pp. 167, 170.

47 Schofield, *JEH*, XII, p. 167. Predecessor Johannes de Prato: Schofield, *AHC*, p. 16; IE, 393, f. 60v; Mandati, 824, f. 87; Pius II, *Brief als Priester*, p. 181; *Briefe aus der*

Laienzeit (1431–5), p. 14. De Mera: letter from Henry VI, Schofield, *AHC*, p. 21, printed Mansi, XXIV, cols. 372–4; XXXI, cols. 132–3.

48 Cotton Cleop. C IV, f. 196v; also *RTA*, X, no. 119.
49 *DK*, XLVIII, p. 285 for Holes; Cotton Cleop. C IV, f. 190v sends bull of dissolution, *Avisamenta* of Sigismund and Cesarini's views to Chichele, with documents on divided views of cardinals. See also G. Christianson, *Cesarini: the Conciliar Cardinal. The Basel Years*, Kirchengeschichtliche Quellen und Studien, X, St Ottilien, 1979, p. 40.
50 Cotton Cleop. C IV, ff. 151v–2.
51 Schofield, *JEH*, XII, pp. 179–80; H. J. Zeibig, 'Beitrag zur Geschichte der Wirksamkeit des Basler Concils in Oesterreich', *Sitzungsbericht der Königl. Akademie der Wissenschaften, Hist.–Phil. Klasse*, VIII, Vienna, 1852, pp. 599–600.
52 Schuchard, pp. 76, 116, 151, 190.
53 Schofield, *AHC*, pp. 10–11, 12; PRO, E404/48/314; *PPC*, IV, p. 120; PRO, E403/703, m. 10; Mandati, 824, f. 137; Rymer, IV/4, p. 181 (X, 514, 515).
54 Schofield, *JEH*, XII, pp. 172, 173–4; *PPC*, IV, pp. 123–4, 125; Paris, BN, MS Lat. 1575, ff. 155–5v, 176; Mansi, XXX, cols. 156–7.
55 *JEH*, XII, pp. 173–4.
56 *CPL*, VIII, p. 280.
57 *MC*, II, pp. 288–91; copy, contemporary: BL, MS Harley 3768, ff. 166–7.
58 Plancher, *Preuves*, IV, no. CV, pp. cxxvii–cxxviii.
59 ADN, B 1945, ff. 59–9v, for messenger.
60 Appointment of delegates: *PPC*, IV,. pp. 119–20; ACO, B 11899/97 for those to look after them.
61 Plancher, *Preuves*, IV, no. CII, pp. cxx–cxxii, request, cxix–cxx, reply, dated 15 June for the whole, whereas ACO, B 11899/21, dated 27 October, tells Chancellor to obey Moisy.
62 ACO, B 11899/19.
63 Above, note 58 and Albergati to Bedford, Paris, AN, X¹ᵃ 8605, ff. 22v–3. Quotation: *regnum Francie libere et in pace dimitti domino suo velud jure hereditario debitum.*
64 Schofield, *JEH*, XII, p. 177; Chichele, *Register*, III, p. 233.
65 *DK*, XLVIII, p. 291; *PPC*, IV, pp. 152–3, 159; PRO, E403/706, m. 15, 19; Rymer, IV/4, p. 189 (X, 536) with PRO, E404/52/397, why Kemp did not go.
66 Salisbury or Sarysbury: Pantin, *Canterbury College*, III, p. 91; *Literae Cantuarienses*, III, pp. 163–5. Letter from him in Rome: Cotton Cleop. C IV, f. 190, 1 June 1433.
67 IE 393, f. 82; Mandati 826, f. 138v; *CPL*, VIII, p. 280.
68 *CPL*, VIII, pp. 212–13; Cotton Cleop. C IV, ff. 208–8v. One of Eugenius's formulae for adherence: BL, MS Harley 3768, ff. 172–2v, cf. *MC*, II, pp. 370–2; Christianson, p. 94.
69 Harley 3768, f. 172, notice of 28 February 1433.
70 Harley 3768, ff. 173–5, dated 16 June.
71 Harvey, 'Andrew Holes', pp. 24–9; 29 December 1432?.
72 Schofield, *AHC*, p. 47; *CB*, I, pp. 316–18, 318–20.
73 Beaucourt, II, p. 453. Burgundians went to Paris, accompanying Anglo-French delegates to conference: ADN, B 1948, ff. 69v, 75, 80, 83.
74 ACO, B 11899/24; Plancher, *Preuves*, IV, no. CVII, p. cxxix: no. CIX, p. cxxxiii.
75 Plancher, *Preuves*, IV, no. CXI, pp. cxxxiv–cxxxv, 14 August 1433; ACO, B 11899/26bis; Toussaint, p. 79.
76 Beaucourt, II, p. 454; Armstrong, p. 371.
77 Schofield, *JEH*, XII, pp. 185, 187–9; *AHC*, pp. 38, 40–2, and add Dublin, MS Trinity College 255, f. 150 to refs. For MS: M. L. Colker, *Trinity College Library,*

Dublin, Descriptive Catalogue of the Medieval and Renaissance Latin Manuscripts, 2 vols., Irthlingborough, 1991, I, pp. 455–69. Harriss, *Beaufort*, p. 227. Burgundian messages: ADN, B 1948, ff. 80, 108v, 109, 109v, 110, and note 75 above.

78 PRO, E403/708, m. 1, 25 April 1433.
79 Schofield, *JEH*, XII, pp. 190–1; *AHC*, pp. 42–3.
80 Henry to Burgundians, Stevenson, II/1, pp. 249–62.
81 Harriss, *Beaufort*, pp. 228–9.
82 *PPC*, IV, pp. 167–8.
83 Beaucourt, II, pp. 455–6; envoy, Hugh de Lannoy: Lannoy, *Hughes de Lannoy*, pp. 96–101 for this episode and further pp. 232–4; ACO, B 11899/25; ADN, B 1948, f. 112v.
84 Stevenson, II/1, pp. 218–49, 18 July. Lannoy includes (documents xxxvii and xxxviii, pp. 232–5) memoir and Beaufort to Burgundy.
85 Armstrong, p. 368.
86 ADN, B 1948, f. 114v, letter to him there from Burgundy.
87 *MC*, II, p. 405.
88 Beaucourt, II, p. 463; Rymer, IV/4, pp. 197–9 (X, 556–61); Plancher, *Preuves*, IV, no. CXI, pp. cxxxiv–cxxxv; ACO, B 11899/26bis; safe-conducts: *DK*, XLVIII, p. 294; PRO, E403/712, m. 1.
89 *CB*, II, pp. 479, 482, 517; *MC*, II, p. 440.
90 ACO, B 11899/26², 26³; Plancher, *Preuves*, IV, pp. cxxxv–cxxxvi, letters of duke's envoy and lieutenant of Calais.
91 Schofield, *JEH*, XII, pp. 193–4 and *AHC*, p. 48, prints much of Henry's letter.
92 Schofield, *JEH*, XII, p. 193; *AHC*, p. 47; Bekynton, *Correspondence*, II, pp. 61–6; Mansi, XXX, cols. 836–9.
93 *CB*, II, p. 467.
94 Vaughan, *Philip the Good*, pp. 210–11.
95 Schofield, *JEH*, XII, p. 193; *AHC*, p. 47; *RTA*, XI, p. 10, note 7.
96 G. de Lannoy, *Oeuvres de Ghillebert de Lannoy, voyageur, diplomate et moraliste*, ed. C. Potvin, Académie de Belgique, 1878, pp. 254–61, for correspondence, report pp. 258–61, p. 256 English among opponents.
97 *CB*, II, pp. 490–2.
98 Schofield, *JEH*, XII, p. 195; *AHC*, p. 47.
99 Dublin, Trinity College MS 255, ff. 200v–2 dated; Cambridge, Emmanuel College, MS 142, ff. 127–8.
100 *RTA*, XI, no. 45, pp. 86–8.
101 Plancher, *Preuves*, IV, no. CXIII, pp. cxxxvii–cxl.
102 Wedding: ADN, B 1951, ff. 103v, 104, 106v–7, 108v, 111–11v, 201, 201v, 202, 215; Beaucourt, II, p. 506.
103 Beaucourt, II, p. 511; ADN, B 1951, f. 40, journey, Lille, England, Ghent, from 23 April to 20 June 1434; Toussaint, p. 85; PRO, E403/715, m. 7.
104 *PPC*, IV, pp. 255–9.
105 ACO, B 11899/28.
106 *PPC*, IV, pp. 259–61.
107 Schofield, *JEH*, XII, p. 195; *AHC*, pp. 50–1.
108 Schofield, *JEH*, XII, p. 196; idem, 'The second English delegation to the Council of Basel', *JEH*, XVII, 1966, pp. 29–64, esp. pp. 30–4; *AHC*, pp. 52–3.
109 Schofield, *JEH*, XVII, p. 34; Harriss, *Beaufort*, p. 239.
110 *CPL*, VIII, pp. 213–15; Schofield, *JEH*, XVII, p. 43; *BRUO*, I, pp. 281–2 and E. F. Jacob, 'Thomas Brouns, Bishop of Norwich', *Essays in British History presented to Sir Keith Feiling*, ed. H. R. Trevor-Roper, London, 1964, pp. 61–83; Le Neve,

Chichester, p. 2.
111 *PPC*, IV, pp. 207–8.
112 *PPC*, IV, pp. 183–4; Harriss, *Beaufort*, p. 240.
113 Haller, *Piero da Monte*, Beilagen no. 18.
114 Haller, *Piero da Monte*, Beilagen nos. 19, 20; Paris, BN, MS Lat. 12542, f. 110v letter to chapter; PRO, E28/55 two letters.
115 Eubel, I, p. 34.
116 Le Neve, *Lincoln*, p. 11.
117 Bekynton, *Correspondence*, II, pp. 251–2.
118 *CPL*, VIII, p. 282.
119 Schofield, *JEH*, XVII, pp. 48–50; *AHC*, pp. 59, 72.
120 Schofield, *JEH*, XVII, p. 43; *AHC*, p. 60.
121 *PPC*, IV, pp. 281–2.
122 PRO, E28/55, 8 November.
123 *PPC*, IV, p. 285.
124 *PPC*, IV, p. 286; PRO, E28/49, undated.
125 *CPL*, VIII, pp. 218–19; Vatican Library, MS Chigi D VII 101, ff. 73–4.
126 *CPL*, VIII, p. 218; Haller, *Piero da Monte*, Beilagen no. 23.
127 *CPL*, VIII, p. 216–18; Haller, *Piero da Monte*,Beilagen no. 21; Vatican Library, MS Chigi D VII 101, ff. 72v–3.
128 *CPL*, VIII, p. 236; Le Neve, *Bath and Wells*, p. 36.
129 *CPL*, VIII, p. 236; Le Neve, *Northern Province*, p. 94.
130 *CPL*, VIII, p. 236; Le Neve, *Coventry and Lichfield*, p. 26.
131 *CPL*, VIII, p. 235; Le Neve, *Northern Province*, p. 65.
132 *CPL*, VIII, p. 233; Le Neve, *Lincoln*, p. 77, but collated.
133 Dickinson, *Arras*, p. 20.
134 Bekynton, *Correspondence*, II, pp. 265–7.
135 Toussaint, p. 113; *RTA*, XI, p. 371, no. 216, pp. 406–8, Sigismund to Henry VI.
136 *PPC*, IV, p. 265; Rymer, V/1, p. 12 (X, 594); PRO, E364/68, m. 7; E403/715, m. 14.
137 Beaucourt, II, p. 513.
138 Beaucourt, II, pp. 514–17.
139 Dickinson, pp. 163–5; Toussaint, pp. 89–90.
140 Toussaint, p. 249.
141 Dickinson, pp. 20–1.
142 Toussaint, pp. 248–9; Vaughan, *Philip the Good*, p. 71.
143 Toussaint, pp. 118, 251–3.
144 Toussaint, p. 90; Dickinson, pp. 219, 221–2, Appendix A, nos. 5, 7.
145 Rymer, V/1, p. 18 (X, 610–11); PRO, E28/55, 5 June.
146 Full story: Dickinson.
147 Haller, *Piero da Monte*, Beilagen no. 2.
148 Haller, *Piero da Monte*, no. 66, p. 56.
149 PRO, E403/719, m. 8; BL, MS Cotton Cleop. E III, f. 76, for Moleyns who probably returned again, Haller, *Piero da Monte*, Beilagen no. 24; *CPL*, VIII, pp. 233, 285–6. Ely returned in July: PRO, E403/719, m. 12; E28/55; E404/51/347.
150 Rymer, V/1, pp. 21, 23 (X, 620, 625) and PRO, E30/1249, *inspeximus*, 12 November 1435.
151 Harriss, *Beaufort*, p. 251.
152 Dickinson, p. 153.
153 Toussaint, p. 102; Mansi, XXX, cols. 950–1.
154 Toussaint, p. 102; Mansi, XXX, cols. 952–3.

155 M.-R. Thielemans, *Bourgogne et l'Angleterre. Relations politiques et économiques entre les Pays-Bas bourguignons et l'Angleterre, 1435–67*, Université Libre de Bruxelles. Travaux de la Faculte de Philosophie et Lettres, XXX, Brussels, 1966, p. 68.

156 Toussaint, p. 103; Rymer, V/1, p. 23 (X, 625).

157 PRO, E403/721, m. 12; E404/52/190.

158 Note 156 above.

159 *PPC*, IV, p. 308; *DK*, XLVIII, p. 308; PRO, E403/721, m. 11; E28/74, 18 January 1445; E404/62/108.

160 Puis II, *Commentarii rerum memorabilium que temporibus suis contigerunt*, 2 vols., ed. A. Van Heck, Studi e testi, CCCXII, CCCXIII, Vatican City, 1984, II, Book 1.6, pp. 48–9.

161 Differing accounts: Pius II, *Privatbriefe*, no. 20, p. 41, 9 April 1436; idem, *De viris illustribus*, Bibliothek des Literarischen Vereins in Stuttgart, I, Stuttgart, 1842, p. 47; J. A. Campano, life of Pius, in *Le Vite di Pio II di Giovanni Antonio Campano e Bartolomeo Platina*, ed. G. C. Zimola, Rerum italicarum scriptores, III part 2, Bologna, 1964, p. 10; J. H. Burns, *Scottish Churchmen and the Council of Basel*, Glasgow, 1962, p. 11.

162 Haller, *Piero da Monte*, no. 20, pp. 12–13; PRO, E364/78, m. 9 dorse.

163 Thielemans, p. 74, note 51.

164 PRO, E403/723, m. 12, 28 August 1435, Sigismund ?Ottlinger sent back 16 November, with message, E403/725, m. 4; E28/58. 1437 John Erkenroth E403/725, m. 10; Sigismund Ottlinger had been and gone 17 July, E403/727, m. 7, 10; E404/53/325. Adam Moleyns dispatched letters 18 June: E404/53/320.

165 PRO, E403/721, m. 12; E404/52/190.

166 Rymer, V/1, p. 25 (X, 629).

167 Thielemans, p. 68.

168 PRO, E28/56, 13 February 1436, Beaupère and Novaro; E28/56, no. 22, Teramo; E28/55, 14 June 1435 Novaro allowed 100 marks benefices, like his relative Ardicino.

169 PRO, E28/56, 20 March 1436, complimentary letter of king to Cardinal Orsini.

170 *DK*, XLVIII, p. 317.

171 Harriss, *Beaufort*, p. 171; Thompson, *The English Clergy*, pp. 21–2.

172 *CPL*, VIII, pp. 230–1.

173 *CPL*, VIII, p. 230; Haller, *Piero da Monte*, no. 26, pp. 211–13.

174 Bekynton, *Correspondence*, I, pp. 4–12; *CPL*, VIII, pp. 252, 254.

175 Bekynton, *Correspondence*, II, pp. 1–18.

176 *CPL*, VIII, p. 292.

177 Cavalcantibus: Mandati 828, f. 134; IE 402, ff. 73, 73v; *CPL*, VIII, p. 292.

178 *PPC*, V, pp. 64, 66.

179 Haller, *Piero da Monte*, no. 52, pp. 40–2.

180 As last note.

181 Haller, *Piero da Monte*, no. 53.

182 Harvey, 'England, the council of Florence and the end of the council of Basel', in *Christian Unity: 500 Years since the Council of Ferrara/Florence 1439/9–1989*, ed. G. Alberigo, Bibliotheca Ephemeridum Theologicarum Lovaniensium, XCVII, Louvain, 1991, pp. 203–25, for aspects.

183 J. W. Stieber, *Pope Eugenius IV, the Council of Basel and the Secular and Ecclesiastical Authorities in the Empire*, Studies in the History of Christian Thought, ed. H. A. Oberman, XIII, Leiden, 1978, pp. 233–5.

184 *PPC*, V, p. 82; A. Gwynn, 'A Franciscan Bishop of Clonfert', *Journal of Galway Archaeological and Historical Society*, XXVIII, 1958–9, pp. 5–11, correcting *BRUO* Appendix.

185 Bekynton, *Correspondence*, II, pp. 37–45.
186 Bekynton, *Correspondence*, II, pp. 83–6.
187 Bekynton, *Correspondence*, II, pp. 86–90.
188 Bekynton, *Correspondence*, II, pp. 46–9.
189 *PPC*, V, p. 81.
190 *PPC*, V, pp. 87, 89; messenger to Austria, *c.* 20 February, PRO, E403/729, m. 11; Bekynton, *Correspondence*, I, pp. 68–9.
191 *PPC*, V, p. 86; Bekynton, *Correspondence*, I, pp. 220–1.
192 Bekynton, I, pp. 246–8. Sigismund Ottlinger retained: PRO, E403/729, m. 18; *RTA*, XIII, no. 150, p. 239.
193 Stieber, pp. 137–8.
194 *RTA*, XIII, pp. 232–3. Letters from Cologne, Bekynton, *Correspondence*, I, p. 131; PRO, E403/731, m. 3; Chaplais, *Diplomatic Practice*, I/I, no. 38.
195 Bekynton, *Correspondence*, I, pp. 94–6, dated 1438; for date 1440: *RTA*, XIII, pp. 337–8, no. 169, reply to *RTA*, XIII, no. 145, pp. 232–3.
196 Haller, *Piero da Monte*, no. 71, pp. 72–3.
197 Haller, *Piero da Monte*, no. 70, pp. 70–1; *PPC*, V, pp. 100, 102; PRO, E403/731, m. 3; also Malden, pp. 94–7.
198 Schofield, *AHC*, pp. 102–3.
199 *PPC*, V, pp. 96–8.
200 Bekynton, *Correspondence*, I, pp. 134–5.
201 PRO, E403/731, m. 15; E403/733, m. 10, 12.
202 PRO, E403/733, m. 4, 14; *DK*, XLVIII, p. 326.
203 Haller, *Piero da Monte*, nos. 44, 72, 73.
204 Haller, *Piero da Monte*, Beilagen no. 29.
205 PRO, E403/731, m. 15; Haller, *Piero da Monte*, no. 35.
206 Haller, *Piero da Monte*, no. 36; *CPL*, VIII, p. 233, for Sutton's prebend; Le Neve, *Lincoln*, p. 77.
207 Haller, *Piero da Monte*, Beilagen nos. 29–35. Barbo's benefices: *CPR Henry VI, 1429–36*, p. 498.
208 Le Neve, *Lincoln*, p. 114.
209 Haller, *Piero da Monte*, nos. 74 and 81.
210 Haller, *Piero da Monte*, no. 38.
211 Mandati 828, f. 199v.
212 Harvey, 'England, the council of Florence', p. 211.
213 Stieber, pp. 156–9.
214 *RTA*, XIV, no. 111, p. 215; Hartung van Klux sent to England partly for this; his instructions: BL, Add. Ms. 48001, ff. 291–4.
215 Schofield, *AHC*, p. 105; Bekynton, *Correspondence*, II, pp. 66–70; *PPC*, V, pp. 364–5, 375; Allmand, 'Documents', pp. 79–149.
216 Harvey, 'England, the council of Florence', pp. 215–16.
217 Copy: Oxford, University College, MS 53, f. 219.
218 Gill, p. 138.
219 Haller, *Piero da Monte*, no. 96, pp. 98–9.
220 Haller, *Piero da Monte*, no. 100, pp. 108–9.
221 Schofield, *AHC*, p. 105; Zellfelder, pp. 360–3.
222 *RTA*, XIV, no. 174, pp. 309–12.
223 Haller, *Piero da Monte*, no. 104, pp. 112–15.
224 Haller, *Piero da Monte*, nos. 103, 108.
225 Mandati 828, f. 230; Hofmann, *Acta*, III/1, p. 77.
226 Bekynton, *Correspondence*, II, pp. 49–51.

227 27 October 1439.

228 Arnold Brempt in London before 5 November: Bekynton, *Correspondence*, I, pp. 73–4; *PPC*, V, pp. 128–9; Bekynton, *Correspondence*, I, pp. 74–5 probably to Brempt. Simon Bochold in London by 15 November, Bekynton, *Correspondence*, I, pp. 75–7; PRO, E403/736, m. 5; credence for Brempt, 21 May 1439, Chaplais, *Diplomatic Practice*, I/I, no. 77.

229 *RTA*, XIV, p. 426.

230 *DK*, XLVIII, p. 331; Rymer, V/1, pp. 67–9 (X, 741–5); Bekynton, *Correspondence*, I, pp. 77–8, 98–9, 214–15; PRO, E403/736, m. 13.

231 Harvey, 'England, the council of Florence', pp. 217–18.

232 Harvey, 'England, the council of Florence', p. 217.

233 *CPL*, IX, p. 46; Eubel, II, p. 7; Bekynton, *Correspondence*, I, pp. 41–7, 50–2.

234 Haller, *Piero da Monte*, no. 134, pp. 247–8, Beilagen no. 39, pp. 227–8; Bekynton, *Correspondence*, I, pp. 39–41, 48–50.

235 M. M. Harvey, 'Eugenius IV, Cardinal Kemp and Archbishop Chichele: a reconsideration of the role of Antonio Caffarelli', *The Church and Sovereignty*, Studies in Church History, Subsidia, 1991, pp. 329–44.

236 Haller, *Piero da Monte*, no. 160, p. 180.

237 Haller, *Piero da Monte*, Beilagen no. 40, pp. 228–9; Stieber, p. 213 for Diet.

238 See below, note 251.

239 Harvey, 'Kemp and Chichele', pp. 335–6.

240 PRO, E403/736, m. 16.

241 Bekynton, *Correspondence*, I, pp. 85–6, 96–8, 343–5; II, 58–9; *DK*, XLVIII, p. 336; Rymer, V/1, p. 78 (X, 770–1); *RTA*, XV, no. 138, pp. 246–7; no. 139, pp. 247–9.

242 Bekynton, *Correspondence*, I, p. 166.

243 *RTA*, XV, pp. 529–30; Rymer, V/1, pp. 103–5 (X, 835–40); PRO, E403/740, m. 2.

244 Bekynton, *Correspondence*, II, pp. 59–60, 70–5. Chaplais, *Diplomatice Practice*, I/I, no 78; *RTA*, XV, no. 306, pp. 588–9.

245 Harvey, 'England, the council of Florence', pp. 213–14.

246 Lunt, II, p. 571; Durham, Archives of the Dean and Chapter, *Locellus* 19, no. 75.

247 Haller, *Piero da Monte*, no. 118, pp. 127–9. Harvey, 'England, the council of Florence', p. 218, esp. note 98.

248 Bekynton, *Correspondence*, I, pp. 34–6.

249 Rymer, V/1, p. 103 (X, 834).

250 PRO, E403/740, m. 8; Bekynton, *Correspondence*, I, pp. 167–8, 168–9, with perhaps idem, II, pp. 94–6.

251 PRO, E403/740, m. 8, 9: *pro tranquilitate ecclesie*. Bekynton, *Correspondence*, II, pp. 96–7, bishop of Rochester with John Grenewell, OCist., with *RTA*, XV, nos. 308, 309, pp. 591–2.

252 *DK*, XLVIII, p. 343; Rymer, as note 241 above; *PPC*, V, pp. 126–30.

253 For him in Cologne: Bekynton, *Correspondence*, II, pp. 58–9; I, 166–7.

254 Bekynton, *Correspondence*, II, p. 58.

255 Stieber, p. 215.

256 *RTA*, XV, no. 300, art. 2.

257 Stieber, pp. 215–17.

258 PRO, E403/740, m. 19. Henry still intending to send previous group: Bekynton, *Correspondence*, II, p. 56; *RTA*, XV, no. 310, pp. 592–3, cf. recommendation to a cardinal, Oxford, Bodleian Library, MS Ashmole 789, f. 261. December 1440 Eugenius thought Kemp on his way: Haller, *Piero da Monte*, Beilagen nos. 40, 41; *RTA*, XV, no. 315, pp. 597–8 but see Bekynton, *Correspondence*, I, pp. 38–9; also idem, II, pp. 97–8.

259   *RTA*, XV, no. 311, p. 593; Bekynton, *Correspondence*, I, pp. 238–9; II, pp. 97–8; Schofield, *AHC*, p. 107; Stieber, p. 217.

260   *RTA*, XV, p. 869.

261   *RTA*, XVI, pp. 18, 34–5; Stieber, p. 218.

262   *RTA*, XVII, p. 55, memorandum by papal representative 1442 (correct reference for *RTA*, XV, p. 574).

263   Stieber, p. 231.

264   *RTA*, XVI, no. 31, pp. 71–2.

265   *RTA*, XV, p. 531; J. Chmel, *Regesta chronologico-diplomatica Friderici IV Romanorum Regis (Imperatoris III) 1440–93*, Vienna, 1838–40, no. 285.

266   *RTA*, XVI, no. 31, pp. 71–2 and p. 18; Bekynton, *Correspondence*, II, pp. 100–2.

267   Stieber, p. 232.

268   Bekynton, *Correspondence*, II, pp. 98–9, 102–3; *RTA*, XVI, no. 33, pp. 73–4; Stieber, p. 234. Edward Hull to Germany 13 July, PRO, E403/741, m. 8; 743, m. 2.

269   PRO, E403/743, m. 2: Moleyns and John Lowe, bishop of St Asaph; Rymer, V/1, p. 110 (XI, 1–2), names Reginald Boulers, abbot of Gloucester with Moleyns, *DK*, XLVIII, pp. 349, 350, 351; E403/743, m. 5; E28/69, nos. 29, 32, 45, 61.

270   Stieber, pp. 235, 237.

271   Bekynton, *Correspondence*, I, pp. 89–90.

272   PRO, E364/75, m. 5, 15; *RTA*, XVI, p. 225, for Boulers and Lowe, with incorrect dates. Lowe left 15 March, Boulers 14 March, returning together 14 August. For Moleyns, Bekynton, *Correspondence*, I, pp. 118–19.

273   Stieber, pp. 237 seq.

274   *RTA*, XVI, pp. 225, 249, no. 203, p. 376, nos. 214–16, pp. 544–57.

275   *RTA*, XVI, no. 214, pp. 544–7.

276   *RTA*, XVI, no. 215, pp. 547–57.

277   PRO, E30/425: vice-chancellor becomes *consiliarius* of Henry VI, 27 July 1442; E30/1436, 3 August, Branda likewise. See also E30/1285.

278   See note 270 above.

279   *PPC*, V, p. 197.

280   Stieber, pp. 241–2; English stance on place: *RTA*, XVII, p. 146, recollection of Carvajal, papal representative.

281   *PPC*, V, p. 206.

282   Stieber, pp. 249–50.

283   Stieber, pp. 264, 266, 274; Pius II, *Briefe aus der Laienzeit*, I, *Privatbriefe*, no. 58, pp. 156–7 (probably with *RTA*, XVII, no. 60, pp. 148–50, asking kings to agree new council, June 1443; Henry's reply *RTA*, no. 84, pp. 188–9, 4 October, he needs to consult further); no. 69, pp. 171–2, Moleyns replying king favourable; no. 143, pp. 324–6, 29 May 1444, hoping Moleyns will come to Nuremburg Reichtag (cf. *RTA*, XVII, no. 119, p. 269). Connected probably: Anstey, *Epistolae Academicae*, no. 166, pp. 226–7, 26 October 1443.

284   Lunt, II, pp. 131–40.

285   *CPL*, VIII, p. 299; IE, 410, f. 153v; Mandati, 830, f. 88v; messengers to him IE, 410 ff. 167v, 177v; IE 412, f. 120; Mandati, 830, ff. 100v, 111v, 126.

286   Stafford, Register, Canterbury, ff. 19, 45–9 for whole. This ref. f. 45.

287   Stafford, Register, ff. 45, 45v.

288   Stafford, Register, f. 19. 25 June Baptista leaving, PRO, E404/61/246; free passage: E28/75, 14 March 1445.

289   Giovanni de Balderonibus returning 14 August, PRO, E404/61/272; E403/757, m. 11; IE, 412, f. 139; Mandati, 830, f. 150v. Letters entrusted to him: Stafford, ff. 45, 45v.

290 Lunt, II, pp. 133–4.
291 Stafford, Register, ff. 45v–6: *Dudum Siquidem*, letters patent, asking payment in six months; *Anno proximo anteacto*, letters close, saying money and men were promised but delay allowed. Letters ask collection now to be completed.
292 Opizzis collector, 15 July 1445: *CPL*, VIII, pp. 319–20, 303–4. Cordona: IE, 412, ff. 138, 143v; Mandati, 830, ff. 150, 158, 168, 197v; *CPL*, VIII, pp. 306, 311.
293 Stafford, Register, ff. 46–6v.
294 Above, note 291.
295 Stafford, Register, f. 46v.
296 Stafford, Register, ff. 47–7v, letter of 8 kal. July (= 24 June) 1446.
297 Stafford, Register, ff. 47v–8.
298 Stafford, Register, ff. 47v–8. Henry Verbondeswyk sent to pope, 3 December 1446, PRO, E403/765, m. 10.
299 Letter of Stafford, Register, f. 48; information on the two letters, ibid. Hope left 8 December. Described as BCL, *nacione teutonicus*.
300 Stafford, Register, f. 48; copy in Hope's letter collection, Cambridge, Corpus Christi College, MS 170, p. 208.
301 Stafford, Register, f. 48v.
302 Stafford, Register, ff. 48v–9. He thanks Grey for helping Frere Byrd, cf. above, Chapter 4 note 93.
303 Stafford, Register, f. 49. Gnele: either Ghele, above, Chapter 2, notes 187–93; or John Neel, for whom Candour later did copying: De la Mare, *Manuscripts at Oxford*, p. 96.
304 Payment to Cordona February 1447, PRO, E403/765, m. 14. Stafford's remunerations: Register, f. 49.

10
Anglo-papal relations 1447–58

Eugenius IV died on 3 February 1447, to be succeeded (as Nicholas V) by Tommaso Parentucelli, formerly in the service of Albergati. In Rome the royal proctor was William Gray,[1] and very rapidly his associates were promoted to be *cubicularii*.[2] This was probably a signal not only of Nicholas V's personal liking for Gray, but also that relations with England were set to improve.

Because of the eagerness of Henry VI's government to play a part in ending the Basel schism, Anglo-papal relations had probably improved since the refusal to allow the grant of one-tenth in 1445–6. Uneasy truce with France was still maintained and just before Eugenius died the French government's possible surrender terms for the anti-pope Felix V, duke of Savoy, were sent both to Eugenius and to Henry VI.[3] To take part in the negotiations the English government appointed William Lyhert, bishop of Norwich, Robert Botill, prior of Rhodes in England and Vincent Clement,[4] with orders that Botill and Clement were afterwards to offer obedience to the new pope.[5] They left England about 24 August 1447.[6]

The transaction in which they were involved included another French and English group, discussing a lasting peace, to involve a visit of Henry VI to France, supposedly in May 1448.[7] The latter discussions formed the background to, and coloured the reception of, the English contribution to the Basel negotiations. The French wanted the credit for ending the schism and the English were present only because allies could not be excluded. But the alliance was wavering and they were unpopular. Most unpopular of all was Clement.[8] He was not only a Catalan but from the first an outspoken critic of Basel:[9] 'Very rigorously confounding the facts and doings of the said council and supporting and sustaining in justice those of Pope Eugenius.' He saw to it that he was present at all important public meetings,[10] and took a major part in drafting the final agreement with Felix.[11]

One aim of these discussions was that the rump council of Basel should continue in existence to extort the best possible terms from the other Christian rulers; the Basel representatives in Geneva late in 1447 tried to arrange that the English would delay offering obedience to Nicholas V until this agreement was complete.[12] This worked: the English group returned to France instead of to the curia.

But Nicholas V was in touch with Henry VI none the less. A serjeant-at-arms went to Burgundy, England and Scotland in March 1447.[13] A friar minor, John Marquetus, came from the pope with messages in November/December,[14] and Thomas Candour was paid on 7 December for going to the curia to await Botill, whose arrival must have been thought imminent.[15] In February, when money for the Basel negotiators was running out, Clement was thought to be about to leave France for the curia.[16] Chester Herald went to the group,[17] their whereabouts evidently uncertain, though on 10 February Botill was still waiting in France.[18] In fact the negotiations lasted longer than had been anticipated.

Finally in July 1448 the English and French set off for the curia independently. The English, arriving first, presented the terms, which were rejected. The French then arrived, and presented them again, this time, of course, with all the force of their king's bargaining power.[19] Nicholas V, anxious to have the support of the French, though reluctant to make terms with Basel, found this bargain the only way to end the schism. While the English waited in Viterbo, marginal to these negotiations, the French bargained. In the end Nicholas grudgingly accepted the full settlement, particularly the need to hold another general council and grant generous terms to Felix V's cardinals. On 10 August some of the French, with Botill and Clement, returned to Lausanne to present the agreement to Felix.[20] Messengers between Nicholas V and Henry VI in early 1449 were probably connected with this.[21]

At last, on 1 April 1449, Felix V accepted. The English signatures to the agreement were Botill and Clement.[22] They wrote to the pope as they were leaving Lausanne for England,[23] sending a copy of the agreement with Felix, warning the pope that ambassadors of Charles VII were coming to try to persuade him to hold a council in France in 1451 and levy one-tenth from the whole church to defray expenses. The English pair said they had not agreed to a general council in France: 'We have no special mandate from our prince about nation or place', and asked the pope to wait until Henry VI sent an embassy to express his wishes. They also reminded Nicholas of the problems Eugenius had had with the last tenth in England. Who knew better than Clement?[24]

Clement finally reached to England on 5 June 1449, no doubt to report on the outcome of the lengthy negotiation.[25] Nicholas was pleased and sent Thomas Candour to thank the king.[26] To know that the English disagreed with the French about place and cost of a council no doubt strengthened the pope's ability to resist the French. William Gray returned to England about the same time as Clement, returning to Rome in September 1449, presumably briefed by the king on the royal attitude.[27]

In subsequent years, while the political situation in England deteriorated, the papacy concentrated on launching a crusade. After the Holy Year of 1450 Nicholas V devoted large sums to this. He was encouraged by the enthusiasm of Burgundy. In 1449 the duke stressed in negotiations with Henry VI that a crusade could follow the pacification of Europe. Henry replied that, though enthusiastic, he could not rely on the treacherous French to keep a truce.[28] The Anglo-French truce had finally collapsed.[29] Burgundy, however, continued to propound the notion. In July 1450 the duke suggested to Nicholas V that he and the king of France could crusade together, provided Anglo-French peace was achieved first.[30]

The papacy took these ideas seriously, since neither England nor France would support a crusade while their quarrel lasted. In July 1451 Marino Orsini, archbishop of Taranto, went to England as papal nuncio,[31] while Cardinal Guillaume D'Estouteville went to France instructed to negotiate the removal of the Pragmatic Sanction, but also to make Anglo-French peace, prior to a crusade.[32] Nicholas V even planned to send Nicholas of Cusa, the papal leader of the crusade, to England, though without result.[33]

Both nuncios had a bad time. D'Estouteville's entry into France was resisted by Charles VII, who thought the pope too favourable to Burgundy and wished for no diversion from French triumphs against the English.[34] The legate, finally allowed to enter in December 1451, only managed to see the king in February 1452,[35] then spent the next few months trying vainly to persuade the clergy to accept a concordat,[36] returning to Rome empty-handed in January 1453.[37] Orsini fared no better. Arriving in England in October 1451,[38] he probably stayed only a few months. At least one letter arrived from Nicholas of Cusa,[39] but what, if any, reply Orsini took home is not apparent.[40]

Henry VI's collapse in early August 1453, precipitated apparently by French success in the field, made an Anglo-French peace settlement even less likely, though from the pope's point of view the fall of Constantinople made it even more urgent.[41] Nicholas V announced a new crusade and the cause was taken up by the emperor. Aeneas Sylvius pressed the English to attend a diet at Regensburg in spring 1454,[42] but the letter arrived only on 15 April.[43] In summer the emperor wrote again.[44] Philip of Burgundy, having promised at the Feast of the Pheasant on 17 February that he would go on crusade, did come to the emperor's meeting, thus signalling that he at least was serious.[45]

In England money-raising for this crusade met a very mixed reaction. In July 1453 the grand master of Rhodes, John Lasci, decided to tax the order for the defence of the island. The castellan wrote to Henry VI asking permission to levy this.[46] The reply was that the imposition, though contrary to the law of the land, would be allowed this once because Botill, the English prior, had done such good service. The castellan, Langstrother, then asked the king to request the pope to allow the Jubilee indulgence to be preached in England in Lent 1455 for the benefit of Rhodes.[47] On 24 July 1454, Henry VI asked this of the pope and cardinals, entrusting the letters to Langstrother, as the king's envoy,[48] furtherance of the business in Rome relying on John Lax.[49] The request succeeded: on 1 December 1454 Nicholas V acquiesced, with, later in the month, further refinements.[50] Lunt described the complicated network which Botill and Langstrother organised[51] to collect the final total of over £4000.[52]

The preaching must have high-lighted the needs of eastern defence; certainly it is noticed in chronicles, whereas the 1450 Jubilee was not. But there was criticism.[53] A friar preached against it at Paul's Cross,[54] and Thomas Gascoigne was fiercely hostile.[55]

Probably in yet another attempt at pacification prior to crusade, Nicholas sent another legate. In spring 1454 the French and Burgundians were discussing crusade,[56] and the pope therefore sent to Burgundy Jean Jouffroy, a loyal councillor, whom Philip had persuaded him to make bishop of Arras the year before.[57] Behind the scenes Jouffroy was probably in touch with the Yorkists in England, both parties trying to persuade the French to consider a long truce, but of course the Yorkist grip on power slackened when Henry VI recovered in March 1455.[58] To England, to complement Jouffroy in Burgundy, Nicholas V sent a Greek named Nicolas Agolo. He went first to France, where, at the beginning of September 1454, Charles VII sent him to D'Estouteville in Rouen.[59] We know what happened next chiefly from Agolo's later report to the French.[60] D'Estouteville advised that as the pope was about to send to England a legate, Bartolemeo Rovarella, Bekynton's friend, now archbishop of Ravenna, Agolo should cross the channel to meet him. D'Estouteville and Dunois said 'that he could greatly help the archbishop of Ravenna in the matter of peace'.[61] So he came in late September 1454,[62] awaiting the archbishop, who arrived about 9 December.[63] Agolo told the French royal council that he accompanied the legate everywhere. Rovarella met the assembled royal council: York, Buckingham, Salisbury, the chancellor, the treasurer and bishops. Agolo reported that, before he (Agolo) left, the king had recovered and Somerset had been released from the Tower, with the archbishop of Canterbury made chancellor. The pope must therefore have been well informed about English politics and of the small likelihood of any crusading help.

To the French Agolo said that the English, though not wanting peace, were not a threat because of internal divisions and shortage of cash. They professed a desire to help the crusade but needed their army against the French. Unfortunately we do not know what the English royal council said to Rovarella, because, by the time Agolo gave his account, he assumed that Rovarella had already reported this to the French. He merely added that though the English wished to help against the Turks, Rovarella had told them that a crusade was impossible without peace or a truce with the French. They thought a truce of two years might be achieved, promising an embassy to notify the pope of their intention to help.

But all this occurred before the king recovered, altering the political scene. Nicolas Agolo was back in France in April 1455.[64] Rovarella probably left England a little later, but on 7 May Charles VII replied to Agolo, assuming that the English attitude was known,[65] and Rovarella probably left before, on 22 May, the battle of St Albans finally killed a definitive peace with France or help for a crusade.[66]

By the time Rovarella returned to Rome Nicholas V had died (24 March) and Calixtus III had succeeded (8 April). The papacy's crusading plans remained unaltered. On 15 May Calixtus renewed Nicholas V's crusading bull,[67] sending a papal serjeant-at-arms, destined also for Lower Germany, Scotland and Ireland, who reached London in July.[68] In September Calixtus planned to send Nicolas of Cusa to England to collect the crusading tenth, but the legation never came. At best it would have had had very little hope, but the unfavourable political climate made it quite unrealistic.[69] Instead a Catalan nuncio called Antonio Ferrar arrived early in 1456,[70] but there is no evidence for any attempt to collect money.[71] Individual Englishmen, surprisingly, continued to take the cross,[72] but the troubled times precluded any national enterprise, even had there been widespread enthusiasm for the ideal.

England's unsettled state reverberated in Rome. When on 18 September 1455 Bishop Lacy of Exeter died, the queen's chaplain, John Hals, chosen as his successor, was named in consistory in answer to royal letters, with Thomas Hope as proctor. The Nevilles, however, were determined to have George Neville. Accordingly the king (and perhaps in the end even the queen), wrote to have the appointment of Hals overturned. The pope, not unnaturally, protested, saying that Hope would explain why, but Hals was induced to resign and, on 3 February 1456, Neville received a provision.[73] The papal registers give no hint of these machinations.

Until the country settled no significant number of Englishmen would share the papal ideas about crusade. They might not have done so in any case, but with the outbreak of civil war went the last hope. Even Calixtus III's new feast of the Tranfiguration, to mark a crusading victory, was not celebrated in England for some years, though bulls proclaiming it were delivered late in 1457.[74]

In this period, therefore, relations between king and pope were without major upheavals. Nicholas V was usually on cordial terms with the government. But the state of English politics and continued tension over France precluded real assistance to the pope, whilst the contradictions of internal policy must have been a nightmare for royal representatives at the curia, when there were any.

Notes

1 Chapter 1, notes 87–99.

2 Chapter 2, notes 159–66.

3 *CB*, VIII, pp. 273, 292; G. Pérouse, *Le Cardinal Louis Aleman, Président du Concile de Bâle et la Fin du Grand Schisme*, Lyons, 1904, pp. 446–7. Truce: M. D'Escouchy, *Chronique de Mathieu D'Escouchy*, ed. G. du Fresne de Beaucourt, 3 vols., Société de l'Histoire de France, Paris, 1864, III, pp. 145–265. Church question, July 1447: pp. 164–8, Henry VI to Charles VII.

4 PRO E403/767 m. 13, 14; E404/63/139, for Clement, 18 August 1447; E404/63/135, 137, for Botill, Lyhert and two others, 31 July; Grunzweig, *Correspondance*, no. 6, p. 7; group to Calais, E404/64/77; D'Escouchy, III, pp. 168–9, Henry to Charles VII, announcing their setting out, 28 July.

5 PRO, E364/84 m. 5 dorse, 24 August 1447; *CB*, VIII, p. 357.

6 PRO, E28/81, no. 73 and E364/84, m. 5 dorse.

7 *CB*, VIII, pp. 306–7, 310–11, 312.

8 *CB*, VIII, pp. 326.

9 *CB*, VIII, pp. 370, 374.
10 *CB*, VIII, pp. 375, 378, 382.
11 *CB*, VIII, p. 390.
12 *CB*, VIII, p. 428.
13 Mandati, 831, f. 1bisv; PRO, E403/767, m. 8, 'regard', July.
14 PRO, E403/769, m. 7; E404/64/97, 12 December, 25 marks.
15 PRO, E403/769, m. 7–8.
16 PRO, E403/769, m. 12; E404/64/14.
17 PRO, E404/64/113, 28 January 1448.
18 PRO, E404/64/122, 10 February 1448; E 403/769, m. 16, four more months' wages.
19 Pérouse, p. 454; J. Chartier, *Chronique de Charles VII, Roi de France*, ed Vallet de
   Viriville, 3 vols., Paris, 1858, II, pp. 55–6.
20 Pérouse, p. 455; Chartier, II, p. 57.
21 PRO, E403/773, m. 14, Miguel Amici and Master Simon de Lotharingiis, 20 February; E404/65/113.
22 Pérouse, p. 458.
23 Oxford, Bodleian Library, MS Ashmole 789, ff. 334–4v, quotation: *de nacione et loco
   nullum haberemus a nostro principe speciale mandatum*; f. 334, letter to Henry VI; f.
   334v, to Zeno di Castiglione, with details of agreement.
24 Above, Chapter 9, notes 294–5, 297.
25 PRO, E364/84, m. 5. Interim payments to members of embassy omitted for brevity.
26 Stafford, Register, Canterbury, f. 50v, thanks and credence, 2 August 1449.
27 *DK*, XLVIII, p. 382.
28 Stevenson, II/2, pp. 471–3, 17 August 1449; Thielemans, p. 159.
29 C. T. Allmand, *Lancastrian Normandy, 1415–1450. The History of a medieval Occupation*, Oxford, 1983, pp. 48–9.
30 Vaughan, pp. 296–7; Beaucourt, V, p. 192, note 6.
31 *CPL*, X, pp. 219–20; Chartier, II, p. 326, two legations confused.
32 Beaucourt, V, pp. 192–3; correcting Beaucourt, P. Ourliac, 'La Pragmatique Sanction
   et la légation en France de Cardinal d'Estouteville, 1451–53', *Mélanges d'Archaeologie et
   d'Histoire* (École Française de Rome), LV, 1938, pp. 403–32, esp. p. 415, 427.
   Reprinted in Ourliac, *Études d'Histoire du Droit Médiéval*, Paris, 1979, pp. 375–98.
   D'Estouteville also: *Lexicon des Mittelalters*, IV/1, article by H. Müller.
33 *CPL*, X, pp. 233–6, esp. p. 233; E. Meuthen, *Die letzten Jahre des Nikolaus von Kues.
   Biographische Untersuchungen nach neuen Quellen*, Wissenschaftliche Abhandlungen
   der Arbeitgemeinschaft für Forschung des Landes Nordrhein-Westfalen, III, 1958, p.
   18.
34 Ourliac, p. 416.
35 Ourliac, p. 417.
36 Ourliac, pp. 418–25. Ursins, *Écrits politiques*, II, p. 291.
37 Ourliac, p. 426.
38 Malden, pp. 94–5, notes, to Salisbury, before 16 October 1451; J. Stone, *The Chronicle
   of John Stone, Monk of Christ Church, 1415–1471*, ed. W. G. Searle, Cambridge Antiquarian Society, Octavo series, XXXIV, 1904, p. 52, to Canterbury 8 October and
   again, pp. 52–3, Christmas. PRO, E403/786, m. 13, E404/68/60, 16 December 1451,
   paid £100. Paid by pope: IE, 422, f. 70, Mandati, 830, f. 268.
39 PRO, E403/788, m. 13; E404/68/93 to Leon de Cruce who brought it.
40 Papal serjeant-at-arms sent mid-1452, IE, 422, f. 87v; PRO, E403/789, m. 16.
41 Griffiths, *Henry VI*, p. 715.
42 Pius II, *Briefe als Bischof von Siena, 1450–1454*, no. 221, pp. 411–12; to Carlo Gigli,
   Italian merchant in London, no. 222, pp. 412–13, 17 January 1454.

43 Rymer, V/2, pp. 58–9 (XI, 355–6). Cf. PRO, E28/85, no. 42, 17 July 1454.
44 K. M. Setton, *The Papacy and the Levant, 1204–1571*, 2 vols., American Philosophical Society, Philadelphia, 1976–8, II, p. 153 quotes references. See PRO, E28/85, no. 68 to herald, 17 July, with letters from emperor.
45 Vaughan, pp. 296–302, 358–66.
46 Rymer, V/2, p. 53 (XI, 340–1).
47 Rymer, V/2, pp. 57–8, 59 (XI, 351–5, 357), letters discussed below, from PRO, E28/85; Lunt, II, p. 577
48 Rymer, as last note.
49 Ferguson, pp. 141–2; PRO, E28/85, no. 34, 24 July; Lunt, II, pp. 578–9; *CPL*, X, pp. 261–6.
50 Lunt, II, pp. 578–81.
51 Lunt, II, p. 582.
52 Lunt, II, p. 582.
53 R. Flenley, *Six Town Chronicles of England*, Oxford, 1911, pp. 141, 158.
54 Flenley, p. 141.
55 e.g. Oxford, Lincoln College, MS Lat. 117, f. 16, and below, Chapter 12, note 58.
56 Beaucourt, V, pp. 408–9.
57 C. Fierville, *Le Cardinal Jean Jouffroy et son temps, 1412–1473*, Paris, 1874, pp. 8, 84.
58 Beaucourt, V, p. 410, for basis for a story that a notable English embassy discussed a twenty-year truce prior to a crusade in February 1455. The Italians thought the English working with Jouffroy, P. M. Kendall and V. Ilardi, *Dispatches with related documents of Milanese Ambassadors in France and Burgundy, 1450–83*, 2 vols., *1450–61*, Athens (Ohio), 1970, I, pp. 155–9, 161–3; E. Sestan, *Carteggi diplomatici fra Milano Sforzesca e la Borgogna*, I, *1453–1475*, Fonti per la storia d'Italia, CXL, Rome, 1985, pp. 27–9.
59 N. Valois, 'Fragment d'un registre du Grand Conseil de Charles VII, Mars-Juin 1455', *Annuaire Bulletin de la Société de l'Histoire de France*, XIX, 1882, pp. 272–308, esp. pp. 283–6, 292–3.
60 Valois, 'Fragment', pp. 283–6.
61 Valois, 'Fragment', p. 284
62 Nicholas the Greek received 50 marks, 4 December, PRO, E404/70/2/39. Valois, 'Fragment', p. 284, arrived *c.* 28 September.
63 Lunt, II, pp. 140–1; *DK*, XLVIII, p. 403; Chaplais, *Diplomatic Practice*, I/2, no. 399; Stone, *Chronicle*, p. 62 at Canterbury 9 and 10 December. Agolo gives arrival about 20 December, Valois, 'Fragment,' p. 284, but Stone would know when he reached the monastery. Safe-conduct 22 November, Rymer, V/2, pp. 60–1 (XI, 360). Next two paragraphs: Valois, 'Fragment', pp. 284–5.
64 Report, 27 April: Valois, 'Fragment', p. 283.
65 Valois, 'Fragment', pp. 292–3.
66 PRO, E403/801, m. 3; Mandati, 822ᵃ, f. 32v. In Rome by 28 June.
67 Setton, II, p. 165.
68 Antonella de Rocha Prioris, Mandati, 832ᵃ, f. 11; paid £20 on 6 August, PRO, E 403/801, m. 7; E404/70/2/96.
69 *CPL*, XI, p. 19; IE, 432, f. 22v, 1000 florins for him at Bruges; I. Parrino, *Acta Albaniae Vaticana*, I, Studi e testi, CCLXVI, 1971, no. 98, p. 26, 13 October 1456, money to go to cardinal of St Angelo, since Cusa has not gone. H. L. Gray, 'Greek visitors to England', *Anniversary Essays in Medieval History by Students of Charles Homer Haskins*, Boston and New York, 1929, pp. 80–116, esp. p. 83.
70 *CPL*, XI, pp. 31–2, 387; IE, 430, f. 128; Mandati, 832ᵃ, f. 75v, with William Ferrar, Mandati, 832ᵃ, f. 94v; Setton, II, p. 191; perhaps for Neville's appointment, see note 71.

71 Lunt, II, pp. 141–2.
72 Examples: C. Tyerman, *England and the Crusades, 1095–1588*, Chicago, 1988, p. 307; Durham, February 1463: Durham, Dean and Chapter Archives, *Registrum Parvum*, III, ff. 121–1v. Canterbury: *Literae Cantuarienses*, III, p. 239.
73 *CPL*, XI, p. 30; Cambridge, Corpus Christi College, MS 170, p. 235: Calixtus to Henry, pp. 235–6: to queen; Rymer, V/3, p. 63 (XI, 367).
74 Mandati, 833ª, ff. 54v, 115; IE, 436, f. 117. R. W. Pfaff, *New Liturgical Feasts in Later Medieval England*, Oxford, 1970, pp. 29–30.

11
Pius II and England

From a papal standpoint the reign of Pius II was dominated by attempts to launch a crusade and by Italian politics. In the English church and state, however, papal interests were eclipsed by internal political struggles, escalating into civil war and a change of dynasty.

Calixtus III died on 6 August 1458. His successor Pius II, elected on 19 August, was crowned on 3 September. On 13 October he summoned the European powers to Mantua for 1 June 1459, where peace-making was to be a prelude to crusade. To understand what followed one must look at the situation in England and at both the pope's policies in Italy and the relations between England and her neighbours, France and Burgundy.

In August 1458 politics in England were dominated by the queen and royal household, who were attempting to isolate the duke of York and his supporters. The Yorkists meanwhile, trying to build their faction, had Warwick established as captain of Calais, collecting booty by piracy and with it support and admiration.[1] Relations between Philip the Good of Burgundy and Charles VII of France were very bad, Charles determined whenever possible to advance at Philip's expense. In summer 1456 the dauphin, Louis, quarrelling with his father, was received by Philip, given a residence with a large allowance and allowed to become a centre of anti-French intrigue.[2] Outwardly Burgundy was neutral between England and France.[3] In reality York fostered good relations with Burgundy from his first protectorate[4] and Burgundy became willing to countenance this, faced with an increasingly pro-French Lancastrian government.

As pontiff Pius II wanted peace between England, France and Burgundy, as a prelude to the crusade. As an Italian prince he preferred the king of France thoroughly distracted at home.[5] On 9 April 1454 had been signed the peace of Lodi, the basis of Italian politics until 1494,[6] followed shortly by formation of the Italian league, which Nicholas V joined, as nominal leader, in February 1455. Lodi accepted that Francesco Sforza, who had seized power in Milan in 1450, was to remain duke there. Claims to the duchy had been being pursued by several candidates, including Alfonso, king of Naples. Faced with this hostility, Sforza and his ally Florence allied with Charles VII (the treaty of Tours), and Duke René of Anjou actually invaded Italy, asserting the ancient Angevin claim to Naples. For a time the dauphin Louis actually pursued a foreign policy contrary to his father's, but Angevin ambitions were ruined because the fall of Constantinople (29 May 1453) made allies in Italy very anxious to make peace at home.

The Italian league maintained only a precarious peace, not least because Calixtus III was implacably hostile to the ambitions of Alfonso, king of Naples. In June 1458 Alfonso died and, since Naples was claimed as a papal fief, Calixtus at once refused to accept the succession of Alfonso's illegitimate son and heir Ferrante. The pope's own death, however, prevented him installing a Borgia nephew.

Pius II, the papal candidate favoured by Sforza and Ferrante,[7] in October 1458 agreed to invest Ferrante with Naples. Against this background Pius called the princes to Mantua, inviting them to unite for crusade. Not for the first time the pope's interests as secular ruler and as churchman were at variance. This had important implications for Anglo-papal relations.

To publicise the crusade in France, Burgundy and England, the pope first sent Franciulo Seruopolos, a Greek from the Morea, who came asking for western help.[8] By the time he set off, for a six-month stay abroad,[9] the Lancastrian government was becoming increasingly alarmed at the good relations between Yorkists and Burgundians and at the strength of the Yorkist hold on Calais. Hence in autumn 1458 an embassy left England for Burgundy and Charles VII, led by Sir John Wenlock, former chamberlain to the queen, and master Louis Galet.[10] The ostensible aim was marriage between the prince of Wales and other nobles and French or Burgundian princesses, to lead to a general peace, preceded by a year's truce. According to French reports, Wenlock told his masters that the French were preparing to invade, which was far from the case.[11] But Wenlock was in fact very much in sympathy with the Burgundians by this time.[12]

In these circumstances Seruopolos came before Henry VI. A French report says that in February 1459 he pleaded before the king for the faith, for peace between Christians, and for a joint enterprise against the infidel. He was to have a reply on 12 February, but the reporter remarked how few magnates were in court to hear him. His plea had no result.[13]

Wandering Greeks were not to be discouraged, but Pius II mainly trusted the council of Mantua. On 10 January 1459 he commissioned Francesco Coppini, bishop of Terni, to come to England and Burgundy to organise delegations to the congress.[14] Coppini's career in England was extremely controversial; eventually deposed as a bishop, ostensibly for what he had done there, he was forced by the pope to end his days as a monk, finding a place in Pius II's memoirs in consequence.[15] By this very fact, however, his activities in England, and even more in Burgundy and France, have been misrepresented, because the pope needed to conceal or disguise his own activites.

Coppini had excellent credentials: clerk of the papal camera, a *referendarius*, one of the collectors of the crusading tenth in Lombardy already under Calixtus III (from December 1456), responsible for recruiting soldiers.[16] The commission to Burgundy allowed him to operate in both countries. It also allowed Pius II's ally, Francesco Sforza, to keep himself informed of various anti-French moves in both. Since Charles VII of France was pressing both the pope and Sforza in late 1458 and 1459 to desert Ferrante and support an Angevin, Sforza in particular was retaliating by secretly fostering hostility to France wherever possible.[17]

Coppini must have set out in late January 1459.[18] On 24 February he had an audience with Sforza, who already knew and trusted him.[19] Almost certainly from this time Coppini considered himself an agent of Sforza as well as of the pope. Pius II must have known and would not have disapproved; the secular interests of the two were the same at that point. Coppini came through France, where he negotiated safe-conducts for the English delegates to Mantua.[20] In late May or early June he reached England, spent a few days in Canterbury, was in London on 8 June,[21] and finally, some time in June, pleaded before the king and royal council at Coventry that delegates be sent to Mantua.[22] His text was Matthew 10 vv. 18, 19 (suggesting that Christ will inspire the Christian who addresses kings), and his theme that the king of England would send ambassadors prepared to negotiate peace, before concerted action against the Turks with the French and the emperor. The council agreed and delegates were named, with a warrant for their expenses dated 25 July.[23] Probably to announce this, John Lax, one of them, was dispatched to the curia on 10 July.[24] The others were to be John Carpenter, bishop of Worcester, the abbot of Peterborough, John Tiptoft, earl of Worcester, Lord John Dudley, and Sir Philip Wentworth.[25] John

Tiptoft was already in Italy at the time, but the others certainly did not go.[26]

Another group – Tiptoft, Robert Flemming, Henry Sharpe and Richard Bole – had already (May 1459) been commissioned to present Henry's formal profession of obedience to the pope.[27] Most were already in Italy: Flemming was named Henry's proctor in October 1458;[28] Sharpe had been *cubicularius* since 1447; Tiptoft had returned from Jerusalem in September 1458 to study in Padua early in 1459.[29] Bole alone was in England; we have met him already as *familiaris* of William Gray, now bishop of Ely, and noticed that he had spent time in Rome with Gray in the late 1440s.[30] Sharpe and probably Flemming, who came to Mantua,[31] may be two 'priests of small account' who, said Pius II angrily, alone came from England.[32]

In July Pius reminded Coppini that it was vital for England to send delegates,[33] and the congress was certainly expecting more Englishmen.[34] In an undelivered speech defending his conduct, Coppini said later that all his good work produced an English delegation which was recalled almost on its journey by the machinations of factious people.[35] Writing to the pope much later Henry VI was made to say that all Coppini's good work 'concerning the meeting' (*circa dietam*), was delayed by ill-wishers.[36] John Whethamstede implied that the outbreak of civil war at the battle of Blore Heath, 23 September, ruined the plan, but probably tensions in July and August were really to blame.[37] By 2 September Pius II had received Henry VI's excuses, which he thought inadequate, brought by the priests who had earlier brought the obedience, and that day his letter to the king, entrusted to Coppini, demanded that delegates be sent.[38] But by the time it arrived Blore Heath had been fought, at least one of the potential delegates, Lord Dudley, had been captured, and there followed the flight of the leading Yorkist lords, after a skirmish at Ludlow on 12/13 October, York to Ireland and Warwick with the young earl of March to Calais.[39] The Lancastrian government proceeded at the November parliament to attaint York and the other leaders.[40]

Presumably Coppini informed Pius of these English problems. By October the curia was assuming that the nuncio's stay would be longer;[41] on 4 December his powers were increased to those of *legatus de latere*.[42] The appointment of a non-cardinal was unusual and the powers given always carefully circumscribed by the mandate.[43] Since Coppini was indicted for his abuses of power, this document was crucial. He was called *nuncium et commissarium cum potestate legati de latere*. He thought that this made him a normal legate *de latere*, but, if so, Pius defined the powers more narrowly than Coppini. As usual in such commissions he was given wide powers to root out abuse:[44] bring back the disobedient, conserve the liberty and authority of the holy see, bring peace and order to church and realm, proceed against all rebels against the church, make peace between barons and make all necessary leagues and pacts 'even if they require more special mandate'.[45] He could hold a general synod of lords and prelates and use censures against opponents. The pope promised to uphold 'the sentences which you correctly pass on rebels'. Coppini thought this gave him fullest power and authority as a *legatus de latere* to compose the civil war.[46]

Coppini's Italian supporters later argued that, trying to fulfil his mandate, he was rebuffed by Henry VI and his advisers, only the Yorkists proving amenable. The Lancastrians therefore became *rebelles* against papal authority.

Coppini's activities in late 1459 and early 1460 are unknown. By late spring Pius II had added the tasks of proclaiming, and collecting for, the crusade called at Mantua and persuading the English to meet the French for a peace conference, since Charles VII's delegates at Mantua maintained that crusade was impossible whilst the English menaced France.[47] A legate went to France, Coppini's friend Ermolao Barbo, bishop of Verona.[48]

In spring 1460 Coppini left England and either contacted or was contacted by the Yorkists in Calais, who persuaded him to join them.[49] One of his advocates stated that the encounter occurred on his way back to the curia to seek further advice, and the Yorkist offered obedience to pope and king, urging him to stay. The account suggests that their fleet and their powerful support convinced him that they would win.[50] On 25 June 1460 the rebels issued public letters, one to Coppini, justifying their actions, saying, among much else, that they had invited the legate because he had power to mediate, which of course was true.[51]

Hence Coppini presented the rebel case to Henry VI, begging him to receive them and hear their grievances, whilst carefully assuring him of their entire obedience. The document publicly issued in London on 3 or 4 July, at a great gathering of supporters, was sent far and wide, including to the pope, for maximum propaganda.[52] At the same time Coppini told Pius II that the Yorkists were very successful and he himself was being treated with great respect.[53]

From London on 5 July the rebels marched to meet the king, accompanied by Coppini, and on 10 July Henry VI was captured at

Northampton, although the queen and Prince Edward remained at liberty. His conduct in supporting the rebels at this juncture brought Coppini most severe criticism from the Roman Rota court. Its judges thought the pope intended his powers only for the crusade, whereas, they maintained, he used them to help faction. They said he issued dispensations for defects of birth and age, dispensed a Benedictine monastery to allow meat-eating, allowed a titular bishop to excommunicate opponents and committed simony. On the journey from London to Northampton he exceeded his mandate by allowing the cross to be borne before him.[54] He vehemently denied simony, which was never proved,[55] and, while admitting some of the rest, pleaded that his actions were within his mandate. His advocates, John of Prato, Federico Capodalista and Antonio Roselli of Padua, argued that raising the cross, which they admitted, was legitimate for a legate *de latere*. John of Prato said that the cross had been carried before him from London to Northampton because the other side was disseminating scandal against the pope, implying a Yorkist idea to which Coppini had agreed. Prato thought that the pope would have had good reason to complain if Coppini had neglected an opportunity to work for peace. Raising the cross was a way of reaching the king in peace, not of rendering the Yorkist army more formidable.[56] Prato denied Coppini any part in the battle itself: 'The legate, fearing lest in the heat of battle the agreements might be deserted and the slaughter of many might follow, against his intention, decided to withdraw and go to pray for the people.' Later: 'All unanimously supported the legate to the king, who, when peace was restored, sent for him, received him honourably and offered him obedience.'[57]

Coppini's advocates pointed out that in the heat of battle it was impossible to clarify the extent of his mandate.[58] Later, on 9 October 1460, Coppini obtained explicit papal permission to have the cross borne before him, presumably necessary because of criticism.[59] Federico Capodalista argued that this showed papal approval of earlier actions, though the Rota judges explicitly denied it.[60] He certainly dispensed for defects of birth and age. In December 1465 Nicholas Dovedale was dispensed again because, when he was eighteen, Coppini had dispensed him, who was also illegitimate, to receive all orders and even to hold a benefice. He had then held a benefice for four years.[61] Coppini's advocates considered such dispensations within the powers of a legate *de latere* and John of Prato asserted that Coppini had had advice from a doctor (of laws, presumably) from the curia.[62]

Writing to Queen Margaret's chaplain, early in 1461, Coppini denied using excommunication as a political weapon.[63] His advocates, blaming enemies, who had even tried to kill him, attributed many hostile stories to slanderers at the curia.[64]

After the triumphs of Northampton, the Yorkists took charge of the king and York proceeded to claim the throne. Pius II's belief that Warwick opposed this may have come from Coppini,[65] as also that the compromise by which York became Henry's heir was devised by Coppini.[66] Coppini claimed in his own defence: 'I reformed the state of the whole of England.'[67]

The Yorkists had independent communications with the curia. The government agent in Rome was John Lax,[68] to whom on 6 August 1460 the Yorkists sent letters for delivery to pope and cardinals.[69] The king's letter gave the pope a Yorkist account, praising Coppini's initial work, slowed by the negligence of certain people, after which the troubles of the kingdom had supervened. Thanks to his authority from the pope, Coppini had produced a settlement, which, the king was made to complain, had been kept from him by ill-disposed persons. At the resulting battle (Northampton) these had been killed, producing new arrangements for government. The legate had been most helpful, so Henry wanted him in England, promoted by the pope (to the cardinalate, understood). Lax would explain the royal wishes. A similar letter went to the cardinals, and one to Lax, in English, asking him to promote the policy. But the Yorkists were perhaps uncertain of Lax's loyalty. Four days later, 'for certain reasons', the government entrusted the same messages to Antonio della Torre, with 'other information'.[70]

Other information concerned Coppini's suggestions to Francesco Sforza that the Yorkists, once established, might combine marriage alliance with Burgundy with invasion of France.[71] Coppini wanted secret papal permission to negotiate and assured Sforza that the policy would help Ferrante, king of Naples, presumably by distracting Charles VII. Coppini also enlisted Sforza's aid for promotion to the cardinalate. Sforza certainly favoured Coppini's personal ambitions and commended the invasion plan to his own ambassador in Rome.[72] Della Torre returned to England on 15 October via Milan, and Sforza wrote to Coppini that the promotion to the cardinalate was being actively pursued; asking Coppini to help plan an invasion of France.[73] A little later Sforza's secretary told Coppini that only if the king (i.e. the Yorkists) asked specially to have a cardinal for England would his name go forward.[74]

By 3 December 1460 Pius II knew the arrangements for the dynasty, and acknowledged receipt of a geneological table, telling Coppini that he had power of a legate *de latere*, even if not a cardinal.[75] Failing the cardinalate, the Yorkist council licensed his acceptance of an English bishopric and letters announced this on 10 December for Della Torre to take to Rome, though they were not in fact sent until 4 January.[76]

The delay resulted from the political situation. York went north about 2 December,[77] met powerful resistance from the Lancastrians, and finally suffered defeat and death at Wakefield on 30 December.[78] Temporarily at least, Wakefield ruined the schemes of Sforza and Pius II.

On 24 December Sforza had sent his agent Prospero Camogli to the dauphin, sheltering with the duke of Burgundy, to continue negotiations for a Franco-Milanese treaty, to last after Louis became king. Camogli also had instructions to approach Burgundy and the Yorkists, follow Louis's line in England, reassure Coppini that his activities were helping Ferrante and try to discover whether the Yorkists would attack France.[79] On 9 January 1461 Della Torre in London announced to Sforza the battle of Wakefield, explaining that the queen's party was slandering Coppini in the curia and England, saying that he was not a legate but had been recalled.[80] Coppini meanwhile told Sforza that he was trying to negotiate a peace,[81] also writing to the queen's chaplain to refute the slanders.[82] On 11 January Warwick sent Della Torre to the pope with a message also for Sforza, playing down the battle of Wakefield, saying that Coppini's promotion would greatly help. The red hat for Coppini had become symbolic of papal support for the Yorkist dynasty.[83] Coppini reassured Sforza at the same time.[84] Della Torre considered that without some tangible help to Coppini, presumably promotion, the 'papal' cause, invasion of France, would be lost.[85] By 15 February Sforza had received these views.[86]

Sforza was dismayed: 'any disaster in that quarter [England] has a disastrous effect here.' Despite the Yorkist victory of Mortimer's Cross, 2 February 1461, he and Pius II must have become convinced that England was useless.[87] In Burgundy Prospero Camogli, Sforza's agent, watched, gloomily, to see who emerged victorious,[88] gloomier still when on 17 February, at St Albans, Warwick lost the king.

Coppini meanwhile left England for safety, escorted to the coast by Warwick's supporters, arriving in Brill on 10 February.[89] His collectorship, as well as the close relations of Burgundians and Yorkists, no doubt attracted him there. He was thus absent when Pius II replied to the Yorkists and Sforza that he was reluctant to promote Coppini because, although pleased with the legate's achievements, some cardinals were saying that the latter had exaggerated to attain his ambitions.[90]

Whilst Coppini waited for the English situation to improve he cultivated the duke of Burgundy. Sforza was still discussing his treaty with the dauphin, whose friendship was being assiduously cultivated by Milan and Pius to counteract his father's hostility. For Burgundy and Milan the political climate began to improve from about 9 March, when news of Edward IV's acceptance as king reached the dauphin's headquarters at Genappe.[91] That day too the Genoese rebelled, secretly supported by Milan, casting off the French. On 22 March Coppini, in Bruges where the duke of Burgundy had made him very welcome, reported to the pope and Sforza the successes of Edward and Warwick,[92] though Camogli was less hopeful and, not surprisingly, doubtful about Louis's attitude.[93]

On 29 March 1461 Edward IV was victorious at Towton and Henry VI fled with the queen. Letters of 7 April brought this news to Bruges,[94] for dispatch to Milan, with the information that England was again controlled by the Yorkists.[95] Already on 17 April Sforza, informed about Towton, told Camogli to cross to England and present his compliments to Edward IV, 'guided by the legate'.[96]

Yorkist intervention on the continent was thus reconsidered. On 17 April Coppini, from Malines, assured Sforza that Edward was in full control.[97] Coppini wished the Yorkists to have papal support, 'with my assistance, provided I have the right authority and prestige', and declared himself ready to devote himself wholly to Sforza's interests. He proposed to meet Camogli in St Omer, where there was to be a meeting of the order of the Golden Fleece, and thence to cross to England: 'I say to your lordship that if I am given the authority I will make the Angevins wish to attend to their home affairs by means of England.' He did not think the curia understood the wonderful opportunity. Edward IV, with support of the church, would be totally secure: 'and there is no other honourable mode of accomplishing this, except for me to return there, with the pretext of reforming the government of the church as I had begun, and, for greater prestige, to return there elevated.'

Camogli, not having met Coppini and more cautious, remarked on 18 April from Bruges that Edward, if completely victorious, might attack France, but that even though Warwick and Burgundy were very friendly, the king of France, weakened by the Genoese rising, might now reconcile with the dauphin.[98] Louis was urging Camogli not to go to England until the situation was clearer.

What Pius II made of this is unclear. Letters from him to Warwick and Henry VI of 10 March 1461, commiserated the losses of Wakefield,[99] urging Coppini to stay with Henry,[100] but whether these reached their destination is unknown. Edward sent obedience at some unknown date, doubtless March or April 1461, announcing that he had taken charge of his hereditary kingdom. Presentation of this may have been the occasion when Sir John Tiptoft moved Pius II to tears by his eloquence.[101] The pope was also kept informed by Sforza and Coppini, but very little is known about his instructions to his legate. On 17 April 1461 Coppini asked the pope for instructions,[102] but on 27 April, after hearing from Chancellor Neville and others that his presence in England would be most welcome, he proposed to write again, not having heard since 4 March (presumably the pope's explanation about the cardinalate). He then intended to see the dauphin, attend the Golden Fleece meeting and finally cross to England.[103]

By 7 May Camogli and Coppini had met. Coppini thought their aims the same: alliance of Milan and the Yorkists with papal approval,[104] though Camogli, needing Sforza's sanction, was more reluctant to cross to England. On 8 May comes a first reference to Coppini talking to the dauphin.[105] During the next weeks their plans fluctuated. Camogli, hesitating too openly to commit Sforza, ostensibly a French ally, to Edward, sought some covert action.[106] He considered Coppini well informed, 'an English Aristotle', and told Sforza the legate's notion that some of the crusading tenth could be used to hire Genoese vessels to give Edward command of the sea, to attack France. Camogli told Sforza 'we have a pope who is well disposed', but that Coppini wanted the idea of thus (mis)-using the funds to come from Sforza. Camogli professed such high matters beyond him, and needed firm orders from his principal. Coppini described for Pius the precarious English situation, with Henry and Margaret in Scotland and the Scots likely to obtain French assistance.[107] The duke of Burgundy was dissuading his niece, the queen of Scotland, from allying with France, but this danger was driving Burgundy and Edward closer and making Louis openly favourable to Edward.

In this letter, dated 1 June, Coppini first mentioned to the pope the dauphin's promise, when king, to abolish the Pragmatic Sanction of Bourges, the French legislation regulating papal provisions, as disliked by the papacy as its English counterpart, the statutes against provisors. Charles VII was very old and ill, and Coppini wanted Pius II to be ready with a legate, to strike while the iron was hot. He thought himself on excellent terms with Louis. This most tempting of carrots was almost certainly dangled by Louis, an accomplished politician who knew how to please the pope.

After the hesitations,[108] Sforza finally authorised the trip to England, on 14 June 1461, in letters reaching Burgundy by 12 July.[109] Sforza gave the necessary letter of credence to Della Torre, Warwick's envoy in Rome, as he came through Milan. Sforza congratulated Edward, assured him of papal good-will and commended Coppini,[110] who was also assured of papal good-will.[111]

Whilst Camogli struggled to complete his business with Louis, delaying their crossing,[112] the death of Charles VII on 22 July and the accession of Louis, known to Camogli in Bruges by 28 July,[113] drastically altered the situation.

As Camogli realised, Louis's interests as dauphin and king would be very different. He would not now favour Warwick and invasion.[114] His attitude to Naples would change too, surrounded as he would be by Angevins, and especially influenced by his mother, Marie of Anjou. The envoy favoured persuading the king to undertake some Christian enterprise (i.e. crusade) under the pope, for which Coppini should visit the king, to sound him on Camogli's behalf. He also favoured Sforza's continued encouragment of Yorkist invasion schemes.

Hence, far from returning to England, Coppini joined Prospero in complicated schemes involving Louis and Pius II, by which the king tried to detach the pope from Milan, by promising to revoke the Pragmatic Sanction, in return for the desertion of Ferrante, and the pope was led to believe that the abolition of the Sanction could be achieved on acceptable terms. The details are unimportant here, but Coppini was deep in negotiations with Louis during August and September 1461, 'as a legate', for which of course he had no mandate,[115] sending regular accounts of Louis's terms to the pope.[116]

Pius II reacted with extreme nervousness and anger, calling Coppini 'too frivolous' (troppo legiero), thinking that he talked too much and professing to believe that Louis's terms – desertion of Ferrante, to be compensated in Italy – were either Coppini's own, or, if Louis's, should have been altered by Coppini.[117] Coppini's hints, that either Coppini or a friend of his should be made legate for France, went unheeded; he entrusted the task to Jean Jouffroy, bishop of Arras, already encountered.[118] On 18 August Jouffroy was commissioned for France, Burgundy, England and Scotland. Pius commended him to Louis, specifically as coming to discuss the abolition of the Pragmatic

Sanction.[119] Jouffroy had orders to go first to Burgundy and be guided by the duke.[120]

At first Pius II tried simply to recall Coppini,[121] but allowed Jouffroy to use him if he thought it helpful.[122] Jouffroy must have accepted Coppini's help; on 23 September Coppini told Sforza of Jouffroy's arrival and suggestion that since the pope intended to make some agreement between England and France, Coppini's long-postponed channel crossing might now occur.[123] On 20 October Pius II rescinded his recall at Jouffroy's request and let Coppini go.[124]

We know only that Coppini found favour in England. Edward IV made him his proctor in Rome, granted an annuity and the right to the white rose on his arms.[125] Louis later professed to believe that he had intrigued against France (all too likely),[126] and his own advocates had to defend him against charges of misappropriation of papal funds and taking too much in presents,[127] which he vehemently denied.[128]

Meanwhile Jouffroy worked with Louis XI and on 27 November 1461 the king announced to the pope the abolition of the Pragmatic Sanction,[129] which Jouffroy hailed on 30 November as 'without bargain, without condition' (*sine pacto, sine conditione*).[130] It seems impossible that Pius II truly believed this, but he certainly disbelieved Coppini's earlier account of Louis's likely conditions. Over the next few weeks Louis's terms became ever clearer[131] in discussions with the Milanese ambassadors, whom he tried to frighten into abandoning Ferrante.[132]

Meetings between Burgundians and English, with Jouffroy present, and English messengers to France in November,[133] did not lessen tension between England and France; relations were strained when Coppini passed through France, returning to Rome. In Tours, where Louis was, from 8 to 12 January 1462, he talked to the Milanese ambassador.[134] Coppini thought the English hostile to Louis, but the ambassador equally considered Louis hostile to Coppini. The king thought the legate had gone to England to foment trouble for France. He accused Coppini, 'a changeable man who does not stand firm in his purposes', of boasting that he had made two kings, presumably some garbled version of Coppini's role in the constitutional crisis. The ambassador told the king that Coppini had been slandered, but warned the legate against boasting. Louis was now wholly trusting Jouffroy, whom, on 18 December, Pius II had rewarded with a red hat.

Jouffroy must have known that the reward the king demanded for abolishing the Sanction would be most unwelcome to the pope, and to prepare Pius's mind he blamed Coppini for giving Louis ideas. On 13 January 1462, replying to Jouffroy's explanation that Louis was now making conditions, Pius recalled that earlier Jouffroy had been full of security, adding the telling sentences: 'The bishop of Terni did not afterwards return to France; if he sowed the seed of evil it must already have put out its shoots when you wrote those splendid words so full of peace and glory. If things changed later, it is up to you to correct this.'[135] On 27 January Sforza's agent in Rome said that Pius II's suspicions against Coppini had been confirmed by Jouffroy, who blamed Coppini for misleading Louis that his ambitions in Italy, especially concerning Naples, would be supported by the pope and Milan.[136]

Sforza did his best to support Coppini, recommending him highly, awarding a pension and making him a member of his council,[137] but Jouffroy's arrival in Rome on 13 March revealed the full details of Louis's conditions and Coppini shared with Jouffroy the extreme papal displeasure.[138] Jouffroy was protected by his mandate and his cardinal's hat, coupled with Pius II's desire neither to antagonise Louis nor fully to admit his own machinations. But Coppini was arrested some time in May 1462.[139] On 10 July, from Castel St Angelo, he told Sforza he believed Jouffroy's accusations were the major cause of his problems[140] and Pius II admitted that he had French enemies.[141] Despite assiduous organisation of a defence by his friend Girolamo Aliotti, he was condemned on 30 August.[142] All the charges concerned England. The pope could not admit publicly that France and Naples played a major part.

Edward IV's government continued to support Coppini; in March 1462 Della Torre even thought that he might receive an English bishopric,[143] but such support cannot have helped.

His fall presented the English government with the question of its representation in the curia. Della Torre represented Warwick. John Lax, who was among those attainted, was said by Della Torre to have been pardoned, along with his servant Thomas (Coventry) in the new year of 1462,[144] but he never enjoyed Edward's confidence.

Early in 1462 Pius II sent his blessing to Edward.[145] Louis XI, announcing an intention to negotiate peace between Henry VI and Edward, prior to a crusade, sent an embassy to England at the end of February.[146] Edward's instructions to a follow-up embassy maintained the façade that peace was needed for a crusade,[147] but as Louis was also negotiating with Queen Margaret, and soon, on 24 June, allied with her, neither the pope nor Edward can have been very impressed.[148]

Not until late 1463 did Pius II again try to raise money from England.

By then Edward had as permanent proctor in Rome Peter Courtenay,[149] protonotary and *referendarius*, who, with Thomas Hope, was sent to England on 7 November 1463 to plead the crusading cause.[150] They brought a bull for the archbishop of Canterbury, explaining that, after a consistory on 22 October, in the presence of Burgundians and Italians, the pope had summoned a crusade, which he would lead in person. Courtenay and Hope were to ask Bourgchier to levy one-tenth.[151] Edward IV reacted like his predecessors, informing the pope that he could not impose such a novelty, but, in May 1464, asking for a gift from the clergy which could be forwarded.[152] Bourgchier, to stir the clergy to pay, argued that the method avoided the use of hated sanctions like excommunication or the granting of *commendams*. At first he asked only 4 pence in the pound but later, on 16 June, at least 6 pence, having, he said, now heard from a notable person recently come from Rome that Pius II was working very hard.[153] By early 1465 the 6 pence had been agreed by diocesan synods and paid by most clergy. But by then Pius II was dead (15 August 1464). Paul II sent an envoy to collect the money, but that is another story.

Pius II was undoubtedly sincere in his desire to organise a crusade, but his preoccupation with Italian politics delayed its onset and marred its chances. The career of Coppini shows, for the first time in Anglo-papal relations in this period, how the ethos of the Renaissance papacy could affect the localities. The blatant politicising by Coppini of his spiritual office was unusual up to that time, but was a portent, and he had a right to feel aggrieved. His master Pius II had undoubtedly condoned his behaviour in England and certainly would have accepted the consequences of his much more serious French intrigues if successful. The failure of the plot, not its content, procured Coppini's sad fate. It is hardly surprising that the nations of Europe henceforward treated the pope as just another secular ruler; Coppini behaved as he did because Pius frequently acted as if he too believed it. The consequences for the history of the church in the next seventy years were dire.

Notes

1 Griffiths, *Henry VI*, pp. 807–10; G. Harriss, 'The struggle for Calais, an aspect of the rivalry between Lancaster and York', *EHR*, LXXV, 1960, pp. 30–53, esp. p. 48.
2 Vaughan, pp. 353–4.
3 Vaughan, p. 110.
4 P. A. Johnson, *Duke Richard of York, 1411–1460*, Oxford, 1988, p. 151; G. Chastellain, *Oeuvres*, 8 vols., ed. Kervyn de Lettenhove, Académie Royale de Belgique, Brussels, 1863–6, III, pp. 427–8.

5 Thielemans, pp. 367–81 for Burgundians. I. Parrino, *Acta Albaniae Vaticana, Res Albaniae Seculorum XIV et XV atque Cruciatum Spectantia*, I, Studi e testi, CCLXVI, Vatican City, 1971, no. 61, letter to French king, August 1456.

6 V. Ilardi, 'The Italian League, Francesco Sforza and Charles VII, 1454–61', *Studies in the Renaissance*, VI, 1959, pp. 129–66, esp. pp. 131–50 for next paragraph.

7 Ilardi, 'The Italian League', p. 150.

8 Setton, II, p. 199 note; Mandati, 834, f. 42v, at pope's command, 6 November 1458, with four horses.

9 Mandati, 834, f. 111v.

10 Griffiths, *Henry VI*, p. 816, and references. Chastellain, III, pp. 479–85, notes, charges against Alençon, said to be involved.

11 Stevenson, I, p. 367, February 1459, misdated November 1458.

12 J. S. Roskell, *The Commons and their Speakers in English Parliaments*, Manchester, 1965, pp. 259–62, 370–1; idem, 'John Lord Wenlock of Someries', *Publications of the Bedfordshire Historical Record Society*, XXXVIII, 1958, pp. 12–48, esp. pp. 33–4.

13 Stevenson, I, p. 368.

14 Activities in England, not including defences (note 35 below): C. Head, 'Pius II and the Wars of the Roses', *Archivum Historiae Pontificiae*, VIII, 1970, pp. 139–78. I have not repeated references to Head. *DBI*, XXVIII, pp. 619–24, article by A. I. Galletti, further bibliography. Letters of credence: Rymer, V/2, p. 83 (XI, 419). Commission to Burgundy: A. Gottlob, 'Des Nuntius F. Coppini Anteil an der Entthronung des Königs Heinrich VI und sein Verurteilung bei Römische Curie', *Deutsche Zeitschrift für Geschichtswissenschaft*, IV, 1890, pp. 75–111, esp. p. 77.

15 Pius II, *Commentarii*, ed. A. van Heck, pp. 231–3, 644–5. Kendall and Ilardi, *Dispatches*, II, *1460–61*, pp. xxii–xxvi. Pius II, *The Commentaries of Pius II*, ed. F. A. Gragg and L. C. Gabel, VII, Smith College Studies in History, XXXV, Northampton (Mass.), 1951, pp. 508–9, takes many points from C. Lucius, *Pius II und Ludwig von Frankreich, 1461–2*, Heidelberger Abhandlungen zur mittleren und neueren Geschichte, XLI, Heidelberg, 1913. Pius II relied on the Rota judgement: printed Gottlob, pp. 108–11.

16 Parrino, *Acta Albaniae*, no. 128. For example IE, 438, ff. 86v, 88v, 119; IE, 440, ff. 104, 109v, 115v; Mandati, 833ᵃ, ff. 98v, 123v; Mandati, 834, ff. 33v, 46, 57, 70.

17 Ilardi, 'The Italian League', pp. 151–2; idem, 'France and Milan: the uneasy alliance, 1452–66', *Studies in Renaissance Diplomatic History*, Variorum Reprints, London, 1986, Chapter 2, esp. pp. 427–8.

18 Mandati, 834, ff. 71, 73v, 79; IE, 440, ff. 117, 117v, 16 and 19 January, for four months.

19 Kendall and Ilardi, II, p. xxii, from Milan archives.

20 21 March 1459, C. L. Scofield, *The Life and Reign of Edward the Fourth, King of England and of France and Lord of Ireland*, 2 vols., London, 1923, I, p. 71. Letter from pope to Coppini in France, Mandati, 834, f. 99v, 16 June 1459 (payment of cursor).

21 Stone, *Chronicle of John Stone*, p. 77; J. Whethamstede, *Registrum Abbatiae Johannis Whethamstede Abbatis Monasterii S. Albani*, 2 vols., ed. H. T. Riley, *RS* XXVIII/6i, London, 1872, p. 331 arrival 4 June; Flenley, *Six Town Chronicles*, p. 147, in London.

22 Whethamstede, *Registrum*, I, pp. 333–6, summary of speech.

23 Scofield, I, p. 72; *PPC*, VI, p. 302.

24 *DK*, XLVIII, p. 437.

25 *PPC*, VI, p. 302.

26 Mitchell, *Tiptoft*, pp. 48, 50, 51, 62, 64.

27 Rymer, V/2, p. 84 (XI, 422).

28 Above, Chapter 1, note 109.

29 Sharpe: *CPL*, X, p. 274. Tiptoft: Mitchell, *Tiptoft*, p. 50.

30 Chapter 3, notes 214–16.

31 *CPL*, XI, pp. 556–7, present 7 September.

32 *Commentarii*, p. 231, line 20.

33 Parrino, no 442, 8 July, perhaps taken by Antonio de Famixiano, Mandati, 834, f. 114, who brought reply by 1 September. Coppini probably brought Pius II to Henry VI dated 17 April, Parrino, no. 408.

34 *Commentarii*, p. 221, lines 31–2.

35 Arezzo City Library (Biblioteca della Citta di Arezzo), MS 400, ff. 43–5 (microfilm only) defence before Paul II, written by Girolamo Aliotti, never delivered. MS is Aliotti's letter book, H. Aliotti, *Epistolae et opuscula*, ed. G. M. Scarmalli, Arezzo, 1769, not including this. See f. 44: *adqueti tandem homines regni illius ut oratores eligerent utque ipsi electi et desinati onus legationis acciperent, implevi igitur omne ex parte pontificis votum preterquam quod horatores ipsos meis humeris ad dietam Mantuanam deferre non potui. Est regnum illud contumax et rebelle factionibusque ac seditionibus plenum sedique apostolice haud multum deferens. Nonnulli igitur illorum hominum qui his artibus et factionibus student sanctum pontificis ceptum fraude ac dolis impedire totque labores meos irritare conati sunt ut scilicet oratores electos atque ad iter . . .? . . . ex ipso pene itinere revocarent.*

36 Oxford, Bodleian Library, MS Ashmole 789, ff. 326v–7, Canterbury, 6 August 1460, after battle of Northampton (7 July).

37 Whethamstede, *Registrum*, I, pp. 336.

38 Parrino, no. 454: pope to Henry, acknowledging *oratores* who explained absence of delegates, but not accepting excuse. 12 August cursor from England via Venice: Mandati, 834, f. 113. Pius II to Coppini to see that Henry's letter delivered: ASV, Arm. XXXIX 9, f. 77.

39 Johnson, *York*, pp. 194–5.

40 Johnson, p. 192.

41 Mandati, 834, f. 120.

42 *CPL*, XI, p. 397. In full: A. Theiner, *Vetera monumenta Hibernorum et Scotorum historiam illustrantia*, Rome, 1864, pp. 423–4. He is called (p. 423): *nuncium et commissarium cum plena potestate legati de latere.*

43 Legatine powers: G. Paro, *The Right of Papal Legation*, The Catholic University of America, Studies in Canon Law, CCXI, Washington, DC, 1947. Further: Blet, Figueira, Lesage, Schmutz, Wasner in bibliography below.

44 Above, note 42. Paro, pp. 92–102 for terminology.

45 Theiner, p. 424.

46 MS Arezzo 400, f. 44: *Unde romanus Pontifex, cupiens illorum principum discidia resque regni pacatas et conpositas reddere, misit ad me plenissimam legationis auctoritatem, summa cum potestate ad omnia eius generis transfigenda..*

47 Parrino, no. 470; *CPL*, XI, pp. 401–2, 403, powers as collector, cf. Gottlob, pp. 80–1. French: *Commentarii*, pp. 230–1; also ASV, Arm. XXXIX 9, f. 107, further announcement of meeting, 10 January 1460.

48 Raynaldus, *Annales*, X, pp. 224–5; payment to bishop: Mandati 834 f. 137, 18 January.

49 Letter dated by Head and Scofield 22 March 1460 is 1461: Scofield, I, p. 74; Head, pp. 150–1. C. Ross, *Edward IV*, London, 1974, pp. 22–38, good for 1460–1.

50 John of Prato's defence: Vatican, MS Reg. Lat. 377, ff. 85–94. For John: *Dictionaire de Droit Canonique*, VI,col. 117. MS, f. 86v: *suspicatus se posse repelli, revertebat ad curiam volens hic referre papae, sed cum obviasse principibus exilitis repulsis de latere regis, exhortatus est ab eis ut non recederet, offerentibus ei obedientiam pro summo pontifice et*

etiam se paratos obedire regi offerentibus . . . et sic exhortati sunt ut dictus legatus cum eis accederet, habentes classem maritinum et portus principales regni in sua potestate et favorem populi . . . .

51 Stone, pp. 78–80, Neville etc. pass Canterbury 26 June, Coppini 27 June. Letter to Coppini: ASV, AA I–XVIII, no. 1443, f. 30, part of dossier for Coppini's trial. Letter in full: H. Ellis, *Original Letters Illustrative of English History*, 3rd series, I, London, 1846, pp. 85–8. See Johnson, *York*, pp. 201–5. Ross, *Edward IV*, pp. 24–5 for propaganda.

52 ASV, AA I–XVIII, no. 1443 ff. 3–34; Ellis, pp. 89–97, Coppini to Henry VI. Also Durham, Dean and Chapter Archives, Misc. Ch. 5655, list of grievances issued from Calais; and previous note.

53 ASV, AA I–XVIII, no. 1443 ff. 34–6.

54 Gottlob, pp. 109, 110.

55 MS Arezzo 400, f. 44.

56 MS Reg. Lat. 377, f. 86v.

57 MS Reg. Lat. 377, f. 87v.

58 MS Reg. Lat. 377, f. 89: *Exercitus principum erat infinitus et quasi in facto esse. Unde tempora non largebantur nec patiebantur hoc notificari pape . . . cum mora modici temporis esset periculosa.*

59 *CPL*, XI, p. 582.

60 ASV, Misc. Arm. II 107, f. 301.

61 *CPL*, XII, pp. 467–8. Gottlob, p. 111, judges blamed Coppini for not telling pope enough.

62 MS Reg. Lat. 377, f. 90. Hieronimo de Sanctuciis de Urbino, with Fra Gabrieli Piccolomini, paid going to England early in 1461: Mandati, 836, ff. 60, 60v, 63v; IE, 446, f. 116v.

63 Hinds, pp. 37–41, 9 January 1461.

64 MS Reg. Lat. 377, f. 92v.

65 Head, p. 161; *Commentarii*, pp. 232–3; Johnson, pp. 212–18.

66 Head, p. 161; *Commentarii*, p. 233.

67 MS Arezzo 400, f. 44: *statum tocius Angliae reformavi.*

68 Hinds, p. 22 for his sending in May 1460.

69 MS Ashmole 789, ff. 326v–7, to pope; f. 327 to cardinals; f. 327v to Lax, in English.

70 MS Ashmole 789, f.327v. For Lax, above, pp. 15–18.

71 Letter, 6 August 1460, Hinds, pp. 28–30; Hinds, p. 31, letter, 15 August, Della Torre is Coppini's messenger to pope and Milan; negotiations with Burgundy, Beaucourt, VI, p. 291.

72 Hinds, pp. 31–2, 33.

73 Hinds, pp. 33–4.

74 Hinds, p. 34, 25 October 1460.

75 ASV, Arm. XXXIX 9, ff. 124–4v; Raynaldus, *Annales*, X, p. 261.

76 Rymer, V/2, pp. 102–3 (XI, 468), named sees excepted; Head, p. 162; Hinds, pp. 35, 36, for Della Torre, 10 December. Request for promotion of William Wayneflete, 8 November, taken by John Lasci, assuming that pope knows of troubles: MS Corpus Christi College 170, p. 216.

77 Johnson, p. 221.

78 Johnson, p. 223.

79 Kendall and Ilardi, II, pp. 48–58; Hinds, p. 37; Louis XI, *Lettres de Louis XI, roi de France*, 11 vols., eds. J. Vaesen and E. Charavaray, I, *1438–1462*, Société de l'Histoire de France, Paris, 1883, pp. 337–41.

80 Hinds, pp. 42–3.

81 Hinds, p. 41.
82 Hinds, pp. 37–41.
83 Warwick to Sforza: J. Calmette and G. Perinelle, *Louis XI et l'Angleterre*, Mémoires et Documents publiés par la Société de l'École des Chartes, XI, Paris, 1930, no. 3, pp. 274–5, 11 January, 1462; Hinds, p. 44, Warwick to Pius II.
84 Hinds, pp. 44–5.
85 Hinds, pp. 46–7, from Della Torre. Coppini to Milan, p. 47, saying Della Torre crossed on 19 January.
86 Kendall and Ilardi, II, pp. 76–8.
87 Kendall and Ilardi, II, pp. 68–9, Camogli to Sforza, 5 February: dauphin has lost interest; ibid., pp. 96–103, 17 February, no hope from England.
88 Kendall and Ilardi, II, pp. 142–5, 3 and 4 March.
89 Hinds, pp. 53, to Richard Caunton, from Brill, 20 February.
90 Kendall and Ilardi, II, p. xxiv.
91 Kendall and Ilardi, II, pp. 146–53.
92 Kendall and Ilardi, II, pp. 214–16; Sestan, I, *1453–1475*, pp. 94–6.
93 Kendall and Ilardi, II, pp. 210–23.
94 Hinds, pp. 63–5, bishop of Salisbury (Beauchamp) to Coppini; pp. 60–3, George Neville to Coppini.
95 Kendall and Ilardi, II, pp. 252–4.
96 Kendall and Ilardi, II, p. 270.
97 Kendall and Ilardi, II, pp. 274–81.
98 Kendall and Ilardi, II, pp. 284–97.
99 ASV, Arm. XXXIX 9, f. 238v, to Warwick; ibid., ff. 239v–40, to Henry.
100 ASV, Arm. XXXIX 9, ff. 239–9v.
101 Cambridge, Corpus Christi College, MS 170, p. 217–19, obedience. Tiptoft's speech: R. Weiss, 'A letter-preface of John Free to John Tiptoft, Earl of Worcester', *Bodleian Quarterly Record*, VIII/87, 1935, pp. 101–3, esp. p. 102. Tiptoft safe-conduct, 16 October, 1460: *CPL*, XI, p. 580. Christ Church, Canterbury, thought he had obtained valuable indulgences: Foreville, *Le Jubilé*, pp. 72–4, 186–7, suggests late 1460. In England 1 September 1461: Stone, *Chronicle*, p. 84.
102 Asking Sforza to forward letter: Kendall and Ilardi, II, p. 278.
103 Coppini to Sforza: Kendall and Ilardi, II, pp. 302–5. Coppini to Neville: Hinds, pp. 78–81, dated 23 April.
104 Kendall and Ilardi, II, pp. 318–21.
105 Kendall and Ilardi, II, pp. 322–9.
106 Kendall and Ilardi, II, pp. 334–41, Camogli to Sforza, 9 May.
107 Sestan, pp. 108–13.
108 Further correspondence June 1461, Kendall and Ilardi, II, pp. 380–85, 394–7, 400, 404–7.
109 Kendall and Ilardi, II, pp. 416–19; B. Mandrot, *Dépêches des Ambassadeurs milanais en France sous Louis XI et François Sforza*, 4 vols., Paris, 1916–23, I, p. 3. Arrival of letters: Kendall and Ilardi, II, pp. 438–49.
110 Hinds, pp. 96–7; similar to various notables, credence for Della Torre, p. 97.
111 Hinds, p. 97.
112 Kendall and Ilardi, II, pp. 420–3, 424–35, 438–49.
113 Mandrot, I, pp. 12–19, possible visit to new king.
114 Mandrot, I, pp. 12–19.
115 Mandrot, I, pp. 56–8, to Pius II, phrase used, p. 57.
116 I hope to publish an account of this elsewhere.
117 On Pius II's state of mind cf. 3 October account by Sforza's agent in Rome about

conversations with pope: Lucius, pp. 92–6.

118 J. Combet, *Louis XI et le Saint Siège*, Paris,1903, p. 4; Fierville, p. 9.

119 Pius II, *Epistolae*, ed. A. Zarothus, Milan, 1487, letter 23, 18 August 1461.

120 Pius II, *Epistolae*, letter 24; Raynaldus, *Annales*, X, p. 317.

121 Lucius, pp. 85–6, 88–9, 89–90; Hinds, pp. 102–4, Sforza to Coppini, 31 August.

122 Lucius, pp. 89–90.

123 Hinds, pp. 104–5.

124 Lucius, p. 97.

125 *CPR, Edward IV*, I, p. 59; Rymer, V/2, p. 106 (XI, 479–80).

126 Mandrot, I, pp. 173–4.

127 Gottlob, p. 109 for charges; refuted in MS Reg. Lat. 377, ff. 92v–3v. Royal appointment gave proctor's salary *donec sibi conpetenter provideretur.*.

128 MS Arezzo 400, f. 43.

129 Pius II, *Opera omnia*, Basel, 1579, p. 863, letter 388.

130 Fierville, pp. 246–7, Jouffroy to pope.

131 Mandrot, I, pp. 103–26, 129–35, 138–42.

132 Mandrot, I, pp. 143–63.

133 Scofield, I, p. 211; Calmette and Perinelle, pp. 9–10, 11 note 3; Chastellain, IV, pp. 160–4, legate's speech at Valenciennes.

134 Mandrot, I, pp. 172–5.

135 Pius II, *Epistolae*, ed. Zarothus, letter 26.

136 Kendall and Ilardi, II, p. xxv.

137 Kendall and Ilardi, II, p. xxv.

138 Fierville, p. 119; *Commentarii*, p. 455 line 17 to p. 457 line 34; for Coppini's unpopularity, letter to Sforza, Hinds, p. 108.

139 Letter in note 138 written when pope leaving for Viterbo *c.* 3 May. Arrested after that: *Commentarii*, p. 644 line 25.

140 Kendall and Ilardi, II, pp. xxv–xxvi.

141 *Commentarii*, p. 644 line 9.

142 Head, p. 173; *CPL*, XI, pp. 675–6.

143 Hinds, pp. 106–8; Italian in Calmette and Perinelle, no. 5, pp. 276–8.

144 Hinds, p. 107; Calmette and Perinelle, p. 277, Lax called Sax.

145 Scofield, I, p. 216; Rymer, V/2, p. 110 (XI, 489).

146 Scofield, I, p. 238; Chastellain, IV, pp. 220–1.

147 Scofield, I, p. 239.

148 Griffiths, *Henry VI*, p. 887.

149 Katterbach, no. 16.

150 *CPL*, XI, p. 654, safe-conduct.

151 Cambridge, Corpus Christi, MS 170, pp. 227–8, not in Lunt, II, p. 145. For events: L. Pastor, *History of the Popes*, English ed., III, London, 1900, pp. 320–33, and Pastor, *Acta inedita historiam Pontificum Romanorum praesertim saec. XV, XVI, XVII illustrantia*, Freiburg, 1904, no. 148, pp. 188–93, 225–33.

152 Lunt, II, p. 146; T. Bourgchier, *Registrum Thome Bourgchier, Cantuariensis Archiepiscopi, A.D. 1454–1486*, CYS, LIV, Oxford, 1957, pp. 117–18.

153 Lunt, II, pp. 148–9; Bourgchier, *Registrum*, pp. 119–22. Sequel: Bourgchier, pp. 122–9. Ross, *Edward IV*, p. 377: rebels in 1469 said government misused collection; cf. J. Warkworth, *A Chronicle of the first thirteen years of the reign of King Edward the Fourth*, ed. J. O. Halliwell, Camden Society, 1st series, London, 1839, p. 49.

III
Theory and belief

12
Pope and council

In the fifteenth century the most important attack on the papacy's view of itself came from general councils. The councils of Pisa, Constance and Basel embodied theories of the supremacy of general councils over popes, but also of the council as the legal and natural vehicle for reform of the church, urgently necessary after the schism. In England there was also a native reforming tradition, rendered more anxious as Wyclif and, in our period, the lollards, seriously criticised the institutional church. This chapter will examine some aspects of that native tradition and ask also what the English made of the conciliar movement. What did they read? What did they think about pope and council?

The most characteristic expression of orthodox 'reforming' thought in England drew its main inspiration from Robert Grosseteste, *noster Lincolniensis*, who had been rediscovered by Wyclif but was also used by several writers by no means lollard, probably because Wyclif had drawn attention to his works, available in the library of the Oxford Franciscans.[1] Grosseteste himself had a pastoral ideal of the papacy, ultimately based on pseudo-Dionysius.[2] The pope was the supreme bishop, but all bishops derived their authority from divine illumination, with the task of diffusing divine light to those in their care. Within his diocese each bishop had the duty and authority from God to follow the gospel.[3] Though bishops derived their light from the pope, he did not 'limit' them, solving in favour of the local bishop the quarrel about the derivation of episcopal power later bitterly fought at the council of Trent.[4] In modern parlance Grosseteste would have found it difficult to accept that papal universal jurisdiction automatically overruled his episcopal *ordo*. Though he said in places that the bishop derived his power from the pope, within his own diocese he thought the bishop was 'the sun' and he became more and more uneasy with papal interference.[5]

A programme based upon these episcopal ideals was taken by the English to the general councils of Pisa and Constance. When in 1408

Robert Hallum asked Richard Ullerston, of Queen's College, Oxford, to prepare a reform programme for Pisa, Ullerston produced *Petitiones* based on Grosseteste's ideals.[6] In so far as he discussed the role of the papacy, he pleaded for the appointment as pope of a man, as far as this was possible to discover, chosen by God for the office, who would refrain from avaricious, legalistic interference with the local church and act as a centre of unity and peace. Within the kingdom, if the church proved too weak to act, the king had the duty to come to its rescue. Within the diocese the bishop was to have a free hand for reform.

The major authorities for Ullerston's views on bishops were, he said, Grosseteste, 'who for his time was a light and lamp of this world':[7] his memorandum to the curia in 1250 and his letters, which were quoted or paraphrased again and again;[8] the *Ecclesiastical Hierarchy* of pseudo-Dionysius, rediscovered as a support for this attitude no doubt first from Grosseteste but quoted or paraphrased continually;[9] and Bernard, *De consideratione*, another Grosseteste favourite.[10]

This fondness for Grosseteste's viewpoint was certainly carried by the English delegates to the general councils of the early fifteenth century. At Pisa, Hallum's protégé, John Luke, quoted Dionysius, *De divinis nominibus*, with Grosseteste's commentary, to show how all unity is grounded in divine unity and flows from it,[11] and also quoted Grosseteste's views on ecclesiastical abuse.[12] At Constance Hallum himself preached a notable sermon *Erunt signa in sole*, on 8 December, 1415.[13] He used the study of optics in a manner certainly derived from Grosseteste, to equate the properties of the sun, at the apex of light, with the role of the pope and bishops, regarded as equals: 'Thus the papal and episcopal order is set above all estates and grades, dignities and orders, in, as it were, similar excellence.'[14] Hallum attacked simony and wished the pope and bishops to be founts of justice, not of indulgence, to their subjects. He proclaimed that we await 'the spiritual sun, the future pope' (*sol spiritualis, papa futurus*), who would purge the curia of all its vices, particularly of avarice and simony, which obscure the sun.

The English used this tradition to further the work of reform at the council. Henry Abendon, fellow of Merton College, Oxford, in a sermon *Sitis repleti fructu justitiae*, delivered on 27 October 1415, quoted Ullerston's authorities in a radical plea against exemptions[15] and an anonymous English preacher on 10 May 1416, quoted him verbatim on the abuse of appeals and on 'daughters of simony'. The abusive extension of ecclesiastical power was said to be at the origin of the schism.[16]

It is known that Chichele particularly wanted a pope who was politically neutral, and especially hoped that Constance would tackle exemptions.[17]

During and after Constance interest in reform along lines traced by Grosseteste had combined in some cases with a conciliar theory. Some writers, William Lyndwood for instance, whom we will meet again, of course take for granted the traditional position: the pope superior to the council.[18] But support for versions of conciliar theory was now more common. In an Epiphany sermon, *Surge illuminare Jerusalem*, pronounced at the council of Constance, Richard Flemming upheld the superiority of the council over the pope, quoting 'that doctor of venerable memory' (*iste doctor memorie venerabilis*), who came before the pope and told him that although he could do all things on earth, the holy see could do nothing against God; if it tried to do so it was to be resisted as Paul resisted Peter; in other words the 1250 memorandum of Grosseteste.[19] Robert Gilbert, welcoming Sigismund and the Spaniards in 1417, argued that the council truly had plenitude of power, even over the pope, and could truly undertake reform. Christ's prayer for Peter, that his faith fail not, referred to the church, not to Peter personally nor to his successors, 'some of whom deviated from the faith' (*quorum aliqui deviabuntur a fide*), a thoroughly conciliar quotation from canon law (Dist. 40 chapter 6).[20]

One needs to ask how far this adoption of conciliar ideas depended on the immediate circumstances and how far on new ideas from elsewhere. What was being read both on councils and on reform?

Though survival of books is notoriously difficult to use as evidence,[21] it appears that material from all the councils was collected, especially from Basel. English *Acta* from Pisa survive from the privy seal office, with conciliar letters in William Swan's collections;[22] there are *Acta* from Constance, for instance a complete set belonging to Thomas Polton and then to Duke Humfrey;[23] there are several collections from Basel, some associated with institutions which sent delegates,[24] with stray *Acta* and collections of letters and speeches, often showing interest in the Hussites.[25] There is one English account of Florence and stray *Acta*.[26]

English scholars were familiar with, and had access to, much polemical literature about papal power from the past. John Whethamstede in his great dictionary, *Granarium*, outlined possible views, with authorities;[27] contemporary collections exist: Cambridge, Emmanuel College 9,[28] Corpus Christi College 157 (copied *c.* 1441),[29] British Library, Harley 631 (associated with the Kemps).[30] Works by Alexander de Elpidio[31] and Augustinus Triumphus (quoted by Thomas Gascoigne whom we will meet again) were still being copied.[32] Polton and his nephew Philip owned a manuscript containing both earlier and contemporary works on papal authority and reform.[33] John of Paris's *De potestate papali et regali* was being read in Oxford in the 1450s and 1460s.[34] Marsilius of Padua's *Defensor pacis*, thoroughly refuted by Thomas Netter, who thought he had inspired Wyclif, as we will see, only began to be known in England in the fifteenth century,[35] perhaps in the first place because Cardinal Adam Easton drew attention to his errors.[36] Easton's books came to rest in Norwich cathedral.[37] Thomas Gascoigne owned a Marsilius, and Harley 631 includes it.[38] Florence of course fostered interest in the Greeks and their church organisation, though not much was known. But significantly Whethamstede used, and others also copied, a *Dialogus inter orthodoxus et cathecumen*, written in 1388 and circulated at Basel,[39] which gave an account of Greek organisation but also pleaded for church reform based on bishops, with an historical repudiation of much of the western church power structure, including the Donation of Constantine.[40]

Until Constance ended the most commonly collected contemporary conciliar treatises in English hands were works of Jean Gerson and Pierre D'Ailly,[41] which continued to be copied.[42] After Constance some material from the earlier schism was collected for the first time; Harley 631 and Harley 3768 (already mentioned) contain some.[43] But there is little evidence for widespread ownership of the writings of the time of Basel. Works of the papal champion Juan de Torquemada were owned.[44] Andrew Holes procured in Florence a copy of a defence of the papacy by Cardinal Juan de Casanova, whom he admired,[45] of which there is another English copy.[46] William Gray bought in Cologne from 1442 copies of Basel speeches along with other schism and conciliar works.[47] His was probably the biggest collection.

Interest in Grosseteste, combined with 'reform', continued. In Corpus Christi College, Cambridge, manuscript 156, a miscellaneous fifteenth-century volume in different hands, letters of Grosseteste with Grosseteste's *Memorandum* of 1250, occur in a section of the manuscript which also includes *Somnium viridarii*, a radical exposition of the Gallican (French anti-papal) position.[48] Cambridge manuscript Trinity College B 15 23, in three, perhaps once separate, parts, now includes Ullerston's *Petitiones*, Pierre D'Ailly's *De ecclesiastica potestate*, and Grosseteste letters,[49] and Bodley 42 has works by D'Ailly as well as Grosseteste letters to the pope.[50]

There is some evidence that during Basel in England criticism of the papacy went hand in hand with demands for reform, at least in some quarters. The lower clergy, unwilling to pay for a delegation to the council of Ferrara which they felt would only concern greater prelates, insisted on hearing the outcome of the statement from the representatives of Basel in May 1438.[51] In April 1440 da Monte heard constant complaints about the greed of the curia and failure to reform. The representatives of Basel had publicised these things and there were particular complaints about expectatives, dispensations to hold in plurality and reservations. It may be significant that stray *Acta* about these matters remain in English sources.[52] There is little evidence about these commmplaints except from da Monte, but one statement is certainly true: the arrest of priests who were heretics for saying that the pope had no power to grant dispensations to hold several benefices and that the holders of pluralities were damned. On 17 June 1440 Richard Wyche, a well-known relapsed lollard, was burned in London, apparently for saying that a layman could as well have two wives as a priest two cures of souls.[53] Riots followed his death in London.[54] Chichele was outraged by the grant *in commendam* to Louis of Luxembourg in 1438 of the see of Ely, 'a thing unheard of and giving very bad example'.[55] Even Henry VI in 1440, supporting Eugenius against the anti-pope, said that in the event of schism the pope should reform the abuses in the church.[56]

Thus the English had developed a theory of episcopal power from Grosseteste, but also had available much 'reforming literature', though not necessarily the very latest polemic. It remains to ask what they made of the materials they had. Did they develop, for instance, an English conciliar theory? To find out I have examined some contemporary writers, who I hope are typical, to show the different results that could be produced.

Not surprisingly the most full-blooded denunciation of the abuses of papal power in this period in England from an orthodox source came from an admirer of Grosseteste. Thomas Gascoigne, Yorkshireman, doctor of divinity, three times chancellor of Oxford, left a *Liber veritatum*, or collection of theological truths, which he put together at the end of his life, (he died in 1458) after a lifetime's collecting of snippets, begun at least in 1434.[57] The *Liber*, now two volumes in Lincoln College, Oxford,[58] may have been an aid to sermon-making.

Gascoigne, irascible, gossipy and unsystematic, was a very serious theologian and student of scripture, as a guide to which he preferred Jerome,[59] whose life he had written before 1444, largely based on Johannes Andreas.[60] He also valued Hugo of St Cher,[61] Thomas

Docking and Clement of Llanthony.[62] But as a guide to both the psalms and the Pauline epistles he preferred the works of Grosseteste, which from 1434 until he died he studied in the library of the Friars Minor in Oxford.[63] He even cites the shelf marks in the library catalogue.[64] In addition to the biblical commentaries, he read, and quoted, Grosseteste's speech to the council of Lyons and submission, with some sermons[65] and Oxford's submission for Grosseteste's canonisation.[66] He probably thought Grosseteste a saint.[67]

Probably Jerome[68] and Grossteste were the main influences shaping Gascoigne's ideas; or perhaps their ideas most agreed with his. The result, however, was a line of thought markedly like that of Hallum or even Richard Ullerston.

A theory of the papacy to answer Wycliffite criticisms occurs in the *Doctrinale* of Thomas Netter of Walden, Carmelite prior provincial.[69] In Book II of this huge work, presented to Martin V in 1426, thus pre-dating the quarrels of Basel, but written with Pisa, Constance, and Pavia/Siena in the background, Netter deals with the body of Christ, the church and its various members.[70] The agenda and the form of the argument were set by Wyclif, especially *De Christo et Antichristo*, *Trialogus*, and *Opus evangelicum*,[71] and also by Marsilius of Padua's *Defensor pacis*, which Netter believed was by William of Ockham and an important influence on Wyclif.[72]

We have already seen that in John Capgrave's *Solace of Pilgrims* he took a conservative look at local legends in Rome and, though a historian by instinct, was more concerned with edification than with historical niceties.[73] But Capgrave too was a serious biblical scholar. From his commentary on the *Acts of the Apostles*, now MS Balliol College, Oxford, 189, presented to William Gray in gratitude for the latter's assistance when Capgrave was sick in Rome during the Jubilee, we can discern further aspects of his thought.[74] Capgrave thought that *Acts* was written to tell us how the early church was run, so his commentary is of interest in the present context.

A further work which must be considered is now in the British Library, in a manuscript copied by John Bobych, a scribe of Exeter, at the time of the council of Basel, called *Actus determinatorius*, which one may take to be a university disputation, *De potestate pape*.[75] The question was: 'Whether the universal church is above the pope?' (*Utrum universalis ecclesia sit supra papam?*). It is theological in traditional scholastic mode, with heavy emphasis on philosophical argument. Whether it is English and who was the author cannot be ascertained. Harley 3768, containing it, is a collection of miscellaneous theological texts, with an emphasis on conciliar ideas.

The author defines his terms and resolves his question into this: whether the congregation of human beings called to faith in Christ taken as a whole had subordinate to it him from whom comes all ecclesiastical development. The corollary is whether a general council is superior to the pope.

Another writer whose views are of interest is Reginald Pecock, the famous bishop of Chichester, whose opinions were condemned as heretical in 1457.[76] In some of his works, in English for the educated layman, he has something to say on the subject of this enquiry.

Even if not reading the very latest polemics, English scholars had material to study conciliarism and conciliarists can be found more frequently after Constance. Da Monte identified Nicholas Bildeston, Beaufort's most trusted offical, as one.[77] Gascoigne was another. He was disgusted that many of the English bishops had not in 1427 maintained their appeal from pope to council in the Chichele affair, but changed their view to say that the pope is above the council and can dissolve it at will.[78] He seems to have blamed Chichele himself and Humfrey, Duke of Gloucester, for this weakness. Councils were for reform and he hoped that a future council would reform the method of appointing bishops, particularly payment of annates.[79] Basel had ordained a remedy against annates but it was not put into effect; he did not know what had happened to this decree in France. On the other hand he accepted the validity of Ferrara/Florence, and was, we know, keenly interested in the union with the Greeks, about which he wrote enthusiastically to a friend.[80]

Thomas Netter is another, unexpected, conciliarist, of a kind. He tackled the question of the authority of general councils, which Wyclif had denied, but did not allow that the pope was superior to the council, only that the council containing the pope had more influence.[81] Netter refuted Wyclif by quoting Matthew 18 v. 20, 'where two or three are gathered together in my name, there am I in the midst of them.' It was, he thought, reasonable that the presence of so many bishops should increase the power of the pope: 'It does not increase in itself as to substance but in the acceptance of those who hear and believe.' Greater authority in correcting both people and clergy was thus achieved.

The apostolic discussion about the mosaic law was a *locus classicus* for those who wanted to discuss general councils and to prove James superior to Peter.[82] Netter interpreted the passage to mean that the whole council, led by Peter, took the decision and James promulgated it:[83] 'as is the custom of the church in modern councils that one of the lesser people promulgates to the whole church the sentence defined by the pope and prelates: thus it is right to think that this is what James did then.'

Capgrave, characteristically, is more uncertain. The passage in Acts also proved for him that the church had authority to call together the clergy: general councils were scriptural.[84] The fact that James summed up the decision, however, posed problems. Nicholas de Lyra was quoted by Capgrave to suggest that Peter, though prince of the apostles, deferred to James because Jerusalem was James's diocese.[85] Capgrave noted that some writers suggested that because the quarrel was in James's diocese and could only by appeal go to another bishop, James had to offer the definitive sentence.[86] The early church was truly very like the later medieval one!

Netter followed his discussion about the authority of the council with a section on the function of the council *De utilitate generalis concilii*, and thought that from the time of Constantine councils had met to combat heresies.[87] He by no means thought the council infallible, however. Councils could contain self-seeking persons, just as the Last Supper had contained Judas, but they were the best that could be achieved:[88] 'thus in the fullest councils of the church, at least if they remain incorrupt, the Holy Spirit is present and defines faith.'

Marsilius had suggested that lay people should be members.[89] Netter denied the necessity, with scriptural references: *Acts* 15 v. 6 where the apostles and elders assemble. 'Elders' is interpreted as either bishops or priests, though lay people may be included if expedient.[90] In the council Netter thought the majority vote should prevail, which he thought Wyclif denied in the *Dialogus*,[91] though in fact Wyclif was speaking especially of papal elections, mindful particularly of the doubtful election of Urban VI in 1378, which had sparked off the schism. Evidently therefore Netter believed in a hierarchy of authority. Primary and fundamental was scripture. Next was a general council, then the pope, then the 'apostolic sees', especially Rome, holy bishops, and then doctors of the church.[92] The majority vote of a council was to be believed unless it was obviously unscriptural.

Not all writers accepted so conciliar a view. When the Harley disputant had settled to his own satisfaction the question of the role of the pope, which I discuss below, he turned to the general council, discussing first what the terms meant.[93] A universal council is a council for unity, a council of all the Christians who are concerned in it. Whether these are only prelates is a matter of dispute. The writer argued that a general council could err even in matters of faith. Christ (Matthew 28 v. 20) did not say to the council but to the church 'I shall be with you always.' The writer notes that a council can assemble in Christ's name and then stay together:[94] 'not in his name but in the name of the devil . . . as perhaps has happened in these days', which suggests that the time of writing was during the council of Basel. The conclusion is that it is probable that a general council can err in faith and therefore in matters connected with faith and can sin mortally and lack divine assistance.[95] General councils have in fact erred and the badness of their rulings may become apparent only later. We do not know when the members are inspired by God and when they are just using natural reason; in other words, a theory of reception.

Hence the work leaves one with a papalist rather than conciliarist view, though not enthusiastically so, rather because the balance of probabilities is on the side of the pope. After the debacle of the later stages of Basel that may have been the position of many.

Pecock was another sceptic. His condemnation included, among other things, a charge of upholding that Christians did not need to accept the rulings of general councils as to faith and salvation of souls, and that they did not need to disapprove what the council disapproved.[96]

Pecock did not believe that general councils were infallible; though clergy used this as an argument to exact obedience.[97] The task of councils was to interpret scripture for the benefit of the people: so councils had the authority of reason only. He thought they only had authority to draw reasonable conclusions from scripture. The council was understood by him to include 'eldist party of the chirche, ioyned to the apostles'. This group could be wrong but was much more likely to be right than a few individuals and should always be obeyed by lay people, unless it could be proved wrong, without question.[98]

Naturally, when it suited the English government, conciliarists could be produced. Thus in 1424/5, Picart and Sulbury went to Rome with a carefully prepared case for speeding up the holding of the council of Basel, for reform of the church, backed with references to Dionysius (though the hierarch is the king) and to Acts 15, interpreted to make the council superior to Peter, with a thinly veiled threat that the secular power would hold the council if the pope refused. Sulbury's task was to convey the threat.[99]

This 'governmental' conciliarism is very difficult to believe. But that does not mean that those propounding it for the government were totally insincere. Clearly by the time Constance was over plenty of churchmen in England and in English France believed in conciliarism in some form. The form and degree varies greatly: Netter apparently believed pope in council the safest, though non-infallible, guide. Pope in council seems to have been Capgrave's ideal too. The Harley writer inclined more towards the pope alone, whereas Pecock in fact was closer to Netter. This tendency to think a council had at least some answer was what the government was able to exploit. The evidence for disillusion about the state of the church during the council of Basel points in the same direction: there were at least some churchmen in England, as elsewhere, for whom Basel, for all its faults, had more to offer than Eugenius IV alone.

Notes

1 Rediscovery: R. W. Southern, *Robert Grosseteste: the Growth of an English Mind in Medieval Europe*, Oxford, 1986, pp. 298–315. Friars' library: K. W. Humphreys, *The Friars' Libraries*, Corpus of Medieval Library Catalogues, British Library, 1990, pp. 224–8, 229.
2 *Dionysiaca*, 2 vols., Paris, 1937.
3 Identification of works of Grosseteste: S. H. Thomson, *The Writings of Robert Grosseteste, Bishop of Lincoln*, Cambridge, 1940.
4 Southern, pp. 263–4. Trent: H. Jedin, *Crisis and Closure of the Council of Trent: a Retrospective View from the Second Vatican Council*, London, 1967, Chapter 5. P. Broutin (after Jedin), *L'Évêque dans la tradition pastorale du XVI siècle*, Museum Lessianum, section historique, 16, Bruges, 1953.
5 *Roberti Grosseteste episcopi quondam Lincolniensis Epistolae*, ed. H. R. Luard, *RS*, 1861, p. 290.
6 M. M. Harvey, 'English views on the reforms to be undertaken in the General Councils, 1400–1418, with special reference to the proposals made by Richard Ullerston', DPhil' for the University of Oxford, 1964. *Petitiones*: above, Chapter 7, note 19.
7 Hardt, I, col. 1144.
8 1250 memorandum: Hardt, I, col. 1142 on appropriation, cf. S. Gieben, 'Robert Grosseteste at the Papal Curia, Lyons 1250: an edition of the documents', *Collectanea Franciscana*, XLI, 1971, pp. 350–69, quotation p. 359, section 21; on promotions: Hardt, col. 1142, from letter 27, Grosseteste, *Epistolae*, pp. 105–8 and letter 53, pp. 161–8; on exemptions: letter 127, *De cura pastoralis* or *Moyses*, Hardt, col. 1144, ed. Luard, pp. 357–431; on plurality: *in suis epistolis* Hardt, col. 1151; letter 25, *Epistolae*, pp. 97–100, quoted, Hardt, cols. 1152–3.
9 *Dionysiaca*, II, pp. 727–1066; on selection of bishop: Hardt, col. 1133, from chapter 2, part 2 and chapter 3, part 3 and at col. 1134 from chapter 16; on relations within hierarchy against exemption: Hardt, col. 1148, from chapter 6 part 3; on status of abbots, against useless privileges: Hardt, col. 1157, from chapter 6.
10 Bernard, *De consideratione ad Eugenium Papam* (*S. Bernardi opera*, 6 vols., Rome 1963, III, eds. J. Leclercq and M. Rochais, pp. 381–493) on exemptions; Hardt, cols.

1144–6 (ed. cit., pp. 442–5); on dispensations: Hardt, col. 1151 (ed. cit., p. 445); on appeals: Hardt, col. 1154 (ed. cit., pp. 435–9); see references to *De dispensatione et preceptis* (printed ed. as above, pp. 243–94): Hardt, col. 1146 (ed. p. 257), on exemptions, and col. 1151, on dispensations.

11 M. Harvey, 'A sermon by John Luke on the ending of the Great Schism, 1409', *Studies in Church History*, IX, 1972, pp. 159–69. Better text: Vatican Library, Archivio S. Pietro D 175, fols. 82–6v. See also Harvey, *Solutions*, pp. 176–9. Dionysius quoted MS, f. 83, summarising *De divinis nominibus*, Chapters 2 and 3 (*Dionysiaca*, I, pp. 57–144), with examples from Chapter 5 (ibid., pp. 343–6). Grosseteste's commentary quoted f. 83 also. For it Southern, pp. 46, 200–3.

12 Archivio, f. 84v; Gieben ed., p. 354, on unqualified prelates; on nepotism, Archivio, ibid., and Gieben, p. 356.

13 Several MSS. I used Oxford, Jesus College MS E 12; excerpts: H. Finke and J. Hollnsteiner, *Acta Concilii Constanciensis*, 4 vols., Münster, 1896–1928, II, pp. 424–5.

14 Finke, *Acta*, II, p. 424. He quotes *Petrus de Salinis et alios perspectivos*; Grosseteste, Jesus f. 213; Dionysius, f. 221. See H. Phillips, 'John Wyclif and the optics of the eucharist', *Studies in Church History*, Subsidia, V, *From Ockham to Wyclif*, Oxford, 1987, pp. 245–58.

15 C. G. F. Walch, *Monumenta medii aevii*, Göttingen, 1757, I/2, for refs. to Ullerston at pp. 190, 192, 193, 202–3.

16 Finke, *Acta*, II, pp. 442–4, for sermon. At p. 443 verbatim from Ullerston, Hardt, col. 1155.

17 Chichele to Hallum, BL Royal and Kings MS 10 B IX f. 59v; E. F. Jacob, *Henry Chichele and the Ecclesiastical Politics of his Age*, Creighton Lecture, 1951, London, 1952, p. 8. Sermon by Richard Flemming, probably Advent 1415, ed. J. B. Schneyer, 'Konstanzer Konzilspredigten: Texte', *Zeitschrift für die Geschichte des Oberrheins*, CXIX, 1971, pp. 175–231, with sermon at pp. 175–221, and another pp. 222–31. Refs. to Grosseteste, pp. 176, 188, 216, and Dionysius with Grosseteste's commentary, pp. 177, 185, 186.

18 *Provinciale*, p. 284.

19 Finke, *Acta*, II. pp. 482–3.

20 J. B. Schneyer, 'Konstanzer Konzilspredigten', *Zeitschrift für die Geschichte des Oberrheins*, CXIII, 1965, p. 387; Finke, *Acta*, II, p. 487.

21 J. Griffiths and D. Pearsall, eds., *Book Production and Publishing in Britain, 1375–1475*, Cambridge, 1989, passim.

22 BL, MS Harley 431; Paris, BN, Fonds Latin 12542. See Harvey, *Solutions*, Index, pp. 223, 224; A. L. Brown, 'The Privy Seal clerks in the early fifteenth century', *The Study of Medieval Records: Essays in Honour of Kathleen Major*, ed. D. A. Bullough and R. L. Storey, Oxford, 1971, pp. 360–81, esp. pp. 261, 278, note 2. Swan's books above, Chapter 2, p. 30.

23 BL, Cotton Nero E V; *Duke Humfrey's Library*, no. 33. Also Oxford, Bodleian Library, e Museo 86.

24 *Acta*: Cambridge, Emmanuel College, 142, associated with Norwich, cf. M. R. James, *The Western Manuscripts in the Library of Emmanuel College*, Cambridge, 1904, pp. 111–15; Oxford, New College, D. 138, owner William Brygon, canon of Salisbury (1447–69) cf. R. W. Hunt, 'The medieval library', *New College, Oxford 1379–1979*, eds. J. Buxton and P. Williams, pp. 317–45, esp. pp. 328–9 and *Duke Humfrey and English Humanism*, nos. 58 and 59; Dublin, Trinity College, 255, see Chapter 9, note 77.

25 Letters and treatises: Emmanuel 142 and TCD 255; also BL, Harley 826; Oxford, Bodleian Library, Digby 66, cf. SC 1667; New College, D. 138; Mynors, pp. 146–72. Stray *Acta*: Harley 3768, cf. Harvey, 'Two *Questiones*', p. 99; a Wellington MS (photo-

graphs kindly supplied by library) cf. M. M. Manion, V. F. Vines and C. de Hamel, *Medieval and Renaissance Manuscripts in New Zealand Collections*, Melbourne, London, New York, 1989, no. 148, p. 130; BL, Cotton, Cleop. E III, among others.

26 London, Lambeth Palace 183, microfilm; Harvey, 'England, the council of Florence', p. 213.

27 Harvey, 'Whethamstede', passim; add J. Miethke, 'Die Traktate *De Potestate Papae*. Ein Typus politik-theoretischer Literatur im späten Mittelalter', *Les Genres littéraires dans les sources théologiques et philosophiques médiévales. Définition, Critique et Exploitation*, Publications de l'Institut d'Études Médiévales, 2nd series, Textes, Études, Congrès, V, Louvain la Neuve, 1982, pp. 193–211. *Granarium*, BL, Cotton Nero C VI; section *Papa*, Cambridge, Gonville, 230, pp. 251–70.

28 James, *Emmanuel College*, pp. 6–9.

29 James, *Corpus Christi College*, pp. 355–6.

30 A. G. Watson, *Catalogue of Dated and Datable Manuscripts c. 700–1600 in the Department of Manuscripts, the British Library*, 2 vols., London, 1979, I, p. 119, no. 637 and pl. 317.

31 Miethke, p. 209. Error in Harvey, 'Whethamstede', p. 116; additional MS Ker, *Medieval Manuscripts*, II, p. 266.

32 Harvey, 'Whethamstede', p. 116; add: P. B. Ministerii, 'De Augustini de Ancona OESA (†1328) vita et operibus', *Analecta Augustiniana*, XXII, 1951, pp. 7–56, 148–262, list: pp. 209–11. Owners: *BRUC*, pp. 532, 618–19; *BRUO*, II, p. 866. Gascoigne, below note 58.

33 Above, Chapter 7, note 35; Harvey, 'Whethamstede', p. 117; add: J. Dunbabin, *A Hound of God, Pierre de la Palud and the Fourteenth-Century Church*, Oxford, 1991, pp. 70–91; A. D. de Sousa Costa, *Mestre Andre Dias de Escobar, Figura Ecumenica do Seculo XV*, Estudos e Textos de Idade Media e Renascimento, II, Rome, 1967, pp. 66–7, 140, 190–1, 202–3.

34 Harvey, 'Whethamstede', p. 119; Miethke, p. 209. In Harley 631, Emmanuel 9, Balliol 146A, with letter to Gascoigne f. 281v, cf. Mynors p. 123; All Souls gift 1467: N. R. Ker, *Records of All Souls' College Library, 1437–60*, Oxford Bibliographical Society, new series, XVI, Oxford, 1971, pp. 18, 114, Addenda, p. 216.

35 Below, p. 219; Harvey, 'Whethamstede', pp. 119–20; Miethke, p. 211.

36 M. Grabmann, 'Das *Defensorium ecclesie* des Magister Adam, ein Streitschrift gegen Marsilius von Padua und Wilhelm von Ockham', *Festschrift Albert Brackmann dargebracht*, ed. L. Santifaller, Weimar, 1931, pp. 569–81; W. A. Pantin, 'The *Defensorium* of Adam Easton', *EHR*, LI, 1936, pp. 675–80; MS Vatican Vat. Lat. 4116.

37 H. C. Beeching and M. R. James, 'The library of the Cathedral Church at Norwich', *Norfolk Archaeology*, XIX, 1917, pp. 67–116, esp. p. 72; N. R. Ker, 'Medieval manuscripts from Norwich Cathedral Priory', *Books, Collectors and Libraries*, pp. 243–72, esp. pp. 253, 254, 260, 261, 271.

38 Gascoigne's MS: BL, Royal 10 A XV, given to Lincoln College.

39 Harvey, 'Whethamstede', pp. 120–1; add E. Meuthen, 'Kanonistik und Geschichteverständnis. Über ein neuentdecktes Werk des Nikolaus von Kues: *De maioritate auctoritatis sacrorum conciliorum supra papae*', *Von Konstanz nach Trient, Festgabe für August Franzen*, ed. R. Baumer, Munich, 1972, pp. 147–70, esp. p. 157.

40 R. Scholz, 'Eine Geschichte und Kritik der Kirchenverfassung vom Jahr 1406', *Papsttum und Kaisertum, Forschungen . . . Paul Kehr zum 65. Gebürtstag dargebracht*, ed. A. Brackmann, Munich, 1926, pp. 594–621; D. Menozzi, 'La critica alla autentica della Donazione di Constantino in uno manuscritto della fine del XIV secolo', *Cristianismo nella Storia*, I/1, 1980, pp. 123–54; I used Harley 631 and Emmanuel 9,

consulting Vatican Reg. Lat. 715.

41 C. M. D. Crowder, 'Constance *Acta* in English Libraries', *Das Konzil von Konstanz*, eds.
    A. Franzen and W. Muller, Freiburg, 1964, pp. 477–517, esp. p. 479.

42 Harvey, 'Two *questiones*', p. 99; idem, 'Harley manuscript 3049 and two *questiones* of
    Walter Hunt, O. Carm', *Transactions of the Architectural and Archaeological Society of
    Durham and Northumberland*, new series, VI, 1982, pp. 45–7, esp. p. 45; Watson,
    Dated . . . British Library, pp. 131–2, no. 725.

43 Harvey, 'Two *questiones*', p. 99, 121–7. See also BL, MS Arundel 11, f. 4; works by
    Nicholas de Clamanges: M. R. James, *A Descriptive Catalogue of the Manuscripts in the
    Library of Sidney Sussex College, Cambridge*, Cambridge, 1895, p. 71; Oxford, New
    College, 128 (*BRUO*, I, p. 35); Sammut, pp. 113–14, no. 23 and *Duke Humfrey's
    Library*, no. 36, for Bodleian library, MS Hatton, 36.

44 Cambridge, Corpus 157 and University Library KK 1. 2, cf. Juan de Torquemada, *A
    Disputation on the Authority of Pope and Council*, trans. T. M. Izbicki, Dominican
    Sources, IV, Oxford, 1988; idem *Protector of the Faith: Cardinal Johannes de
    Turrecremata and the Defense of the institutional Church*, Washington, DC, 1981.

45 Harvey, 'Andrew Holes', pp. 28, 35–7, with literature. MS Bodleian Library, Bodley
    339.

46 Corpus 157.

47 Mynors, pp. 146–72.

48 M. R. James, *A Descriptive Catalogue of the Manuscripts in the Library of Corpus Christi
    College, Cambridge*, 2 vols., Cambridge, 1912, I, pp. 351–4.

49 M. R. James, *The Western Manuscripts in the Library of Trinity College, Cambridge: A
    Descriptive Catalogue*, 4 vols., Cambridge, 1900–4, I, pp. 487–8.

50 SC 1846, two volumes, bound together in the fifteenth century.

51 M. Harvey, 'England, the council of Florence'p. 208; Haller, *Piero da Monte*, p. 275.

52 Haller, *Piero da Monte*, nos. 129, pp. 142–5; 136, pp. 150–5. See *Acta* above, note 25.

53 J. A. F. Thomson, *The Later Lollards, 1415–1520*, Oxford, 1965, pp. 148–50; G. L.
    Harriss, and M. A. Harriss, eds. 'John Benet's Chronicle', *Camden Society*, 4th series,
    IX, 1972, p. 187; J. L. Kingsford, *Chronicles of London*, Oxford, 1905, pp. 147, 153;
    Flenley, *Town Chronicles*, pp. 101, 114.

54 See last note and J. Stafford, *The Register of John Stafford, Bishop of Bath and Wells*, 2
    vols., ed. T. S. Holmes, Somerset Record Society, XXXI, XXXII, 1915–16, II, pp.
    262–4, 266–9.

55 Chichele, *Register*, III, p. 165.

56 Bekynton, *Correspondence*, II, pp. 93, 94, as sent to pope.

57 Oxfords Lincoln College, MS Lat. 118, p. 14.

58 Lincoln College, MSS, Lat. 117, 118; further extracts, Oxford, Bodleian MS Lat. th. e.
    33. W. A. Pronger, 'Thomas Gascoigne', *EHR*, LIII, 1938, pp. 606–26; LIV, 1939,
    pp. 20–37; *BRUO*, II, pp. 745–8; Southern, *Grosseteste*, pp. 313–15. For selection by
    Thorold Rogers, above, Chapter 5, note 18; hereafter called *Loci*.

59 Lincoln 117, p. 457: *Ego Thomas, professor sacre pagine vocatus,testificor quod numquam
    vidi aliquem doctorem ita veraciter et pure exponentem sensum primarium [MS p'memi]
    sacre scripture . . . .*

60 Oxford, Magdalen College MS 93, item 31. Joannes Andreas: E. F. Rice, *Saint Jerome
    in the Renaissance*, Baltimore, London, 1985, pp. 64–8.

61 Lincoln 117, p. 457. Hugo: B. Smalley, *The Gospels in the Schools*, London, 1985, pp.
    125–43; N. R. Ker, 'Oxford College Libraries before 1500', in *Books, Collectors and
    Libraries*, ed. A. G. Watson, London, 1985, pp. 300–20, esp. pp. 318–19 and R. E.
    Lerner, 'Poverty, preaching and eschatology in the Revelation Commentaries of
    "Hugo of St Cher", *The Bible in the Medieval World. Essays in Memory of Beryl Smalley*,

ed. K. Walsh and D. Wood, Studies in Church History, Subsidia IV, Oxford, 1985, pp. 157–89.

62 Docking: Lincoln 117, p. 415; B. Smalley, *The Study of the Bible in the Middle Ages*, Oxford, 1952, reprinted, South Bend (Ind.), 1964, pp. 278–9, 280, 323–4; A. G. Little, 'Thomas Docking', in *Franciscan Papers, Lists and Documents*, Manchester, 1943, pp. 98–121; J. I. Catto, 'New light on Thomas Docking, OFM', *Medieval and Renaissance Studies*, VI, 1968, pp. 135–49, esp. p. 138 for Gascoigne. Clement of Llanthony: see B. Smalley, 'Which William of Nottingham?', *Medieval and Renaissance Studies*, III, 1954, pp. 200–38, esp. pp. 201–2.

63 Southern, *Grosseteste*, pp. 314–15, quoting Lincoln 118, p. 14.

64 Dates when reading: Lincoln 118, p. 14; Lincoln 117, pp. 117, 409. Grosseteste's commentary in margin of Peter Lombard's common gloss, Lincoln, 117, p. 350. Still reading Grosseteste on psalter, 1456, Bodley Lat. th. e. 33, p. 47. Registrations: are noted Lincoln 117, p. 69, epistles; Bodley lat. th. e. 33, p. 47, psalter.

65 Lincoln 117, p. 30, a sermon; p. 403, letter 127; p. 486 and Bodley lat. th. e. 33 p. 60, Lyons speech.

66 Bodley lat. th. e. 33, pp. 28–9.

67 Lincoln 118, p. 89: Grosseteste's sandals in Friar's library *sed non in libraria studencium fratrum*; *Loci*, p. 141.

68 Pronger, *EHR*, LIV, p. 21.

69 Netter: *BRUO*, II, 1343–4; K. S. Smith, 'The ecclesiology of controversy: scripture, tradition, and church in the theology of Thomas Netter of Walden', Ph.D, Cornell University, 1983; idem, 'An English Conciliarist? Thomas Netter of Walden', *Popes, Teachers and Canon Lawyers in the Middle Ages*, ed. J. R. Sweeney and S. Chodorow, Ithaca and London, 1989, pp. 290–9. For *Doctrinale*, I used photo-reproduction of the ed. in three volumes by B. Blanciotti, Venice, 1757, by Gregg Press, Farnborough, 1967. Volume numbers from it, not from books of *Doctrinale*.

70 *Doctrinale*, I, cols. 274–696.

71 Netter refers to *De Christo et Antichristo* as *De veritate et mendacio*; *Opus evangelicum, Tractatus II* is referred to as *De sermone Domini in monte*. I have used Wyclif Society editions as indicated in notes, identifying works from W. R. Thomson, *The Latin Writings of John Wyclif: An Annotated Catalog*, Pontifical Institute of Medieval Studies, Subsidia medievalia, XIV, Toronto, 1983.

72 *Doctrinale*, I, cols. 270–4. *Marsilius von Padua, Defensor Pacis*, ed. R. Scholz, Fontes iuris Germanici antiqui, Hannover, 1932.

73 Above, p. 62.

74 Preface: Capgrave, *Liber de illustribus Henricis*, p. 221.

75 BL, MS Harley 3768, ff. 203–17v. W. Krämer, *Konsens und Rezeption: Verfassungsprinzipien der Kirche im Basler Konziliarismus*, Münster, 1980, p. 320, with author as Johannes Gobych, in fact scribe; see M. Harvey, 'Two *questiones* on the Great Schism by Nicholas Fakenham, OFM', *Archivum Franciscanum Historicum*, LXX, 1977, pp. 97–127, esp. p. 99.

76 C. W. Brockwell, Jnr., *Bishop Reginald Pecock and the Lancastrian Church. Securing the Foundations of Cultural Authority*, Texts and Studies in Religion, XXV, Lewiston, 1985, with refs. there.

77 Haller, *Da Monte*, p. 108.

78 Lincoln 117, p. 438; *Loci*, p. 52.

79 Lincoln 117, p. 438; *Loci*, p. 52.

80 Pronger, *EHR*, LIII, p. 612, from Cambridge, Trinity College, MS B 4 23, fly leaf.

81 *Doctrinale*, I, cols. 376–81; refuting J. Wyclif, *Sermones*, III, *In epistolas*, ed. J. Loserth, London, 1889, sermons 45, 46: pp. 384–401, esp. pp. 390–1, 392–3,

82 Acts 15 vv. 5–29.
83 *Doctrinale*, I, col. 261.
84 Balliol 189, f. 107v.
85 Balliol 189, f. 110.
86 Balliol 189, f. 111.
87 *Doctrinale*, I, cols. 381–7.
88 Col. 382.
89 *Doctrinale*, I, col. 382; *Defensor pacis*, ed. Scholz, II, chapter 20, sect. 2, 13, pp. 393–4, 400–1.
90 *Doctrinale*, I, col. 383.
91 *Dialogus* chapter 11 (not 16 as Netter), p. 22.
92 *Doctrinale*, I, col 384; see Smith, 'An English conciliarist', p. 294, and note 28.
93 Harley 3768, f. 215.
94 Harley 3768, f. 216: *non in nomine suo sed in nomine diaboli . . . sicut fortassis accidit hiis diebus*.
95 Harley 3768, f. 216v–17.
96 Abjuration: Brockwell, pp. 243–5.
97 R. Pecock, *Book of Faith*, ed. J. L. Morison, Glasgow, 1909, p. 111. Also pp. 250, 282–3.
98 *Book of Faith*, pp. 222–5.
99 Above, Chapter 8, notes 30, 49, 50. Picart: Brown, *Fasciculi* pp. x–xvii; Sulbury: ibid., pp. xix–xxi. Add to MSS in Harvey, 'Martin V and the English', p. 78, note 124, Württembergische Landesbibliothek, Stuttgart, Ms Poet. et Phil., 4° 31, ff. 260–71, cf. *Die Handschriften der Wurttembergischen Landesbibliothek Stuttgart*, series I/2, Wiesbaden, 1981, pp. 96–8.

13
Episcopate and papacy

John Wyclif and the lollards attacked the papacy with such thoroughness that no contemporary English ecclesiastical scholar could ignore the assault. The effect might have been to drive the English to extreme defences of the papacy, or even of infallible general councils. This did happen in Bohemia, under the threat of Hussitism, yet not in England.[1] As we saw there were conciliarists, though few extreme ones, but a much more characteristic reaction may be dubbed a theory of 'episcopalism', which owed some of its inspiration to Robert Grosseteste. This was a sort of English Gallicanism, which believed in reform of the church relying on the local episcopate, with minimum papal interference. The beginnings of such ideas can be seen in Richard Ullerston's *Petitiones* taken to Pisa as the English reform programme.

Ullerston was not hostile to the papacy as an institution, but was unsympathetic to its claim that universal jurisdiction overrode local authority, and if he had had his way its activities in the diocese would have been drastically curtailed. In line with this ideal, as we saw earlier, the chapter of Salisbury, headed by Hallum, was pressing for the canonisation of Osmund, a bishop notable for his work for the diocese and cathedral.[2]

According to Ullerston some kinds of papal interference were so contrary to the natural order of the church that they were simply not allowed: for instance appropriation of parish churches to religious orders, or exemptions. These, together with the service taxes, which smacked of the 'heresy' of simony, should cease wholly. Other papal activities, such as grants of privileges and dispensations, as well as *motu proprio* appropriations, in other words assigning tithes to corporate bodies solely on the pope's mandate, should be subject to scrutiny at provincial or diocesan level, and there should be no direct appeals to Rome, over the heads of the local ecclesiastical judges.[3]

Ullerston's ideas were not forgotten at Constance, as we saw: Henry

Abendon, quoted him against exemptions[4] and an anonymous English preacher quoted him word for word on abusive appeals and simony.[5]

Theories about the relative power of pope and bishop continued and not surprisingly the most fierce defender of the episcopate was Grosseteste's champion, Thomas Gascoigne.

According to Gascoigne the bishop was crucial to the rule of the local church. He thought he could discern episcopacy immediately from the apostles and his ideal, like that of so many pre-Tridentine reformers, was a resident episcopate, elected locally.[6] Under *Episcopus* he rehearses at enormous length his ideals and current abuses, with themes repeated again and again:[7] residence,[8] local election,[9] bishops who must preach personally and oversee their own flock.[10] Hence his obsession with Reginald Pecock, whose chief sin was saying that the episcopal office did not *ipso facto* involve preaching. This stirred anti-clericalism.[11]

Gascoigne's concern was that the papacy should allow the bishops to do their job. He believed in the papal office, but nearly all his extracts concerned limiting its power.[12] Rome was the final authority, to which the church could appeal for a ruling,[13] but: 'The Lord gives great power to his vicar the pope of the church that he may reform great ills and give great edification of good acts.'[14]

The opposite occurred. The papacy undermined the local church with licences to be non-resident,[15] with appropriations, always involving the impoverishment of the local church and non-residence,[16] with plurality,[17] and with indulgences, leading to belief that conversion of heart was unnecessary.[18] A seperate tract on indulgences, probably from his ordinary lectures, also remains.[19]

A much fuller study of Gascoigne's contacts in Rome would be of great interest. His stories may be scurrilous but his technical vocabulary is usually correct. Presumably Thomas Spofforth, then abbot of York, an eye witness who told him about the death of Hus and Jerome of Prague at Constance, was one.[20] He also mentions John Carpenter, bishop of Worcester,[21] and Erasmus Fullar, a Hungarian who had been in Rome.[22]

For his knowledge of the schism and of recent councils, apart from personal information, Gascoigne read, and quotes several times, *De gestis et factis concilii Pisani et concilii Constanciensis et concilii Basiliensis*, three paper volumes in the library of Durham College, which also included a continuous history of the schism (perhaps the indictment of the popes at Pisa).[23]

Pecock, whom Gascoigne so disliked, was not in fact very interested in the papacy. He thought that it, with other ranks in the church, was ordained by Christ, but if he had not so ordained, the body of Christians would have been able to set up its own priesthood.[24] It is unclear whether Pecock thought papacy and bishops a 'higher' order, or whether he considered the arrangement simply expedient for good order. When attacking lollards, he says that it does not matter whether priesthood is founded by Christ or later by the church.[25] He makes a distinction between 'this preesthode which is apostilhode and . . . this preesthode which is hizest popehode', but wherein lies the subtle theological difference, if any, we are not informed, except that hierarchy is ordained by God.[26]

Because Netter's agenda was set by Wyclif he showed much more concern with the papacy than with bishops. Wyclif had argued that the power of bishops had no scriptural foundation.[27] It was usual to maintain (and Netter did) that the bishops were the successors of the apostles and the priests the successors of their subordinates, the seventy-two who were sent out.[28] But Netter is quite firm that bishops have no special power *iure divino* making them different in order from priests. The bishop indeed is superior to the priest and for instance presides at synods:[29]

> But I think this arose not so much from divine institution as from human custom, because the opinion not of one but of many ought to prevail. And thus it is commonly said that the pope presides in the council, not however that he is superior to it, because the church ought to be ruled in common . . .

He probably thought the authority of the church was an organic whole: the pope *in the council* the highest authority and the pope separated from the council not considered an authority, nor, presumably, the council apart from the pope.

Since Netter's priorities were set by Wyclif he considered the role of Peter first. He deals with the *petra* upon which the church was founded, arguing that it was Peter's faith, backing this by a quotation from Ambrose.[30] When faced with the question of Peter as the rock, Matthew 16 vv. 18–19, Netter is attacking the ideas of both Wyclif and Marsilius.[31] All admitted that there was considerable disagreement among their authorities, where Jerome, discussing this very passage,[32] said that Peter was the rock, whereas Augustine maintained that the rock was Christ, though he did admit that the other meaning was acceptable.[33] Netter suggested that the church was built on both: first on Christ, then on Peter, his vicar.

Netter also discussed Peter's name *Cephas*, which he thought meant head, an interpretation which Wyclif had denied in *De Christo et Antichristo*.[34] In order thoroughly to refute Wyclif, Netter attempted to show that early writers accepted that Peter was the head,[35] whereas Wyclif thought that Peter and the other apostles were equal, sharing 'full power'.[36] Wyclif's belief concerning Peter was shocking because it removed all hierarchy: 'if you remove order, you remove the church.'[37] In attempting to prove that hierarchy was present at the origins he quoted Jerome, for whom he had a deep respect, in *Contra Jovinianum*, to show that the other apostles accepted Peter as head to avoid schism, though he acknowledged that there was no evidence that Peter behaved like a fifteenth-century pope, for instance using coercive power, explaining that the church was still an infant.[38] Later he gave a weak defence of citations of the type sent to Wyclif.[39] He thought he could see from the (pseudo) decretals of the early popes that the pope's use of power increased with time. Marsilius and Wyclif had denied the papacy any coercive power. The scriptural examples supporting papal coercive power are Christ ejecting the moneychangers, in Matthew 21 v. 12, and Matthew 16 v. 19 about binding and loosing. Wyclif had tried to base any authority the pope might wield entirely upon the moral worth of the individual.[40] Netter argued that Christ's church needed to continue; to leave discernment of authority in this way would cause the church to fail.[41]

Wyclif denied that Paul and the other apostles ever consulted Peter,[42] but Netter quoted Galatians 1 v. 18, where Paul goes to see Peter and stays fifteen days, and suggested that Galatians 2 v. 6, where Paul claims that those who 'were something' added nothing to him, simply meant that the other apostles approved of Paul.[43] That Paul criticised Peter (which Peter accepted) was a sign of Peter's humility.[44] Peter even praised Paul. Wyclif tried to prove that James was superior to Peter, quoting Galatians 2 v. 9, where James is mentioned first, so Netter cited many other cases where Peter was mentioned first and a pseudo-decretal of Anacletus, which said that James was consecrated by Peter, James and John.[45]

Pecock, also countering lollards, dealt with the same points. He too interpreted *Cephas* as head; a Greek word, used to show that Peter was head in a way that none of the other apostles were.[46] Some of Pecock's contemporaries would have thought it of crucial importance whether Peter was made head by Christ, or after Christ's ascension, i.e. by the other apostles, or whether not he but his successors became head. Pecock thought this unimportant.[47] The list of possibilities was probably that discussed in his own day, but to him even the third, that the papacy existed 'by eleccion and ordinance of men', proved that it existed by God's providence.[48] He thus very much shared Netter's desire to uphold hierarchy and with it order. A further argument of Pecock's in favour of the papacy was that, as Christ commended monarchy, so a monarchical constitution for the church was indicated.[49]

When discussing the passage in Matthew 16 v. 18, 'Thou art Peter and upon this rock I will build my church' etc., Pecock admits that 'some men' interpret this to refer to the faith of Christ, which is the rock, whereas some say that Peter's faith in Christ, not Peter's person, was the rock.[50] He personally thinks that Peter's person is intended, but is more concerned that it followed that Christ also willed all the subordinate powers in the church under Peter.

In Capgrave's commentary on Acts Peter of course plays a prominent part; where he is not prominent enough, Capgrave supplies explanation. This is particularly true of the discussion of the section of Acts 15 vv. 1–21, where the Christian group in Jerusalem discussed the obligation to obey Jewish law, when Paul and Barnabas had been sent from Antioch to seek an opinion, since some Jews thought circumcision obligatory for converts. This was understood traditionally as the first council of the church; it was therefore important that at it Peter expressed the view that the law should not bind them. But it was equally a problem for this tradition that James gave the final statement.

Capgrave argued that the passage revealed the need for more important cases to go to the principal church:[51]

> Paul thought that the church of Jerusalem ought to be consulted because the apostle Peter, with the rest of his brethren, was still presiding there and had not yet come to the city of Rome. Thus we find from the decision of the ancients that the Roman church presides over all churches.

It was true that Peter went first to Antioch, but that in no way prejudiced the fact that the Roman church was the mistress and queen of all churches. To prove this Capgrave quoted a letter of Marcellus, from pseudo-Isidore via Gratian's *Decretum* (Causa 24 q. 1. c. 15), where the letter quoted *Tu es Petrus* and said that Rome had superseded Antioch 'by God's command' (*iubente Deo*).

Another question which Acts raised, of course, was who had authority to appoint preachers. Capgrave discussed this at 13 v. 3 where Paul and Barnabas were sent by the church at Antioch to preach, after laying-on of hands. This proved to Capgrave how elections ought to be conducted and preachers, that is bishops, chosen.[52] He had noted earlier, discussing the election of Matthew, Acts 1 vv. 21–6, that elections ought to be free, but said that, his task being to produce peace, not disturbance, he would not expatiate about modern situations where there was no free election nor how 'they sometimes elect contrary to their vows, by the letter of secular powers . . .'[53] In the case of Paul and Barnabas he supposed one of those present must have been a bishop, noting that 'some say', though he did not accept, that though chosen at Antioch, the pair must have been sent to Jerusalem to be commissioned.[54] For him, however, this text is proof that freelance preaching is not scriptural.[55]

Thus Capgrave does not take the opportunity which this commentary might have given him to produce a defence of the bishop. His discussion is cautious and conservative, as one might expect.

Behind Gascoigne's denunciations of the many abuses he observed lay a distinct theory of the power and role of the papacy, and also of its early history.[56] The pope was not given by Christ more power than other bishops. All the apostles (that meant all bishops) were equally *petre* upon whom Christ founded his church.[57] Paul was sent not 'from men, therefore not from the apostles, nor through a man, therefore not through Peter', but by God. The apostles in Acts 13 vv. 1–3 merely declared the sending by God. Acts 13 did not indicate ordination.

Gascoigne believed that the pope's power was limited by the end for which it was given: *edificacio*, upbuilding. Modern extremist theories, which would have made the very words of the pope into law,[58] and popular notions that the pope was inspired, were equally dismissed:[59]

> Once it was commonly said, and still is among some of the common herd, that the pope daily speaks with God three times to know what is to be granted and what not, what is to be established and what not and that he may know what laws made by men are to be annulled and destroyed. Although this is just the credulity of the masses we ought to pray that for our sins the inspiration of God which is always necessary for the pope for the members of the church, will not be taken away from him.

Papal power was thus not absolute. He several times quotes with approval Augustine of Ancona, *De Ecclesisatica Potestate* to show that:[60] 'The pope cannot dispense in things against divine institution, the order of nature nor the commands of divine law'. He was prepared to allow the pope to act as *epykes* or interpreter of positive law where there was a gap or a need for flexibility,[61] but no one must rely on a papal ruling to make evil acts good.[62] Licences which allowed what scripture did not could not be granted.[63] The power of binding and loosing, given to Peter and thence to the pope,[64] was interpreted as: 'What is truly loosed on earth is truly loosed in heaven. But Christ did not say to St Peter, nor to his successor: "Whatever you wish to loose in earth . . ." '[65] God may not ratify the pope's ruling, so one's conscience is not automatically clear.[66] 'The sentence of the pope should conform to the judgement of God.'

None of this was necessarily revolutionary.[67] It would have been accepted by all traditionally-minded western Christians. Application, however, made it more controversial. Gascoigne was well read in recent church history, disliking what he found. Of modern popes he approved only Nicholas V, but all popes were apt to be badgered into making grants which were *ultra vires*.[68] Eugenius IV was criticised,[69] as was Calixtus III, who not only promoted his nephew (Rodrigo Borgia) cardinal deacon at twenty-four in 1456,[70] but made George Neville bishop of Exeter at twenty-two.[71] The way king and pope colluded to achieve episcopal appointments in consistory, allowing promotion of non-resident courtiers who paid annates and tips (*propina*) in Rome, roused his wrath.[72] Nicholas Carent with his rival for the deanery of Wells is cited frequently.[73]

Gascoigne thought that annates (taxes paid on appointment) were simoniacal;[74] it was wicked to withhold a bull of appointment until payment was made.[75] But the real problem was that papal interference 'destroyed the vineyard'.[76] Episcopal power was almost wholly destroyed by papal grants. He quoted a story about Richard Praty, bishop of Chichester from 1438 to 1445,[77] whose answer to a claim to papal exemption from his jurisdiction was: 'This letter which you say the pope has granted you undermines all power granted by God to bishops'. The pope was fallible and could be deceived; *cubicularii* and *camerarii* often included clauses in bulls signed *fiat* or *fiat ut petitur* which the pope neither knew nor granted. In any case: 'I know that in reality he cannot grant this. For his power is given him by Christ to bind what is rightly bound by men.' This, whether Praty or merely Gascoigne, is also Ullerston's view. The prior of Durham, Wessington, agreed, saying of a permission for a monk of Durham to come to the curia: 'I wonder not a little at such graces and concessions which give religious persons means of wandering and licence to stray',[78] and, in the course of the quarrel of William Partrike with the priory, the prior's supporter, Robert Westmoreland, wrote to Partrike:[79] 'I wot wele ye pape has graunte your bulle after ye suggestion was made till hym whilk I suppose will not be fin all trewe.' Durham collected authorities to prove that not even the pope can dispense a monk to hold property; St Albans preserved a discussion of whether the pope could dispense from monastic vows, with the conclusion that he could not.[80]

One place where the pope displayed his power to affect the mass of lay people was in granting indulgences. Consequently they were very controversial. In theory Gascoigne accepted them; his beloved St Bridget had said in a revelation that her house ought to have an indulgence modelled on (*ad instar*) St Peter ad Vincula.[81] In the separate work on indulgences, probably from his ordinary lectures, he is completely orthodox.[82] He explained that only God could forgive the guilt (*culpa*) of mortal sin, the church only acting in a declaratory manner (*denunciative sive ministerialiter*). True repentance, a prerequisite for forgiveness, meant turning away from sin and towards good. He then asked what pains the pope could remove. Once sin was forgiven there remained either penalties which canon law had imposed, including excommunication, or penances given secretly in confession. These the pope could 'indulge'. Indulgences varied: at the stations of Rome pilgrims from far off were treated differently from Roman citizens. Indulgences indicated that a man deserved that much indulgence from God: they indicate rather than confer an indulgence (*pocius se habet ut indicans quam ut indulgenciam conferens*). He disliked plenary indulgences; Simon Magus did not obtain full indulgence from Peter, but was told to do penance, (Acts 8 v. 23). He explained carefully the 'treasury of merits' by which the pope is empowered and we can all share the prayer and virtue of the saints; but also carefully explained that what was being relaxed was temporal penalties, not purgatory: 'from the treasury of the church, an indulgence of temporal pain, to be paid here, not in purgatory.'

In practice Gascoigne disliked indulgences intensely; in the *Liber veritatum* the tone is markedly more hostile than in the lectures. Indulgences lured people into thinking that absolution was easy and automatic,[83] giving false hope.[84]

> The ignorant untutored multitude say that in the twinkling of an eye they have total pardon of all fault and all penalty following the grant of the pope, as they say. But, as important evidence makes clear, there are penalties due by the judgement of God for sins, which indulgences granted by the pope neither do nor could in any manner remove.[85]

The only power which indulgences certainly had was to remove temporal penalties. 'Full remission' in God's eyes could only come if God 'conceded or promised that he wanted what the pope wanted', or if the pope were certain of God's will.[86]

Gascoigne was deeply critical of particular contemporary indulgences, saying that the knights of Rhodes misused the money.[87] He accused Piero da Monte of misusing the collection for the Greeks coming to Florence in 1439/40;[88] ill-informed and chauvinistic criticism but ideologically based.[89]

One can compare this with William Lyndwood's gloss in the *Provinciale*, a collection of the provincial constitutions of the English church, completed probably between 1422 and 1430, where there is also a veritable *questio* on indulgences, its length suggesting a contemporary controversy.[90]

Lyndwood gave as the arguments against indulgences firstly that there is no mention of them in the Bible and secondly that they were a superstitious invention. Furthermore they tended to destruction, not edification, Gascoigne's argument: 'free remission of sin tends to destruction . . . ease of pardon gives incentive to crime . . .'

But against this was that indulgences went back to time immemorial; all theologians accepted them; and Peter had power to bind and loose. Lyndwood quoted Boniface VIII's constitution *Antiquorum* establishing the Jubilee, and justified the Jubilee indulgence from Exodus 21.[91] He then explained that the church shared in one mystical treasury,[92] and finally pointed out that only the truly penitent could use indulgences: 'for the pope has the highest power and in him who represents the church by indulging seems to us to communicate the works of the saints and of the passion of Christ.'[93] Elsewhere he contended that if the form of the indulgence allowed, it could be used to help souls in purgatory. He acknowledged differences of opinion about this, but relied on Aquinas.[94] In the final section he stressed: 'beware lest anyone accept this grace with an evil heart, neglecting because of the indulgence good works for the future.' The emphasis is thus different from Gascoigne's.

One St Albans manuscript, Arundel 11, contains a discussion of the same points, noting that some thought that absolution *a pena et culpa* merely announced forgiveness already granted after repentance. The doctrine is orthodox: the pope does not remit purgatory. Indulgence is not an easy option: it requires contrition, confession, and, in the case of the Jubilee indulgence, 'a great part of the necessary satisfaction is in the labours of the pilgrimage'.[95]

Unlike the other writers here considered, the Harley disputant was not discussing scripture but arguing from reason. He had a high doctrine of the papacy, though he believed that popes can be deposed if incorrigible, and certainly thought they may err.[96] The pope is the spouse of the whole church. To counter arguments against this line of reasoning Duns Scotus is quoted, on the Sentences, to show that ultimately all the baptised are received into the college of Christians with the pope as its president, and although the pope may delegate the power for practical reasons, in fact he has power to baptise anyone.[97] The pope is the bridegroom of the church, meaning, according to the law of nature, supreme head. 'The pope' is the office, not the individual who holds it.

The writer considers the contention that unless the pope is thought of as a part of the church, there can be no remedy against his misconduct.[98] Matthew 18 vv. 15–17, on fraternal correction, is quoted to show that 'Tell the church' must mean that the pope is open to judgement by the church. The argument in this section moves from the right ordering of communities, quoting Aristotle's *Metaphysics*, to applying these notions to the church as the community *par excellence*, requiring one ruler to bring it to unity. A multitude cannot be a regulating force unless it is ruled.[99]

The corollary of thinking the pope subordinate to the church is that he can be suspended in any case at all, whether he errs or not.[100] 'Adversaries', not named, considered the church was above the pope in case of heresy, but if the church's power were truly greater, it would be greater in all cases.

In the disputation the pope's role as father of the Christian family was spelled out also in terms of his position as vicar of Christ, meaning that he could do whatever Christ would do for the church if he were still alive in the flesh.[101]

Discussing what could be done about an erring pope, the disputant argued that the pope should first be privately admonished, in confession, and then by the cardinals, but with reverence.[102] If he is still unwilling to listen, because perhaps he does not trust the prudence of his critics, others, 'skilled men of good character',[103] should intervene, especially a general council. If he still persists in his error Christians 'who are fitted for this' (*qui ad hoc apti sunt*) should assemble and take counsel about a remedy, 'not claiming any authority over him'. The pope must then correct himself. This procedure is supported from Gratian's d. 21, c. 7, *nunc autem*, referring to the council which dealt with the case of Pope Marcellinus. The bishops in that council did not pass sentence on the pope; he did it by his own words.

But what if the pope refused to condemn himself? Then *ipso facto* he proved unworthy of office and deprived himself, and all ought to withdraw obedience and proceed to a new election.[104] He would have proved incorrigible; a situation threataning the destruction of the Christian community, which Christians must do all they can to improve; the best is to provide a new pope.

The final section of the Harley disputation deals with faith. Church, not pope, is to be believed in matters of faith, relying on the scriptures ('Behold, I am with you always', Matthew 28 v. 20). But what about Christ saying to Peter 'I have prayed for thee . . .' and 'Confirm thy brethren' (Luke 22 v. 32)? These suggest that Peter's faith was firmer. If Christ said that the church cannot err, then some part cannot.[105] We therefore assume that, error in faith being most dangerous in the pope, he is most likely to be preserved from it. Furthermore his role as ruler of the church for salvation necessitates the same assumption. Scripture (Luke 22 v. 32) supports this. Peter's subsequent denial was not a failure in faith but a temporary lapse; Peter, when converted, when returned to the faith temporarily betrayed, was to confirm his brethren. We also presume the pope superior in virtue, since his office involves instructing others.

So we are to assume that in what pertains to salvation the pope has not erred, 'until error is manifestly proved',[106] and are obliged to obey his commands relating to faith.

Discussion of theory was accompanied by historical investigation. Capgrave the historian struggled to date events, for example Paul's stay in Rome, attempting to fit in a time in Spain, and the date of Paul's death, as well as trying to envisage the organisation of the early church.[107] He noted, for instance, that there were Christians in Rome to greet Paul.[108] Perhaps not surprisingly, Capgrave's early church turns out not unlike that of the fifteenth century, or, where it was not, he felt bound to explain away the problem.

Netter too had to tackle the historical questions. He attacked Marsilius's argument that Peter was never in Rome, where Marsilius had said that Peter's presence was supported only by 'apocryphal legends' (*legenda apocripha*).[109] Netter scornfully dismissed arguments from silence: for instance that Peter's presence is not mentioned in Acts: saying that John does not mention Christ's birth, nor any part of the New Testament Mary's perpetual virginity. But the fathers do refer to Peter's presence in Rome, for instance Dionysius to Timothy,[110] and Eusebius,

who added that the Babylon mentioned in 1 Peter 5 v. 13 is Rome.[111]
The *Quo vadis* story came from Ambrose *Contra Auxentium*.[112] In
chapter 41 Netter commended the fittingness of Rome as the centre of
the Christian church, in answer to Wyclif in *De Antichristo*.[113]

Chapters 31 and 33 of *Doctrinale* attempted to establish early papal
history, to show the continuous succession of popes, though Netter
admits disputes about placing Linus, Cletus and Anacletus after Peter; he
thought they might have been Peter's coadjutors.[114] He cited the false
decretals to prove that long before Constantine popes were claiming
primacy, against Wyclif's assertion that the papacy was established by
that emperor.[115] Chapter 38 discussed the title *papa*, where he confesses
ignorance about its length of use by the bishop of Rome, though he
thinks it means *pater patrum*, and knows that other bishops used it.[116]

Election by the cardinals, attacked by Wyclif, is next tackled,[117]
though not allowing for Wyclif's context, the election of two popes in
1378, and the appalling conduct of the cardinals.[118] Netter simply tried
to establish how Matthew was chosen,[119] and, contrary to Wyclif, says
that the choice of the apostles was then further refined by lot; God
intends the church to be ruled by human judgement. He accused Wyclif
of gloating over the schism, in the supplement to the *Trialogus*, whereas
Wyclif became increasingly disillusioned with mutual
excommunications, crusades and power struggles.[120]

Wyclif contended that cardinals, being non-scriptural, had no true role
in the church.[121] Netter argued that their titles were ancient, and though
ignorant of the age of the office, was clear that the Roman church had
always had subordinate members, though the main authority for this was
Gratian's *Decretum*.[122] He realised that the name cardinal was unknown
in the early Roman church, but quoted Jerome to show that the ministers
were a 'senate of priests'.[123] Thus Netter avoided contentious arguments
about the role and power of the cardinals, not relevant to his quarrel with
Wyclif.

Lyndwood also discussed cardinals, in the context of whether the pope
must take their advice. He concluded that, on balance, he was not
obliged to do so, though noting that not all authorities agreed. The
opinion of Johannes Monachus, that the pope was obliged to consult
them, was rejected because, as a cardinal, he was biased, as Domenicus of
St Geminiano had noted.[124]

Were the English, with their statutes against provisors, truly anti-
papal? Did the judges who enforced, or the litigants who invoked, these
act out of hostility to the papal office?

No doubt motivation varied, but concerning the statutes one can be fairly sure that usually not hostility to the papacy *per se* prompted clergy but desire to win a particular lawsuit using every available weapon.[125] Enforcement of the statutes depended upon their invocation by individuals. When William Partrike, prior of Lytham, obtained a bull allowing him to be prior of Lytham 'in perpetuity', he also, prudently, obtained a royal pardon for importing it,[126] but Durham priory, on which Lytham depended, mobilised all its resources, especially secular aid; rapidly the king wrote to Partrike saying that, had he known that the bull was so prejudicial to Durham he would not have granted the pardon. The royal letter revoked the pardon, issued 'us not lernyd nor enformyd of ye treuth',[127] and Partrike received a writ of *praemunire facias* ordering him to desist.[128] Yet the prior of Durham eagerly sought and used papal graces: to have a portable altar, not to have to refrain from meat at certain times, for the prior to have increased spiritual jurisdiction over his monks, and to obtain the Jubilee indulgence at home.[129] The excuse for the resistance over Lytham was that the pope was ill informed, though the prior may genuinely have believed also that the pope had no power to grant so unnatural a grace. Gascoigne would have understood either claim.

Statements by individual common lawyers look very anti-papal at times,[130] but Professor Storey concluded that in Henry IV's reign common lawyers usually respected the sphere of ecclesiastical jurisdiction, though defending tenaciously the common law monopoly of the grey area where jurisdictional boundaries were unclear.[131] At least once the two chief justices arbitrated where a papal provision was in question, compensating the defeated provisor.[132]

Despite the statutes, England shared the common ecclesiastical law of western Christendom. Lyndwood noted certain legal areas where local ecclesiastical law did not agree with Roman canon law: for example defamation,[133] and testamentary law,[134] but the church in England was not a law unto itself.[135] On the contrary, Roman canon law was the accepted norm. Professor Helmholz has pointed out also that the English practice whereby, except in criminal cases, clergy appeared in the king's court was regarded as invalid by the Rota, yet never attacked by the bishops.[136] Helmholz notes too that divergence between theory and customary practice, with considerable room for dispute, was an accepted feature of medieval canon law,[137] arguing that the old canon law did not function like modern statute law.[138] English ecclesiastical courts had some wider jurisdiction than their French counterparts, for instance the right to have excommunicates imprisoned.[139] But there were areas of constant conflict: testamentary jurisdiction, recovery of debt owed to or by the dead, defamation, rights of sanctuary[140] and compurgation to prove innocence.[141] In all these cases in the later fifteenth century the common lawyers began to deliver a serious and fairly continuous assault on ecclesiastical jurisdiction,[142] but why the assault began then is not clear, and though there are some clerical complaints about misuse of *praemunire* against local church courts already in 1461,[143] no evidence has so far been produced by the legal historians that any concerted attack was under way in the period with which I am dealing.

The most striking thing about the writers whom I have been discussing is the variety of their opinions about the papacy and its relation to the universal church, especially to the bishops. Like Richard Ullerston, Gascoigne thought some interference by the papacy in the local churches was simply wrong. Pecock would not have objected if the papacy had been proved a human invention. Netter did not believe in *iure divino* local power of bishops, nor in an all-powerful pope. He founded the church on Christ and then Peter, whereas Gascoigne was sure that Christ founded the church on bishops, rather than on Peter alone. There seems to have been no standard orthodoxy on these points and it is not perhaps surprising that the pope was vulnerable to attack. Rehearsal of exactly the same points of scripture could produce remarkably different theories about ecclesiastical power and there were apparently widely diverging views of the power of the episcopate relative to the pope, though it would appear that many prelates must have shared the views of Richard Ullerston and Thomas Gascoigne.

Notes

1 H. J. Sieben, *Traktate und Theorien zum Konzil vom Beginn des Grossen Schismas bis zum Vorabend der Reformation (1378–1521)*, Frankfurter Theologische Studien, XXX, Frankfurt, 1983, pp. 154–6.
2 Above, Chapter 6, pp. 114–15.
3 Appropriation: Hardt, I, cols. 1140–3; Exemption: cols. 1144–51; services: col. 1136; privileges: cols. 1154–7; dispensations: cols. 1150–1; appeals: 1152–5.
4 Above, Chapter 12, note 15.
5 Above, Chapter 12, note 16.
6 e.g. Lincoln 117, pp. 316, 320.
7 Lincoln 117, pp. 298–441 is *Episcopus*.
8 e.g. Lincoln 117, pp. 10, 299.
9 e.g. Lincoln 117, p. 291.
10 e.g. Lincoln 117, pp. 314, 342.
11 Lincoln 117, pp. 143, 317, 343–4, 355, 403.

12 *Papa*: Lincoln 118, pp. 157–94.
13 Lincoln 117, p. 497.
14 Lincoln 117, p. 497: *Magnam enim potestatem dedit dominus vicario suo pape ecclesie ut magna mala reformeret magnamque faceret edificacionem bonorum actuum*; also Lincoln 117, p. 262.
15 Lincoln 118, pp. 17–27: *licencia seu dispensacio*.
16 Lincoln 117, pp. 55, 56, 60.
17 e.g. Lincoln 117, p. 483.
18 Lincoln 117, under *absolutio*, pp. 1–52; *dispensare*, pp. 260–1; *indulgencia*, pp. 575–611.
19 BL, MS Royal 8 G VI, ff. 188–91.
20 *Loci*, p. 10; Lincoln 117, p. 112.
21 Lincoln 117, p. 49; repeated e.g. *Loci*, p. 8.
22 *Loci*, p. 172; Lincoln 117, p. 111.
23 Lincoln 117, p. 594; chapter XI *De ortu cismatis* mentioned 1390 Jubilee. Other refs: *Loci*, pp. 121, 187; Lincoln 117, pp. 596–7.
24 R. Pecock, *The Repressor of Over Much Blaming of the Clergy*, ed. C. Babington, 2 vols., RS, London, 1860, part 4 chapter 4, pp. 436–49.
25 Ibid., pp. 438–9.
26 R. Pecock, *The Reule of Crysten Religioun*, ed. W. C. Greet, Early English Text Society, CLXXI, 1927, p. 312; *Repressor*, pp. 442–3.
27 Refuting *De gradibus cleri*, J. Wyclif, *Opera Minora*, ed. J. Loserth, Wyclif Society, London, 1913, pp. 142–3; *De quattuor sectis*, *Polemical Works in Latin*, 2 vols., ed. R. Buddensieg, Wyclif Society, London, 1883, I, pp. 241–90; quotation p. 267.
28 *Doctrinale*, I, chapter 60, col. 564.
29 *Doctrinale*, I, col. 563; quoted Smith, 'An English conciliarist', p. 295 and note 35, saying Netter contradicts himself, p. 298, but does not consider my point.
30 *Doctrinale*, I, col. 241; Ambrose, *De incarnatione*, ed. O. Faller, Corpus scriptorum ecclesiasticorum latinorum, LXXIX, Vienna, 1964, chapters 4–5, pp. 235–47.
31 *Doctrinale*, I, cols. 266–70; *Defensor pacis*, ed. Scholz, *Dictio* II, chapter 28 sect. 2, p. 519, sect. 5, pp. 532–4, sect. 25, pp. 569–70; *Opus evangelicum*, ed. J. Loserth, Wyclif Society, London, 1896, III, chapter 28, p. 105.
32 *Doctrinale*, I, col. 267.
33 *Retractationes*, chapter 21 (section a), quoted Marsilius, ed. Scholz, p. 533, from Aquinas, *Catena aurea*, without last sentence. See Augustine, *Retractationum libri II*, ed. A. Mutzenbecher, Corpus Christianorum, Series Latina, LVII, Turnhout, 1984, I, 21, p. 62.
34 Chapter 5, pp. 663–5.
35 *Doctrinale*, I, col. 245, from Jerome, *De viris illustribus*, ed. E. C. Richardson, Texte und Untersuchungen zur Geschichte der altchristlichen Literatur, XIV/1, Leipzig, 1896 and cols. 246–7, Chrisostom, perhaps from canon law; Isidore, *De ortu et obitu sanctorum Patrum*, PL, LXXXIII, chapter lxviii, cols. 149–50.
36 *De Christo et suo adversario Antichristo*, Wyclif, *Polemical Works in Latin*, 2 vols., ed. R. Buddensieg, London, 1883, II, pp. 653–92, esp. chapter 6, pp. 665–8; *Doctrinale*, I, col. 248.
37 *Doctrinale*, I, col. 249.
38 *Doctrinale*, I, col. 250; Jerome, *Contra Jovinianum*, PL, XXIII, cols. 211–338, esp. col. 247.
39 Answering what Netter *Doctrinale*, I, cols. 421–6, calls *De praevaricantia sectae*, now *De nova prevaricantia mandatorum*, *Polemical Works*, I, pp. 128–9.
40 *Opus evangelicum*, III (*De Antichristo*), I, chapter 29, pp. 108–9.

41 *Doctrinale*, I, cols. 426–30.
42 *De Christo et Antichristo*, chapter 6, pp. 665–8, on Galatians 2 vv. 6–14.
43 *Doctrinale*, I, cols. 253–7, citing Haymo of Faversham.
44 *Doctrinale*, I, col. 256–7.
45 Matthew 10 v. 2; Luke 6 v. 14; Acts 1 v. 13; P. Hinschius, *Decretales Pseudo-Isidorianae et capitula Angilrami*, Leipzig, 1863, p. 75 (*Epistola secunda*).
46 *Repressor*, pp. 437–8 quoting Jerome on Galatians, *PL*, XXVI, cols. 335–42.
47 *Repressor*, pp. 438–9.
48 *Repressor*, p. 439.
49 *Repressor*, pp. 443–4.
50 *Repressor*, pp. 440–2.
51 Balliol 189, f. 107v.
52 Balliol 189, f. 95v.
53 Balliol 189, f. 15: *per literam secularium potestatum contra vota sua quandoque eligant.*
54 Balliol 189, f. 94v.
55 Balliol 189, f. 95v.
56 In general: L. Buisson, *Potestas und Caritas. Die Päpstliche Gewalt im Spätmittelalter*, Forschungen zur Kirchlichen Rechtsgeschichte und zum Kirchenrecht, II, Cologne, 1958.
57 Lincoln 117, pp. 73–4, quoting Jerome on Amos 3 chapter 6. See Jerome, *Opera*, Pars I, *Opera exegetica*, VI, *Commentarii in prophetas minores*, Corpus Christianorum, Series Latina, LXXVI, Turnhout, 1969, p. 310. Quotation: *non ab hominibus, scilicet non ab apostolis nec per hominem, id est non per Petrum.*
58 Lincoln 117, p. 262; Lincoln 118, p. 163.
59 Lincoln 118, p. 23.
60 Questio 53, art. I; quoted e.g. Lincoln 117, p. 160; Lincoln 118, p. 167. Also Lincoln 117, p. 265; II8, p. 583.
61 Lincoln 117, p. 498, quoting Francis de Meyronnes, *in suo libro de virtutibus moralibus*. B. Roth, *Franz von Mayronnes*, Frankiskanische Forschungen, III, Werl, 1936.
62 Lincoln 117, p. 483.
63 Lincoln 118, p. 19.
64 Mathew 16 v. 19.
65 Lincoln 117, p. 41.
66 Lincoln 117, pp. 498–9, from Holcot.
67 See note 56.
68 Nicholas V: Lincoln 118, p. 171; *Loci*, p. 157.
69 Below, note 77.
70 Lincoln 117, p. 257; *Loci*, p. 12.
71 Lincoln 117, p. 320, *Loci*, p. 16–17; Griffiths, *Henry VI*, p. 757. Gascoigne dated it 1456, but the grant was 1454.
72 Lincoln 117, p. 291; *Loci*, p. 13, reading *propinis*; Lincoln 117 p. 299, lamenting royal dispensations from statutes against provisors.
73 e.g. Lincoln 117, pp. 386–7.
74 Lincoln 117, pp. 344; *Loci*, p. 38.
75 Lincoln 117, p. 379.
76 Lincoln 117, p. 291.
77 Lincoln 117, p. 360; *Loci*, p. 13.
78 Durham, Dean and Chapter Archives, *Registrum Parvum*, III, f. 46v.
79 Durham, Dean and Chapter Archives, *Locellus 9*, no. 8.
80 Durham, Dean and Chapter Archives, Misc. Ch. 5637/15; BL, MS Arundel 11, f.

233v (from St Albans).

81 Lincoln 117, p. 597; Bridget, *Sancta Birgitta revelaciones extravagantes*, ed. L. Hollman, Samlingar utgivna av Svenska Fornskrift-Sällskapet, 2nd series, V, Uppsala, 1956, p. 161, chapter 44.

82 MS, above, note 19. See Pronger, *EHR*, LIV, 1939, pp. 21–3 for this. Quotation below: f. 190v: *ex thesauro ecclesie indulgenciam pene temporalis hic, nichil in purgatorio solvende.*

83 Lincoln 117, p. 11: *iam dicunt, iam Roma est ad ostium nostrum quia licencie et indulgencie papales ut placet nobis conceduntur et nobis conferuntur*; repeated p. 576.

84 Lincoln 117, p. 14.

85 Lincoln 117, p. 29.

86 Lincoln 117, p. 586.

87 Lincoln 117, pp. 16, 610–11; *Loci*, p. 125.

88 Lincoln 117, pp. 606, 610–11; *Loci*, pp. 123, 126.

89 Lunt, II, p. 573.

90 Lyndwood: *BRUC*, pp. 379–81 and appendix. C. R. Cheney, 'William Lyndwood's *Provinciale*', *The Jurist*, XXI, 1961, pp. 405–34. Indulgences: *Provinciale*, III, tit. 23, *De celebratione Missarum*, c. *Altissimus*, pp. 231–2, and at V, tit. 6, *De Poenitentiis*, c. *cum salubriter*, pp. 336–7.

91 *Bullarium Romanum*, Turin, 1859, IV, p. 156–7; H. Thurston, *The Holy Year of Jubilee*, London, 1900, pp. 13–14, for translation. Quotation below: Lyndwood, p. 231.

92 Further: Lyndwood, *De poenitentiis*, c. *cum salubriter*, p. 336.

93 Lyndwood, p. 232.

94 Lyndwood, p. 337. Quotation p. 232.

95 BL, MS Arundel 11, ff. 233–3v.

96 MS Harley 3768: Chapter 12, note 75. *Sponsus* discussed ff. 204–7.

97 *Joannis Duns Scoti . . . opera omnia*, ed. according to the Paris edition of L. Wadding, 26 vols., Paris, 1891–5, XVI, ed. A. Hickey, p. 531, *Sentences*, IV, d. 6, q. 1 no. 3.

98 Harley 3768, ff. 207–12.

99 Metaphysics, Book XII, chapter 10, 1122; Harley 3768, ff. 208–9v.

100 Harley 3768, f. 209v.

101 Harley 3768, f. 210.

102 Harley 3768, f. 210v–11.

103 Harley 3768, f. 211: *peritos et bene morigeratos* (R. E. Latham, ed., *Medieval Latin Word List*, London, 1965, gives 1400 for first use of *morigeratos*). Also f. 211: *nullam vendicantes auctoritatem super ipsum*. Marcellinus: J. N. D. Kelly, *Oxford Dictionary of Popes*, Oxford, 1986, pp. 24–5; B. Tierney, *Foundations of the Conciliar Theory*, Cambridge, 1955, pp. 38, 57.

104 Harley 3768, ff. 211–11v.

105 Harley 3768, f. 214.

106 Harley 3768, f. 215: *donec error manifeste probetur.*

107 Balliol 189, ff. 177–7v.

108 Balliol 189, f. 175.

109 *Doctrinale*, I, cols. 270–4; *Defensor*, ed. Scholz, pp. 352–3 (*dictio* II, cap. 16, sect. 16).

110 ?Dionysius of Corinth, in Eusebius, *Historia ecclesistica*, Sources Chrétiennes, 4 vols., Paris, 1952–60, I, p. 93 (Book II, cap. 25/8).

111 Eusebius, *Historia Ecclesiastica*, I, p. 71 (Book II, cap. 15/2).

112 Reference: Ambrose, *Contra Auxentium*, 5, letter 32: Ambrose, *Epistolarum liber decimus*, ed. M. Zelzer, Corpus scriptorum ecclesiasticorum Latinorum, LXXXII/iii, Vienna, 1982, letter 75a, pp. 89–90.

113 *Doctrinale*, I, cols. 453–8; answering *De Antichristo*, I, chapter 28 (*Opus evangelicum*, III, p. 104).

114 *Doctrinale*, I, cols. 405–9; 415–21; 406, role as coadjutors.

115 *Doctrinale*, I, col. 417, against *De Christo et Antichristo*, chapter 7 (*Polemical Works*, II pp. 669–71).

116 *Doctrinale*, I, cols. 438–43.

117 *Doctrinale*, I, cols. 443–52; against *De Christo et Antichristo*, Chapter 9 (*Polemical Works*, II, pp. 674–6); *Dialogus sive Speculum Ecclesiae Militantis*, ed. A. W. Pollard, Wyclif Society, London, 1886, chapter 11 (not 16 as Netter), p. 22.

118 *De Christo et Antichristo* (*Polemical Works*, II p. 678).

119 Acts 2 v. 23.

120 *Doctrinale*, I, cols. 476–81, answering supplement to *Trialogus*, ed. G. Lechler, Oxford, 1869, chapter IX, pp. 448–9.

121 *De Antichristo*, I chapter 29, (*Opus evangelicum*, III), p. 109.

122 *Doctrinale*, I, chapter 54, cols. 525–32; Gratian, d. 79, c. 3 (*oportebat*), quoted col. 527.

123 *Doctrinale*, I, col. 529.

124 *Provinciale*, p. 104.

125 Storey, 'Clergy and common law', p. 351. R. E. Rodes, *Lay Authority and Reformation in the English Church, Edward I to the Civil War*, Notre Dame, 1982, pp. 59–65.

126 Dobson, *Durham Priory*, p. 330; *CPL*, IX, p. 318; *CPR 1441–6*, p. 237.

127 Durham, Dean and Chapter Archives, *Locellus* 9, no. 9.

128 *Locellus* 9, nos. 4, 45.

129 Dobson, *Durham Priory*, pp. 207–9.

130 e.g. Storey, 'Clergy', p. 346.

131 R. H. Helmholz, *Roman Canon Law in Reformation England*, Cambridge Studies in Legal History, Cambridge, 1990, pp. 21–2.

132 Storey, 'Clergy', pp. 351–2.

133 Helmholz, *Roman Canon Law*, p. 6; Helmholz, *Select Cases on Defamation to 1600*, Selden Society, CI, 1985, pp. xvi–xx.

134 Helmholz, *Roman Canon Law*, p. 7.

135 Helmholz, *Roman Canon Law*, p. 8.

136 Helmholz, *Roman Canon Law*, p. 10.

137 Helmholz, *Roman Canon Law*, pp. 11–12, 14.

138 Helmholz, *Roman Canon Law*, p. 19.

139 Helmholz, *Roman Canon Law*, p. 21.

140 Helmholz, *Roman Canon Law*, p. 23; Spelman, *The Reports of Sir John Spelman*, ed. J. H. Baker, 2 vols., Selden Society, XCIII, XCIV, 1976, 1977, pp. 64–70; 326–36.

141 Helmholz, *Roman Canon Law*, p. 24.

142 Helmholz, *Roman Canon Law*, p. 25, 26; Spelman, pp. 326–36.

143 1460 Convocation: A. K. E. Rose, 'The political career of Cardinal Thomas Bourghier, Archbishop of Canterbury, 1454–1486', University of Maryland, Ph.D Thesis, 1986, pp. 274–5; Bourgchier, *Registrum*, pp. 77–93.

Conclusion

Relations between England and Rome underwent many changes from 1417 to 1464, though it is doubtful whether contemporaries would have noticed some of them. It will be easier to separate the point of view of politics, at government-to-government level, from the point of view of religion, seen by clergy and laity, who, in theory at least, considered the pope the successor of St Peter and Rome the centre of the western church.

At the level of 'high' politics the main change was that after the congress of Arras the English ceased to use papal arbitration in their quarrel with France. The Yorkists still hoped to use the papacy politically but the needs were different. The willingness of Pius II to allow Coppini to be involved in pure politicking, based on Italian interests, was as much a measure of the change in the role of the papacy in its own Italian world as it was a change in English attitudes. The failure of Henry VI's government to keep permanent proctors in Rome was probably not a deliberate decision that Rome was unimportant, but rather the result of faction-fighting and carelessness. It produced problems; probably the change after 1464, whereby the English ambassador was a much more important person than hitherto, was partly a result of lessons learned. But the curia of Pius II was different from that of Martin V; politically much more powerful, even if still chronically short of money.

The popes still demanded obedience largely by requests for cash (clerical taxes) or kind (papal provisions) but by 1464 the provisions question had been settled to the satisfaction of all Englishmen. There was no chance that the statutes would be repealed. More importantly, no Englishman supposed that this, much less the refusal of clerical taxation, constituted a failure of obedience. English and papal ideas about obedience differed! By 1464 the pope had largely ceased to demand annulment of the statutes; the main source of revenue from England was the services, of course very lucrative. The changed papal attitude may be a measure of the changing sources of papal revenue; reliance on sale of office and local taxation as much as anything caused the pope to stop pestering the English to rescind the statutes.

The changed situation of Rome in Italy was matched in 1464 by improvements in the city itself. English institutions there, like those of other nations, developed with the city. The English centre in Rome, the hospice of St Thomas, had by 1464 absorbed St Edmund's and was dominated by the small group of English *curiales*, led by the royal representative. In new buildings, it had either achieved or was in process of achieving a new chapel.

In England the papal collector was the pope's recognised representative, at the centre of a network of contacts, expected to play politics. But the existence of the curia, and the need to do business with it, produced a set of informal relationships by which individuals and institutions made contact with influential courtiers, thus hoping to speed their business. English *curiales* were by no means the only members of the court with English connections. Italians were of great and increasing importance; cultivation of the right friends and contacts was not confined to relationships of English with English. This of course was important culturally as well as religiously and politically. Contact with the curia did not make a man a humanist, though few humanists in England at this period were without such contact.

The relationship between the English and the pope, however, was not ultimately based on cultural links, nor on politics, nor even on money, though the pope often stressed the financial aspects of obedience, in ways which were, to some modern eyes, scandalous. Ultimately Rome was the centre of the western church and obedience to it, or at least communion with it, was obligatory if one wished to avoid schism. There is no evidence that this was doubted by anyone in England considered orthodox. But within the bounds of that belief there was wide scope for disagreement about what constituted obedience. Theoretical writings of Englishmen on these matters strike at once by the wide variety of views: evidently there was no single orthodoxy, either about the limits of papal power or about the proper relations of pope to council or pope to bishops. On the last point there seems to have been a widespread acceptance of, and admiration for, the opinions of Grosseteste, a very high view of episcopal power which would have left bishops as the main activators of church reform in their areas. If, as I suspect, many English bishops accepted some form of this, it would explain how they could quite happily accept the statutes and resist the pope's view that these symbolised lack of obedience.

With unhistorical prevision one might say that nothing in the history of Anglo-papal relations in 1417–64 prepares one for a break with Rome. The relationship was indeed often strained and not always cordial, but it seems to have been accepted as 'given' and as theologically necessary. The English could have accepted neutrality during the Basel troubles, but did not. Nor is there any evidence that such a scheme was seriously canvassed. The superiority of a general council might be accepted by some, but the pope was always considered as having a part to play, even if a much less influential part than he would have liked. Abolition of the papacy, however, was another matter. Even in the darkest days of the council of Basel no non-lollard Englishman seems to have thought of that.

Bibliography

Manuscripts

Only manuscripts cited and actually seen by me are listed. Those cited but not seen are noted with the reference from which I derived the information.

Arezzo
Biblioteca della Citta: 400 (Microfilm only)

Cambridge
University Library: KK.1.2.
Corpus Christi College: 156, 157, 170
Emmanuel College: 9; 142
Gonville and Caius College: 230
Trinity College: B 15 23, B 4 23

Dijon
Archives de la Côte D'Or: B 11615, 11897, 11898, 11899

Dublin
Trinity College: 255

Durham
Archives of the Dean and Chapter: *Registrum Parvum*, II, III; *Locelli* 9, 19, 21, 25; Misc. Ch. 1024, 1066, 4367, 5637/15, 5655, 7246.

Lille
Archives du Nord: B 1929, 1931, 1935, 1942, 1945, 1948, 1951.

London
British Library: Additional, 14848, 48001; Arundel 11; Cotton, Cleop.

C IV, Cleop. E II, Cleop. E III, Nero C. VI, Nero E V; Harley, 431, 631, 826, 861, 3049, 3768, 3972; Royal and Kings, 7 E X, 8 G VI, 10 B IX
Inner Temple Library: Petyt 538 no. 55
Lambeth Palace Library: 183 (photocopy only)
Public Record Office: E28; E30/425, 1249, 1285, 1436; E36/195; E 364; E 403; E 404; SC 1/43/147

Oxford
Bodleian Library: Arch. Seld. B 23; Ashmole 789; Bodley 42, 339; Digby 66; Hatton 42; Lat. Th. e 33; e Museo 86; Tanner 165
All Souls College: 47
Balliol College: 165B, 189
Jesus College: E 12
Lincoln College: Lat. 117, Lat. 118
Magdelen College: Lat. 4, Lat. 93 (microfilm only)
New College: Lat. 128, Lat. D 138
University College: 53

Paris
Archives Nationales: J 653; LL 4^a; P2298; X^{1a} 8605
Bibliothèque Nationale: Collection de Bourgogne 70; Fonds Latin 12542, 1575; Français 4485, 4491, 20590, 26048; Nouvelles Aqu. Françaises 7626

Rome
Archivio di Stato: Fondo Camerale I, Mandati di Camera, 824, 826, 828, 829, 830, 831, 832a, 833a, 834, 836, 837, 838
English College Archives: Membranes 171–208; *Libri* 16, 17, 33, 232, 272

Stuttgart
Württembergische Landesbibliothek: Poet. et Phil 4° 31 (photo only)

Uppsala
University C I (photos only)

Vatican
Archivio Segreto Vaticano: Acta. Misc. I; Archivium Arcis I–XVIII no. 1443; Armarium XXIX, 7; Armarium XXXIX, 4, 5, 6, 7a, 9; Misc.

Arm. II 107; Introitus et Exitus 379 to 455
Penitentiaria (housed in the Archivio): Registri 2 to 11 inclusive, including 2bis
Biblioteca Vaticana: Archivio S. Pietro D. 175, Archivio S. Pietro, Censuali, Arm. 41/42, nos. 4 and 5; Chigi D VII 101; Reg. Lat. 377, 715; Vat. Lat. 3878, 4116, 12159

Vienna
Oesterreichisches National Bibliothek: 4139

Wellington
New Zealand National Library, Alexander Turnbull Library: Acc. 115,004, ff. 1–3v (photcopy only)

Bishop's Registers on microfilm

Aiscough, William, bishop of Salisbury, from Wiltshire Record Office
Alnwick, William, bishop of Lincoln, from Lincoln Archives Office
Alnwick, William, bishop of Norwich, from Norfolk and Norwich Record Office
Beauchamp, Richard, bishop of Salisbury, from Wiltshire Record Office
Chedworth, John, bishop of Lincoln, from Lincoln Archives Office
Heyworth, William, bishop of Coventry and Lichfield, from Lichfield Joint Record Office
Kemp, John, archbishop of York, from Borthwich Institute, York
Lyhert, Walter, bishop of Norwich, from Norfolk and Norwich Record Office
Stafford, John, archbishop of Canterbury, and John Kemp, ditto, from Lambeth Palace Library

Printed sources

Albertini, F., *Francesci Albertini opusculum de mirabilibus urbis Rome*, ed. A. Schmarsow, Heilbronn, 1886
Albizzi, R., *Commissioni de Rinaldo degli Albizzi per il Commune de Firenze dal 1399–1433*, ed. C. Guasti, 3 vols., Florence, 1867–73.
Aliotti, H., *Epistolae et opuscula*, ed. G. M. Scarmalli, Arezzo, 1769.
Ambrose, *De incarnatione*, ed. O. Faller, Corpus scriptorum ecclesiasticorum Latinorum, LXXIX, Vienna, 1964, pp. 235–47.
Ambrose, *Epistolarum liber decimus*, ed. M. Zelzer, Corpus scriptorum

ecclesiasticorum Latinorum, LXXXII/iii, Vienna, 1982.

Amundesham, J., *Annales Monasterii S. Albani a J. Amundesham*, ed. H. T. Riley, 2 vols., *RS*, XXVIII, London, 1870, 1871.

Anstey, H., ed., *Munimenta Academica, Documents illustrative of Academical Life and Studies at Oxford*, 2 vols., *RS*, L, London, 1868.

Anstey, H., ed., *Epistolae Academicae Oxonienses (Registrum F)*, Oxford Historical Society, XXXV, XXXVI, 1898.

Augustine, St, *Retractationum libri II* ed. A. Mutzenbecher, Corpus Christianorum, Series Latina, LVII, Turnhout, 1984.

Bernard, *S Bernardi Opera*, 6 vols., Rome, 1963.

Bekynton, T., *Official Correspondence of Thomas Bekynton*, ed. G. Williams, 2 vols., RSLVI, London, 1872.

Bekynton, T., *The Register of Thomas Bekynton, Bishop of Bath and Wells, 1443–65*, ed. H. C. Maxwell-Lyte and M. C. B. Dawes, 2 vols., Somerset Record Society, XLIX, L, 1934–5.

Bisticci, V. di, *Le vite*, ed. A. Greco, 2 vols., Florence, 1970, 1976.

Blomfield, F., *An Essay Towards a Topographical History of the County of Norfolk* ed. C. Parkin, 11 vols. (Index, 1862), London, 1805, 1810.

Boulay, E. du, *Historia Universitatis Parisiensis*, V, Paris, 1668.

Bourgchier, T., *Registrum Thome Bourgchier, Cantuariensis Archiepiscopi, A.D. 1454–1486*, ed. F. R. H. Du Boulay, CYS, LIV, Oxford, 1957.

Bridget: *Sancta Birgitta revelaciones extravagantes*, ed. L. Hollman, Samlingar utgivna av Svenska Fornskrift-Sällkapet, 2nd series, V, Uppsala, 1956.

Brown, E., ed., *Fasciculi rerum expetendarum*, 2 vols., London, 1690.

Bullarium diplomatum et privilegiorum Sanctorum Romanorum Pontificum, V, Turin, 1860.

Cagni, G. M., *Vespasiano da Bisticci e il suo epistolario*, Temi e testi, XV, Rome, 1969.

Calendar of Close Rolls, His Majesty's Stationery Office, London, 1902 onward.

Calendar of Entries in the Papal Registers relating to Great Britain and Ireland: Papal Letters, ed. W. H. Bliss and J. A. Twemlow, London, 1893 onward.

Calendar of Patent Rolls, His Majesty's Stationery Office, London, 1901 onward.

A Calendar of Signet Letters of Henry IV and V (1399–1422), ed. J. L. Kirby, London, 1978.

Campano, G. A., *Le vite di Pio II di Giovanni Antonio Campano e Bartolomeo Platina*, ed. G. C. Zimola, *Rerum Italicarum Scriptores*, III, part ii, Bologna, 1964.

Capgrave, J., *Liber de illustribus Henricis*, ed. F. C. Hingeston, *RS*, London, 1858.

Capgrave, J., *Ye Solace of Pilgrims*, ed. C. A. Mills, Oxford, 1911.

Capgrave, J., *Abbreviacion of Cronicles*, ed. P. J. Lucas, Early English Text Society, CCLXXXIII, Oxford, 1983.

Capra, L., 'Nuove lettere di Guarino', *Italia medioevale e umanistica*, X, 1967, pp. 165–218.

Caro, J., 'Liber Cancellariae Stanislai Ciolek', *Archiv für Oesterreiches Geschichte*, XLV, 1871, pp. 319–545, and LII, 1875, pp. 1–273.

Chaplais, P., *English Medieval Diplomatic Practice*, Part I, 2 vols., *Documents and Interpretation*, London, 1982.

Chartier, J., *Histoire de Charles VII Roi de France*, ed. A. Vallet de Viriville, 3 vols., Paris, 1858.

Chastellain, G., *Oeuvres* ed. Kervyn de Lettenhove, 8 vols., Académie Royale de Belgique, Brussels, 1863–6.

Chichele, H., *The Register of Henry Chichele, Archbishop of Canterbury, 1414–43*, ed. E. F. Jacob, 4 vols., CYS, XLII, XLV, XLVI, XLVII, Oxford, 1938–47.

Chmel, J., *Regesta Chronologico-diplomatica Friderici IV Romanorum Regis (Imperatoris III) 1440–93*, Vienna, 1838–40.

Concilium Basiliense: Studien und Quellen zur Geschichte des Concils von Basel, ed. J. Haller et al., 8 vols., Basel, 1896–1936.

Cramaud, S. de, *De Subtraccione Obediencie*, ed. H. Kaminsky, Cambridge (Mass.), 1984.

Decrees of the Ecumenical Councils, 2 vols., ed. N. P. Tanner, London and Washington, DC, 1990.

Deputy Keeper, *Annual Report of the Deputy Keeper of the Public Records*, XLIV, London, 1883; XLVIII, London, 1887.

D'Escouchy, M., *Chronique de Mathieu D'Escouchy*, ed. G. du Fresne de Beaucourt, 3 vols., Société de l'Histoire de France, Paris, 1864.

Devillers, L. ed., *Cartulaire des Comtes de Hainault*, 6 vols., Collection de chroniques Belges inédites, Brussels, 1889.

Dionysiaca, 2 vols., Paris, 1937.

Documents illustrating the activities of the General and Provincial Chapters of the English Black Monks, 1215–1540, ed. W. A. Pantin, 3 vols., Camden Society, 3rd series, XLV, XLVII, LIV, 1931–7.

Egidi, P., ed., *Necrologi e libri affini della provincia Romana*, II, *Necrologi della citta di Roma*, Fonti per la storia d'Italia, XLV, Rome, 1914.

Ellis, H., ed. *Original Letters Illustrative of English History*, 3rd series, I,

London, 1846.

Eubel, C., *Hierarchia Catholica Medii Aevi*, 8 vols., Münster, 1913.

Eusebius, *Historia ecclesiastica*, Sources Chrétiennes, 4 vols., Paris, 1952–6.

Fauquembergue, C., *Journal de Clément Fauquembergue, Greffier du Parlement de Paris, 1417–35*, ed. A. Tuetey, 3 vols., Société de l'Histoire de France, CVIII, Paris, 1909.

Fink, K. A., 'Die politische Korrespondenz Martins V nach den Brevenregistern', *QFIAB*, XXVI, 1935–6, pp. 172–245.

Finke, H. and Hollnsteiner, J., *Acta Concilii Constanciensis*, 4 vols, Münster, 1896–1928.

Flenley, R., *Six Town Chronicles of England*, Oxford, 1911.

Gascoigne, T., *Loci e libro veritatum*, ed. J. E. Thorold Rogers, Oxford, 1881.

Gieben, S., 'Robert Grosseteste at the Papal Curia, Lyons 1250: an edition of the documents', *Collectanea Franciscana*, XLI, 1971, pp. 340–93.

Griffi, P., *De officio collectoris in regno Angliae di Pietro Griffi da Pisa (1496–1516)*, ed. M. Monaco, Uomine e dottrine, XIX, Rome, 1973.

Grosseteste, R., *Epistolae*, ed. H. R. Luard, *RS*, London, 1861.

Grunzweig, A., ed., *Correspondance de la Filiale de Bruges des Medici*, Commission royale d'Histoire, Brussels, 1931.

Hallum, R., *The Register of Robert Hallum, Bishop of Salisbury, 1407–1417*, ed. J. M. Horn, CYS, LXXII, 1982.

Handbook of British Chronology, 3rd ed., London, 1986.

Hardt, H. von der, *Magnum Oecumenicum Constancientie Concilium*, 4 vols., Frankfurt and Leipzig, 1700.

Harriss, G. L. and M. A., 'John Benet's Chronicle', *Camden Society*, 4th series, IX, 1972, pp. 151–233.

Helmholz, R. H., ed., *Select Cases on Defamation to 1600*, Selden Society, CI, 1985.

Hinds, A. B., ed., *Calendar of State Papers and Manuscripts in the Archives and Collections of Milan*, I, London, 1912.

Hinschius, P., *Decretales Pseudo-Isidorianae et Capitula Angilrami*, Leipzig, 1863.

Historical Manuscripts Commission, *Calendar of Manuscripts of the Dean and Chapter of Wells*, 2 vols., London, 1914.

Historical Manuscripts Commission, *Ninth report*, Part I, London, 1883, Appendix, pp. 349–50.

Hofman, G., *Acta Camerae Apostolicae et Civitatum Venetiarum*,

Ferrariae, Florentiae, Januae de Concilio Florentino, Concilium Florentinum documenta et scriptores, series A, III/1, Rome, 1950.

Hofman, W. von, *Forschungen zur Geschichte der Kurialen Behörden vom Schisma bis zum Reformation,* 2 vols., Bibliothek des Deutschen Historischen Instituts in Rom, XII, XIII, Rome, 1914.

Jerome, *De viris illustribus,* ed. E. C. Richardson, Texte und Untersuchungen zur Geschichte der altchristlichen Literatur, XIV/1a, Leipzig, 1896.

Jerome, *Opera,* Pars I, *Opera exegetica,* VI, *Commentarii in prophetas minores,* Corpus Christianorum, Series Latina, LXXVI, Turnhout, 1969.

Kempe, M., *The Book of Margery Kempe,* ed. S. B. Meech, with H. E. Allen, Early English Text Society, CCXII, 1940.

Kendall, P. M. and Ilardi, V., *Dispatches with related documents of Milanese Ambassadors in France and Burgundy, 1450–1483,* 2 vols, *1450–61,* Athens (Ohio), 1970.

Keussen, H., ed., *Die Matrikel der Universität Köln,* I, *1389–1475,* 2nd ed., Bonn, 1928.

Kingsford, J. L., *Chronicles of London,* Oxford, 1905.

Koeppen, H., ed., *Die Berichte der Generalprokuratoren des Deutschen Ordens an der Kurie,* Veröffentlichungen der Niedersächischen Archivverwaltung, XXIX, 3/2, *Jehan Tiergart,* Göttingen, 1971.

Lacy, E., *The Register of Edmund Lacy, Bishop of Exeter, 1420–53: Registrum Commune,* ed. G. R. Dunstan, 5 vols., CYS, LX–LXIII, LXVI, 1963–72.

Lacy, E., *Register, Exeter, Institutions,* ed. F. C. Hingeston Randolph, London, 1909.

Lannoy, G. de, *Oeuvres de Ghillebert de Lannoy, voyageur, diplomate et moraliste,* ed. C. Potvin, Académie de Belgique, Brussels, 1878.

Le Neve, J., *Fasti ecclesiae Anglicane, 1300–1540,* revised ed., 12 vols., London, 1960–7.

Literae Cantuarienses: the letter books of the monastery of Christ Church, Canterbury, ed. J. B. Sheppard, 3 vols., *RS,* LXXXV, 1887–8.

Louis XI, *Lettres de Louis XI, Roi de France,* ed. J. Vaesen and E. Charavaray, 11 vols., Société de l'Histoire de France, Paris, 1883.

Luce, S., *Jean D'Arc à Domremy,* Paris, 1885.

Lyndwood, W., *Provinciale,* Oxford, 1676, reprinted Farnborough, 1969.

Malden, A. R., *The Canonisation of St Osmund,* Wiltshire Record Society, Salisbury, 1901.

Mandrot, B. de, *Dépêches des Ambassadeurs milanais en France sous Louis XI et François Sforza*, I, Paris, 1916.

Mansi, J. D., *Sacrorum Conciliorum nova et amplissima collectio*, 31 vols., Venice, 1759–98.

Margaret, *Letters of Queen Margaret of Anjou*, ed. C. Monro, Camden Society, 1st series, LXXXVI, 1863.

Marsilius of Padua, *Defensor pacis*, ed. R. Scholz, Fontes iuris Germanici antiqui, Hannover, 1932.

Martène, E. and Durand, U., *Veterum Scriptorum et Monumentorum . . . Amplissima Collectio*, 9 vols., Paris, 1724–33.

Martin of Troppau, *Chronicon pontificum et impersatorum*, ed. L. Weiland, Monumenta Germanica historica, Scriptores, Hannover, 1872.

Mercati, A., ed., *Raccolta di Concordati*, I, *1098–1914*, Vatican City, 1954.

Migne, J. P., *Patrologiae cursus completus . . . series prima, patres doctores, scriptoresque ecclesiae latinae*, 221 vols., Paris, 1844 onwards.

Monumenta conciliorum generalium seculi decimi quinti, I–II, Vienna, 1857–73; III, Vienna/Basel, 1886–1932; IV, Basel, 1935.

Morosini, A., *Chronique d'Antoine Morosini. Extraits rélatifs à l'histoire de France*, ed. L. Dorez and G. Lefevre-Pontalis, Société de l'Histoire de France, 4 vols., Paris, 1898–1902.

Netter, T., *Thomae Waldensis . . . doctrinale antiquitatum fidei Catholicae ecclesiae*, ed. B. Blanciotti, 3 vols., Venice, 1757, photo reprint Farnborough, 1967.

Nicolas, H., ed., *Proceedings and Ordinances of the Privy Council of England*, 7 vols., London, 1834–7.

Ottenthal, E. von, ed., *Regulae Cancellariae Apostolicae*, Innsbruck, 1888.

Pantin, W. A., *Canterbury College, Oxford*, 4 vols., Oxford Historical Society, new series, VI, VII, 1947, VIII, 1950, XXX, 1985.

Parrino, I., *Acta Albaniae Vaticana*, I, Studi e testi, CCLXVI, Vatican City, 1971.

Paston, *Paston Letters and Papers of the Fifteenth Century*, ed. N. Davis, 2 vols., Oxford, 1971 and 1976.

Pastor, L. von, ed., *Acta inedita historiam pontificum Romanorum precsertim saec. XV, XVI, XVII illustrantia*, Freiburg, 1904.

Pecock, R., *The Repressor of Over Much Blaming of the Clergy*, ed. C. Babington, 2 vols., *RS*, London, 1860.

Pecock, R., *Reginald Pecock's Book of Faith. A fifteenth century theological tractate*, ed. J. L. Morison, Glasgow, 1909.

Pecock, R., *The Reule of Crysten Religioun*, ed. W. C. Greet, Early English Text Society, CLXXI, 1927.

Pius II, *Pii II commentarii rerum memorabilium que temporibus suis contingerunt*, ed. A. van Heck, Studi e testi, CCCXII, CCCXIII, 1984.

Pius II, *The Commentaries of Pius II*, ed. F. A. Gragg and L. C. Gabel, Smith College Studies in History, XXXV, Northampton (Mass.), 1951.

Pius II, *De viris illustribus*, Bibliothek des Literarischen Vereins in Stuttgart, I, Stuttgart, 1842.

Pius II, *Der Briefwechsel des Eneas Silvius Piccolomini*, ed. R. Wolkan, I, *Briefe aus der Laienzeit (1431–1445)*, 1, *Privatbriefe*, 2, *Amtlichebriefe*, Fontes rerum Austriacarum, II, Diplomataria et acta, LXI, LXII, Vienna, 1909; II, *Briefe als Priester und als Bishof von Triest (1447–1450)*, same series, LXVII, Vienna, 1912; III, *Briefe als Bischof von Siena, 1450–1454*, same series, LXVIII, Vienna, 1918.

Pius II, *Epistolae*, ed. A. Zarothus, Milan, 1487.

Pius II, *Opera omnia*, Basel, 1579.

Plancher, U., *Histoire générale et particulière de Bourgogne*, 4 vols., Dijon, 1739–81.

Poggio Bracciolini, *Opera omnia*, ed. R. Fubini, Turin, 1964, reprint.

Poggio Bracciolini, *Lettere*, ed. H. Harth, 3 vols., Florence, 1984–7.

Raynaldus, O., *Annales*, 15 vols., Lucca, 1752.

Reichstagsakten, *Deutsche Reichstagsakten*, ed. J. Weizsacker et al., VII–XVII, Munich, and elsewhere, 1867 onwards.

Registrum Cancellarii Oxoniensis, ed. H. E. Salter, 2 vols., Oxford Historical Society, XCIII, XCIV, 1933.

Repertorium Germanicum. Regesten aus den päpstlichen Archiven zur Geschichte des deutschen Reichs und seiner Territorien im XIV und XV Jahrhundert, Deutsches Historiches Institut in Rom, various editors, Berlin, Tübingen, 1897 onwards, still appearing. For this period: IV, 1957–79, for Martin V; V, for Eugenius IV, 1897; VI, for Nicholas V, 1985–9; VII, for Calixtus III, 1989.

Rotuli parliamentorum ut et placita et petitiones in parliamento, 6 vols., London 1767–77.

Rucellai, G., *Giovanni Rucellai ed il suo Zibaldone*, I, *Il Zibaldone quaresimole*, ed. A. Perosa, Studies of the Warburg Institute, XXIV, London, 1960.

Rymer, T., ed., *Foedera, conventiones et literae . . .*, 3rd ed., 10 vols., The Hague, 1739–45. I quote the photo reprint of 1967, citing the references to the earlier edition from its margins.

Salter, H. E., ed., *Snappe's Formulary and other Records*, Oxford Historical Society, LXXX, 1924.

Schneyer, J. B., 'Konstanzer Konzilspredigten: Texte', *Zeitschrift für die Geschichte des Oberrheins*, CXIII, 1965, pp. 361–88; CXIX, 1971, pp. 175–231.

Scott, E. and Gilliodts van Severen, L., eds., *Le Cotton Ms Galba B I*, Collection des chroniques belges inédites, Brussels, 1896.

Scotus, *Johannis Duns Scoti . . . Opera Omnia*, ed. according to the Paris edition of L. Wadding, 26 vols., Paris, 1891–5.

Serravalle, J. de, *Fratris Johannes de Serravalle . . . translatio et commentum totius libri Dantis Aldhigerii*, ed. F. B. a Colle, Prato, 1891

Sestan, E., ed., *Carteggi diplomatici fra Milano Sforzesca e la Borgogna*, I, *1453–75*, Fonti per la storia d'Italia, CXL, Rome, 1985.

Spelman, J., *The Reports of Sir John Spelman*, ed. J. H. Baker, 2 vols., Selden Society, XCIII, XCIV, 1976, 1977.

The Stacions of Rome, ed. F. J. Furnival, Early English Text Society, XX, Oxford, 1867.

Stacyons, *The Stacyons of Rome*, ed. F. J. Furnival, in: *Political, Religious and Love Poems*, Early English Text Society, XV, Oxford, 1866.

Stafford, J., *The Register of John Stafford, Bishop of Bath and Wells*, ed. T. S. Holmes, Somerset Record Society, XXXI, XXXII, 1915–16.

Stevenson, J,. ed., *Letters and Papers illustrative of the Wars of the English in France during the Reign of Henry the Sixth, King of England*, 2 vols., RS, XXII, 1861.

Stone, J., *The Chronicle of John Stone, Monk of Christ Church, 1415–1471*,, ed. W. G. Searle, Cambridge Antiquarian Society, Octavo series, XXXIV, 1902.

Theiner, A., *Vetera monumenta Hibernorum et Scotorum historiam illustrantia*, Rome, 1864.

Thompson, A. H. and Clay, T., *Fasti parochiales*, Yorkshire Archaeological Society, Record Series, LXXXV, 1933 (vol. I of a set).

Torquemada, J. de, *A Disputation on the Authority of Pope and Council*, trans. T. M. Izbicki, Dominican Sources, IV, Oxford, 1988.

Uginet, F. C., *Le Liber Officialium de Martin V*, Archivio di Stato, Fonti e sussidi, VII, Rome, 1975.

Ursins, J. J. des, *Écrits politiques*, ed. P. S. Lewis, 2 vols., Société de l'Histoire de France, 1978, 1985.

Valois, N., 'Fragment d'un registre du Grand Conseil de Charles VII, (Mars-Juin 1455)', *Annuaire Bulletin de la Société de l'Histoire de France*, XIX, 1882, pp. 273–317; XX, 1883, pp. 209–45.

Vincke, J., *Briefe zum Pisaner Konzil*, Beiträge zur Kirchen und Rechtsgeschichte, I, Bonn, 1940.

Visitations of Religious Houses in the Diocese of Lincoln, 1420–49, II, *Records of Visitations held by William Alnwick . . . (1436–1449)*, ed. A. Hamilton Thompson, 2 vols., CYS, XXIV, XXXIII, 1919, 1927.

Walch, C. G. F., *Monumenta Medii Aevi*, 3 vols., Göttingen, 1757.

Warkworth, J., *A Chronicle of the first thirteen years of the reign of King Edward the Fourth*, ed. J. O. Halliwell, Camden Society, 1st series, London, 1839.

Wey, W., *The Itineraries of William Wey, fellow of Eton College, to Jerusalem, AD 1458 and Ad 1462, and to St James of Compostella*, Roxburghe Club, 1857.

Whethamstede, J., *Registrum Abbatiae Johannis Whethamstede Abbatis Monasterii S. Albani*, 2 vols., ed. H. T. Riley, *RS*, XXVIII/6, London, 1872.

Wilkins, D., *Concilia Magnae Britanniae et Hiberniae*, 4 vols., London, 1737.

Woolley, R. M., *The Officium and Miracula of Richard Rolle of Hampole*, London, 1919.

Wyclif, J., *Dialogus sive speculum ecclesiae militantis*, ed. A. W. Pollard, Wyclif Society, London, 1886.

Wyclif, J., *Opera minora*, ed. J. Loserth, Wyclif Society, 1913.

Wyclif, J., *Opus evangelicum*, 2 vols., ed. J. Loserth, Wyclif Society, 1895, 1896.

Wyclif, J., *Polemical Works in Latin*, 2 vols., ed. R. Buddensieg, Wyclif Society, London, 1883.

Wyclif, J., *Sermones*, III, *In epistolas*, ed. J. Loserth, Wyclif Society, London, 1899.

Wyclif, J., *Trialogus cum supplemento Trialogi*, ed. J. Lechler, Oxford, 1869.

Zippel, G., ed., *Le vite di Paolo II di Gaspare da Verona e Michele Canensi*, Rerum italicarum scriptores, III, part XVI, 1904.

Zonta, G. and Brotto, C. A., *Acta graduum Academicorum ab anno MCCVI ad annum MCCCCL*, Padua, 1922.

Secondary Works

Ait, I., 'La dogana di S. Eustachio nel XV secolo', in Esch, *Aspetti*, pp. 83–147.

Allmand, C. T. 'The relations between the English government, the higher clergy and the papacy in Normandy 1417–1450', Oxford University DPhil., 1963.

Allmand, C. T., 'Un conciliariste Nivernais du XVe siècle, Jean Beaupère', *Annales de Bourgogne*, XXXV, 1963, pp. 145–54.

Allmand, C. T., 'Documents relating to the Anglo-French negotiations of 1439', *Camden Miscellany*. Camden Society, 4th series, IX, 1972, pp. 79–149.

Allmand, C. T., *Lancastrian Normandy, 1415–1450. The History of a Medieval Occupation*, Oxford, 1983.

Andrews, A., 'The lost fifth book of the Life of Pope Paul II by Gaspar of Verona', *Studies in the Renaissance*, XVII, 1970, pp. 7–45.

Armstrong, C. A. J., 'La double monarchie et la Maison de Bourgogne 1420–1435', *Annales de Bourgogne*, XXXVII, 1965, pp. 81–112.

Armstrong, C. A, J., *England, France and Burgundy in the Fifteenth Century*, London, 1983, contains the previous article at pp. 343–74.

Barber, M. J., 'The Englishman abroad in the fifteenth century', *Medievalia et Humanistica*, XI, 1957, pp. 69–77.

Baumgarten, P. M., 'Miscellanea Cameralia', *Römische Quartalschrift*, XIX, 1905, pp. 163–76.

Beaucourt, G. du Fresne de, *Histoire de Charles VII*, 6 vols., Paris, 1881–91.

Beeching, H. C. and James, M. R., 'The library of the Cathedral Church at Norwich', *Norfolk Archaeology*, XIX, 1917, pp. 67–116.

Behrens, B., 'Origins of the office of English resident ambassador in Rome', *EHR*, XLIX, 1934, pp. 640–56.

Bennett, J. A. W., 'Andrew Holes, a neglected harbinger of the English Renaissance', *Speculum*, XIX, 1944, pp. 314–35.

Biscaro, G., 'Il Banco Filippo Borromei e compagni di Londra (1436–39)', *Archivio Storico Lombardo*, fourth series, XL, 1913, pp. 37–126; 283–386.

Blet, P., *Histoire de la représentation diplomatique du S. Siege des origines à l'aube du XIX*, Collectanea Archivi Vaticani, IX, Vatican City, 1982.

Bliemetzrieder, F., 'Traktat des Fr. Nikolaus de Fakenham', *Archivum Franciscanum Historicum*, I, 1908, pp. 577–600; II, 1909, pp. 79–91.

Bliemetzrieder, F., *Literatur Polemik zu Beginn des grossen abendländischen Schismas*, Vienna/Leipzig, 1910.

Boese, H., *Wilhelm von Moerbeke als Übersetzer der Stoicheiosis theologike des Proclus*, Abhandlungen der Heidelberger Akademie der Wissenschaften, Phil.-Hist. Klasse, Heidelberg, 1985.

Boitani, P., *Chaucer and the Italian Trecento*, Cambridge, 1983, repr.

1985.

Bonenfant, P., *Du Meutre de Montereau au Traité de Troyes*, Brussels, 1958.

Brandmüller, W., 'Der Übergang vom Pontifikat Martins V zu Eugen IV', *QFIAB*, XLVII, 1967, pp. 598–629; reprinted in *Papst und Konzil im Grossen Schisma (1378–1431). Studien und Quellen*, Paderborn, 1990, pp. 85–110.

Brandmüller, W. 'Simon de Lellis de Teramo. Ein Konsitorialadvokat auf den Konzilien von Konstanz und Basel', *AHC*, XII, 1980, pp. 229–68, reprinted in *Papst und Konzil*, as above, pp. 356–96.

Brandmüller, W., *Das Konzil von Pavia-Siena, 1423–4*, 2 vols., Vorreformationsgeschichtliche Forschungen, XVI, Münster, 1969, 1974.

Bray, J. R., 'Concepts of sainthood in fourteenth-century England', *BJRL*, LXVI/2, 1984, pp. 40–77.

Brockwell, C. W., Jnr., *Bishop Reginald Pecock and the Lancastrian Church. Securing the Foundations of Cultural Authority*, Texts and Studies in Religion, XXV, Lewiston, 1985.

Broutin, P. (after H. Jedin), *L'Évêque dans la tradition pastorale du XVI siècle*, Museum Lessianum, Section Historique, XVI, Bruges, 1953.

Brown, A. L., 'The Privy Seal clerks in the early fifteenth century', *The Study of Medieval Records: Essays in Honour of Kathleen Major*, ed. D. A. Bullough and R. L. Storey, Oxford, 1971, pp. 260–81.

Buisson, L., *Potestas und Caritas. Die Päpstliche Gewalt im Spätmittelalter*, Forschungen zur kirchlichen Rechtsgeschichte und zum Kirchenrecht, II, Cologne, 1958.

Burns, J. H., *Scottish Churchmen and the Council of Basel*, Glasgow, 1962.

Buxton, J. and Williams, P., eds., *New College, Oxford, 1379–1979*, Oxford, 1979.

Cagni, G. M., *Vespasiano da Bisticci e il suo epistolario*, Temi e testi, XV, Rome, 1969.

Calmette, J. and Perinelle, G., *Louis XI et l'Angleterre*, Mémoires et documents publiés par la Société de l'École des Chartes, XI, Paris, 1930.

Catto, J. I., 'New light on Thomas Docking, OFM', *Medieval and Renaissance Studies*, VI, 1968, pp. 135–49.

Cerchiari, E., *Capellani Papae et Apostolicae sedis, auditores causarum Sacri Palacii Apostolici seu Sacra Romana Rota ab origine ad diem usque 20 Septembris 1870*, 4 vols., Rome, 1919–21.

Chambers, D. S., *Cardinal Bainbridge in the Court of Rome 1509–1514*,

Oxford, 1965.

Cheetham, F., *English Medieval Alabasters with a Catalogue of the Collection in the Victoria and Albert Museum*, Oxford, 1984.

Cheney, C. R., 'William Lyndwood's *Provinciale*', *The Jurist*, XXI, 1961, pp. 405–34.

Christianson, G., *Cesarini: the Conciliar Cardinal. The Basel Years, 1431–38*, Kirchengeschichtliche Quellen und Studien, X, St Ottilien, 1979.

Cnattingius, H., *Studies in the Order of St Bridget*, Stockholm Studies in History, VII, Uppsala, 1963.

Colker, M. C., *Trinity College library, Dublin, Descriptive Catalogue of the Medieval and Renaissance Latin Manuscripts*, 2 vols., Irthlingborough, 1991.

Combet, J., *Louis XI et le Saint Siège*, Paris, 1903.

Cosneau, E., *Le Connetable de Richemont (Artur de Bretagne) 1393–1458*, 2 vols., Paris, 1886.

Crompton, J., 'Fasciculi Zizaniorum', *JEH*, XII, 1961, pp. 35–45; 155–185.

Crowder, C. M. D., 'Henry V, Sigismund and the Council of Constance', *Historical Studies*, IV, 1963, pp. 93–110.

Crowder, C. M. D., 'Constance *Acta* in English libraries', *Das Konzil von Konstanz*, ed. A. Franzen and W. Muller, Freiburg, 1964, pp. 477–517.

Damiatto, M., *Alvaro Pelagio, Teocratico scontento*, Studi Francescani, Florence, 1984.

D'Amico, J. F., *Humanism in Papal Rome. Humanists and Churchmen on the Eve of the Reformation*, Baltimore (Md), 1983.

Davies, M. C., 'Poggio Bracciolini as rhetorician and historian: unpublished pieces', *Rinascimento*, 2nd series, XXII, 1982, pp. 153–82.

Davies, R. G. 'Martin V and the English episcopate', *EHR*, XCII, 1977, pp. 309–44.

De la Mare, A. C., 'Vespasiano da Bisticci and Gray', *JWCI*, XX, 1957, pp. 174–6.

De la Mare, A. C., 'Vespasiano da Bisticci and the Florentine manuscripts of Robert Flemming in Lincoln College', *Lincoln College Record*, 1962–3, pp. 7–16.

De la Mare, A. C. and Barker-Benfield, B., *Manuscripts at Oxford: an exhibition in memory of Richard William Hunt, 1908–1979*, Oxford, 1980.

De Roover, R., *The Rise and Decline of the Medici Bank*, Cambridge (Mass.), 1963.

Dickinson, J. G., *The Congress of Arras, 1435. A Study in Medieval Diplomacy*, Oxford, 1955.

Dictionaire de droit canonique, 7 vols., Paris, 1935–65.

Dizionario biografico degli italiani, Rome, 1960 continuing.

Dobson, R. B., 'The last English monks on Scottish soil: the severance of Coldingham Priory from the monastery of Durham, 1461–78', *Scottish Historical Review*, XLVI, 1967, pp. 1–25.

Dobson, R. B., *Durham Priory, 1400–1450*, Cambridge Studies in Medieval Life and Thought, 3rd series, Cambridge, 1973.

Du Boulay, F. R. H., 'The fifteenth century', *The English Church and the Papacy in the Middle Ages*, ed. C. H. Lawrence, London, 1965, pp. 197–242.

Dunbabin, J., *A Hound of God, Pierre de la Palud and the Fourteenth-Century Church*, Oxford, 1991.

Dykmans, M., *Le Cérémonial papale de la fin du Moyen Age à la Renaissance*, III, *Textes Avignonais jusque'à la fin du Grand Schisme d'Occident*, IV, *Le Retour à Rome ou le cérémonial du Patriarche Pierre Ameil*, Bibliothèque de l'Institut Historique Belge de Rome, fascs. XXVI, 1983, and XXVII, 1985.

Emden, A. B., *Biographical Register of the University of Oxford to A.D. 1500*, 3 vols., Oxford, 1957–9.

Emden, A. B., *A Biographical Register of the University of Cambridge to 1500*, Cambridge, 1963.

Esch, A. and D., 'Die Grabplatte Martins V und andere Importstücke in den römischen Zollregistern der Frührenaissance', *Römische Jahrbuch für Kunstgeschichte*, XVII, 1978, pp. 211–17.

Esch, A., Ait, A. and Polica, G. S., eds., *Aspetti della vita economica e culturale a Roma nel quattrocento*, Fonti e studi per la storia economica e sociale di Roma e dello Stato Pontificio nel tardo medioevo, III, Rome, 1981.

Fages, H., *Histoire de Saint Vincent Ferrier*, 3 vols., Paris, 1901–4.

Fechner, H., *Giuliano Cesarini (1398–1444) bis zu seiner Ankunft in Basel am 9 September, 1431*, Berlin, 1907.

Ferguson, J., *English Diplomacy, 1422–1461*, Oxford, 1972.

Fierville, C., *Le Cardinal Jean Jouffroy et son temps, 1412–1473*, Paris, 1874.

Figueira, R. C., 'The classification of medieval legates in the *Liber Extra*', *AHP*, XXI, 1983, pp. 211–28.

Fink, K. A., *Martin V und Aragon*, Historische Studien, CCCXL, Berlin, 1938.

Flynn, V. J., 'Englishmen in Rome during the Renaissance', *Modern Philology*, XXXVI, 1938–9, pp. 121–38.

Foffano, T., 'Umanisti italiani in Normandia nel secolo XV', *Rinascimento*, series 2, IV, 1964, pp. 3–34.

Foreville, R., *Le Jubilé de St Thomas Becket du XIIIe au XVe siècle (1220–1470)*, Paris, 1958.

Franzen, A. and Müller, W., eds., *Das Konzil von Konstanz. Beiträge zu seiner Geschichte und Theologie*, Freiburg, 1964.

Ganz, M. A., 'A Florentine friendship: Donato Acciaiuoli and Vespasiano da Bisticci', *Renaissance Quarterly*, XLIII, 1990, pp. 372–83.

Gill, J., *Eugenius IV Pope of Christian Union*, London, 1961.

Giovannoni, G., *Roma da Rinascimento al 1870*, part III of Castagnoli, F. et al., *Topografia e urbanistica di Roma*, Bologna, 1958.

Göller, E., *Die Päpstliche Pönitentiarie von ihrem Ursprung bis zu ihrer Umgestaltung unter Pius V*, Bibliothek des Kgl. Preuss. Historischen Instituts in Rom, III, IV, VII, VIII, Rome, 1907, 1911.

Gottlob, A., 'Des Nuntius F. Coppini Anteil an der Entthronung des Königs Heinrich VI und seine Verurteilung bei Römische Curie', *Deutsche Zeitschrift für Geschichtswissenschaft*, IV, 1890, pp. 75–111.

Grabmann, M., 'Das *Defensorium ecclesie* des Magister Adam, ein Streitschrift gegen Marsilius von Padua und Wilhelm von Ockham', *Festschrift Albert Brackmann dargebracht*, ed. L. Santifaller, Weimar, 1931, pp. 569–81.

Gransden, A., *Historical Writing in England*, II, *c. 1307 to the Early Sixteenth Century*, London, 1982.

Gray, H. L., 'Greek visitors to England', *Anniversary Essays in Medieval History by Students of Charles Homer Haskins*, Boston and New York, 1929, pp. 80–116.

Griffiths, J. and Pearsall, D., eds., *Book Production and Publishing in Britain, 1375–1475*, Cambridge, 1989.

Griffiths, R. A., *The Reign of King Henry VI. The exercise of royal authority, 1422–1461*, London, 1981.

Grothe, M. J., 'The Kronenburse of the Faculty of Law of the University of Cologne', *Franciscan Studies*, IX (XXXI), 1971, pp. 235–99.

Guillemain, B., *La Cour Pontificale d'Avignon (1309–1376). Étude d'une Société*, Bibliothèque des Écoles Françaises d'Athènes et de Rome, CCI, Paris, 1962.

Gwynn, A., 'A Franciscan Bishop of Clonfert', *Journal of Galway Archaeological and Historical Society*, XXVIII, 1958–9, pp. 5–11.

Haines, R., 'The practice and problems of a fifteenth century Bishop; the episcopate of William Gray', *Medieval Studies*, XXXIV, 1972, pp. 435–61.

Haines, R., 'The associates and *familia* of William Gray and his use of patronage while Bishop of Ely (1454–78)', *JEH*, XXV, 1974, pp. 225–47.

Haller, J., *England und Rom unter Martin V*, *QFIAB*, VIII, 1905, pp. 249–304, 1905, and separately, Rome, 1905.

Haller, J., *Piero da Monte, ein Gelehrter und päpstlicher Beamter des 15 Jahrhunderts. Seine Briefsammlung*, Bibliothek des Deutschen Historischen Instituts in Rom, XIX, Rome, 1941.

Hallman B. M., *Italian Cardinals, Reform and the Church as Property, 1492–1563*, Berkeley (Cal.), 1985.

Harriss, G. L., 'The struggle for Calais, an aspect of the rivalry between Lancaster and York', *EHR*, LXXV, 1960, pp. 30–53.

Harriss, G. L., *Cardinal Beaufort, a study of Lancastrian ascendancy and decline*, Oxford, 1988.

Harvey, M. M., 'English views on the reforms to be undertaken in the General Councils, 1400–1418, with special reference to the proposals made by Richard Ullerston', DPhil. for the University of Oxford, 1964.

Harvey, M. M., 'England and the Council of Pisa: some new information', *AHC*, II, 1970, pp. 263–83.

Harvey, M. M., 'A sermon by John Luke on the ending of the Great Schism, 1409', *Studies in Church History*, IX, 1972, pp. 159–69.

Harvey, M. M., 'Two *questiones* on the Great Schism by Nicholas Fakenham, OFM', *Archivum Franciscanum Historicum*, LXX, 1977, pp. 97–127.

Harvey, M. M., 'Harley manuscript 3049 and two *questiones* of Walter Hunt, O. Carm', *Transactions of the Architectural and Archaeological Society of Durham and Northumberland*, new series, VI, 1982, pp. 45–7.

Harvey, M. M., *Solutions to the Schism: a study of some English attitudes, 1378–1409*, Kirchengeschichtliche Quellen und Studien, XII, St Ottilien, 1983.

Harvey, M. M., 'John Whethamstede, the Pope and the General Council', *The Church in Pre-reformation Society, Essays in Honour of F. R. H. Du Boulay*, ed. C. M. Barron and C. Harper-Bill, Woodbridge, 1985, pp. 108–22.

Harvey, M. M., 'Martin V and Henry V', *AHP*, XXIV, 1986, pp. 49–70.

Harvey, M. M., 'The benefice as property', *Studies in Church History*, XXIV, 1987, pp. 161–73.

Harvey, M. M., 'An Englishman at the Roman Curia during the Council of Basel: Andrew Holes, his sermon of 1433 and his books', *JEH*, XLII, 1991, pp. 19–38.

Harvey, M. M., 'Martin V and the English, 1422–1431', *Religious Belief and Ecclesiastical Careers in late Medieval England*, ed. C. Harper-Bill, Studies in the History of Medieval Religion, III, Bury St Edmunds, 1991, pp. 59–86.

Harvey, M. M., 'England, the council of Florence and the end of the council of Basel', *Christian Unity: 550 Years since the Council of Ferrara/ Florence, 1438/9–1989*, ed. G. Alberigo, Bibliotheca ephemeridum theologicarum Lovaniensium, XCVII, Louvain, 1991, pp. 203–25.

Harvey, M. M., 'Eugenius IV, Cardinal Kemp and Archbishop Chichele: a reconsideration of the role of Antonio Caffarelli', *The Church and Sovereignty*, Studies in Church History, Subsidia, 1991, pp. 329–44.

Head, C., 'Pius II and the Wars of the Roses', *AHP*, VIII, 1970, pp. 139–78.

Hefele, C. J., *Histoire des Conciles*, VII/1, Paris, 1916.

Helmholz, R. H., *Marriage Litigation in Medieval England*, Cambridge Studies in English Legal History, Cambridge, 1974.

Helmholz, R. H., *Roman Canon Law in Reformation England*, Cambridge Studies in Legal History, Cambridge, 1990.

Helmrath, J., *Das Basler Konzil, 1431–1449, Forschungsstand und Probleme*, Vienna, 1987.

Helmrath, J., 'Kommunikation auf den spätmittelalerlichen Konzilien', *Die Bedeutung der Kommunikation für Wirtschaft und Gesellschaft*, ed. H. Pohl, Stuttgart, 1989, pp. 116–72.

Hill, M. C., *The King's Messengers, 1199–1377*, London, 1961.

History of the University of Oxford, I, *The Early Oxford Schools*, ed. J. I. Catto, Oxford, 1984.

Hollaender, A. E. J. and Kellaway, W., *Studies in London History*, London, 1969.

Holmes, G. A., 'Florentine merchants in England, 1346–1436', *Economic History Review*, 2nd series, XIII, 1960, pp. 193–208.

Holmes, G., 'Cardinal Beaufort and the crusade against the Hussites', *EHR*, LXXXVIII, 1973, pp. 721–50.

Humfrey, *Duke Humfrey and English Humanism in the Fifteenth Century*, Oxford, 1970.

Humfrey, *Duke Humfrey's Library and the Divinity School, 1488–1988*, Oxford, 1988.

Humphreys, K. W., *The Friars' Libraries*, Corpus of Medieval Library Catalogues, British Library, London, 1990.

Hunt, R. W., 'The medieval library', *New College, Oxford 1379–1979*, eds. J. Buxton and P. Williams, Oxford, 1979, pp. 317–45.

Hurtubise, P., *Une Famille-Témoin, les Salviati*, Studi e testi, CCCIX, Rome, 1985.

Huskinson, J. M., 'The crucifixion of St Peter: a fifteenth century topographical problem', *JWCI*, XXXII, 1969, pp. 135–61.

Ilardi, V., 'The Italian League, Francesco Sforza and Charles VII, 1454–61', *Studies in the Renaissance*, VI, 1959, pp. 129–66; reprinted in idem, *Studies in Renaissance Diplomatic History*, Variorum, London, 1986, chapter 2.

Ilardi, V., 'France and Milan: the uneasy alliance, 1452–1466', repinted as before, chapter III.

Izbicki, T., 'The canonists and the treaty of Troyes', *Proceedings of the Fifth International Congress of Medieval Canon Law*, ed. S. Kuttner and K. Pennington, Monumenta iuris canonici, series C, Subsidia VI, Vatican City, 1980, pp. 425–34.

Izbicki, T., *Protector of the Faith: Cardinal Johannes de Turrecremata and the Defense of the Institutional Church*, Washington, DC, 1981.

Jacob, E. F., 'The Bohemians at the Council of Basel', *Prague Essays*, ed. R. W. Seton-Watson, Oxford, 1949, pp. 81–123.

Jacob, E. F., *Henry Chichele and the Ecclesiastical Politics of his Age*, Creighton Lecture in History, London, 1952.

Jacob, E. F., 'A note on the English Concordat of 1418', *Medieval Studies Presented to Aubrey Gwynn, SJ*, ed. J. A. Watt, J. B. Morrall and F. X. Martin, Dublin, 1961, pp. 349–58.

Jacob, E. F., 'Thomas Brouns, Bishop of Norwich', *Essays in British History presented to Sir Keith Feiling*, ed. H. R. Trevor-Roper, London, 1964, pp. 61–83.

Jacob, E. F., *Essays in Later Medieval History*, Manchester, 1968.

Jacob, E. F., 'To and from the court of Rome in the early fifteenth century', *Essays in Later Medieval History* as above, pp. 58–78.

James, M. R., *A Descriptive Catalogue of the Manuscripts in the Library of Sidney Sussex College, Cambridge*, Cambridge, 1895.

James, M. R., *A Catalogue of the Manuscripts in Peterhouse*, Cambridge,

1899.

James, M. R., *The Western Manuscripts in the Library of Trinity College, Cambridge: A Descriptive Catalogue*, 4 vols., Cambridge, 1900–04.

James, M. R., *The Western Manuscripts in the Library of Emmanuel College*, Cambridge, 1904.

James, M. R., *A Descriptive Catalogue of the Manuscripts in the Library of Pembroke College Cambridge*, Cambridge, 1905.

James, M. R. *A Descriptive Catalogue of the Manuscripts in the Library of Corpus Christi College, Cambridge*, 2 vols., Cambridge, 1912.

Jedin, H., *Crisis and Closure of the Council of Trent: a Retrospective View from the Second Vatican Council*, trans. N. D. Smith, London, 1967.

Johnson, P. A., *Duke Richard of York, 1411–1460*, Oxford, 1988.

Kaeppelli, T., *Scriptores Ordinis Praedicatorum*, 3 vols., Rome, 1970–80.

Katermaa-Ottela, A., *Le casetorri medievali in Roma*, Commentationes humanarum litterarum, LXVII, Helsinki, 1981.

Katterbach, B., *Referendarii utriusque signaturae a Martino V ad Clementem IX et praelati signaturae supplicationum a Martino V ad Leonem XIII*, Studi e testi, LV, Vatican City, 1931.

Kelly, J. N. D. *The Oxford Dictionary of Popes*, Oxford, 1986.

Ker, N. R., *Medieval Libraries of Great Britain. A List of Surviving Books*, 2nd ed., Royal Historical Society Guides and Handbooks, III, London, 1964. *Supplement to the Second Edition*, ed. A. G. Watson, Royal Historical Society Guides and Handbooks, XV, London, 1987.

Ker, N. R., *Medieval Manuscripts in British Libraries*, 3 vols., Oxford, 1969–83.

Ker, N. R., *Records of All Souls' College Library, 1437–60*, Oxford Bibliographical Society, new series, XVI, Oxford, 1971.

Ker, N. R., *Books, Collectors and Libraries. Studies in the Medieval Heritage*, ed. A. G. Watson, London, 1985.

Kirby, J. L., *Henry IV of England*, London, 1970.

Kleinberg, A. M., 'Proving sanctity: selection and authentication of saints in the later Middle Ages', *Viator*, XX, 1989, pp. 183–205.

Knowlson, G. A., *Jean V, duc de Bretagne et l'Angleterre*, Cambridge, Rennes, 1964.

Krämer, W., *Konsens und Rezeption: Verfassungsprinzipien der Kirche im Basler Konziliarismus*, Münster, 1980.

Kraus, A., 'Die Sekretäre Pius II', *Römische Quartalschrift*, LIII, 1958, pp. 25–80.

Kraus, A., 'Secretarius und Sekretäriat', *Römische Quartalschrift*, LV, 1960, pp. 43–84.

Lannoy, B. de, *Hughes de Lannoy, le Bon Seigneur de Santes*, Brussels, 1957.

Latham, R. E., ed., *Medieval Latin Word List*, London, 1965.

Leader, D. R., *A History of the University of Cambridge*, I, *The University to 1546*, Cambridge, 1988.

Lerner, R. E. 'Poverty, preaching and eschatology in the Revelation Commentaries of "Hugh of St Cher", *The Bible in the Medieval World. Essays in Memory of Beryl Smalley*, eds. K. Walsh and D. Wood, Studies in Church History, Subsidia IV, Oxford, 1985, pp. 157–89.

Lesage, G. L., 'La Titulaire des envoyés pontificaux sous Pie II', *Mélanges d'Archaeologie et d'Histoire. École Française de Rome*, LXVIII, 1941–8, pp. 206–47.

Lexicon des Mittelalters, Munich and Zurich, 1980 continuing.

Little, A. G., *Franciscan Papers, Lists and Documents*, Manchester, 1943.

Lombardo, M. L., *Spinti di vita privata e sociale in Roma da atti notarili dei secoli XIV e XV*, Archivi e cultura, XIV, Rome, 1981.

Lucas, P. J., 'John Capgrave, OSA (1393–1464), scribe and publisher', *Transactions of the Cambridge Bibliographical Society*, V, 1969, pp. 1–35.

Lucius, C., *Pius II und Ludwig von Frankreich, 1461–2*, Heidelberger Abhandlungen zur mittleren und neueren Geschichte, XLI, Heidelberg, 1913.

Lunt, W. E., *Financial Relations of the Papacy with England, 1327–1534. Studies in Anglo-papal Relations during the Middle Ages*, II, Cambridge (Mass.), 1962.

Lyall, R. J., 'Scottish students and masters at the Universities of Cologne and Louvain in the fifteenth century', *The Innes Review*, XXXVI, 1985, pp. 55–73.

Maas, C. W., *The German Community in Renaissance Rome, 1378–1523*, Römische Quartalschrift für Christliche Altertumskunde und Kirchengeschichte, XXXIX Supplementheft, Rome, 1981.

McFarlane, K. B., 'Henry V, Bishop Beaufort, and the red hat, 1417–21', *England in the Fifteenth Century*, ed. G. L. Harriss, London, 1981, pp. 78–113.

Manion, M. M., Vines, V. F. and Hamel, C. de, *Medieval and Renaissance Manuscripts in New Zealand Collections*, Melbourne, London and New York, 1989.

Martin, V., *Les Origines du Gallicanisme*, 2 vols., Paris, 1939.

Maxwell-Lyte, H. C., *A History of Eton College*, 4th ed., London, 1911.

Menozzi, D., 'La critica alla autentica della Donazione di Constantino in un manuscritto della fine del XIV secolo', *Cristianismo nella storia*, I/1, 1980, pp. 123–54.

Meuthen, E., *Die letzen Jahre des Nikolaus von Kues*. *Biographische Untersuchungen nach neuen Quellen*, Wissenschaftliche Abhandlungen der Arbeitsgemeinschaft für Forschung des Landes Nordrhein-Westfalen, III, Cologne, 1958.

Meuthen, E., *Nikolaus von Kues, 1401–1464 Skizze eines Biographie*, Münster, 1964.

Meuthen, E., 'Kanonistik und Geschichteverständnis', *Von Konstanz nach Trient, Beiträge zur Geschichte der Kirche von der Reformkonzilien bis zum Tridentinum. Festgabe für August Franzen*, ed. R. Baumer, Munich, 1972, pp. 147–70.

Meuthen, E., *Kölner Universitätsgeschichte*, I, *Die Alte Universität*, Cologne, 1988.

Meuthen, E., 'Die Artesfakultät der alten Kölner Universität', *Die Kölner Universität im Mittelalter*, Miscellanea medievalia, XX, Cologne, 1989, pp. 366–93.

Meyer, A. de, 'John Capgrave', *Augustiniana*, V, 1955, pp. 400–40; VII, 1957, pp. 118–48, 531–75.

Miethke, J., 'Die Traktat *De potestate papae*. Ein Typus politik-theoretischer Literatur im späten Mittelalter', *Les Genres littéraires dans les sources théologiques et philosophiques médiévales. Définition, critique et exploitation*, Publications de l'Institut d'Études Médiévales, 2nd series, Textes, Études, Congrès, V, Louvain la Neuve, 1982.

Ministerii, P. B., 'De Augustini de Ancona, OESA (†1328), vita et operibus', *Analecta Augustiniana*, XXII, 1951, pp. 7–56, 148–262.

Mitchell, R. J., 'English students at Padua 1460–75, *TRHS*, 4th series, XIX, 1936, pp. 101–17.

Mitchell, R. J., 'English law students at Bologna in the fifteenth century', *EHR*, LI, 1936, pp. 270–87.

Mitchell, R. J., *John Tiptoft, 1427–70*, London, 1938.

Müller, H., 'Zur Prosopographie des Basler Konzils: Französiche Beispiele', *Archivum Historiae Conciliorum*, XIV, 1982, pp. 140–170.

Müller, H., *Die Französen, Frankreich und das Basler Konzil, 1431–1449*, 2 vols., Konziliengeschichte, Reihe B: Untersuchungen, Paderborn, 1990.

Munby, A. N. L., *Essays and Papers*, London, 1977.

Murray, P., *The Architecture of the Italian Renaissance*, 3rd ed., London, 1986.

Mynors, R. A. B., *Catalogue of the Manuscripts of Balliol College, Oxford,*,

Oxford, 1962.

Nigota, J. A., 'John Kemp, a political prelate of the fifteenth century', Ph.D for Emory University, 1973.

O'Malley, J. W., 'The feast of Thomas Aquinas in Renaissance Rome. A neglected document and its import', *Rivista di Storia della Chiesa in Italia*, XXXV, 1981, pp. 1–27.

Ourliac, P., 'La Pragmatique Sanction et la légation en France du Cardinal d'Estouteville, 1451–53', *Mélanges d'Archaeologie et d'Histoire*, (École Française de Rome), LV, 1938, pp. 403–32; reprinted in idem, *Études d'histoire du droit médiéval*, Paris, 1979, pp. 375–98.

Ouy, G., 'Paris, l'un des principaux foyers de l'humanisme en Europe au début du XV siècle', *Bulletin de la Société de l'histoire de Paris et de l'Ile de France*, years 94–5, 1967–8, pp. 71–98.

Ouy, G., 'La recherche sur l'humanisme français des XIVe et XVe siècles. À propos d'un ouvrage récent', *Francia*, V, 1977, pp. 693–707.

Ouy, G., 'Simon Plumetot (1371–1443) et sa Bibliothèque', *Miscellanea codicologica F. Masai dicata*, 2 vols., ed. P. Cockshaw, M.-C. Garard and P. Jodogne, Ghent, 1979, pp. 353–81.

Ouy, G., 'Les premiers humanistes et leurs livres', *Histoire des bibliothèques françaises: Les bibliothèques médiévales du VIe siècle à 1530*, ed. A. Vernet, Paris, 1989, pp. 267–83.

Owen, D. M., *The Medieval Canon Law. Teaching, Literature and Transmission*, Cambridge, 1990.

Pantin, W. A., 'The *Defensorium* of Adam Easton', *EHR*, LI, 1936, pp. 675–80.

Parks, G. B., *The English Traveller to Italy*, I, Rome, 1954.

Paro, G., *The Right of Papal Legation*, The Catholic University of America. Studies in Canon Law, CCXI, Washington, DC, 1947.

Partner, P., *The Papal State under Martin V*, London, 1958.

Partner, P., *The Pope's Men. The Papal Civil Service in the Renaissance*, Oxford, 1990.

Pastor, L. von, *History of the Popes*, I–III, English ed., London, 1899–1906.

Pastura Ruggiero, M. G., *La Reverenda Camera Apostolica e i suoi archivi (secoli XV–XVIII)*, Rome, 1987.

Pearce, E. H., *The Monks of Westminster*, Cambridge, 1916.

Pecchiai, P., 'Banchi e Botteghe dinanzi alla Basilica Vaticana nei secoli XIV, XV e XVI', *Achivi*, series 2, XVIII, 1951, pp. 81–123; idem, 'I segni sulle case di Roma nel medio evo', same journal, volume and series, pp. 227–51.

Pérouse, G. *Le Cardinal Louis Aleman Président du Concile de Bâle et la Fin du Grand Schisme*, Lyons, 1904.

Perret, P.-M., 'L'ambassade de l'Abbé de Saint Antoine de Vienne et d'Alain Chartier à Venise', *Revue Historique*, XLV, 1891, pp. 198–307.

Pfaff, R. W., *New Liturgical Feasts in Later Medieval England*, Oxford, 1970.

Phillips, H., 'John Wyclif and the optics of the eucharist', *Studies in Church History*, Subsidia, V, *From Ockham to Wyclif*, Oxford, 1987, pp. 245–58.

Pollard, A. F., 'The medieval under-clerks of Parliament', *Bulletin of the Institute of Historical Research*, XVI, 1938–9, pp. 65–87.

Poquet du Haut-Jussé, B.-A., *La France gouverné par Jean Sans Peur*, Paris, 1959.

Pronger, W. A., 'Thomas Gascoigne', *EHR*, LIII, 1938, pp. 606–26; LIV, 1939, pp. 20–37.

Quaglioni, D., *Pietro da Monte a Roma. La tradizione del Repertorium utriusque juris (c. 1435). Genesi e diffusione della letteratura giuridico-politica in età umanistica*, Studi e fonti per la storia dell' Università di Roma, III, Rome, 1984.

Queller, D., *The Office of Ambassador in the Middle Ages*, Princeton, 1967.

Ramsey, N., 'Scriveners and notaries as legal intermediaries in later medieval England', *Enterprise and Individuals in Fifteenth Century England*, ed. J. Kermode, Stroud, 1991, pp. 118–31.

Re, E., 'The English colony in Rome in the fourteenth century', *TRHS*, VI, 1923, pp. 73–92.

Rice, E. F., *Saint Jerome in the Renaissance*, Baltimore, London, 1985.

Richmond, C., *The Paston Family in the Fifteenth Century: The First Phase*, Cambridge, 1990.

Rodes, R. E., *Lay Authority and Reformation in the English Church, Edward I to the Civil War*, Notre Dame (Ind.), 1982.

Rodocanachi, E., 'Les Couriers pontificaux du quatorzième au dixseptième siècle', *Revue d'Histoire Diplomatique*, XXVI, 1912, pp. 392–428.

Roper, H. E. G., 'A Salopian pilgrim to the Hospice in 1448', *Venerabile*, X, 1942, pp. 265–8.

Rose, A. K. E., 'The political career of Cardinal Thomas Bourgchier, Archbishop of Canterbury, 1454–1486', Ph.D University of Maryland, 1986.

Roskell, J. S., *The Commons and their Speakers in English Parliaments*, Manchester, 1965.

Roskell, J. S., 'John Lord Wenlock of Someries', *Publications of the Bedfordshire Historical Record Society*, XXXVIII, 1958, pp. 12–48.

Ross, C., *Edward IV*, London, 1974.

Sammutt, A., *Unfredo Duca di Gloucester e gli Umanisti Italiani*, Medioevo e umanismo, XLI. Padua, 1980.

Sanford, E. M., 'Gaspar Veronese, humanist and teacher', *Transactions and Proceedings of the American Philological Association*, LXXXIV, 1953, pp. 190–209.

Sanford, E. M., 'Juvenalis', *Catalogus translationum et commentoriorum*, I, Washington, DC, 1960, pp. 175–240.

Schmutz, R. A., 'Medieval papal representatives, legates, nuncios, and judges delegate', *Studia Gratiana*, XV, 1972, pp. 443–63.

Schofield, A. N. E. D., 'The first English delegation to the Council of Basel', *JEH*, XII, 1961, pp. 167–96.

Schofield, A. N. E. D., 'The second English delegation to the Council of Basel', *JEH*, XVII, 1966, pp. 29–64.

Schofield, A. N. E. D., 'England and the Council of Basel', *AHC*, V/1, 1973, pp. 1–117.

Scholz, R., 'Eine Geschichte und Kritik der Kirchenverfassung vom Jahr 1406', *Papsttum und Kaisertum. Forschungen . . . Paul Kehr zum 65. Gebürtstag dargebracht*, ed. A. Brackmann, Munich, 1926, pp. 594–621.

Schuchard, C., *Die Deutschen an der päpstlichen Kurie im späten Mittelalter, 1378–1447*, Bibiothek des Deutschen Historischen Instituts in Rom, LXV, Tübingen, 1987.

Scofield, C. L., *The Life and Reign of Edward the Fourth, King of England and of France and Lord of Ireland*, 2 vols., London, 1923.

Setton, K. M., *The Papacy and the Levant, 1204–1571*, 2 vols., American Philosophical Society, Philadelphia, 1976–8.

Sieben, H. J., *Traktate und Theorien zum Konzil vom Beginn des Grossen Schismas bis zum Vorabend der Reformation (1378–1521)*, Frankfurter theologischen Studien, XXX, Frankfurt, 1983.

Smalley, B., *The Study of the Bible in the Middle Ages*, Oxford, 1952, repr., South Bend (Ind.), 1964.

Smalley, B., 'Which William of Nottingham?', *Medieval and Renaissance Studies*, III, 1954, pp. 200–38.

Smalley, B., *The Gospels in the Schools*, London, 1985.

Smith, K. S., 'The ecclesiology of controversy: scripture, tradition and church in the theology of Thomas Netter of Walden', Ph.D for Cornell University, 1983.

Smith, K. S., 'An English conciliarist? Thomas Netter of Walden', *Popes, Teachers and Canon Lawyers in the Middle Ages*, eds. J. R. Sweeney and S. Chodorow, Ithaca and London, 1989, pp. 290–9.

Souchon, M., *Die Papstwahlen in der Zeit des Grossen Schismas*, 2 vols., Braunschweig, 1898–9.

Sousa Costa, A. D. de, *Mestre Andre Dias de Escobar, Figura Ecumenica do Seculo XV*, Estudos e textos de Idade Media e Rinascimento, II, Rome, 1967.

Southern, R. W., *Robert Grosseteste: the Growth of an English Mind in Medieval Europe*, Oxford, 1986.

Spingarn, J. E., 'Unpublished letters of an English humanist', *Journal of Comparative Literature*, I, 1903, pp. 47–65.

Stieber, J. W., *Pope Eugenius IV, the Council of Basel and the Secular and Ecclesiastical Authorities in the Empire*, Studies in the History of Christian Thought, XIII, ed. H. A. Oberman, Leiden, 1978.

Stinger, C. L., *The Renaissance in Rome*, Bloomington (Ind.), 1985.

Storey, R. L., 'Clergy and common law in the reign of Henry IV', *Medieval Legal Records, Edited in Memory of C. A. F. Meekings*, eds. R. F. Hunniset and J. B. Post, London, 1978, pp. 341–408.

Summary Catalogue of Western Manuscripts in the Bodleian Library, Oxford, various editors, Oxford, 1895–1953.

Sumption, J., *Pilgrimage: an Image of Medieval Religion*, London, 1975.

Swanson, R. N., *Universities, Academics and the Great Schism*, Cambridge, 1979.

Swanson, R. N., 'Titles to orders in episcopal registers', *Studies in History Presented to R. H. C. Davis*, ed. H. Mayr-Harting and R. I. Moore, London, 1985, pp. 233–45.

Swanson, R. N., *Church and Society in Late Medieval England*, Oxford, 1989.

Tamburini, F., 'Il primo registro di suppliche del l'Archivio della Sacra Penitenzieria Apostolica (1410–11)', *Rivista di Storia della Chiesa in Italia*, XXIII, 1969, pp. 384–427.

Tamburini, F., 'Nota Diplomatiche intorno a suppliche e lettere de Penitenzieria (sec. XIV–XV)', *AHP*, XI, 1973, pp. 149–208.

Tamburini, F., 'Per la storia dei Cardinali Penitenzieri Maggiori e dell'archivio della Penitenzieria Apostolica. Il tratto *De Antiquitate Cardinalis Penitentiariae Majoris*, di G. B. Coccino (†1641)', *Rivista di Storia della Chiesa in Italia*, XXXVI, 1982, pp. 332–86.

Tanner, N. P., *The Church in Late Medieval Norwich, 1370–1532*, Pontifical Insitute of Medieval Studies, Studies and Texts, LXVI, Toronto, 1984.

Thielemans, M.-R., *Bourgogne et Angleterre: relations politiques et économiques entre les Pays-Bas bourgignons et l'Angleterre 1435–67*, Université Libre de Bruxelles, Travaux de la Faculté de Philosophie et Lettres, XXX, Brussels, 1966.

Thompson, A. H., *The English Clergy and their Organisation in the Later Middle Ages*, Oxford, 1947.

Thomson, J. A. F., *The Later Lollards, 1415–1520*, Oxford, 1965.

Thomson, J. A. F., 'The 'Well of Grace': Englishmen and Rome in the fifteenth century', *The Church, Politics and Patronage in the Fifteenth Century*, ed. R. B. Dobson, Gloucester, 1984, pp. 99–114.

Thomson, S. H., *The Writings of Robert Grosseteste, Bishop of Lincoln*, Cambridge, 1940.

Thomson, W. R., *The Latin Writings of John Wyclif: An Annotated Catalog*, Pontifical Institute of Medieval Studies, Subsidia Medievalia, XIV, Toronto, 1983.

Thrupp, S. L., 'Aliens in and around London in the fifteenth century', in A. E. J. Hollaender and W. Kellaway, *Studies in London History*, London, 1969, pp. 251–72.

Thurston, H., *The Holy Year of Jubilee*, London, 1900.

Tierney, B., *Foundations of the Conciliar Theory*, Cambridge, 1955.

Tomei, P., *L'architettura a Roma nel quattrocento*, Rome, 1942.

Töth, P. de, *Il Beato Cardinale Nicolo Albergati ed i suoi tempi, 1375–1444*, 2 vols., Viterbo, 1934.

Toussaint, J., *Les relations diplomatiques de Philippe le Bon avec le Concile de Bâle, 1431–1447*, Recueil de travaux d'histoire et de philologie, 3rd series, IX, Louvain, 1942.

Toussaint, J., 'Philippe le Bon et le Concile de Bâle (1431–1449)', Académie Royale de Belgique, Bruxelles, Commission Royale d'Histoire, *Bulletin*, CVII, 1942, pp. 1–126.

Tyerman, C., *England and the Crusades 1095–1588*, Chicago, 1988.

Vale, M. G. A., *English Gascony, 1399–1453*, Oxford, 1970.

Valois, N., 'Fragment d'un registre du Grand Conseil de Charles VII, Mars–Juin 1455', *Annuaire Bulletin de la Société de L'Histoire de France*, XIX, 1882, pp. 272–308.

Valois, N., *Histoire de la Pragmatique Sanction de Bourges sous Charles VII*, Archives de l'histoire réligieuse de la France, Paris, 1906.

Valois, N., *La Crise religieuse du XVe siècle: Le Pape et le Concile*,

1418–1450, 2 vols., Paris, 1909.

Vauchez, A., *La Sainteté en Occident au derniers siècles du Moyen Age, d'aprés les procès de canonisation et les documents hagiographiques*, Bibliothèque des Écoles Françaises d'Athènes et de Rome, CCXLI, Rome, 1981.

Vaughan, R., *Philip the Good. The Apogée of Burgundy*, London, 1970.

Venerabile, 'The English Hospice in Rome', *Venerabile*, XXI, May 1962.

Victoria County History, Cambridgeshire, III, *The City and University of Cambridge*, London, 1959.

Victoria County History, History of the County of Berkshire, ed. P. H. Ditchfield and W. Page, II, London, 1907.

Victoria County History, History of the County of Yorkshire, ed. W. Page., III, London, 1913.

Virgoe, R., 'The divorce of Sir Thomas Tuddenham', *Norfolk Archaeology*, XXXIV/4, 1969, pp. 406–18.

Walravens, C. J. H., *Alain Chartier*, Amsterdam, 1971.

Walser, E., *Poggius Florentinus, Leben und Werke*, Beiträge zur Kulturgeschichte des Mittelalters und Renaissance, XIV, Leipzig, 1914.

Wasner, F., 'Fifteenth-century texts on the ceremonial of the papal *Legatus a latere*', *Traditio*, XIV, 1958, pp. 295–358.

Watson, A. G., *Catalogue of Dated and Datable Manuscripts c 700–1600 in the Department of Manuscripts, the British Library*, 2 vols., London, 1979.

Watson, A. G., *Catalogue of Dated and Datable Manuscripts c 435–1600 in Oxford libraries*, 2 vols., Oxford, 1984.

Watt, J. A., Morrall, J. B. and Martin, F. X., eds., *Medieval Studies presented to Aubrey Gwynn, SJ*, Dublin, 1961.

Weiss, R., 'A letter-preface of John Free to John Tiptoft, Earl of Worcester', *Bodleian Quarterly Record*, VIII/87, 1935, pp. 101–3.

Weiss, R., 'Per la conoscenza di Dante in Inghilterra nel quattrocento', *Giornale Storico della Letteratura Italiana*, CVIII, 1936, pp. 357–9.

Weiss, R., *Humanism in England during the Fifteenth Century*, 3rd ed., Medium Aevum Monographs, IV, Oxford, 1967.

Weiss, R., *The Renaissance Discovery of Classical Antiquity*, 2nd ed., Oxford, 1988.

Williams, M. E., *The Venerable English College, Rome, 1579–1979, A History*, London, 1979.

Winstead, K. A., 'Piety, politics and social commitment in Capgrave's *Life of St Catherine*', *Medievalia et Humanistica*, new series, XVII,

1991, pp. 59–80.

Württembergische Landes Bibliothek, Stuttgart, *Codices Poetici et Philologici*, series I, vol. II, Wiesbaden, 1981.

Wylie, J. H. and Waugh, W. T., *The Reign of Henry V*, 3 vols., Cambridge, 1914, 1919, 1929.

Zeibig, H. J., 'Beitrag zur Geschichte der Wirksamkeit des Basler Concils in Oesterreich', *Sitzungsbericht der Königl. Akademie der Wissenschaften Hist.-Phil. Klasse*, VIII, Vienna, 1852, pp. 515–616.

Zellfelder, A., *England und das Basler Konzil, mit einem Urkundenanhang*, Historische Studien, CXIII, Berlin, 1913.

Zimmermann, A., ed., *Die Kölner Universität im Mittelalter. Geistige Würzeln und sociale Wirklichkeit*, Berlin, 1989.

Index

vv. 5–29, 220–1
Exodus, 21, 237
Galatians, 1 v. 18, 232; 2 v. 6, 232; 2 v. 9, 232
Luke, 22 v. 32, 239
Matthew, 16 vv. 18–19, 231–3; 18 vv. 15–7, 238; 18 v. 20, 220; 21 v. 12, 232; 28 v. 20, 222, 239
1 Peter 5 v. 13, 240
Biconyl, William, registrar of Canterbury, 172–3
Bildeston, Nicholas, 39, 83, 145, 220
Biondo, Flavio, of Forlì, 87, 120
Bird, Thomas, 170
bishop(s), 4
  equal to pope, 214–15, 234
  ordo of, 214, 231
  origin of, 230–1
  power of, in diocese, 214–15, 218
  under-age, *see* Bourgchier; Neville, George
  undermined by pope, 230, 235
bishoprics, Italians in English, 93
  see also provisions, papal
Blakedon, James, 32
Blodwell, John, 30, 40, 83, 135
bloodshed, *see* clergy, crimes by and against
Bloxwych, John, 32
Bobych, John, 219
Boccaccio, Giovanni, 40
Bohemians, *see* crusade; Hussites
Bole, Richard, 42, 67, 196
Bologna, University of, English at, 29–30, 32–3
Bona Ayra, Ralph de, 55
Boniface IX, pope, 26, 53, 65
Boninsegna, Lionardo de, 81
Borromeo, Jacopo, 80
Borremeo bank, 79, 81, 84; *see also* Palestrellis
Botyll, Robert, 114, 170, 184–5, 187
Boulers, Reginald, abbot of Gloucester, 170-1
Bourgchier, Thomas, 15, 28, 95
  benefices of, 159–60
  and Ely, 163
  and tenth, 206
  and Worcester, 158-9
Brabantia, Andrea de, 84
Bracciolini, Poggio, 115
  and Beaufort, 40, 42
  and benefices, 98, 133
  and Bildeston, 39

and Candour, 34
and Constance, 40
letters of, 34, 39, 41–2
as papal secretary, 42
and Petworth, 24, 39
Bradway, John, 61
Brese, Roger, 103
Brittany, ambassadors of, 158, 160
Brittany, Jean, duke of, and brother Artur, 142
Broun, Richard, *see* cordon
Brouns, Thomas, 83, 95, 158–60
Bruges, 78
Brygham, William, 61
Bubwith, Nicholas, 40
Burg, Robert, 106
Burgundy, Burgundians, 86, 110, 131 132, 135–6, 139; *see also* Amiens; Philip the Good
Burgundy, duke of, *see* Philip the Good
Bury, abbot of, *see* Babyngton
Byllyngham, Richard, 60, 86–7
Byrtley, John, 61

caballarii, 84–5
Cade, Jack, 28, 60
Calais, Antonius de, 57
Calixtus III, pope, formerly Alfonso Borgia, 16, 77, 117
  and crusade, 188–9, 195
  and England, 15, 118, 188–9
  and Ferrante, 194
  and nephews, 235
  see also Lax, John
Cambridge, university of, 13, 32, 115
  student *familiaris* at, 109
  see also privileges, for King's
camera, papal, 27, 79
  auditors of, 27; *see also* Prene
  clerks of, 27–8
  clerks of, English, *see* Caunton; Clitherow, John; Moleyns;
  notary of; *see* Aucton
  scriptor of, *see* Pollart
Camerarius, 27, 235
Camogli, Prospero, 200–3; *see also* Sforza
Candour, Thomas, 116, 185–6
  books of, 34, 40–1
  as *cubicularius*, 34, 41
  in Padua, 34, 42
  see also Bracciolini, Upton
canonisation, 14, 114–18; *see also* Alfred;

and St James, 220–1, 232
and St Paul, 232, 234
as vicar of Christ, 231
St Peter's, *see* Rome, city of, churches
St Thomas Aquinas, *see* Aquinas
St Thomas Becket, 32, 64–5; *see also*
    Hospice of St Thomas
St Vincent Ferrer, 115–17
sale of office, 42, 248
Salisbury, bishopric of, *see* Bekynton;
    Hallum
    dean of, Moleyns, 28
    precentor of, Upton, 66
Salisbury, dean and chapter of, 228
    bankers of, 81
    proctors of, 34, 36, 65, 82–3, 117
    records of, 34
    see also St Osmund, canonisation of
Salisbury, John, 155
Saltewell, *see* Morden
Salviatis, Jacopo de, 79–80
Sancta Cruce, Andreas de, 117
Sancte Crucis, Blasius, 55
Sandwych, Walter, 33, 173
Sartre, Johannes, 55
Savoy, duke of, *see* Felix V
Saxton, Nicholas, 42, 67
Scerwe, Corradus, 55
Schism, Great Western, 2–4, 26, 31
Schofield, A. N. E. D., 153
Scotus, Duns, 41, 238
scriptor of apostolic letters, 30
    in chancery, 29
    see also abbreviators; penitentiary
scutifer honoris, squire, 34, 56; *see also*
    Gattola; Ildriton
secretary, papal, 26, 28, 42
    English, *see* Lax, John; Swan
    see also Biondo; Bracciolini
sergeant-at-arms, 33; *see also* Asculo;
    Elense; Ely, John
Seroblyghby, *see* Caylart
Serravalle, Giovanni de, 40
Sertor, John, 55
Seruopolos, Franciulo, 194–5
services, 74, 78, 229
Sforza, Francesco, duke of Milan, 194–5,
    199–205
    agent of, 200; *see also* Camogli
Sharpe, Henry, 35, 40, 67, 79, 196
Shepherd, Alice and John, alias
    Paternoster, 52–3, 67
Shirwood, John, 33, 40

Siena, *see* Pavia/Siena
Sigismund, emperor, 141, 153, 158, 160,
    164–5, 216
simony, sin of, 111–12
    attacked, 215, 229–30, 235
    and Coppini, 198, 204
    laws against, 112
Sion, abbey of, 27, 87
Skipwiche, Aline, widow of John, 108–9
Smith, Thomas, *see* Lambert
solicitator, 31
Sollay, Thomas, 31, 65, 107
Somnium Viridarii, 217
Spalding, Hugh, 82, 87
Spencer, John, 92
Spofforth, Thomas, 131, 134, 230
Spoleto, cardinal of, *see* Eroli
Staciouns of Rome, 64
Stafford, John, 160
    and papal tenth, 170–3
    proctor of, 37
Stanley, William, 67
Stappe, John, alias Steppe, 112
Stokes, John, 160
Storey, R. L., 241
Strete, William, 16, 62
subdeacon, papal, 37
Suffolk, duke of, 60, 62, 119
Sulbury, William, 222
Sutton, Henry, 105
Sutton, Robert, 30–1, 35, 83
    benefices of, 160
    see also Humfrey
Swan, William, 85, 149, 155, 169–70
    as abbreviator, secretary, *scriptor*, 26,
        28–9, 30
    and banks, 81
    and Chichele, 11, 30, 87
    clericus conjugatus, 30
    at councils of Basel, Constance and Pisa
        26, 30–1, 56, 65
    family of, brother Richard, 82
        nephews, 82, 95
        wife Joan, 30
    house of, in Rome, 30, 56
    and Kemp, 30, 94, 134
    letters, letter books, 30, 35, 65–6, 87,
        148, 153, 216
Sweziko, Wenceslaus, 36
Symonde, William, 33

Taillour, William, 61
Taranto, bishop of, *see* Orsini, Marino